Thin Description

Thin Description

ETHNOGRAPHY AND THE AFRICAN HEBREW
ISRAELITES OF JERUSALEM

JOHN L. JACKSON, JR.

HARVARD UNIVERSITY PRESS

Cambridge, Massachusetts ▪ London, England

2013

Library of Congress Cataloging-in-Publication Data

Jackson, John L., Jr., 1971– .
Thin description: ethnography and the African Hebrew Israelites of Jerusalem /
by John L. Jackson, Jr.
pages cm
Includes bibliographical references and index.
ISBN-13: 978-0-674-04966-6
1. African Hebrew Israelite Nation of Jerusalem.   2. Black Hebrews—Israel—Dimonah—
Social conditions.   3. African Americans—Relations with Jews.   4. Ammi,
Ben, 1939–   5. Dimonah (Israel)—Ethnic relations.   I. Title.
BP605.B63J33 2013
305.8'9605694—dc23   2013008005

Contents

Thin Description

Passover

M OST MEMORABLE ABOUT that particular flight from New York to Tel Aviv? Three things: the balancing acts performed by *tefillin*-adorned believers in black suits and yarmulkes; the considerable number of African Americans, sleepy-eyed but excited, sprinkled throughout our packed coach cabin; and the thinnest veneer of polite distance softly barricading those two sets of travelers away from one another.

Emergency exit rows on our plane to Israel in May of 2006 provided just enough space for several Orthodox Jewish men to stand in the aisles for morning prayers, bracing their hips and knees against plastic and metal seats in anchored readiness for any hints of turbulence, arms and heads wrapped with leathery black boxes housing Torah verses worn in adherence to a sacred injunction: *Never forget ancient Israel's Egyptian captivity and divinely orchestrated escape.*

These cube-covered entreaties weren't quite like anything I'd seen before, but they showcased the same unapologetic indifference to public scrutiny that always impresses me about certain religious practices, including the exceptionally flamboyant kinds that involve, say, catching

the Holy Spirit and speaking in tongues.[1] One of the strangers seated
closest to me, an African American from Baltimore, didn't look the least
bit fazed by these pious rites unfolding in front of us, though I couldn't
help feeling a little suspicious of his nonchalance, as he should have been
of mine, conspicuous demonstrations of disinterest that sometimes take
as much effort and focus as the ogling they are meant to replace.

I was still noticing news stories in 2010 about Jewish air travelers,
some of them even teenagers, inauspiciously removed from flights for
using phylacteries, for publicly praying with such exotic accessories.
Mix post-9/11 concerns about transportation safety with religionists
"strapped" to "strange" black boxes and you get high-flying jets diverted
to nearby airports and passengers summarily escorted from planes—
boxes, carry-on bags, checked luggage, and all. The "suspects" in those
news reports were usually visiting places like Kentucky or Kansas,
Missouri or Montana, *not* the modern state of Israel, and the flight crew
for our trip to Ben Gurion International Airport had clearly seen such
devout performances many times before, which meant that they didn't
deviate from their typical airline-scripted dispositions, a perch along
that spacious continuum from disingenuous sycophancy to self-assured
insouciance, mostly trying, it seemed, to simply ignore us all, those with
black boxes and those without.

The Baltimorean I met on that flight wasn't laying *tefillin*. He considers himself an Israelite, not a Jew, and this distinction is incredibly
important to him—and to any of the various groups that stress it.[2] This
was his first journey to the Promised Land, though he could chronicle
more than a decade's worth of trips he almost took, plans that fell through
because of finances or family emergencies, because of health crises or the
temporary persuasiveness of naysayers, but he was finally on his way this
time. And we were both headed there for the same reason: to experience
New World Passover (NWP), an annual holiday commemorating the
late-1960s relocation of several hundred African Americans from the
Southside of Chicago to southern Israel. The other black passengers on
our flight, dozens of them, from senior citizens to toddlers, were on their
way to the same Israeli city, Dimona (not too far away, those in the know
always remind me, from the country's "nuclear research facility"), a town
that hosts this event every May. All of us were invited to participate in a

celebration put on by that very community of African American expats in honor of their transatlantic journey almost forty years earlier.[3]

This was just one flight on one day at the start of one year's New World Passover ceremony, but that annual fete seems a justifiable place to begin any discussion about the fascinating group of African American émigrés known as the African Hebrew Israelites of Jerusalem (AHIJ). And this is not just because anthropologists have a long history of emphasizing the social value of grand public rituals (though that is, admittedly, part of the draw).[4] The assortment of activities that make up New World Passover reveals just about every central theme and concern of this <u>transnational spiritual community</u>, a "Kingdom" with its organizational <u>hub lodged squarely in the Israeli desert</u> but also composed of "saints," as members are called, scattered across five different continents and dozens of countries, a truly global phenomenon with a social influence and historical significance that arguably outstrips its relatively obscured and muted place in most discussions of African American or Jewish life.

New World Passover is designed to bring many of the community's dispersed saints together, to carry them "back home," at least for a short time. Even saints who have never spent a single day in Israel, who were born and raised in Chicago or Newark, Los Angeles or Bermuda, consider their first trips to Israel *homecomings,* pilgrimages to their ancient homeland.[5] The Baltimorean I met on that plane certainly spoke in those terms. He was, as he memorably put it, "going home for the first time."

Every facet of the AHIJ community's worldview and all of its emblematic social practices are on display during this annual affair: their committed and creative use of old and new media technologies, their decidedly international constituency, their mandated veganism (and related "preventative health" initiatives), their concerted investments in the musical and theater arts, their revisionist historical narratives, their patriarchal and polygamous family structure, their reinterpretations of the Hebrew Bible and Christian Scriptures, all of which help to constitute, as philosopher Walter Isaac labels it, a distinctively "black midrash."[6] Colloquially described as a kind of "family reunion," a time for saints to join in "feasting, sporting activities, and entertainment," New World Passover is a distillation of just about everything the AHIJ believe about the world, a translation of those beliefs into specific cultural practices, and a demonstration of the many ways in which they self-consciously represent themselves to themselves and to a wider eavesdropping public.[7]

The second time I saw that aforementioned Baltimorean during the same year's NWP event, briefly catching his eye and nodding my head from across a throng of high-spirited saints, was in the main parking lot of the community's *kfar* (village), transformed into a theater-in-the-round for part of the NWP festivities. One skinny youngster, a member of the community who was born in Israel (along with more than 1,200 other saints these past forty-plus years), played the main character, a twenty-something-year-old Ben Ammi Ben Israel, under the scorching sun. Ben Ammi, in his late sixties by that year's tribute, is the community's "anointed spiritual leader," their *mashiach* (messiah), and the teenager playing Ben Ammi's younger self that hot day had real acting ability, especially in terms of physical comedy, which he used to great effect, sweating and thrashing about his asphalt stage with a masterful combination of wildness and restraint.

Depicting Ben Ammi's 1966 interaction with an adamant angel Gabriel back in Chicago, one of the AHIJ's quintessential origin stories, this teenage thespian was spiritedly lighthearted about the exchange, going for a tone close to slapstick in his portrayal of that sacred visitation. In the young actor's depiction of things, Ben Ammi hears a voice, an angelic voice, but he doesn't believe it, not at first. Or better yet, he doesn't want to believe it. He's terrified. He even thinks he might be going crazy. So, this unwilling anointee tries, in vain, to ignore the call, to block it out, to disregard its very clear command: *Lead Yah's flock out of modern-day Babylon, the United States of America.*

A gray-bearded Ben Ammi watched this performance of his past from an elevated platform at the edge of the parking lot only a few yards away, his twelve *Nesikim* (Princes), elder saints within the community, seated right alongside him, all thirteen men laughing heartily at the zany rendition of this special moment. It was a public performance of AHIJ history put on for "family," local and foreign saints, but also acted out in unmistakably mixed company, including at least one anthropologist, his future readers, dozens more American guests, the Israeli press, and several Jewish and Muslim residents from other parts of Israel.[8] It was a particularly stylized retelling of this important tale, a version that demonstrated the community's sometimes self-deprecating playfulness, even about an event so sacred and significant. Saints clearly recognize how outlandish many of their claims seem to outsiders, but in a world overrun with lies and deceptions, they proclaim, "the truth" is bound to look strange. How could it be any other way? Still, ultimately, as one saint explained after the performance, "the joke is on you black folks; you all still trapped in America."

That same parking lot served as a volleyball court for another portion of the holiday stretch, with good-humored competitiveness about the game's final outcome producing almost as much laughter and fanfare as the performance of Ben Ammi's angelic exchange. The AHIJ's "holistic health maintenance" program mandates recurring no-salt days, no-sugar weeks, raw food days, "solar food" days (food cooked directly and exclusively by the sun's rays), Shabbat fasting, periodic enemas, and physical exercise at least three times a week ("to the point of sweating"). The volleyball match, much like the community's frequent softball games and long-distance runs (with even a few septuagenarians apparently preparing for marathons), is meant to flaunt the group's commitment to physical activity as well as its dedication to bold claims about the inextricable links between physical and spiritual well-being, between everyday life and immortality, between the unfolding of human history and the fulfillment of biblical prophecy. These are all interconnected parts of the AHIJ's intriguing story, which includes their international chain of vegan "soul food" restaurants, their many development projects throughout Africa, and their complicated associations with several members of an "Ethiopian Hebrew congregation" in Chicago currently headed by an African American man who has been called Barack Obama's Rabbi.[9]

The AHIJ is composed of several ministries, one of which is the Ministry of Information (MOI), guardian of its systematic approach to self-representation and public outreach—and responsible for documenting special events like New World Passover. The MOI is charged with capturing and archiving the community's exploits, as it did by videotaping that aforementioned parking-lot performance of Gabriel's visitation, along with portions of the volleyball match (doing this all with multiple mini-DV cameras and production crews consisting of saints from their teens to their late-fifties). But the MOI also recorded almost everything else that happened over those 48 hours of NWP, from staged presentations by community-based dance troupes and singing groups to scheduled parades and processions, including the "Nation Dance," where every saint in attendance boogies to a drum beat across the *kfar*'s main green, all of them dressed in Torah-inspired garb, members of each polygynous household in matching outfits, cords of blue cloth extending from the hems of their garments.[10]

Everything about this holiday is revealing, even its name: New World Passover. The AHIJ constantly affirm their "power to define," a commitment to renaming objects and ideas in direct opposition to standard definitions. This "power to define" is central to their entire global agenda and spiritual mission. They aim to redefine what it means to be African, what it means to be Jewish, and even what it means to be human. Attempting to rewrite the very science of human life, the basic parameters of our existence, requires that everything we say, think, and do (no matter how casual and seemingly unremarkable) becomes fodder for purposeful reconceptualization, for daily deconstruction, starting with language itself—each word reconsidered, every phrase carefully parsed.

So people shouldn't talk of "falling in love," the way one would "stumble to the floor or off a cliff," as one saint put it; they must "rise in love," deemed a much more uplifting and authentic way to characterize the sanctity of a romantic bond ordained by God. (Even the word "romantic" has been abandoned by some saints for its etymological allusion to "Roman" sources.) And other rhetorical recalibrations abound, examples of what social theorist Priscilla Wald calls (in her discussion of Frantz Fanon's efforts to redefine the limits of organic life in service to his anticolonialist politics) an "Adamic power," the divine right "to name and define as an act of creation."[11] This is quite literally how the AHIJ describe their venture into rethinking organic life and its recoverable potential, as a direct extension of Adam's God-given power to name. And every expression rewards inspection.

Take the term *diet.* It is the perfect word, saints will point out, for how many people on this planet (especially Americans!) eat, since most of the food we consume—meat and meat byproducts—will certainly kill us. And the AHIJ's entire spiritual and cultural mission pivots quite single-mindedly on life and death, on the many ways in which people easily confuse the two, death for life, and sometimes even on purpose.[12] So saints prefer *live*-it to *die*t as a way of talking about their own eating habits. They eat to live and live *forever*.

Another example of this heralded "power to define": the body-replenishing properties of a mineral-rich "Dead Sea" mean that it is much more accurately described, community members insist, as "the Sea of Life" not of death.[13] And that Live Sea is one of the first places saints take any guests who visit the Kingdom from abroad, providing them with cotton swimwear in place of polyester (saints wear only all-natural fibers that allow the skin to "breathe") and rejecting the idea, as one community leader put it to a group of saints in Durban, South Africa, that "somehow underwear, bras and panties, magically transform into public outfits called 'bikinis' as soon as you step foot on a beach." None of this, they say, is just semantics. It is the frontline of spiritual warfare. *Dead*lines are even called *life*lines whenever saints organize their work schedules, and all of these linguistic gestures (along with the community's elaborate veganism, mandatory athletic activity, and everything else they've gradually incorporated into their revamped cultural universe) are meant to rewire the brain's neurological circuitry. Strengthened synapses, they maintain, naturally follow from truly obeying Yah's divine laws and questioning commonsensical ideas about living and dying.[14]

Claiming this "power to define" means that nothing is off limits or unworthy of close reading and rereading. It is all-encompassing, an elaborate new dictionary for an old and corrupted language. And even what counts as "new" requires careful deliberation. In the case of New World Passover, for instance, the "new world" is on the African side of the Atlantic Ocean, relegating the "old world" to the one that European explorers and the history books written about them once labeled *new*— the Babylonian world that saints rejected in the 1960s.[15]

Everything is up for grabs here, ripe for the rhetorical picking, and this topsy-turvy existence is crucial to understanding the AHIJ's interconnected spiritual, cultural, and political goals. It all would have prompted anthropologist Anthony Wallace and other social scientists of cultural change during the mid-twentieth century to describe the AHIJ as a kind of "revitalization movement," a group invested in reimagining every single aspect of their sociocultural world—and led by Ben Ammi, a Weberianly charismatic authority figure, to boot, which is another quintessential aspect of such movements.[16]

NWP is also a reminder of the complex configurations of all communities, the ways they often blur their insides and their outsides. Ruptures with tainted and misrepresented pasts fuse—sometimes seamlessly, sometimes not—with the inescapable recuperations of those same disputed histories. Listening to the community's Hebrew-singing gospel choirs and soloists during NWP performances provides a sonic reminder of the Christianities that some saints have left behind.[17] Even the designation "saint" seems to signal a palimpsest. These prior experiences with Christianity (or with the various Islamic groups that some members have left behind) inform the AHIJ's sophisticated rereadings of the Bible, including a somewhat tepid acceptance of the New Testament and a major recasting of its central messianic figure, *Yeshua* (Jesus).

Some of the New World Passover's attendees are biological family members of saints and not actual AHIJ members themselves—mothers and fathers, brothers and sisters, who use the occasion as an opportunity to reconnect with loved ones "lost" to Ben Ammi, lost to the Kingdom. Or they are saints in varied states of compliance with the community's stringent tenets, some even backsliders hoping to get reenergized with a short bath in the Israeli sun. Fewer than the proverbial "six degrees of separation" connect the most far-flung segments of the African and Jewish diasporas to members of the AHIJ community, to saints residing in Dimona or linked to any of its many "jurisdictions" around the world.[18]

Those African Americans closer to the community's constitutive peripheries may simply have cousins, nephews, or lifelong friends who are now saints, or once were, or are contemplating the idea of future sainthood. Or they themselves used to be members and have now moved on to something new, something else, maybe Hinduism or Islam, or more orthodox versions of Black Jewry—the latter being a different rendering of things altogether, a difference not always negotiated with ease and mutual acceptance.[19] In fact, there are even other communities of African Americans who call themselves "Hebrew Israelites," communities hostile to Ben Ammi and the AHIJ's spiritual project, groups with irreconcilably different takes on what the label "Hebrew Israelite" actually demands in terms of theological beliefs and everyday behavior, including street preachers on urban American sidewalks who are consistently lampooned in free weekly newspapers all across the country as an almost laughable caricature of "Black Supremacist" hate, extremism, and religious confusion.[20]

Historian James Landing argues that earlier institutionalized forms of Black Hebrewism/Judaism in the United States (dating back to the late nineteenth century) provided models for the kinds of political and economic organizing that would later develop in the Nation of Islam and some versions of late twentieth-century African American Christianity.[21] And such links highlight an important point about the cultural and historical importance of this community, an importance not easily reducible to the total number of saints currently residing in Israel (usually quoted as somewhere between 2,500 and 4,000), or to whatever that number would be if we counted up all the saints living everywhere else.

The story of the AHIJ is not just a quirky tale about an eccentric spiritual "cult," a characterization often used to justify dismissing any serious engagement with their more idiosyncratic (to some, even offensive) ideas and endeavors. Instead, it is a valuable example of the complicated, ongoing negotiations with race, religion, and globalization that have always informed African Americans' social, political, and economic aspirations, ever since the first shipment of African captives arrived in a "new world" that the AHIJ has made "old." The AHIJ's new "new world" is not simply about leaving an old life behind, firewalling oneself away from the past, as if such impossibly ahistorical ambitions could ever be realized. It is an attempt to think the unthinkable, to prove that the seemingly impossible is really inevitable, doggedly forging (in ways that are not always liberating or inspiring, but sometimes certainly can be) a world into being that refutes and even transcends longstanding denials of African humanity.[22] At the same time, writing about a group like the African Hebrew Israelites of Jerusalem, an organization on guard against hostile criticisms of their atypical theories and increasingly capable of challenging an anthropologist's seemingly privileged ability to package their saga for outside audiences, helps to illustrate something noteworthy about the changing nature of social science today, about how the ethnographic branch of human research is made to bend and twist (and maybe even break) in shifting twenty-first century winds.

TWO

Introductions

IDENTITIES RELY ON archives.[1] Public recognition requires supporting documentation, which is part of the reason why saints in the Kingdom spend so much time gathering scholarly details to justify their pronouncements, so much time videotaping their everyday lives: New World Passovers, community sporting events, elders' wedding anniversaries, and more, from the extraordinary to the mundane. It is about actively building an archive, collecting and assembling records that prove a particular version of the past. But there are always other people with conflicting histories to promote, alternative accounts buoyed by their own data.

Scholarly and popular stories about "black Jews" or "Hebrew Israelites" often end up defending or denying the value of specific archives, vetting them as potential proof of autobiographical contentions.[2] *Are you really a Jew? How? What's your evidence?*[3] It is easy to criticize Jewish versions of this dynamic as particularly fetishistic, but all groups have litmus tests for belonging. All identities have doubters: *You aren't who you say you are! You aren't even who you think you are!* Some doubters drag their own documents into the conversation, or they provide contrary interpretations of everyone else's archival material. Of course, many people wouldn't even feel the need to invoke any documentation at all to dismiss seemingly counterintuitive conflations of blackness with Jewishness, simply ignoring black Jews/Israelites altogether, especially given the fact that there are so many other pressing issues to focus on when the topic is contemporary Jews and Jewish life, including the ongoing ethnic, religious, and geopolitical tensions that constitute "the Middle East."[4]

Anthropologists who study the claims that groups make about their own histories and identities are careful not to check vernacular contentions and archives solely against scholarly or "official" ones, an admittedly compelling starting point in a world where the assertions people make about their own pasts often come with declarations about how the planet should be organized for everybody else.[5] There is value in assessing the legitimacy of people's identity claims, but there are other questions worth asking, too.

Many authors who have taken the time to write about the AHIJ or about other Hebrew Israelite communities, some of the very authors I rely on throughout this book, often begin and end with either a pointed defense or harsh refutation of the most fundamental claim these groups espouse: that they are direct genealogical descendants of Abraham, Isaac, and Jacob.[6] Some offerings are only and exclusively about repudiating or affirming that allegation. Others quickly reject it outright and then try to explain why African Americans would cling to an identity that is ostensibly not their own, emphasizing psycho-pathology, political expediency, metaphorical overreach, or just plain disingenuous conniving as an explanation.[7] This book deals with some of the evidence and counterevidence summoned in such debates, but it isn't focused on corroborating or condemning the AHIJ's contentions. Instead, it is much more interested in trying (1) to capture a bit of the design and architecture of the Kingdom's intricately interwoven beliefs, along with the journeys of some of its believers, (2) to make some small sense of the complicated ways in which the AHIJ's practices and practitioners rehearse and recalibrate a set of ongoing questions about the links between race and spirituality, and (3) to highlight emergent concerns about the challenges of conducting social research today, even and especially research on groups already researching themselves (and using some of the very same methods and means that anthropologists employ).[8]

Thin Description is also a response to a certain kind of overconfidence in anthropology, an arrogance borne of the powers that "thick description" (one of its most famously borrowed terms) is believed to grant adherents. This is not just about critiquing anthropologist Clifford Geertz's revered description of thickness. It isn't necessarily a dispute with the way that he, in particular, tried to make a case for the centrality of symbolic interpretation to cross-cultural understanding and analysis. But it does ponder the idea that some contemporary investments in thick description might warrant reconsideration.

Geertz emphasizes that what separates a "thin description" of human behavior (the famous example he borrows from philosopher Gilbert Ryle is about someone "rapidly contracting his right eyelid") from a "thick description" of it (which Geertz parses, hypothetically, as an overly self-conscious and cunning eye-blinker who might just be "practicing a burlesque of a friend faking a wink to deceive an innocent into thinking a conspiracy is in motion") is an understanding of the "stratified hierarchy of meaningful structures" that make the latter interpretation possible.[9] For Ryle and Geertz, thin description is what you can see with the naked eye. It is a raw and baseline empiricism, the necessary starting point for social investigation but not nearly enough all by itself. Part of an anthropologist's job is to contextualize social behaviors for readers, behaviors that are never purely self-evident and that always reward more careful scrutiny. And these days, even shorn of its strictest Geertzian moorings, "thick description" is used like a mystic metaphor or methodological talisman that denotes an attempt at—an ambition for—rich, rigorous, and even *full* social knowing. Headlines or statistics are thin, even when they provide some potentially useful information, but thick description proffers nuance and detail hidden or misconstrued by truncated captions, crude observationalisms, and too-crunched numbers.[10]

The popular imagery anthropologists use to mark this thickened knowledge is revealing, discussions of anthropologists morphing into "flies on the wall" or "seeing through other people's [blinking and winking and fake-winking] eyes"—or even (at the frowned-upon extreme) simply "going native." These aspirations and characterizations signal some of the hubris at the center of the anthropological project, a hubris that has probably always imagined ethnographic thickness to be far thicker than it actually is.

Thick description, in a sense, has always been thin, but just as saints distinguish between two "new worlds" (or even between two different Passovers), we should also recognize that there is *thin* and then there is *thin*. One tries to pass itself off as more than it is, as embodying an expertise that simulates (and maybe even surpasses) any of the ways in which the people being studied might know themselves. Ethnographic spaces become dense with the swelling, the inflation, of resident anthropologists, and all the thicker, ironically, when they choose to shrink from view, omnisciently offstage, puppeteering things from far above the storyline. It is a thinness invested in an occulted version of anthropology, one that would pretend to see *everything* and, therefore, sometimes sees less than it could. What's left to see or say once a "thick description" has purported to decipher *the* definitive meaning of something, even the faux conspiratorial plots of would-be fake-winkers. Geertz's classic example, multiple levels of self-conscious eyelash-batting tomfoolery, is offered up with a sense of explanatory finality. Thick descriptions can even unmask the byzantine intricacies of convolutedly fake conspiracies, an unmasking that seems to leave little need for alternative interpretations.[11]

Paschal Beverly Randolph, an African American spirit medium from the mid-nineteenth century who flitted through time and space at the most canted of angles, represents a kind of precursor to the assumed inscrutableness of Hebrew Israelite claim-making. His work also reinforces this notion that the exact same terms can bolster oppositional undertakings, and the aforementioned *thin* versus *thin* distinction can be mapped quite evocatively onto the difference he embodies between contradictory forms of occultism. One version, as Randolph renders it, might allow people agency to do the seemingly impossible (to speak to the dead or teleport themselves around the world in an instant), while another forecloses human possibilities (let alone seemingly superhuman ones) almost entirely (by turning people into little more than mesmerized slaves). At worst, it is a way of viewing what otherwise cannot be seen (across vast stretches of time and space) because of a self-inflicted obliviousness to what is right in front of your face.

Thick description can be complicit with the more unproductive occultings of anthropological research, especially since seeing through another person's eyes is not the same thing as actually seeing that person. In fact, one precludes the other, by definition, unless the gaze is (tellingly) merely into a mirror. And talk of anthropologists turning into inconspicuous insects—or of peering out through other people's eye sockets—might suggestively be likened to old-fashioned sci-fi and horror genre allegories of body-snatching, soul-stealing, and spirit possession, yet another reason why a figure like Randolph, one of the forefathers of American occultism, will deserve some space in this discussion.

Even if technology allows us to peek at what someone else is seeing, usually in some relatively skimpy way (like giving cameras to "the natives"), what any of us actually sees—and how we see it—is about so much more than what's refracted by the mechanics of an eyeball or a camera's lens. And there is purported thinness there too, in the flatness of a video screen, the constraints of its constructed borders. Some critics claim that cameras cut out too much of the real action, leaving the full story far beyond the boundaries of any image's frame, replacing it with those spectacular and comparatively superficial mesmerisms of emotion and aesthetics.[12] Talking heads that cry or shout are usually considered more cinematic than the larger macro-structural forces that converge to produce their angst, and social scientists have long been suspicious of the camera's capacity to capture the subtler sides of cultural life.[13] That includes the father of American anthropology, Franz Boas, who believed that cameras could depict only the surface of reality on their flat screens, not true cultural depth. Gilbert Ryle specifically cited the camera's lens as an example of something that renders reality thinly, marking the stuff of thick description as relatively "unphotographable."[14]

This accusation of representational flatness is tangled up with any discussion of thick and thin descriptions. When philosophers like Ian Bogost argue for the value of "flat ontology," an analytical position that "grants all objects the same ontological status," everything on earth receiving its own spotlighted moment in front of the camera, these theorists are pushing back against what they consider to be counterproductive efforts "to contain and explain things in a neat and tidy way," efforts that usually begin and end, they argue, with the presumption of human exceptionalism and privilege as a basic organizing principle for all curiosity.[15] The flattening out they call for is an "ideal" meant to displace theoretical grandiosity and pontification with the simplicities that "could be rendered via the screen print on a trucker's cap."[16] This is the thinness of a slogan, no less substantial than the thicker volume it distills—the wink unpacked by Geertz perhaps most elegantly captured above the brim of that same cap, its "microstylings" less invested in total and longwinded completeness.[17]

So much of this difference between flatness and fullness, thinness and thickness, is about a murky middle ground fusing the literal to the metaphorical (a particularly auspicious habitat, some would say, for any discussion of black Jews). Thick descriptions have always occupied this middle ground, its social interactions glossed as occult entanglements. (Talk of seeing out of other people's eyes is no less mystical when described as, say, "stepping into someone else's shoes," a phrase that anthropologist James Frazer would have chalked up to the powers of "sympathetic magic," just a different kind of supernaturalism.)[18]

Anthropology has helped to create a rich archive of human life and history, an archive that gets consulted and challenged from many different perspectives, repurposed to indulge varied political goals. And anthropologists, those erstwhile "handmaidens to colonialism," have rarely been just modest witnesses along the way in all of this.[19] Invocations of thin description are hardly meant to reward that immodesty with even more license to rewrite the social record, willy-nilly, to our own ideological and self-interested ends.[20] It just reminds us that thick description never inoculated us from such tendencies in the first place.

Thin Description is also about how lives and ethnographic information flow, a story about how we all travel—like Randolph, at odd angles—through the thicket of time and space, about the way that both of those trajectories might be constructively thinned, theorized, concretized, or dislodged in service to questions about how we relate to one another in a digital age. I would want to call this a kind of flat ethnography, where you slice into a world from different perspectives, scales, registers, and

7

angles—(all)distinctively useful, valid, and worthy of consideration. And the thinness of these slices is central. A flat ethnography values such thin-slicing, even if the scope of the questions posed are, in some ways, as massive as ever.

But with everything that *Thin Description* purports to do (and this might very well be dismissed as the folly and futility of "fighting fire with fire," the conceit of thickness challenged by arrogance of a different kind), there is so much more that it does not:

(a) The stories of the AHIJ speak to Black Power and Black Liberation struggles in contemporary America writ large. The minister who serves as senior filmmaker in the Ministry of Information, for instance, is a former Black Panther, and many other saints have gone through groups like the Black Panthers or the Nation of Islam. But this book isn't an attempt to delineate those links—or to produce a detailed archaeology of how and why a city like Chicago served as an incubator for all of these groups.

(b) Inextricable connections between and among the categories of "race," "religion," and "nation" are thematized throughout these pages, but this book isn't a strict analytical parsing of exactly how those connections should be retheorized in the contemporary moment, though others have provided roadmaps for ways that that might be done most productively.[21]

(c) This is also not a detailed genealogy of contemporary forms of Jewish normativity, not another version of the argument about "how the Jews became white" (or black). It is just an example of some of the ways in which common assumptions about Jewishness get reimagined in one particular Africana context.[22]

(d) This book tries to provide some sense of how and why the AHIJ decided to embrace veganism, but there is so much more that could be done to connect their dietary evolution to other vegan movements taking shape in America and around the world just as the Kingdom banned the consumption of meat and meat byproducts.[23]

(e) Clearly, this is also not a comprehensive and complete mapping of the ongoing back-and-forth that constitutes the AHIJ's version of the Black Atlantic, even though it is only the specificities of these continual transoceanic crossings that make the Kingdom possible.[24]

And these are just some of the themes that are only glimpsed in these pages, just a portion of this book's egregious incompleteness, an incompleteness underscored by the flow of the narrative itself, which might be jarring to some, with seemingly important facts coming much later than they should. For instance,

(f) This isn't a study of masculinity within the Kingdom per se, but it does mark some portions of a larger discussion about how gender constitutes and is constituted by race, nation-building, and transnationality for saints. The issue gets its most explicit articulation relatively late in the book, and there is still much more that could be said.

But there is always more to be said, other potential readings. And *Thin Description* does its own cultural reading recursively—forty-five different ways of telling the same story, forty-five ways of blinking and winking and twitching through decidedly ethnographic eyes, at different speeds and with constant backtracking and revisitations:

(g) So that the "Power to Define" not only justifies why one "rises" in love (as opposed to "falling"); it also helps to explain why the AHIJ explicitly use a name for God, *Yah* in Hebrew, especially when they pray, even though most practicing Jews understand His name as unutterable. Saints define the phonetic landscape of the Hebrew language as sacred and connect that belief to cymatics, the science of sound's impact on matter.[25] What sound, they argue, would be more intrinsically powerful than the sound of God's Hebrew name? Speaking it, saints contend, produces material effects, even potentially redesigning matter itself, including DNA—the "power to define" as alchemy, or even genetic engineering. And challenging scientific claims about the architecture of DNA and the validity of genetic tests for Jewish ancestry are two more fronts on which the AHIJ's definitional powers operate.

Whenever he has time to ask me for an update on this project, my colleague Elihu Katz, the eminent sociologist, always ends up asking me a version of the same piercing question: "How generalizable is a project on Black Jews?" In other words, can it teach us about anything other than the Black Jewish experience? Some might even argue that his polite skepticism is not nearly skeptical enough. At one level, research on the Kingdom and its saints doesn't begin to explain—definitively or representatively—anything about "the Black Jewish experience" more generally. In terms of sheer numbers, most self-described Afro-Jews or Black Jews were born to Mizrahi, Sephardi, or Ashkenazi parents. Or they converted to Orthodox, Conservative, or Reform Judaism through institutionalized routes. So, there are many black people who embrace the label "Jew" and have nothing whatsoever to do with the AHIJ. If anything, they would adamantly dispute many of the Kingdom's central claims.

As policed and patrolled as any thick line separating Black Jews from Hebrew Israelites (like the AHIJ saints) might be, however, there are also interesting points of connection and convergence, many strong and weak ties that potentially bridge portions of the chasm. And with a certain kind of evocative flattening/thinning, a story of the African Hebrew Israelites of Jerusalem often resonates, in uncanny ways, with seemingly disparate tales of African and European Jews, of "Lost Tribes" in India and China, of "Overcomers" and Afrocentrists, of polygamous Mormons and vegan Hare Krishnas.[26] But not just these groups. So many stories of collective and individual identity-making share the same intonations and inflections. And maybe the AHIJ aren't so fringe and peculiar in an increasingly flat world where everyone can potentially get online, and far more outrageous claims are being championed in the bright, virtual, and screen-savered light of day.[27] *Thin Description* is an attempt to introduce readers to a group that is largely hidden right in front of their eyes, a group that most people choose, actively or passively, not to see. It proffers many different ways of making that brief introduction, of mining a community's archives and everyday activities for potential points of entry into an unabashedly unfinished—and unthick—version of their ethnographic world.

THREE

Artscience

I REMEMBER WATCHING MARLON Riggs tell the story of his own death. It was 1994, and I was in graduate school, scrutinizing his ghostly image in a classroom on the fourth floor of the Schermerhorn building, home to Columbia University's Department of Anthropology.

The dying, the death, was no less real for its televisuality, for the fact that I witnessed it by way of a rolled-out video console's totemic stacking of a TV monitor on top of multiple VHS players, audio/video wires and AC power cords dangling carelessly off to the sides. With a degree of brutal introspection more gripping than anything I'd seen before, Riggs, a controversial documentarian who had already been denounced as a pervert (undeserving of government funding) on the floor of the U.S. Congress for his previous film, *Tongues Untied,* a meditation on black gay manhood, had decided to use his final documentary, *Black Is, Black Ain't* (a film about the openness, though not the emptiness, of blackness as a socially meaningful category) to record his own end, his own death, a body more and more emaciated from the HIV virus with every passing scene.[1]

Black Is, Black Ain't, anthropological in its ambitious holism, spotlights all the many markers of supposed black difference: hair textures, facial features, skin tones, body types, striding gaits, musical genres, political predilections, vernacular styles, existential anxieties, stereotyped burdens, somatic movements, sexist acculturations—everything, including (literally!) a kitchen sink, the preparation of gumbo, southern Louisiana's quintessential stew, being its central metaphor of African American eclecticism and heterogeneity.

By the end of the film, two sets of sequences lingered in my mind: a bony Riggs, out of focus, naked and alone, jogging, as best his sickly body could, through sunlit woods; and a bed-ridden/hospitalized Riggs explaining how he wants his documentary to end, an ending that he would not live to witness. Riggs's narration, by the final few sequences of the film, is punctuated by precise calculations of plunging T-cell counts and lost body weight, a hot-pad on his bloated and non-digesting stomach, nods to the withering materiality and unyielding finality of human life, what Ralph Waldo Emerson once called "the irresistible democracy" of physical decomposition itself, of all earth going back to earth—*ashes to ashes, dust to dust.*[2] (At its core, the AHIJ cosmology is a refutation of such fatalist truisms, redefining "ashes to ashes" as proof of the human body's hidden capacity for "physical immortality," not as testimony to the inevitability of death.[3])

I have always considered *Black Is, Black Ain't* an audacious autoethnography, an autobiography in service to cultural analysis—and with an extra special knack for casting viewers as unrepentant voyeurs.[4] I easily nestled into my own voyeurism (an anthropologist's stock-in-trade, after all), locking eyes on Riggs's death and refusing to turn away—unable to do so. The kind of film that pricks and prods, I couldn't stop rewinding scenes in my head, as it offered me an early trip to one virtual field-site from which a portion of my own anthropological subconscious has never completely returned. My more formal ethnographic interest in the Hebrew Israelites had been sparked most directly, as I tell myself these many years later, by a brief encounter on a New York City subway train not too many months earlier, but watching this Riggs film on Columbia's campus served as something like this project's unofficial launching pad, its depiction of AIDS resonating with Siddhartha Mukherjee's characterizations of tuberculosis and cancer in the nineteenth and twentieth centuries, respectively, as diseases for which *"dying,* even more than death, defines the illness."[5] This recognition of AIDS as a disease that would seek to contort life into little more than death's shiny chrysalis helps to dramatize the central premises of the AHIJ's biological claims, which are adamant renunciations of both Riggs's homosexuality and his gumbo's ham hocks.

Several years later, I would get my first chance to see anthropologist Barbara Myerhoff's cinematic rendering of her own attempt to deal with death, *In Her Own Time,* the 1985 portrayal of one ethnographer's attempt to figure out if Orthodox Jewish customs might help her come to terms with cancer.[6] She was given a proper Jewish divorce (to disentangle her soul from her husband's), even a new Hebrew name (in hopes it might fool the angel of death), and spends much of the film describing her newfound respect for this community despite its gender inequalities, which rankled her political sensibilities. *In Her Own Time* connected some of the dots between Riggs's offering and my own interest in the AHIJ's beliefs and practices, especially those beliefs and practices linked to the community's redefinitions of sickness and health, life and death. Some of the AHIJ's objectives hover inside the very space where Myerhoff's touching experience with Orthodox Judaism brushes up against Riggs's catholic treatment of blackness, extending and transforming both in unique ways.

Myerhoff died two weeks after her main interview was recorded, and the film was released just one year before the publication of *Writing Culture,* an edited collection that helped to foreground and popularize reflexivity as one of anthropology's central conventions—and eventually, its most ridiculed: a supposed solipsism and disciplinary self-consciousness taken, critics claim, to unproductive extremes.[7] These days, Myerhoff's film is not cited or invoked nearly as much as it should be, and for reasons that might have something to do with how it carries its poignant and personal investments in reflexivity, a reflexivity that is, for her, as much art as science, part "self-help" (or retrospectively intelligible under such a maligned rubric) and part *auto-eulogy as cultural critique* (and not so different, in that sense, from what Riggs would produce less than a decade later).

I devoured *Writing Culture* as a graduate student, and it had me chomping at the bit to conduct my own ethnographic research. Admittedly, less because of the intrinsic lure, the interactive rough and tumble, of actual fieldwork (with its sometimes threatening and unwieldy exchanges, the sorts of interactions for which I conjured up *Anthroman*©™, my ethnographic alter ego, as a self-defense mechanism), and more because that book provided license for thinking unabashedly about writing itself, challenging erstwhile anthropological assumptions about ethnographic monographs being simple and transparent windows onto the world.[8] It represented a valuable rethinking of ethnographic representation itself (as opposed to what I considered some of social science's more naively positivist longings), demonstrating the genre's irresolvable complexities and contradictions, delineating those narrative techniques that help create a sense of scientific authority. This provided a powerful paradox: explication and mystification at one and the same time. Though critiques of "the *Writing Culture* turn" and its racial and gendered exclusions (made by scholars such as bell hooks, Ruth Behar, Faye Harrison, and others) felt justified and inspired, I was still stubbornly determined to write myself into that project, to embrace its flights of representational fancy, acknowledging the indubitable aesthetics/rhetorics of all anthropological writing—anthropology being a social science, like any other, co-produced through rhetorical flourishes and literary tools, not just disinterested assessments of objectively culled data.[9]

Anna Grimshaw describes the difference between *aesthetics,* often considered a distraction from social scientific goals, and *objectivity,* the ultimate aspiration for many social scientists, as one of the foundational fault lines disqualifying filmmaking from full academic legitimacy.[10] Grimshaw's framing of the discussion harkens back to Clifford Geertz famously chastising researchers for trafficking in "intuitionism and alchemy," mere "sociological aestheticism."[11] Such concerns and critiques help clarify, Grimshaw argues, some of the reasons why even though anthropologists have used film and then video technology in their ethnographic work since the early twentieth century, the American Anthropological Association would still need to put out a statement almost 100 years later imploring academic institutions to take films into account when assessing scholars for tenure and promotion.[12] That explains why ethnographic films aren't given nearly the same weighty significance as books or articles in most academic assessments of scholarly productivity. Film's problem, Grimshaw says, is that it always bends toward the aesthetic, the emotive, the artistic, the affective, and maybe even, as Csordas would put it, the "preobjective."[13] (It might be ethnographically thin, but it is creatively and affectively overwrought.) This aestheticization of ethnographic inquiry has always been, for some anthropologists, precisely what beckoned, enticingly, with books like *Writing Culture* opening up more and more points of entry into just such scholarly desires.

Media historian John Durham Peters maintains that new media technologies, from telegraphy to telephony, radio to television, photography to film, have always been predicated on complex academic and everyday desires, including an existential yearning to beat back death itself, to transcend our own mortality (our very humanity, implies Peters) in search of ways to communicate like angels or gods (unmediated, without the low tawdriness of mere words or gestures), smashing our way through the walled-up interiors that seem to alienate us from one another.[14] All media communication is, in a sense, communication with the dead, Peters says, which is one interpretation of what Roland Barthes describes as the existential power of all photographs. They are always really *spirit photographs*, ways to glimpse our own pending demise, to peer across that great divide. It is an attempt to watch ourselves dying, our celluloid ghosts forever staring back at us from the future's past.[15] Riggs and Myerhoff provide just one way of literalizing that interpretation.

Films are primary examples of what my colleague Greg Urban calls "metaculture," humanity-made commentaries on other aspects of cultural life (and death).[16] But this is an understanding of film that is no longer just "film" at all, a decidedly twentieth-century term and commercial product that also chronicles its own demise in an increasingly digital age. Film's days are numbered, it seems, given the nonlinear, temporally textured, and even potentially death-defying logics of new digital technologies. The "digital" is often boasted about as having a power to rupture time and space in many contemporary articulations of its prowess. An array of questions follows from such proclamations, some of which ground this book and the stories it seeks to tell. What might the "digital" imply for writing and studying culture today? Is the digital to "thin" what analog's hiss-filled imperfections (in a musical context) are to "thick"? And to what extent does watching Riggs's or Myerhoff's films (admittedly, via the analogics of VHS tapes back in the 1990s, not DVDs) demand new definitions of "ethnography" in the twenty-first century?[17] How about viewing a documentary about Orthodox Jewish practices in California that doubles as a last will and testament for its anthropological investigator? Should writing-up such viewings for anthropological consumption demand new tactics? That is, what kind of writing does a "digital culture" afford or oblige? And how representative and intriguing are the answers to these questions when the object of scrutiny is the African Hebrew Israelites of Jerusalem, a group whose biocultural endgame is eternal life itself—and their story only half-told without a lead role reserved for "new media" technologies?[18]

The AHIJ project starts from a contention that nobody has to die— not Riggs, not Myerhoff, not you, not me, nobody.[19] Saints don't simply want to digitally document the inevitability of life's end, to leverage the indexical power of photochemical, electromagnetic, and digital picture-taking as a monument to fallen saints. They intend, instead, to demonstrate a very different way of theorizing how human beings might defeat death. Not metaphorically, via video documentaries that permit us to see the dead in reanimated life (Riggs still in his hospital bed, Myerhoff in her wheelchair), but literally, allowing human bodies qua bodies to live longer, much longer. Even forever. The AHIJ community uses veganism, their "Edenic" *live-it,* as a central component of a science-sifting contention that human cells have the capacity to regenerate into perpetuity.[20] That our physical bodies were physiologically designed for everlasting life.

This immortality might be evocatively thematized as another way to circumvent chronological timekeeping, a different idiom for discussions about "the digital" as something that short-circuits or confounds time itself—that might even, in a way, last forever. At the most basic level, a "sexist" blog post, a "racist" Youtube rant, or an "offensive" tweet all continue to circulate in something close to their original forms well after their authors have tried to remove them from cyberspace. But they don't die. Not anymore. They multiply, go viral, the web's version of cancerous excess and mass-mediated timelessness.

The faint and forced links between Riggs's and Myerhoff's medita-
tions on death and identity (one tied to Blackness, the other to Orthodox
Judaism) and the AHIJ's social and spiritual project of synching a particular kind of "Blackness" to a specific brand of "Judaism/Hebrewism"
in the fight against existential uncertainty and "social death" actually
simulate some of the convoluted ways in which ethnographic research
itself typically unfurls, in fits and starts, disconcerting ebbs and flows,
differently shaped bits and pieces, a string of differently connected short
stories only subsequently understood as novelistic, a cobbling together
of disparate scales of experience and moments of cathected social
exchange mostly smoothed out afterward, a clunky empirical process
that this book's peculiar flow attempts to mime.[21] This may be another
way to think about what it could mean to fashion "a mode of ethnography that undermines its empiric."[22] At least a little bit, along with its
own *temporic,* its expected timetable. Ethnographic time has always
been nonlinear, especially if we include traditional ethnography's
attempts to place Western researchers and non-Western research subjects at decidedly different points along a trajectory of progress from
"primitive" to "modern," slotting them in vastly distant time zones of
developmental history.[23] Anthropology stands accused and convicted of
this specific brand of nonlinear thinking. Critiques of such temporal dis-
tancing usually emphasize ethnographic *writings,* but gathering anthropological information is also never a strictly linear affair.

Ethnographic research occupies what Jane Guyer calls "punctuated
time," a readily telescoped and tampered with sense of time that requires
us to diligently consider "ethics and temporality together."[24] Ethnography
should not just be cast as the mechanism for spying and deconstructing
the timescapes of Mayan calendars, financial derivatives, and evangelical
apocalypticisms, examples from Guyer's evocative work. Ethnographers
play with and punctuate time as well. In fact, as *Writing Culture* helped
to argue, too-linear narratives may be most misleading of all, crooked
data points and varied time scales actually constituting the disparate
dots strung together in service to all cultural portraiture, no matter how
magnificent or miniscule.

Vicky Kirby makes a case for how each one of these dots/points might
(even must) contain the entirety of the portrait, what she describes (in

her reading of Derrida's undervalued importance to science studies) as "dimensional condensations within linearity" and the "harmonies of the whole within the fragment," making all of the aforementioned points/ dots "quantum 'entities' that have a specific, delimited locality as well as a global presence or efficacy."[25] In some ways, this is a differently pitched commitment to flat or tiny ontologies, and she offers up a kind of thought experiment: What if the tiniest instinctual choreographies of insects or symbiotic micro-workings of cells actually demonstrate reasoned actions of a piece with other cultural practices? What if culture doesn't have a monopoly on thinking? (This is an AHIJ claim, if ever there was one.)[26]

In Kirby's version of things, ethnography is the partial study of a planet that is already studying itself. If the world is in the wafer and tornadoes stir the contents of teacups, it is all because of nature's ongoing self-experimentations.[27] Nature theorizes itself, which compels us, she argues, to reexamine our assumptions about its inaccessibility vis-à-vis language—as well as related claims about humanity cornering the market on semiotic complexity. In what might be described as a tenselessly digital version of time, Kirby also posits a world where the past, present, and future comingle inextricably, thwarting attempts at simple chronology. Being is recursive, allowing for worm-holed shortcuts through time and space, even demanding quantum leaps of sociocultural analysis. How might ethnographies negotiate these quantum dynamics and expectations, and what modes of both/and "artscience," to use David Edwards's framing, do they ultimately promote?[28] Edwards champions artscience labs where the production of good ideas can get "accelerated," unconventional places organized against the grain of disciplinary boundaries, spaces that capitalize on the differential strengths of art and science. Couldn't the so-called "social" laboratory be thought of as a kind of artscience space *par excellence,* even if the term is usually expressed as a way to highlight the science side of things?

Given its ambitious reach across the humanities, social sciences, and physical sciences, anthropology seems especially primed for demonstrating the inadequacies of pitting art against scientific activity, nature against culture, life against death, or even linear against nonlinear time. Guyer, Grimshaw, and Kirby differently suggest that the genre of ethnography might help us to reconsider such potentially straitjacketing binaries, approaching anthropological research in ways that allow for actual *thinking*, as opposed to the forms of "disciplinary decadence" that philosopher Lewis Gordon persuasively shows can make such thoughtfulness appear almost "indecent" within the confines of certain discipline-specific insularities—even within as intrinsically interdisciplinary a field as anthropology.[29]

Ethnography loves gesturing toward new models of (and for) the world, reimagining cultural life's social scientific staging, and studying the AHIJ encourages an appreciation of the many connections to be drawn between seemingly agonistic and mutually exclusive domains that cut across scholarly fields and faultlines: nature, culture; new, old; art, science; Africa, Israel; primitive, modern; fiction, fact; living, dying; thin, thick. Unbelievable connections. Implausible associations. Maybe just perfect for the foolhardy aspirations of quantum anthropologies and the stories they might want to tell.

FOUR

Megiddo

THE Y2K BUG was supposed to end the world, or at least our version of it. Technology would be humanity's downfall, catapulting us back to the Stone Age, the entire thing almost laughable, were the stakes not so high, for its bottom-line simplicity: binary computation's inability to accommodate a switch from 99 in the year 1999 to 00 in 2000 (a major concern given our ubiquitous and completely reasonable practice of abbreviating years just this way). Computers might render January 1st of the new millennium as 1900, the experts said, or as 19100. Or even just as a "fatal error" of some kind. And then global chaos would ensue, the computers that powered everything from ATMs to electrical grids and nuclear power plants ceasing to function properly—or at all.

As many of us remember, governments around the world took these fears very seriously, frantically trying to fix the problem. Just in case the worst happened and modern life was flung back to a prehistoric moment (another kind of challenge to the assumed inevitability of progressive, linear time), the U.S. government put together a list of potential terrorist groups that might try to capitalize on any overnight slide into planetary pandemonium. Some of the organizations on its watch-list already considered the year 2000 ominous. They prophesied that it would mark the start of Armageddon, the apocalyptic final battle of Good versus Evil, with Y2K as its imagined trigger. According to an FBI report issued in October of 1999, several different groups were being monitored as a precaution, including a few white supremacist organizations, some antigovernment militias, and the "Black Hebrew Israelites."

The AHIJ have been trying to distance themselves (in terms of rhetoric, ideology, and public posturing) from other Hebrew Israelite "camps" throughout urban America, camps that are popularly dismissed as delusional, anti-Semitic, hyperparanoid, and extremist in their hatred toward white America.[1] When the FBI was releasing its Y2K watch-list, I was going to nightly classes with one of those other Israelite camps in Harlem, an experience that gave Anthroman©™ several opportunities to hear young Israelite men talk about Project Megiddo and the government's preemptive approach to threats posed by these "biblically driven cults." The young Israelite men described law enforcement's anxious march to December 31st as a "set-up," just another way to justify attacking black neighborhoods. At the same time, though, some of them boldly pondered the potential upside to an all-out "race war," since it would finally allow Yahweh to provide them with an opportunity to slay His enemies and restore His righteous people to power.

The first time I visited Dimona in 2005, saints were still concerned that they were being conflated and confused with these other camps back in the States, collectives infamous for soapboxing on city sidewalks in less than wholly civil ways. One *Village Voice* headline from 2011 labeled the camp that I'd visited as a graduate student "New York's Most Obnoxious Prophets," describing them as "bushy-bearded" black men who "scream and curse" at pedestrians with some of "the craziest shit you've ever heard in your life."[2] Sar Ahmadiel Ben Yehuda, the AHIJ's Minister of Information in Dimona, likes to talk about a time in the 1970s when he naively came upon this very camp in Harlem, the same one that I had briefly examined in the months and years leading up to January 1, 2000. He was still relatively new to the Hebrew Israelite community in those psychedelic 1970s, but he had "long been searching for its truth," even before he ever realized he was doing so. Many of the saints frame their personal stories about "finding" the Kingdom with this exact logic: they had been looking, searching, all along; they just didn't know what they were looking *for* until they found it.[3]

Sar Ahmadiel grew up in a working-class neighborhood in Washington, DC. His family wasn't particularly religious, but he did go to church, somewhat grudgingly, eventually deciding between two options (after his parents divorced), his father's nearby Catholic diocese or his mother's Methodist congregation across town. He made his choice based on the length of their respective Sunday services; as far as he was concerned, the shorter, the better. He already considered Christianity suspect. Its message "wasn't adding up."

Ahmadiel's birth name, his "Jake name," as the community calls it, was Donald, and young Donnie split time between his parents' homes, with summer breaks bringing visits from his fraternal grandmother, a Jewish woman he would increasingly distance himself from as a function of his growing anger at white American racism.[4] He made his politics very personal.

After high school, he had dreams of a professional life on Capitol Hill, but a college internship there soured him on the idea, destroying any illusion he might have had about electoral politics "as an avenue for black liberation," which was his explicit goal by then, once the Black Power ethos had gotten a hold of him. He could easily have become a Black Panther, Ahmadiel says, and he "probably would have" had he not met *Nasik* (Prince) Asiel at Howard University in the early 1970s.

Asiel was the AHIJ's most famous international spokesperson, and he had convened a gathering at that historically black university, my alma mater, to discuss the community's relatively recent emigration to Israel with faculty, students, and staff on campus and any curious members of the local community. They were actively trying to recruit more settlers, and Ahmadiel immediately felt the truth of their message. The saints were talking directly to him, and their story, their truth, was the one he had been longing to hear. Their story was his story, and he immediately began the process of internalizing their teachings and sharing that knowledge with family and friends. A few accepted it and joined the community, including his closest buddy and roommate at the time, but most of the people he knew and loved didn't. After listening to his son rattle off the many reasons he had for joining the Kingdom and embracing its truth, Ahmadiel's father rejected the idea unequivocally. "You read yourself into it," he said gruffly. "Now read yourself out."

Though his father's incredulity was painful, and would influence their complicated relationship for the next four decades, Ahmadiel would not be deterred. Within a couple of years, he was one of the community's most reliable foot soldiers, responsible for the thankless job of shuttling saints to and from New York's JFK airport. Sometimes he'd have to fly with them from, say, Chicago or Atlanta, get them to their airline terminal, and then fly right back out the very same day. Or he'd pick saints up at JFK after their long flights from Tel Aviv and escort them to whatever American city was slated to serve as their stateside destination for the next few weeks or months (as they prepared more saints in the United States for emigration to Dimona). The 1970s were a busy time for the community. Saints were still recovering from a brief stint in Liberia, their first stop after leaving America in 1967, and battling almost daily for the right to remain in Israel, where they'd arrived in 1969, only a couple of years after the Six-Day War allowed Israel to expand its national borders.[5]

Whenever Ahmadiel's schedule got really busy back then, saints coming from and going to New York at a particularly intense clip, he would spend more time hanging out in the Big Apple, combining pickups and drop-offs, entertaining himself by walking around Manhattan in search of people to talk to, spreading the news about what Ben Ammi was doing for the hundreds of African Americans that he had already successfully relocated abroad.

During one of those extended stints in New York, Ahmadiel happened upon a building on 125th Street that boasted huge, colorful placards in several of its tattered windows, placards decorated with spray-painted images of a lion and lamb peacefully posed together inside an iconic Star of David, one strong indication that the Harlem building probably housed an Israelite group. Excited by the sighting, he immediately went inside to introduce himself, informing them that fellow Israelites had already left America and were looking for many more recruits to make the exodus. Ahmadiel expected them to be inspired by his revelation, to fall all over themselves in an effort to join their brothers and sisters in the

Holy Land, but when he stayed for that evening's class, he was pummeled with a series of biblical arguments about why their emigrationist decision was wrongheaded and ill-timed. Ben Ammi should have been waiting for "the ships of Tarshish," they shouted, a sign that was required before any such journey was acceptable in the eyes of God.[6] Ben Ammi was stubborn and misguided, they'd decided, maybe even a spell-casting minion of Satan (possibly in possession of some kind of magical ring that allowed him to mesmerize his duped followers).

By the end of that contentious session, Ahmadiel was crestfallen and bewildered, but he had also learned a fundamental lesson, one that he would never forget: not every black group that called its members Israelites would be receptive to Ben Ammi's message, a fact that only became more intense and undeniable over the years. And the same way Ahmadiel didn't assume any hard-and-fast difference between the Israelite teachings he had just started following and the ones espoused by that group on 125th Street circa 1973, the U.S. government didn't make fine-grained distinctions between and among African Americans calling themselves Israelites during the lead-up to 2000, especially not with the possibility of global bedlam waiting for us all on the other side of the millennium. All self-described Hebrew Israelites were suspect.

Of course, programmers diligently went to work debugging and reprogramming our computers, hundreds of billions of dollars bankrolling the massive Y2K conversion/compliance process, and the doomsday scenarios people dreaded never materialized. In fact, we seemed to stop talking about the entire thing on January 2nd of the new year, but Project Megiddo would still be invoked by AHIJ saints many years later, even as recently as 2012, another year of prophesied global annihilation (according to some interpretations of the Mayan calendar), when several AHIJ community members from Dimona, Israel, were traveling throughout South Africa for what were billed as "Brain Seminars," opportunities to provide local saints in Durban, Johannesburg, and Capetown with valuable information about how to protect and improve their cognitive abilities. One of the Dimona-based seminar instructors, Aturah, born in Bermuda and trained on the *kfar* in the School of the Prophets, the AHIJ's self-accredited and advanced-degree-granting tertiary institution, specifically brought up the government's Y2K accusations during her portion of the lecture one afternoon in Durban, expressing doubt that a subsequent written apology from U.S. officials was really the end of the matter with respect to the American government's attempts to defame the Kingdom and sabotage its efforts. Most of the people in the class grunted and matter-of-factly nodded their agreement.

The AHIJ are at least mildly invested in such apocalyptic talk. In fact, they had prophesied the world's end at least once before in the late-1970s. These days, however, they are even more interested in highlighting things like President Barack Obama's continued embrace of the Patriot Act and its potential for justifying the "targeted killings" of Americans abroad, which his administration has tried to define as constitutional, doubling down, critics argue, on at least one aspect of the so-called Bush Doctrine. In an email to me several weeks after he'd visited Philadelphia and met with some of my Penn students (and before we'd reconnect in Durban, South Africa, for those Brain Seminars), Ahmadiel invoked Maurice Bishop to frame the AHIJ's contemporary concerns about American foreign policy under Obama. Bishop, prime minister of Grenada until he was overthrown and executed in 1983, served as an example, Ahmadiel explained, of how certain messengers get deemed a "threat" to American national security, which then "justifies" violent action against them—with clear implications, he contended, for a future governmental response to Ben Ammi's radical teachings, once their paradigm-shifting and world-redefining impact is fully understood.

If America was in trouble in the 1960s, when the community first decided to leave for Liberia (and then Israel), it is in even worse shape by the second decade of the new millennium, saints believe, and at a certain point, the AHIJ will have to declare its work in the United States done, turning its attentions more fully to the communities they are cultivating, the new saints they are teaching, throughout Africa, "the Edenic lands." Ahmadiel emphasizes this shift in geographical focus without any apologies as he lectures to a group of saints in North Philadelphia at the end of a Shabbat service in March 2012. "A fire chief dealing with a burning house has to decide when to pull the firefighters back," he says, "when it's not worth sacrificing more good men for the people who are still trapped inside. They have to know when it's a lost cause."

Those blacks who have continued to ignore the truth will soon be left to fend for themselves, and the government's explicit willingness to circumvent constitutional protections (in the name of "National Security") heralds, saints argue, another kind of apocalypse-like scenario: a time when African Americans in the United States, not protected by the truth of Yah's message (because they continue to reject it) will be among those groups bearing the brunt of the Patriot Act's assaults in the form of indefinite detentions and preemptive assaults. That time, they claim, is almost here.

A day after Andrew Breitbart's right-wing organization released a video of President Barack Obama hugging law professor Derrick Bell during a diversity rally at Harvard Law School (footage that dated back to when Obama was editor of that school's law journal), Sar Ahmadiel sent me a heartfelt email that included a note about how much he enjoyed the short story, "Space Traders," penned by Bell and invoked that very week by right-wing media pundits to condemn the legal scholar as anti-American. Ahmadiel also mentioned the film adaptation, produced by Reginald and Warrington Hudlin of *House Party* fame. "Space Traders" is a tale about late-twentieth-century Americans effectively selling all of the nation's African Americans to a battalion of nonhuman aliens from some far-off galaxy—in exchange for enough gold and other valuable resources to eliminate the nation's financial problems once and for all. For the blacks forced, at gunpoint, to leave on those alien ships, their removal would be labeled "selective service" (again, "the power to define"), a noble sacrifice for the national good—and certainly not a replay of the transatlantic slave trade. For all people knew, these aliens might have been relocating blacks to "an interplanetary version of the biblical land of milk and honey." Or even just "a new start in a less competitive environment."[7] The aliens' only stipulation was that their ultimate plans remain a mystery. Americans promised not to inquire about the fate of these extraterrestrials' new charges. So people simply speculated, and thinking well of themselves (for white Americans) meant imagining the best.

This short story and its filmed adaptation were labeled "racist" by some members of the right-wing media in early 2012, and Obama's detractors were gearing up to use his past connections with Bell, who had just died the year before, in an effort to portray the president as an ideological extremist. Ahmadiel found this Bell-Obama "controversy" silly, and he certainly wasn't waiting for space aliens to invade the planet in search of black people. But he did consider it ironic that in an era of the Patriot Act and global fiscal crises, a story like this one, premised on an American president unapologetically bypassing the Constitution (to sell his own citizens), would be at the center of such a bizarre political firestorm, as though it were bubbling up from very real anxieties about threats to individual liberty rooted deep in the country's collective unconscious. But more than that, Ahmadiel also expressed genuine concern for me and for the safety of my family here in "Babylon."

Between the irrational ratcheting up of hostile political partisanship and the Obama White House's embrace of expanded governmental powers, "these times are unlike any other we've seen," Ahmadiel wrote. He wanted me to keep my eyes open, to really consider his words, to think about what kind of future appeared to be on the horizon. Per his musings on the power and insight of Bell's story, I immediately read it online, for the first time, and rewatched several clips from that 1994 made-for-TV adaptation.

The story's lead character, Professor Gleason Golightly, played in the film with an inappropriate amount of dignity (given the outlandish circumstances of the plot) by Robert Guillaume, is a well-connected black political operative who is part of the president's inner circle. He is also a man who fights the emigration plan right from the very beginning, only finding out (the day after the national referendum mandating blacks' intergalactic relocation finally passes) that he and his family will not be given asylum or "granted detainee status" in another country on Earth—as the president's administration had insincerely promised. Instead, on Martin Luther King Jr. Day, Golightly and his kin, along with the rest of the country's African American population, are forced to line up along the national coastline for teleportation to alien ships hovering high above them. "There was no escape, no alternative," the story's last lines make clear. "Heads bowed, arms now linked by slender chains, black people left the New World as their forebears had arrived."

FIVE

Chicago

B EN CARTER WAS working as a metallurgist at a foundry in Chicago in 1964 when an elder in the community began to teach him about his true Israelite roots. According to a couple of accounts, the year was 1963, not 1964. And his name might have been Gerson Parker at the time, not Ben Carter. Some historians have even perpetuated the erroneous claim that he was a bus driver. The story of the African Hebrew Israelites of Jerusalem, like any tale sustained through the necessary retellings that create collective memory, consists of many overlapping historical narratives and disputes of recapitulated fact—some easy to reconcile, others irremediably discrepant. Of course, this makes the AHIJ's history no different from "official" narratives about, say, the founding of the American republic or the fall of ancient Rome, no less prone to the privileging of certain pasts over others, mistakenly or on purpose.

I have heard community members relay details about this founding moment in that foundry many times. They have heard it from elders in the community and studied the tale from some of the same books I've consulted. As the story goes, Carter was getting a drink at a water fountain on the job when an Elder Eliyahu Buie asked him a single question: "Have you ever heard of Black Israelites?" In fact, he had. It was hard to live in urban Chicago at the time and not notice the exploits of various black Israelite groups, even if the sightings were nothing more, for some residents, than fleeting distractions from their peripheral vision. Different black Israelite groups were sprinkled all throughout the city, and Carter had taken note of their presence, but he'd never paid a great deal of serious attention to them. Describing his early life, Ben Carter [Ben Ammi] would later say that "a certain voice," a still voice, was always in the back of his head, poised but paused, waiting for the right time to let him know when it was necessary to pay heed. On that day, at the company's water fountain, Carter was moved to listen more closely than usual.

Carter and the early émigrés talk a lot about the powers of the "the Spirit" in explanations of their actions during the 1960s. Their grand ideas, especially the thought of leaving America for good, were all powered by "the spirit," they say, which they consider as relevant to the story as the early émigrés' own stick-to-itiveness and hard work. Looking back some forty years later, they make it clear that the heavy dose of substantive human labor they've all put into the construction of this new New World would have been a waste of time without the blessing and buoyancy of "the Spirit." And the same spirit, they say, opened Ben Carter's heart and mind to "the truth" that very day by an unassuming and anything-but-sacred water fountain.

Elder Eliyahu immediately began to show Carter how to read the Bible against the grain of Christian misconceptions and misinterpretations, unlocking biblical secrets to ancient history and modern American life that had long been hidden in plain sight, right there in the words of a sacred text they had all been trained to misunderstand. Their first discussion about the Bible and Israelite identity at the water fountain in that foundry where they both worked morphed into regular conversations, almost daily, and the two men kept talking—early mornings, late nights— meeting anywhere they could for more dialogue.

Carter was in his midtwenties. He'd already done a short stint in the Armed Forces and was no longer a newlywed, his marriage, a relationship approaching close to five years, already marked and marred by a young wife's unfortunate miscarriages. The two of them would eventually separate.

This was 1960s Chicago; full of conflict and corruption, but also rife with seemingly unprecedented possibilities. Like many cities during that turbulent decade, Chicago had a hyperpolitical public sphere: people taking to the streets; legal institutions slowly bending to the project of formal social inclusion; religious organizations retooled for racial protest. To African Americans on the Southside, or even the Northside, closer to where Carter was born, it meant an urban context informed by an ethos of change, of more or less radical machinations in the ripeness of the political moment—all plotted along a continuum from Civil Rights to Black Power.

Many of the early AHIJ pioneers, the folks who found their way to the community right before or after Ben Carter did, feature life histories energized by incessant and existential searching: stints in various Christian denominations, experiments with the asceticisms of Islam, membership in street/political organizations such as the Black Panther Party for Self Defense. They knew that their lives could be different. Like almost everyone else at the time, they were also talking a lot about politics, even revolution, making the case for drastic changes to the structure of American society. The many Chicagoans who found their place in some version of the black Israelite community in the 1950s and 1960s were part of a larger zeitgeist, participating in ongoing public debates about varying proscriptions for the ultimate advancement of African Americans.

Ben Carter was one of those garrulous Chicagoans, someone quite comfortable talking politics and social liberation—but also not above hustling to make some money in the meantime. As far as Carter was concerned, the Hebrew Israelites were offering a form of liberation far more expansive than anything else he'd heard out there in the streets, and he'd heard it all. Before long, Carter wasn't just a student of the truth. He became a teacher. Even in his twenties, he had an electricity about him, a charisma that some people described as infectious and hypnotic. First, he started sharing this truth with friends, meeting them at their jobs, visiting their homes, rendezvousing with them at public parks and eateries, all the while pointing out links between black revolutionary struggles raging in America's streets and facts about an ancient Israelite disobedience that caused those current realities. He would walk around town with his Bible in his hands so that he could show people how and why their ancestors, the ancient patriarchs, had been cursed by God for turning their backs on His commandments. This wasn't the same thing as the "Curse of Ham," which supposedly turned Canaan's light skin dark and ordained African servitude. To the contrary, this was a curse on God's special people. It started with the presupposition that blacks were chosen, set apart, decidedly *not* disqualified from the holy family. It was also a curse, Carter excitedly proclaimed, which would be permanently rescinded as soon as the descendants of Abraham, Moses, and Jacob repaired their relationship with the Creator, a reparations project that began with His people's collective reclamation of their true identities.

Carter flung himself into this new worldview, into this new sense of self. He had done something of a reversal in his life, from someone prone to hatching "get-rich-quick schemes" to an expert on the Bible who could challenge many of its taken-for-granted and popular interpretations in powerful detail. Ben Carter also began studying Hebrew in classes offered by Chicago's black Israelite community, and before long, he would change his name to Ben Ammi, Hebrew for "son of my people," forming substantive bonds with other members of Chicago's diverse black Israelite community.

Carter wasn't an island. The elder who had first taught him, Eliyahu Buie, was just one point of entry into a sprawling African American Jewish/Hebrew/Israelite community in the Windy City with roots that dated back quite a while—to people like Rabbi Horace, a man who had been arguing that Adam was black as early as the 1920s, and Elder Warien Roberson, one of the early-twentieth-century links between Black Jews in New York and Chicago.[1]

By the time Ammi was teaching and learning from fellow Black Israelites in Chicago, Roberson, Horace, and others had already begun to pass the baton to some of their younger followers. Prophet Lucius Casey started the Negro Israelite Bible Class in the 1940s. He railed against integrationism, called African Americans "the original Jews," was known to call white people Edomites/Esau's seed (as opposed to true Jews/Israelites), and moved his followers to Pulaski County, Illinois, by the 1950s. Elders such as Rabbi Joseph Lazarus, who had been a follower of Roberson, and Rabbi Abihu Reuben (who studied with—and got "ordained" by—New York's Rabbi Wentworth Matthew, one of the country's most famous African American Jews during the 1940s and 1950s), formed another group of Israelite elders in the Chicago community, the Congregation of Ethiopian Hebrews. Invocations of Ethiopia were deployed both as a nod to long-standing Pan-Africanist positions (Ethiopianism) and as a way of linking black Israelites in America to Ethiopian Jews in East Africa. Rabbi Robert Devine, originally affiliated with Matthew's group, started his own by the late 1950s, the House of Israel Hebrew Culture Center, and all of this was Chicago's version of the splintering and differentiating that had also created multiple Israelite communities among black Israelites in other parts of the country.

Even if some of these organizational names quickly fade from memory, it is important to realize that each one of these groups represented a somewhat distinctive set of behavioral and ideological answers to the same question: What does it take to be a Hebrew Israelites? Other scholars have done a good job delineating all the ritualistic and doctrinal particularities of these groups (and several more besides), their varied and changing positions on the incorporation of "white"/Ashkenazi Jewish traditions, on the very legitimacy of Ashkenazi Jewry, on degrees of acceptable militancy and confrontationalism vis-à-vis American society, on the feasibility of creating a viable black Israelite identity/nation in the land of Babylon—as opposed to leaving for someplace else.[2] And this last issue, emigration, would become the major bone of contention within Chicago's Israelite community, especially once Ben Ammi began to establish himself as a worthy truth-teller and an up-and-coming leader within the group.

Louis "L.A." Bryant was also a member of Chicago's Israelite scene in the 1960s. An independent entrepreneur who owned his own publishing company, Bryant was born into the Church of God in Christ, a Pentecostal denomination, but left there to preach and publish pamphlets on black America's Israelite pedigree, which he'd learned from family members and other believers of his former church. Bryant started an Israelite group called "One, Incorporated" and produced materials espousing African American descent from the ancient Israelites. He

would later change his name to Shaleak Ben Yehuda and become one of
the most important scholars in the African Hebrew Israelite movement.
He and Carter found their way to the Israelites' teachings separately,
meeting up and joining forces once the two men had each independently
established their reputations. Bryant would say, in a derivation on an
already-mentioned theme, that he was looking for Ben Ammi before he
ever knew that he needed to find him.

And there were still other black Israelite groups in Chicago as well:
the Camp of the Lost and Found Sheep of the House of Israel, the House
of Judah, the B'Nai Zaken Ba Shalom, the A-Beta Hebrew Israeli Culture
Center. Ben Ammi, Elder Eliyahu Buie, and others would often attend
meetings with more than one of these cross-fertilizing organizations,
going back and forth between them, trying to find ways of reconciling
doctrinal differences as they aspired to build a bigger, stronger, and more
unified movement. They were also raising money for new meeting spots,
manufacturing and distributing literature for their Chicago neighbors,
and debating the pros and cons of any initiatives that might cultivate a
more vibrant black Israelite community in the city. They talked to one
another (and to other Israelites of various persuasions) constantly—
comparing notes, merging practices, discarding or reinventing rituals
and beliefs bequeathed to them by earlier teachers, prophets, and priests.
They also continued to bring their message to nonaffiliated black
Chicagoans, slowly increasing their ranks, fulfilling a biblical charge to
wake up Yah's chosen people. And they were sometimes pretty effective
on that front, which meant that their numbers continued growing.

Anthropologist Merrill Singer, one of the first American anthropologists to conduct any sustained research with the community, chalked up
the success of their proselytizing efforts in the 1960s to the fact that it was
a fertile time for such missionizing activities, an era when "many blacks
were actively seeking a more satisfying identity."[3] There was clearly curiosity about these Israelites in and around black Chicago, especially as
their project of teaching the truth became even more adamantly linked
(by the likes of Ben Ammi, Elder Buie, and Shaleak Ben Yehuda) to emigrationist impulses. Though Marcus Garvey died without ever visiting
Africa, Arnold Ford, his one-time confidant, had taken a group of African
Americans with him to East Africa in the 1930s. Of course, even before

that, African slaves and freedmen had a major part to play in the early nineteenth-century founding of Liberia in West Africa. And there had always been explicit, if somewhat intermittent, talk about blacks leaving the United States throughout the nation's history, especially during moments when the country strayed furthest, often violently, from its ideals of democracy and inclusion.[4] But talk was one thing, and many of the newest members of the Israelite community, the relatively younger believers like Ben Ammi, had had enough talk. It was time for action, and some of them started to research methods for actual emigration. And sooner rather than later.

Ethiopia was the front-runner among potential destinations. "Ethiopia shall stretch forth her hand" was an often-cited biblical quote, and Garvey had already identified that nation-state as one of the plausible capitals for a future black empire. Not to mention the fact that Emperor Haile Selassie had specifically set aside land in that country for Africans in the Diaspora, an option that some Jamaican Rastafarians (positing their own genealogical links to ancient Israel through King Solomon's relationship with the Queen of Sheba) had already started to pursue. Ethiopia was also home to the so-called "Falasha" Jews, a group of Ethiopians brought to global attention by several different European Jews who championed their cause, most famously Jacques Faitlovich.[5] Some Ethiopians had declared themselves descendants of ancient Israelites and were persecuted in that country as a consequence. According to some of the black Israelites in Chicago (and Rabbi Wentworth Matthew had made this case in New York much earlier) the Ethiopian Jews were their genealogical brothers and sisters, descendants of the same group of scattered Israelites who left Judea with the destruction of the first temple by the Babylonians in 586 BCE

Even while Ben Ammi and many other black Israelites in Chicago were actively researching potential routes of return to Africa, and as that same message was resonating with other black urbanites in the city, a few members of the black Israelite community were still unconvinced about the benefits transatlantic relocation would bring. Some agreed with the idea of emigration in principle, but the timing wasn't yet right, they said. Their readings of the Scriptures demanded that any such exodus await an as-yet-unrevealed sign—again, maybe the "ships of Tarshish"—or for

an undisputed and undeniable messiah to lead it. Anything else was premature, they said, a version of the same response that Ahmadiel received
when he visited that Israelite camp in Harlem a decade later.

Other Israelites weren't keen on the idea of relocating at all, now or
later. The community's work was in the belly of the beast, right in the
heart of the land of captivity, and avoiding that task was an evasion of
their political responsibilities. There was work to be done in America,
souls to be saved, the lost to be found, which left little time for any utopian
dreams of a new life in any parts of an old and long-forgotten world.

SIX

Exiles

THE AFRICAN HEBREW Israelites inhabit a *new* New World, the
desert city of Dimona (redefined as "the new Jerusalem"), and so
does their eager ethnographer, even though ethnography (as anthropologists traditionally conceived of it) wasn't necessarily meant to study anything new, wasn't designed to probe the emergent realities of "modern"
life. We knead and warp it to address them anyway—in part, with the
hope that we might avoid the intellectual apocalypse known as irrelevance. And this rethinking of traditional assumptions about ethnographic research also recalibrates other taken-for-granted conventions
within the field, longstanding logics and principles that justify our
research methods and animate the arguments of our storytelling. It begs
a bundle of questions about what ethnography is and isn't, questions that
others have analyzed and advanced before, questions like (picking a subject not so arbitrarily), what is the status of "the arrival scene" in contemporary ethnography?[1]

Arrival scenes have long helped to "confer authority" (as I was first
taught to state things in graduate school) on the fieldworker while

delineating some of the most immediate, conspicuous, and observable differences between the communities being studied and the ones from which those who study them hail. But we no longer simply *arrive* at our field-sites anymore, at least not like before. Those field-sites already come knocking at our doors or flitting across our computer screens long before we get out of bed—and in ways that actually look and feel much different from the cross-cultural state of affairs just ten or fifteen years ago. What does that really mean for ethnographic work? Of course, this is well-trod territory in a discipline like anthropology (again, loved and hated for its self-reflexive bent), but I want to emphasize some of what I think still bears reiterating and even rethinking about such long-standing concerns.

Like many ethnographic offerings, this book's "arrival scene" (about a flight to Israel as part of an annual AHIJ holiday festival) is already not completely Bronislaw Malinowski's version of imagining oneself "suddenly set down" in a strange new land.[2] For one thing, hundreds of people are making the trip with me. It isn't a lone anthropologist pitching his tent in the remote "bush" somewhere, unplugged and off the grid, which was never the only model of ethnographic activity anyway.[3]

This account starts with travel itself, the plane ride over, not just my wide-eyed disembarkation in the Dimona desert. The journeying merits attention as more than just a means to an end. Granted, my shortened rendition of that trip quickly gives way to sights and sounds from NWP festivities, but it still places some of what might be considered the ethnographic margins, stuff traditionally relegated to field-notes or footnotes (or even just "headnotes," sometimes only shared at cocktail parties) onto the story's main stage.[4] This apparently frivolous move, and others like it that characterize what contemporary ethnographers do to represent the "multisited," peripatetic, unwieldy, and arguably "nonlinear" nature of anthropological research and practice, demonstrates a few important things about ethnography's newest mandates as a methodological approach and a literary genre. Or, as Erica James rehearses in her convincing take on family portraiture in the Caribbean, we might think about this discussion as an example of how "the guise of genre" proves useful for pushing back against some (though clearly not all) of the troubling complacencies and complicities of ethnographic convention.[5]

Cultural anthropologists who conduct their research in the United States have long known what some of our colleagues working overseas have come to accept, perhaps, only more recently: that the typical dividing line between "fieldwork" and "writing up" (one traditional way of carving up ethnographic practice) hardly captures the sloppier realities of anthropological research. There is something quaint about this particular dualism, gesturing backward to a time when anthropologists more readily disconnected from their own worlds and immersed themselves entirely in another.[6] And the supposed discreteness of those two places went without saying.

Reconsidering the research/write-up divide means, among other things, recognizing that there sometimes isn't a singular ethnographic "arrival scene" at all. The "arrival" happened before formal research ever began, maybe even before the ethnographer self-identified as one. Anthropologists born into their field-sites or considered members (in one way or another) of the groups they study—or just able to "pass" as such—used to be called, before the term was deconstructed out of popular favor, "native anthropologists," a rhetorical move that bracketed their efforts from the investigatory exploits of true outsiders, cultural strangers who only become friends, insiders, if at all possible, as a function of scholarly pursuits—a peculiar path to intimacy, indeed![7] Native ethnographers might have been described as either more quintessentially authentic or irredeemably subjective than other researchers, but native or not, everyone was asked to abide by a two-world model of ethnographic knowledge production: a field-site (way over *there;* the farther, the better) where data gets carefully collected/categorized and a home base (back *here*) that serves as a perch from which to pound those field observations into new analytical insights.

As a graduate student, I embraced the idea of cordoning off my fieldwork from my writing. It made sense to me. At a certain level, it still does. Ethnographers need the time and space to appreciate new worlds amply *before* their conceptual lenses or theoretical frameworks predetermine what they can even see and experience. Fieldwork takes real time. It is a slow burn, a slog, and demands our fullest, extended attention. And the write-up phase is, of course, just as important, requiring a different kind of immersion. At some point, ethnographers make a break with the field and head back "home" to the academy, specifically so that they can work through field-notes and recordings and anything else culled from time *out there,* sequestered with that data until they can emerge from their studious cocoons with new stories to share.

Anthropologists working in the United States have often found this two-worlding of ethnography a fairly difficult trick to pull off, though we still sometimes try to do it anyway, the equivalent of ramming square ethnographic blocks into round experiential holes. But such contortions don't always carry the day. For some anthropologists, ethnography has always meant writing (more than just field-notes) *while* conducting research, a "fly on the wall" writing on the fly, especially when and if the writing and fieldworking happen in roughly the same place, but not just then. Nowadays, it almost doesn't matter what kind of ethnographic research is getting done, where that research takes place, or with whom; the ethnographer is already and always in the field. And the idea of exiting it is increasingly becoming a kind of myth that we tell ourselves so that we can sleep a little more soundly at night.

When I was writing the earliest draft of the manuscript that would become my first book, *Harlemworld,* I lived on 125th Street in Harlem, about seven blocks from where that anti-emigrationist Israelite camp was located, the one that rebuked Ahmadiel in the 1970s, and I never moved out of that neighborhood to write. I did the bulk of my writing in the same weirdly configured two-bedroom apartment (almost as much square footage in the lone hallway as in all the actual rooms combined) where I scribbled fieldnotes and hung out with Harlemites, my "research subjects." And those same Harlemites didn't stop hanging out there once my focus shifted to writing. I just closed my bedroom door every once in a while as they kept on watching TV, listening to music, or arguing about profound and inane points of dispute in my living room, some of the same arguments that Anthroman©TM had participated in many times before. I did request and receive a "cubicle" in Columbia University's main library (a locked metal-mesh cage with nothing more than a desk, a chair, and a power outlet), and I tried to spend more time there than in anyone's Harlem apartment, even my own, but I never stopped *doing field-work.* There was no way I could. My task, instead, was to figure out how to balance a ramped up emphasis on "data analysis" with my continued, seemingly nonstop, access to more and more original material.[8] I remember sitting in that metal cage and actually lamenting my unbroken access to the field, considering it a kind of disadvantage, an anthropological Achilles' heel. I envied colleagues who conducted their research abroad and seemed to effortlessly disentangle themselves from their field-sites, a move that demands more of a herculean effort at self-deception now than it ever did before.

As banal as it sounds to talk about advances in communication and transportation technologies making the world feel smaller, a slightly different point can be made about the relative size of ethnography's two worlds, old and new, field and home, which continue to flatten onto one another in ostensibly irreversible ways. Modern technological advances might create a global village, but they also make ethnographic field-sites (including most actual villages) feel larger than ever before. That is part of the reason why anthropology must be global. Technology has shrunk the field/home divide for every ethnographer by expanding the field-site, allowing it to overrun its erstwhile opposite.

When I moved down to North Carolina for my first tenure-track academic job in 2002, I kept telling my new colleagues that it felt like I saw more Harlemites in Durham than I ever did in New York City. They would stop by when they visited extended family in the area. Or they'd call from up North and ask me to look in on relatives down there. Or maybe I could lend some of those same nephews and cousins a little money, since they were trying to make it through a particularly rough patch. These are all scenarios that just about any anthropologist would find familiar, even unremarkable, and Harlem, my field-site, was not so far away from Durham, my job-site, that I didn't have to continue negotiating some of the same dynamics that characterized the give-and-take of ethnographic life across 125th Street.

We get to our field-sites in an instant these days, via YouTube postings (clips from the AHIJ's 2012 NWP were already online before the end of the first day's events that year), or emails sent to our in-boxes from out of the blue. An unfamiliar phone number popping up on the caller ID, or maybe just through online glances at an edition of a local newspaper that you only used to be able to find in that blue metal bin at that one coffee shop in a small village square on the outskirts of some charming little town. For me, it also means periodic text-messaging with saints from Israel or Jamaica, Los Angeles or Philadelphia, Harlem or Chicago—to pass along information about an upcoming performance or event, to offer a take on one particularly bizarre news story, to send along a personal note, maybe recommending a book to read or film to watch. None of this justifies jumping to the conclusion that all ethnography can be conducted virtually; it only foregrounds the obvious: that some of it already and inescapably is—and has been for a while now.[9] But more than that, it also means that we are all constantly living, in a sense, in the field, which might require producing not just ethnographies "of the everyday," but maybe even a theory of "the ethnographic" *as a kind of everyday mode of being in the world.*[10] This book, then, would be less a work *of* ethnography (with the AHIJ as its ostensible subject matter) than a story *about* doing ethnography, an "everyday ethnography" practiced by researchers and research subjects alike, ethnography as a particular "way of living," to quote Mary Catherine Bateson, an approach to answering nagging questions (about good and evil, us and them, oppression and freedom, life and death) that is becoming more difficult to compartmentalize with each passing day. Ethnographers find themselves exiled to "the field," and there is no going home anymore.

SEVEN

Backstage

EVERYTHING IS ETHNOGRAPHY. That's something I'm constantly proclaiming to students. "Everything is ethnography. Everything!" An exile's anxious exhortation? It is, I admit, a seemingly silly thing to say, vapid in its catchall triteness—and evaporating into analytical use-lessness, many would protest, as a consequence. But this "everything is ethnography" ethos comes in handy sometimes, even just as a kind of academic parlor trick, a pragmatic and "serious game" played so that you don't work yourself up into a lather over relatively minor (or not so minor) frustrations.[1] In that way, "everything is ethnography" closely shadows the urban colloquialism for Zen-like social acceptance of one's lot in life, "everything is everything," and with similar implications for potentially lowered levels of psychological angst and ire.[2]

Whenever students complain to me about a course they are taking (because they find classroom conversations unfocused or incoherent, or because they don't consider their interlocutors particularly inspiring), I tell them to treat those sessions as "ethnographic opportunities." (I'm sure that other professors do the same. I probably stole it from one of my own professors and just can't remember.) Try to figure out how and why the people in your class are doing what they're doing when they're doing it, I (and others) say. See if you can determine what academic conventions your instructor and classmates believe themselves to be following or breaking, enforcing or challenging. This exercise sometimes helps to determine and domesticate what students find most annoying about the classes in question, even just by distracting themselves from those annoyances until the end of the semester, their colleagues more easily tolerated as unaware informants. Ethnographers are invested in their research subjects, and they usually try not to demonize or dismiss them, which students in a "bad seminar" are prone to do: condemn the course, berate the participants (to others), and then disengage. Ethnographic fieldwork, at its best, won't allow for such luxuries, and getting students to treat classrooms like field-sites can help them to think more like anthropologists, to search for unexpected cultural value in *all* social practice, even and especially the stuff that they take for granted—or don't particularly enjoy—in their own daily lives.

This is something like a flipside to any assertion that the ethnographic field is expanding, imposing itself on us in ways that aren't easily quarantined from everyday life. Only in this instance, students impose an ethnographic fieldworker's sensibility on their institutional lives "back home." This doesn't mean everything has equal heuristic weight or that we no longer need to be diligent about carefully sifting through ethnographic materials for possible patterns and larger implications, with an eye toward degrees of representativeness or generalizability. If it is conceivable that we are, increasingly, almost always "in the field" (and that any attempt to escape that reality is futile, ethnographically impossible), then at its best, this might portend more leveling of the ethnographic playing field, making social researchers accessible in unprecedented ways, even subject to a kind of countersurveillance.[3]

I was asked to give a lecture out West on my AHIJ research in 2007, a lecture advertised on that host school's website months in advance as part of a semester-long speaker series. Just before my trip, I received an unexpected message from a saint in Washington, DC, someone I'd met only once before, who wished me luck on my West Coast swing and asked, politely, for more information about what I was planning to say about the Kingdom out there. I hadn't sent anyone in the community a heads up about my pending talk, but the saint had little difficulty finding information on it. A simple Google search of my name and the community would have pulled it up at the time. And after such campus talks take place, they are often posted online, presentations of works-in-progress that continue to be accessible on the web long afterward. So, any saints who did not catch wind of the talk ahead of time (and had access to the Internet) could still watch the video many months (even years) afterward if they wanted to. Or they could read the campus newspaper's gloss online.

Given the way we increasingly mirror our social and professional lives on the Internet, it is becoming easier for research subjects to "study back," to track the ethnographer's movements, even showing up at academic talks and seminars, more examples of "the ethnographic" ostensibly flattening to include spaces once considered categorically beyond its purview, places where the researcher and the researched once rarely met. With respect to that West Coast lecture's after-the-fact existence online, we have one small illustration of the easier public access to ethnographers' backstages that the contemporary moment affords. And it has emerged with a renewal of interest in basic questions about the very practice of ethnography—practical questions, ethical questions. For instance, does an ethnographer talk about his project the same way at his university as he does when he's in southern Israel representing himself and his work to saints in the *kfar*? There are so many new ways for ethnographic self-presentations to get corroborated or critiqued. Of course, there was always the possibility of misunderstandings between researchers and research subjects, or of those subjects feeling misled or betrayed by their anthropological renderings. But now any devilish duplicities once hidden from ethnographic view (until, at least, after the fieldwork has been done and formally published) are much easier to observe—in something closer to "real time"—from across the ethnographic tracks.[4] If all human communication is postlapsarian—post-Edenic, as the AHIJ might phrase it—and constituted by and through miscommunication, the kinds of cross-cultural communiqués that ground ethnographic research are even more fundamentally susceptible to such misfires and mutual unintelligibilities when ethnographic subjects are newly privy to both sides of the code-switching (or tongue-holding) that can sometimes get euphemized as "building rapport."

The ethnographic project has traditionally been built on the back of an uneven exchange, anthropologists accessing a great deal of the "primitive" others' backstage without necessarily divulging too much of their own—at least not in the same way or to the same extent. Ethnographers have been managing this complicated and lopsided cross-cultural dance for a long time, and there has always been the possibility of performing missteps that portray them in ways that they would have preferred masking—or of ethnographers finding themselves caught in vulnerable situations that belie any effort to dehumanize or neatly sanitize qualitative social scientific research.[5] Even still, anthropologists could feel fairly confident about their ability to hide a good chunk of their everyday lives from the brighter lights of the ethnographic stage. And they would leave "the field" for "home" with a kind of finality that kept such distant locales at bay, even for the most interested of letter-writing informants.

With academia's ramped-up commitments to using the Internet for pedagogical and promotional ends, ethnographers' formerly backstaged presentations (in a relatively impenetrable Ivory Tower) are more easily accessed and assessed than ever before. Plus, there are many things gained from such backstage entrée. Research subjects mining this growing two-way permeability represents an important aspect of the changing terms of ethnographic practice. It makes sense to think about how ethnographers are redisciplined in a world where their backstages (back home) continue to shrink while their field-sites expand to encompass something approaching their entire lives. It suggests that we might reconfigure ethnographic context and content to include the kinds of feedback loops and post-fieldwork exchanges that the Internet and other new (increasingly inexpensive) technologies facilitate.

Anthropologist Johannes Fabian has written about an emergent "virtual archive" that allows ethnographers to circulate their research quickly while also providing for an almost immediate critique of their contentions from research subjects themselves.[6] This real-time exchange is not just another way to think about traditional ethnographic writing or to call for "dialogic" narratives. It also marks a recalibration of relations between ethnographers and their subjects. Fabian imagines a time when that glacial pace of ethnographic research and the books produced from it lose status, prestige, and authority as responses to ethnographic monographs or counternarratives of cultural analysis (from people who are not academic anthropologists!) "go viral" in ways that might one day even outpace citations in academic journals as an indication of scholarly impact. No matter where they are (and increasingly, no matter how much formal education subjects have completed), the Internet is becoming more useful as a mechanism for humbling the ethnographer's aspirations for a kind of one-sided voyeurism. Researchers are increasingly researchable, observable, even in their native habitats. And if a fundamental portion of the bygone backstage is no longer off limits, we might very well be witnessing a seismic shift in the nature of ethnographic research and the kinds of ways in which social scientists can be held accountable.

I would use the term "ethnographic sincerity" as a way to point out some implications of this relatively new configuration of ethnographic regions and relations, its center stages (in the field) and institutional rafters (in the academy) coming together, the borders between them thinned to nonexistence. But this invocation of "sincerity" doesn't imply universality, or analytical applicability always and everywhere. Anthropologists have provided compelling evidence of social groups around the world that do not share "Western" understandings of subjectivity and selfhood, the kinds that serve to anchor certain folk conceptions of in/sincerity. Linguist Bambi Schieffelin, for instance, talks about communities in Papua New Guinea with little notion of subjective interiority or potential individual insincerity, no language for imagining an alternative to taking what people say at something close to face value—that is, until relatively recent and sustained contact with outsiders.[7] For the AHIJ, my own intentions and motivations for engaging their community are almost, sincere or not, beside the point, prophetic mandate and divine intervention serving as more powerful explanatory frameworks than any tale I might tell about how I ended up conducting research with/on them. (The difference between "with" and "on" clearly has major implications for this discussion, but my own ostensible sincerity is part of what's at stake in either prepositional iteration of things.[8])

I started reflecting on that West Coast lecture as soon as I got back to Philadelphia, and I cringed at some of my overly flippant answers to several audience questions, at an occasional tone or terminological choice I made for academic colleagues that ventured some distance away from how I think I hear myself speaking to saints in Dimona—or to saints at the AHIJ's jurisdiction headquarters on Germantown Avenue in Northern Philadelphia. I might not be duplicitous, at least I hope not, but that is an empirical question, one that saints will answer. And they have access to more and more of the previously concealed data that they would need to do so.

But "everything is ethnography" should not just imply the expansion of field-sites or the newfangled ability some research subjects have to monitor researchers even after they've left the field. For a community like the African Hebrew Israelites of Jerusalem, it is both of those things, but it is even more importantly a way to talk about how saints live *their* daily lives, which they constantly and self-consciously expose to ethnographic scrutiny, much of it their own. Saints are consistently doing the work of ethnographic representation vis-à-vis themselves and the outside world, gathering and disseminating descriptions and theories of their own cultural evolution and of the bankruptcies intrinsic to Western civilization. This is not just "ethnographic" in condescendingly metaphorical ways. And it doesn't take the place of living. It is what survival for a group like the AHIJ seems to demand.[9] Stakes are high, and the entire world is also *their* field-site, bulbous and inexorably interconnected, which might explain why even if the field is getting larger and larger, flatter and flatter, it feels more crowded than ever.

EIGHT

Analogies

IN 2008, JEWISH studies scholar Tudor Parfitt published a provocative claim about the Ark of the Covenant. The Ark is that most sacred
of Old Testament objects, built at Yahweh's behest for the housing of His
holy commandments, a quintessential locus for His material presence on
Earth, and all the more valuable for having disappeared since the parting
of the Red Sea and the seizure of Jericho, two well-known biblical stories
that specifically noted its presence. The Bible last places that Ark in
Solomon's temple, which was destroyed by the Babylonians in 586 BCE,
and there hasn't been another commonly accepted sighting since.

Filmmaker Steven Spielberg's first Indiana Jones movie, *Raiders of
the Lost Ark,* makes finding that powerful relic its central plotline, and
Parfitt (dubbed "the British Indiana Jones" by the *Wall Street Journal*)
created international headlines by declaring that he had done just that:
successfully located the ancient receptacle for God's divine tablets. But
what made Tudor's story all the more fascinating was where he claimed
he'd discovered it. Not in Israel or Palestine. Not in Iraq or modern-day
Iran. Not even in Egypt, which might also seem plausible to many

interested parties. Instead, Parfitt maintained that it was all but dis-
carded and ignored among other noncatalogued detritus in an unassuming museum in southern Africa. He had tracked down the Ark of the
Covenant in Zimbabwe's northern city of Harare, one of many cultural
artifacts belonging to the Lemba people, a community that has reinvigorated age-old debates about the contours of the Jewish Diaspora.

Parfitt had popularized, several years earlier, the Lemba's folkloric
accounts of a long-ago exodus from Judea, and of their self-proclaimed
descent from the ancient Hebrew patriarchs.[1] They had already begun
to publish their oral histories, narratives of migration from a place called
Sena (actually, two different places called Sena), and of the part they
played in the building of Great Zimbabwe, royal capital for a grand
kingdom that fell into ruin by the fifteenth century. Those same Lemba
didn't eat pork, circumcised their baby boys, and sported clan names
that sounded, to many, more Semitic than Bantu.[2] Parfitt retraced the
steps of their putative journey, clearly intrigued by its implications.

In 1999, Parfitt controversially took that interest a step further, testing
the community for a specific genetic tag transmitted from fathers to sons,
information bundled together on the Y chromosome, the portion of
human DNA exclusive to men.[3] This specific marker is called the Cohen
Modal Haplotype, because contemporary Cohanim, members of a
Jewish priestly class (determined patrilineally), boast a disproportionately high percentage of men that carry it. Lemba priests, the Buba, were
found to have an even higher percentage of the Cohen Modal Haplotype
carriers than the Ashkenazi and Sephardi Cohanim, potentially corroborating the Lemba's cultural contentions about Israeli descent and
earning their story international coverage in mainstream media venues
all around the world.

Parfitt's claim, more than a decade later, that he had identified the
long-lost Ark added an even more controversial wrinkle to the Lemba's
story. He maintained that this container of divine presence (only handled, of course, by the Cohanim) was simply the hallowed out insides of
a drum, that quintessential representation of Africana difference.[4] This
drum, the *ngoma saba,* which the Lemba say they carried with them
from Sena to Zimbabwe, possessed, according to local legend, many of

the powers of the biblical Ark, and Parfitt used all of this data to offer a theory of ancient history that revisited (profaned, according to some) the ancient Israelite narrative with paradigm-shifting implications for how we might discuss links between Africans and Jews, the same links that play a central role in the AHIJ's reclamation project.[5]

Africans in the Americas have long wondered aloud about (or declared with confident certainty) the ties between themselves and ancient Israelites, making the AHIJ part of a very rich and well-known tradition. For instance, canonical histories of African slavery in the New World often start with discussions of Olaudah Equiano's slave narrative—one of the earliest penned and published in English, to international notoriety. And even if one accepts (which many critics do not) historian Brycchan Carey's theory that Equiano was a trickster who completely fabricated his birth in Africa and his personal journey via slave ship during the Middle Passage (because it provided a more compellingly exotic and expansive narrative arc for his abolitionist propaganda, allowing him to speak in the first-person about a past life snatched from him while situating his story well beyond the South Carolina slave plantation where Carey contends he was actually born), it is still worth flagging Equiano's many musings on the similarities between West African and Jewish cultural practices.[6]

Equiano makes several specific comparisons between the exploits of his kinfolk in Benin and those of "the Jews." It is a recurring point in the early sections of his autobiography. "We practised circumcision like the Jews," he writes, noting his natal community's "many purifications and washings; indeed, almost as many, and used on the same occasions, if my recollection does not fail me, as the Jews." To a contemporary reader, Equiano might look obsessed, preoccupied with this singular association, returning to it again and again. "Like the Israelites in their primitive state," he declares, "our government was conducted by our chiefs, our judges, our wise men and elders." The ancient Jews didn't corner the market on such political organizing, he says, wondering if they handed it down to his closest kin while also taking note of at least one predictable objection to this entire line of thinking. "As to the difference of colour between the Eboan Africans and the modern Jews," he states, "I shall not presume to account for it." But that (unaccounted for) physical difference will not sway him from his point:

> Such is the imperfect sketch my memory has furnished me with of the manners and customs of a people among whom I first drew my breath. And here I cannot forebear suggesting what has long struck me very forcibly, namely, the strong analogy which even by this sketch, imperfect as it is, appears to prevail in the manners and customs of my countrymen, and those of the Jews, before they reached the Land of Promise, and particularly the patriarchs, while they were yet in that pastoral state which is described in Genesis—an analogy, which alone would induce me to think that the one people had sprung from the other.[7]

Equiano references several specific scholars and theologians who argue for African descent from ancient Israelite stock, a clear attack on the fundamental premise of polygenesis, the idea that Africans were not children of Adam and Eve and, therefore, could be justifiably enslaved—guilt-free and (more importantly) sin-free. But Equiano is not simply positing a "strong analogy," as he puts it. He's talking the language of phylogeny. His claims are literal, not just metaphorical—invocations of succession and pedigree, lineage and bequeathal. Of course, some would say, it is little more than his early exposure to Christianity (maybe even as a child on a South Carolina plantation) that accounts for his adamant concoction of such African-Jewish similarities—his fetishization of those supposed links serving as a way for him to ground African membership in the human family, a key weapon in any antebellum abolitionist's rhetorical arsenal. But even if that is the case, Equiano might be overreaching and underestimating at the very same time. Calls for social inclusion hardly need to pivot on strictly Israelite origins, even in antebellum America. One could be a part of the human family without being Yah's "chosen" people, though the latter certainly sealed the deal. And lobbying for Israelite descent still wasn't quite enough to counter the most popular forms of Bible-based racism anyway, which could accommodate some genealogical ties and still dismiss claims of universal commonality and egalitarian community.[8] Not to mention the fact that being deemed

Jewish has never meant inoculation from the threats of existential invali-
dation and social extirpation. History documents just the opposite. Even
still, there is a power in those ancient tales of chosen people, and
Equiano's pursuit of demonstrable historical ties between Africans and
Jews continues to this day, the AHIJ's revisionist commitments representing just one expression of these ongoing and contested efforts.

In 2005 I received my first guided tour of the AHIJ's African/Edenic
Heritage Museum, an elaborate explication of Africa's links to Ancient
Hebrew Israelites and the modern state of Israel. The exhibit is a series
of flat, two-sided, floor-standing Plexiglas panels that include an assortment of maps, photos, drawings, excerpted references, and captions
documenting "the presence of African/Edenic people in the Holy
Lands." The museum was commissioned by Ben Ammi in 1986 and created by Sar Ahmadiel when he was based in Nashville in the early 1990s.
It was crafted to contextualize the kinds of research questions that drive
scholars' interests in black Judaism, to provide more detailed evidence
for Equiano's strong analogy. It is one of the community's most exhaustive attempts at "documenting Hebrewisms throughout Africa."[9]

My wife, Deborah, also an anthropologist, took that first museum tour
with me in Dimona. It was some two years before we would bump into
AHIJ saints in the woods of rural Jamaica, where Deborah conducts a bit
of her research, as some of those saints collaborated with local Rastafarians
on a health-food business for area residents, even brainstorming about
the idea of launching a new vegan restaurant on the island. For that initial
trip to Israel, we also brought along a research assistant from New York
City, a Jewish American graduate student who had visited Israel many
times before, though never Dimona. She toured the museum with us,
along with dozens more guests visiting the *kfar* that same week—some of
them experiencing the museum with us, others touring it on their own.
There was an older African American woman from a U.S.-based slavery-
reparations organization (who seemed to know shockingly little about
the Bible: "Who was Jesus again?"), a small contingent of African American men from a different (traditionally hostile) Israelite camp based in
Philadelphia, a governmental official from Ghana's Ministry of Health,

and many African American visitors from various Christian missionary projects and church groups.

Sar Ahmadiel made sure that the exhibit was set up for viewing, the heavy panels removed from storage and carefully arranged into discretely themed sections in the community's central meeting hall, the Hilltop Manor, right in the middle of the *kfar*, but he didn't lead the tour himself. He was on a tight "lifeline" (deadline) for another project, which meant that he couldn't spare the three or four hours that a proper tour would demand. And he had already spent a lot of time training other saints to curate the exhibit, including graduates from their Kingdom-based university, The School of the Prophets. With several versions of the museum mounted and capable of being moved around different parts of the world at a moment's notice, Sar Ahmadiel wanted to have an assortment of saints fully prepared to lecture on its exhibits.

Our guide on that day was Crowned Brother Elyakeem, a tall and muscular man in his late-fifties with a full beard speckled in gray. He gave us a two-hour lecture on the history of Israel, including a short biography of Theodor Herzl, one of the fathers of political Zionism, and several extended descriptions of cultural groups and tribes that practice "Hebrewisms" in different parts of Africa. But those topics would come up in the second part of our tour. He didn't start there. Instead, he began with a discussion of the project's methods, explaining the logic behind the community's museological approach, the organizing principle that guides their Divine Investigations. "We use the Bible as evidence," he says, facing our small group of ten, his back to the exhibit's panels. "We use biblical evidence, supported by academic sources of different kinds, a variety of them, and basic common sense, to prove that man's ancestral and sacred home is right here in Africa."

"But why do you call it Edenic?" The questioner, a man in the back, is feverishly taking notes, flipping to a new page in his yellow notepad, it seemed, every few seconds.

"We'll get to that," our tour guide assures us. "We'll get to that. But I should just say that Eden is the biblical name for Africa. And we can prove it. I'll show you how. Let me explain it to you."

Elyakeem turns to one of the museum panels and points at the laminated cover of a *Newsweek* magazine. Its headline reads, "The Search for Adam and Eve." He gives us a quick-and-dirty definition of mitochondrial DNA, talks about its discovery and its status as evidence for the theory that "the mother of all human beings, everybody, came out of Africa." Reading the caption placed alongside the magazine cover, he jokes about the fact that the article calls this theory "controversial," using the moment to drive home a point about Africa's centrality to any of the most important milestones in human history. "Africa is the cradle of all civilization," he says. "And if that's controversial to you, I don't know what to tell you. It is just a fact." He then begins piecing together tales of several different African communities' demonstrating "Hebraic practices" and espousing "Israelite" or "Jewish" identities.

I would hear other saints make similar points many times, both before and after that museum tour. During a 2010 trip to a conference on "African Jews" at the School of Oriental and African Studies in London, Sar Ahmadiel arrived at the event with a thoroughly weathered and multiply dog-eared copy of the book *African Apocalypse,* which combines the story of 200 "millenarian Israelites" slaughtered by South African police in 1919 (as they awaited a prophesied apocalypse) with the related saga of a charismatic Xhosa woman, Nontetha Nkwenkwe, born just south of that massacred group, a woman who also proclaimed her people's genealogical links to the ancient Israelites.[10] Nkwenkwe's unflinching adamancy on the matter would help get her committed to an insane asylum and later buried in an unmarked pauper's grave. Stories like these are found throughout the African/Edenic museum exhibit, as are those two famous relocations of Ethiopian Jews to Israel.[11] And the point of all this is to argue, unabashedly, for genealogical ties, for logical descent. All across the continent, this exhibit argues, Africans have been making similar claims about ties to ancient Israel, claims that many other scholars have been ignoring, discounting or avoiding. Saints dare people to refute their research or the museum's central contention: that these Africans are absolutely right.

"All of this has been documented," Elyakeem continues. "Language patterns, name similarities, circumcision, marriage rites, the separation of women during menstrual cycles and after childbirth. This is all what we call Biblical culture. Hebrewisms, pure and simple. And they are all over Africa, all over Eden."

Even before I made that first trip to Dimona, I had heard Sar Ahmadiel break off pieces of the museum exhibit's counterhistory for interested listeners—the first time, in a discussion with several twentysomething-year-old African American women who had stopped by the *kfar* for a very short visit, not more than a few hours long. They were headed back home to Tennessee after a trip to Japan and decided to stop in Israel for a couple of days along the way. The year was 2003, and I asked a Duke University graduate student to do me a huge favor. She was going to spend the summer in Tel Aviv, conducting some preliminary research on her future dissertation project, and she agreed to visit the community for a day. I was working on my second book, *Real Black,* which included a discussion of the Israelite Church of Universal Practical Knowledge (ICUPK) in New York City. Members from that Israelite camp had brought up, in decidedly unflattering terms, the story of these "crazy Negroes in Israel" several times, and I was contemplating the idea of visiting the AHIJ in Dimona, maybe using the occasion to write some kind of short coda for that book.

That Duke University graduate student decided to take a mini-DV camera along with her, and she used it to document a good chunk of her daylong visit to the *kfar,* including lunch in the community cafeteria and several conversations between Kingdom leaders/teachers and that day's guests. Ahmadiel was one of those leaders, and the ten-minute clip of him on the mini-DV tape that my student brought back to Durham, North Carolina, in 2003, would be my first time hearing him make the AHIJ's case.

"Why weren't the ancient slaves singing about the Niger River when they got to the New World?" Ahmadiel asked his visitors, everyone seated in two rows of chairs set up in the *kfar*'s library. "First of all, what happened during the slave trade? You have newcomers arriving to West Africa from Israel after 1,000 years migrating and at about the same time that Europeans arrived in Africa on their boats, rowing into the harbors to carry away millions of our people. There was most certainly collaboration on the part of Africans. But a very particular kind. Who do you think they'd go to the interior and bring back to sell except for newcomers? People who were outsiders, who had just arrived, who brought different cultural practices with them, which made them easy to identify. We give Europeans a lot of credit for something they didn't do alone, and we talk about African complicity without understanding the specific rationale that informed it." I could hear the amplified rumble of that Duke student shifting her weight behind the camera.

"Let's go to the Western Hemisphere, South America, Brazil," Ahmadiel continued. "Santeria has deep Yoruba roots with an icing of Portuguese Christianity on top. That's the icing; the cake is Yoruba. So go to the Yoruba. Go back to Nigeria and ask them about themselves and the Yoruba say they are descendants of whom? Israel. They have a totem pole called the staff of Oranyan, a huge monolith, over a thousand years old. And on top of it is the Hebrew letter *Yud.* The first letter in the name of the God of Israel. That's how you get the *y* sound, *ya,* in *Halleluyah.*" He lectured to these African Americans without a script and without a pause, all of his details plucked effortlessly from memory.

"In Jamaica, where did Bob Marley get the idea to sing 'Exodus'?" He went on. "Where did the Rastafarians get the connections back to Haile Selassie, His Imperial Majesty, King of Ethiopia? And it didn't stop there, because he was descended from Solomon and Sheba. The cultural thread comes through West Africa and Ethiopia and back to Israel."

Eventually, Ahmadiel brought the discussion back to the United States of America for his (mostly) African American audience. "In the U.S., which you all probably know better than Brazil or Jamaica or Ethiopia, we were forbidden to read or write. Capital punishment was the response to breaking that law. Our ancestors, being wise (you've seen *Roots*), how did they keep alive that cultural remembrance? How did they keep alive our cultural heritage?"

"Singing," one of the black women responded.

"Through song," he confirmed. "That's right. We sang. And what did slaves sing about in the fields? Did they sing about the River Niger? The River Gambia? The River Volta? The River Zambezi? No, we sang about the River Jordan. Did we sing about Mali or Timbuktu? No, we sang about Jericho, Jerusalem, and Canaan's Land. Now, there are those who would say that we got that from missionaries. The missionaries brought us their doctrine and the Bible. But that's not true." Sar Ahmadiel pulled out a bound copy of the museum's many citations and searched for a quotation.

"This is documented by a Scottish explorer named Mungo Park," he said, flipping through that manuscript, "which you'll find in the book *Black Song: The Forge and the Flame: The Story of How the Afro-American Spiritual was Hammered Out,* by John Lovell, Jr., pages 31 to 32. Those are the pages. You can look it up yourself. Anything I tell you, I'll give you the full citation. You can verify that I'm not just making this stuff up. And I'm quoting here. 'If the American white man fancies that he is the first to teach the Bible to his black slave, he is quite mistaken. Mungo Park, as affirmed by Marion L. Starkey, found that Fantooma, the Kaffir schoolmaster'. . . . Wait, you all know what a Kaffir is, right?

He waited for nods of recognition before continuing.

"'Fantooma, the Kaffir schoolmaster, had Arabic versions of the Pentateuch, the first five books of the Bible, the Psalms of David, and the book of Isaiah.'"

Ahmadiel closed the manuscript, keeping his place with an index finger and deciding to provide a bit more context for his excerpt.

"The Bible as we know it today is a collection of books," he explained, "but the Bible wasn't always like we know it today. It was handwritten in the ancient times. Why was it in Arabic when it's a Hebrew text? Because Arabic was the language of scholarship in West Africa at that time, because of things like the invasion of the Moors. That was the ruling language of the day, just like English is the ruling language in the world today. It was the language of the imperial powers. So, you have this brother who is in possession of Arabic copies of sacred Hebrew texts. I'll keep on reading. 'The unlettered Mandingoes entertained him,' Mungo Park, 'with stories of Joseph and his brothers, Moses, David and Solomon. They gave out these stories as part of their own folklore and were very much surprised to learn that white men had heard them.' So, our exposure in the States, or anywhere, to the Bible and to this idea of being connected to Hebrews, descendants of ancient Israelites, did not come from European missionaries. It was already a part of our culture. It was already our culture."

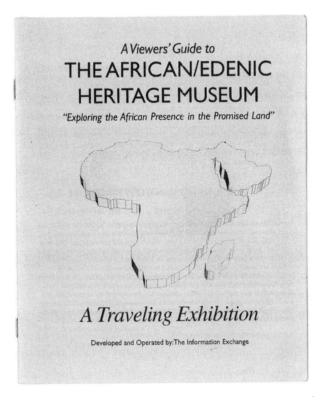

An example of the AHIJ's conceptualization of "Africa," on the cover of a viewer's guide to the African/Edenic Heritage Museum. The continent includes the entire Arabian Peninsula and extends to the Euphrates River (the biblical boundaries of "the Promised Land" extended "from the Nile to the Euphrates"). Most African maps and ornamental representations currently depict Africa as ending at what would be the Suez Canal, which the AHIJ consider geologically and geographically misleading. *(Designed by Atur Yatsiliel Ben Nasik Immanuel.)*

Ahmadiel put down the manuscript to turn off his ringing cell phone, apologizing for the intrusion.

"So, that explains why we sang those songs. But it also explains why, in the late 1880s, you had a 'prophet' named William S. Crowdy who was moving around the South and teaching that African Americans were descendants of ancient Israelites. That we were the lost sheep of the house of Israel. That continued on, little threads of history being taught and held onto. And you can take that all the way up to Marcus Garvey talking about getting our people back to Africa. And Garvey is on record as saying that we, African peoples, were 'the rulers of Israel.' His mentor, his theological arm, was Rabbi Josiah Ford, who was the forerunner of the Black Jewish/African Hebrew Israelite congregations in New York. This is what he was teaching. He was teaching 'back to Zion,' and he was calling his followers 'Black Zionists.'" Ahmadiel provided the women with a few more citations to read and reread after they get back home, finally checking his phone and taking his leave for an impromptu meeting with one of the community's Princes.

Some two years later, our exhibit guide, Elyakeem, one of Ahmadiel's hand-picked curators, holding court in front of the full museum exhibit set up in the *kfar*'s Hilltop Manor for the day, spent quite a bit of time talking to our group about that particular relationship between Garvey and Ford. He came back to it several times, finding their interconnected story particularly instructive for what it said about how versions of the past are misremembered in the present.

"Even most things you hear about African leaders," he emphasized, shaking his head from side to side, "have been stripped of their Hebrew elements, of their links to Hebrew-Israelite history. Our people don't know it. They've never heard it. This exhibit, the panels in this exhibit, are a response, a powerful response, to those lies, half-truths and omissions. This is the antidote to that poison. The whole truth."

NINE

Asiel

IT WASN'T JUST the sparkling allure of new African possibilities that
energized emigrationist impulses within segments of Chicago's black
Israelite community during the 1960s. There was also a push factor,
something more than the worrisome fact that many of America's urban
neighborhoods were going up in flames. If anything, urban rioting in
America was simply a spectacular distraction, a "smokescreen," as several saints describe it, which Yah provided so that His people could exit
the country with little resistance, undetected. Like thieves in the night.
And they left not because of the riots themselves. The real issue was *culture,* African American *culture* in particular, which black Israelites were
committed to abandoning.

Though still only beginning to formulate their more elaborate critiques of African American life in the early 1960s, they were clear about
black culture's most unacceptable attributes. To many black Israelites in
Chicago during the early 1960s, black cultural beliefs and actions were
the problem: the music blacks listened to, the clothes they wore, the kinds
of families they raised, the food they ate (including all of the pig's least

lofty body parts), the educations they received, the lessons they drew from Bible stories, and just about anything else that could be classified as quintessentially African American. From the tone and tenor of their analysis, it could almost seem like a kind of "culture of poverty" argument, a claim that African American culture was a hothouse for pathological mal-adaptations.[1] The Israelites weren't just running into the outstretched arms of a mythical African homeland; they were also running away, and decidedly so, from what black people were doing in the United States. But if this was a "culture of poverty," it wasn't based on black exceptionalism.

African Americans had been duped into perpetuating and glorifying the wrong things, destroying themselves and their traditional value system, passing on that self-destructive ethos to their children and creating a cycle of spiritual and cultural depravity. African Americans were reduced to nothing more than a perversion of their true and authentic selves, their culture a warped and hollowed-out version of its former glory. They were even worshipping the wrong God, a white one, reinforcing their sense of inferiority. The rules that black Israelites like Ben Ammi and Shaleahk Ben Yehuda would help to develop within the Kingdom—before and after they left America—were direct refutations of these cultural shortcomings, divinely inspired correctives to many generations of dysfunction.

As critical as their take on African American culture might have been, however, there were a couple of important details about this critique. For one thing, it wasn't material (or, ultimately, cultural) poverty that *caused* it. The engine was an even more intractable *spiritual* poverty. Black American culture was pathological, but not because black Americans were socially marginalized (though they readily condemned America for its self-interested and racist perpetuation of racial inequalities). And the point surely wasn't that blacks needed to cultivate more mainstream cultural values. In fact, the problem was that they were too much like the mainstream. In the black Israelites' interpretation of things, American culture, writ large, was the apogee of cultural pathology, a godless society steered toward damnation by the seductiveness of sin. The problem wasn't black American incompatibility, the idea that they didn't carry the same sensibilities as good, God-fearing, "middle-class"

Americans. It was that they had fooled themselves into aping the actions of that "middle-class" and going against all of God's commands, shrinking farther and farther away from His light, "victims of mental and spiritual genocide" that was not just inflicted on them from the hostile white world.[2] They were complicit, helping others to kill them every single day.

"In all of the black communities," Ben Ammi argued in 1973, just a few years after they first left Chicago, "it's blacks who are stealing the cars and raping the women. And who are you afraid to go outside because of, because you are afraid they are going to rip you off? Black people. But that's not our nature. What happened? Soul music and soul food and soul brother. What kind of 'soul brother'? They don't understand what they're saying, because that is not their soul. The soul of the black man in America is a righteous soul. It's a loving soul, by nature. These are loving, merciful individuals by nature, but they sold their souls to the devil."[3]

Key to this entire process was what anthropologist St. Clair Drake described as the longstanding African commitment to Providential Design: the "divine intention latent in the sufferings of black people" and the accompanying "great work of liberation, to be wrought by God and man" in the eventual "redemption of Africa" and African peoples.[4] For the AHIJ, transatlantic slavery, contemporary global white supremacy, and Africana cultural dysfunctions are all a function of Yah's plan, punishments enacted as a consequence of the ancient Israelites' disobedience, "Euro-Gentiles" less culprits than pawns. Or maybe, culprits *and* pawns. But once His people disavow their foolish and disobedient ways, once they relearn His Holy commands, Yah will redeem them and restore them to their rightful place as His ambassadors and leaders here on Earth.

Of course, aside from the Israelites, most of Yah's people (Africans throughout the Diaspora) have yet to truly realize their exceptional status, one of Yah's punishments being this very cultural amnesia (necessary to facilitate acceptance of a lowly and tragic lot in life). But once Yah's people began to awaken, a little at a time, they would need to separate themselves from the pathologies of Babylon, which made leaving for Africa (for just about anywhere) a good way to start anew.[5] But even

while the black Israelites have been trying to free themselves from spiritual and cultural bondage in America (and from African American culture), they have remained invested in the idea of writing themselves into
the center of "the African American experience," too. Black culture was
problematic, but it was also impressive insofar as it did show glimmers of
a divine ability to push back against Western forms of indoctrination and
degradation.

The story of black Israelites in the United States is not simply about
one group of African Americans trying to escape African American culture. It is an example of a more complicated two-step maneuver: marking
the distance between "divine culture" and a corrupted version of black
American culture while simultaneously making an argument for the
black Israelites' own legitimate inclusion in any accurate discussion of
African American history and culture. The community's contemporary
take on the 1960s, on their own ambitious exploits during that period,
hinges on appreciating and denunciating black culture at the same time.

When Prince Asiel, formerly the AHIJ's International Ambassador
Plenipotentiary Extraordinaire, turned sixty-five years old back in 2006,
the Ministry of Information's Audio Visual Truth Center produced a
forty-minute documentary about his life, including the parts that took
place in 1960s Chicago *before* he became a part of the Kingdom. The
video narrates his birth (as Warren Brown) on the Southside in the early
1940s and his early childhood in the infamous Ida B. Wells housing
project. Asiel's individual story is presented in the context of a broader
African American historical narrative highlighting the Great Migration
of black Southerners to that "promised land" of the urban North, the
brutal murder and open-casket funeral of teenager Emmitt Till, the creation of Motown Records, the Sixteenth Street church bombing, Rosa
Parks's refusal to relinquish her seat at the front of a public bus in
Montgomery, and the founding of the Black Panther Party for Self-
Defense, all canonized aspects of most retellings of African American life
in the mid-twentieth century.

With that as backdrop, the documentary also covers Brown's gradua-
tion, at the top of his class, from Dunbar High School, public recognition

of his status as one of the most celebrated high school graduates in Chicago that year, and his enrollment at DePaul University—again, all of which took place before he had even heard of Israelites. While getting his undergraduate degree, Brown joined Alpha Phi Alpha, Inc., an African American fraternity, met his future wife, Harriet, and began to sell juke-boxes to local black bars as part of his father-in-law's business. By age twenty-six, Warren and Harriet were able to purchase their own house in a middle-class Chicago neighborhood, and the people who knew Warren best thought that his combination of intelligence and sociability might eventually make him a good bet for citywide public office one day, maybe even Chicago's first black mayor. He was successful by most community standards, but according to his wife, "he was still not satisfied."

In 1966, Warren met Shaleahk Ben Yehuda, received some written material about black America's links to the ancient Israelites, and began to devour more and more of the community's message. The information changed his life completely, and by 1971, he and his wife had moved to Israel with the rest of that vanguard group of black Israelite émigrés, and Warren Brown was well on his way to becoming one of Ben Ammi's most important Princes, Nasik Asiel, the Prince of Blessings. He was tasked with bringing people into the Kingdom, for which he spent as much time away from Israel as not, and he proved to be an incredibly effective community ambassador, responsible for introducing more future saints to the AHIJ message than anyone else. That 2006 documentary, a respectful homage to one of the group's elders, is a visual "thank you" for his life-long service to the community, but it is also an interesting example of the AHIJ's complicated relationship with African American culture.

The first striking feature of this short film is its above-mentioned inte-gration of the AHIJ story into a related one of African American cultural distinctiveness and political strength. For a group often categorically disqualified from valid racial belonging due to its distance from conven-tional (and stereotypical) notions of African American spirituality (based on normative claims about black people's more robust and substantial con-nections to Christianity and Islam, Molefi Asante's Afrocentric critique of such religions notwithstanding), this folding of Nasik Asiel's biography into a conventional reiteration of African American cultural and political history is a very important and calculated move. If the community's identification with the ancient Israelites makes them different from most of black America, marking them as "strange" and "bizarre," their connection to—and invocation of—recognizable black cultural moments is meant to temper that strangeness. Even though their own assumptions about African American cultural pathology usually prompt them to define themselves as safely removed from that cultural formation, this video demonstrates a much more nuanced and multifaceted version of how they think through their relationship to black life in America.

Again, the reason why they represent a "revitalization movement" is because of their adamant attempt to challenge all of black America's cultural moorings. For the AHIJ, this is the essence of their reclaimed "power to define," an ability to recast their actions against the grain of African American (and American) cultural sensibilities. Every aspect of black life is suspect, in need of rehabilitation, nothing is innocent or harmless, which makes the documentary's move to immerse Nasik Asiel's story within canonical moments of twentieth-century African American popular and political culture—Rosa Parks, Emmitt Till, Motown—so fascinating. The AHIJ have a much more intriguing connection to an African American culture that they have (and have not) forsaken, a call to escape black culture while remaining tethered to it. This video of Warren Brown's transformation into Nasik Asiel Ben Israel lumps and splinters, providing avowals and disavowals of black culture at the same time.

Nasik Asiel's birthday video plays like any other PBS documentary about African American life in the twentieth century, in ways that are purposeful, self-conscious, and rhetorically powerful. As interesting as its narrative frame (which would otherwise be fairly unexceptional were it not for the community's general refusal to endorse conventional African American cultural practices) is the documentary's meticulous use of iconic images and sounds to reinforce its dramatic arc. The film begins with recognizable footage (stills and video) from famous documentaries about African American life, some of the same PBS-like documentaries that its stylized third-person narrator and carefully paced editing techniques expertly simulate.

These scenes are noticeable for their own canonical status: oft-replayed black and white video of Emmitt Till's photo above his open casket, classic footage of segregation's public pronouncements of Whites Only water fountains, images of peaceful black protesters, mere children, met by dogs and police batons. Americans have seen these grainy sequences many times before, even if mostly on MLK Day and during Black History Month. Some of these visuals are still under copyright protection, but they are recycled from DVDs and VHS tapes (from documentaries such as *Eyes on the Prize,* a film with its own copyright issues) and integrated into this celebratory video—and without any explicit mention of where these clips have come from. I've never seen this elaborate "thank you" DVD sold, only gifted to members of the community, including all of the many family members and close friends interviewed in the video. Its closing credits list none of the original films excerpted for this docu-biography, but home videos don't engage in such market-driven techniques anyway, and this DVD circulates around the Kingdom (in Israel and the United States) much like a home video would—passed on, watched together, and put on a shelf for other saints to enjoy.

The video's soundtrack reinforces much of the recuperative work that the DVD's images perform. Its Midwesternly (non)accented narration is delivered above recognizable jazz compositions (including "All Blues" by Miles Davis) and various classic Motown hits, reinforcing the images of (and the narrator's references to) early Motown. Several of Chicago's black Israelites were accomplished R&B recording artists in the 1960s, a fact that would determine some of the AHIJ's actions in Liberia and Israel, and it would certainly help to keep the community afloat during many of the toughest times to come, these musicians raising money for the community by performing on the road and sending some of their profits back to the community. But they don't just profile their own members' music on Nasik Asiel's DVD. They use massive hits, broadly popular black music—and again, with none of the songs or artists explicitly listed in any credit sequence. Instead, they are sampled, ostensibly without permission or compensation—in a manner similar to early hip-hop expropriations of musical recordings. Such infringements of copyright indicate a certain indifference to the cultural logic of contract-driven capitalism, but they also speak to the hybrid nature of the DVDs produced—part (private) home movie, part (public) documentary.

Nasik Asiel's birthday DVD toys with the trappings of commodification. Like other items made by and through the AHIJ's media production offices, some of which quite clearly carry ISBN numbers and noticeable price tags, a substantial portion of the community's video productions seem to mobilize the accoutrement of commodities as a kind of ruse for gifting—both within the community and vis-à-vis interested outsiders. When I visit the *kfar,* I almost always have to pay for books (especially any of the many writings by Ben Ammi) and musical CDs, but I'm often plied with DVDs for free. And not just because I'm an over-interested anthropologist. I've seen the same DVDs freely distributed to other visitors as well, both in Dimona and in "extensions" of the Kingdom throughout the United States. In a sense, "the commodity-form" almost seems to be simulated as protective cover for a different mode of exchange, a mode that puts community building in productive tension with the necessities of commercialization, the central architecture of "redemptive enterprises." Such a dynamic is hardly new, especially as more and more social groups become increasingly invested in heritage and identity tourism, attempts (in tough economic times) to capitalize on the potential market value of ethnic and racial difference itself.[6] Nasik Asiel's birthday DVD mobilizes copyright-protected audio and video commodities to produce a film without formal genuflection to standard legal expectations about such usage, and its status as a sellable commodity appears to play with the design and iconography of commercial transactions without making the sales themselves absolutely mandatory. Of course, such gifts demand other obligations, but those aren't necessarily reducible to the workings of a capitalist marketplace.

I was given my copy of that Nasik Asiel DVD during my second trip to Dimona, but I would see many copies of it in other Ministries of Information or saints' homes in Chicago, Atlanta, and Washington, DC. By 2010, I started hearing rumors that Nasik Asiel was no longer a member of the Kingdom, no longer on speaking terms with Ben Ammi. He was back in Chicago trying to figure out his next move, which sounded like another example of the splintering that had produced new versions of black Israelites in America for almost 100 years.

TEN

Hustling

FIVE YEARS AGO I started using the American Anthropological Association's annual conference as my own private ethnographic overflow room, a time for reaching out to saints or former saints (or other Hebrew Israelites unaffiliated with the AHIJ) who live in places where I have *not* done any extended research. Over the past decade or so, Philadelphia, New York, Washington, DC, and North Carolina have each served as more *bona fide* field-sites during different phases of this project, but there is hardly a region in the country without at least a spattering of Hebrew Israelites of one kind or another, even cities that are not one of the AHIJ's official "jurisdictions," hubs for the Kingdom's ministerial missions.

Washington, DC, Atlanta, and Chicago are home to three of the AHIJ's largest communities in the United States, so I always try to schedule interviews and meetings with saints during trips to those locations. Usually, I'll meet people at one of the community's vegan restaurants or health food stores, obvious institutional anchor points. Or I might get a quick look at the jurisdiction's media facilities, their local branch of the Kingdom's Ministry of Information. Or I could simply rendezvous with a former saint to hear details about why he or she decided to leave the fold.

But even when the AAA meetings are in places like New Orleans or San Francisco, not AHIJ jurisdictions, there are still Israelites or former Israelites to track down. That sometimes means blowing off half-a-day of the conference or getting to town a little early, but for the past few years, saints and former saints have also been meeting up with me at the AAA meetings themselves, usually in the main conference hotel, sometimes because the venue is conveniently located near their homes or jobs and sometimes because it just so happens that they are attending the conference, too, watching the watchers more closely or even self-identifying as one. We'll find an open conference room or, more likely, pull some empty chairs up to a coffee table in a relatively quiet stretch of hotel hallway space and chat, my digital audio recorder lazily lavaliered to a blouse's or shirt's front placket.

During the 2010 AAA conference in New Orleans, I was actually trying to recruit a young saint to apply to the PhD program in Africana Studies at the University of Pennsylvania. Ahmahlyah received her BA at a public university on the West Coast, and she had entered a Master's program in sociology at a school in New England, a school that wasn't shaping up to be a great fit. For one thing, some faculty there didn't seem to think that she could/should be doing a social scientific study of her own eccentric community, but that's exactly what she was determined to do. She had already started conducting formal interviews with many of the AHIJ saints that she'd grown up with (even doing a few of those interviews for me), and she presented some of that material as part of her own AAA presentation during the 2010 conference. Her mother, Semhiah, was also a member of the community, or at least once was—describing herself as having a kind of "complicated" relationship with both her husband, Shivooel, a saint who was back in Israel at the time, and with the AHIJ Kingdom as a whole. Ahmahlyah's mother had earned a PhD in African studies decades earlier, and she was interested in assisting me with my AHIJ research, which was one of the reasons why she tagged along with her daughter to the same AAA meetings, which is where she and I first met. She assumed that her insights on the community—as a "complicated" insider with a formal academic pedigree—could be helpful. And she was right. She was also excited about supporting her daughter's attempt to follow in her scholarly footsteps.

Born in California in the early 1980s, Ahmahlyah joined the AHIJ community as a preteen, after her mom and one of her mom's closest friends met Ben Ammi and several other senior leaders in southern California about a decade earlier. This was just after the beating and trial of Rodney King—and the deadly protests/riots they sparked in Los Angeles. Those events traumatized Ahmahlyah's mother so much that she seriously contemplated suicide as an escape from the dark, cold shadow those incidents cast on the lives of Angelenos. Black life still seemed to have such little value. But then she met Ben Ammi, "Abba," and that, she says, "changed everything." He gave her the confidence to leave American racism behind.

The fact that she had already earned a PhD made her particularly valuable as a prospective saint. Saints were re-educating themselves for a new "Edenic," post-American millennium, and they needed to include scholars in that effort, especially if those scholars weren't completely "brainwashed" by the academy. The elders were very pleased about the possibility of Ahmahlyah's mother joining their ranks, and the AHIJ's overtures provided her with a new reason for living, even thriving. It gave her life a new purpose, a more profound significance, and within a few years, she was living in southern Israel with a new husband, someone who had been born into the community, a saint that she met during her yearlong "absorption" process in Atlanta and Chicago.[1]

The couple set up shop in Eilat, one of Israel's southernmost cities, competing with Ethiopians to braid the hair of European tourists vacationing there. They had beaten the Ethiopians to the hair-braiding industry in and around that port city, setting up shop on the gamble that they could convince Europeans to embrace exotic hairstyles during their short respites at various Red Sea resorts, but their Ethiopian competitors caught up fast. And there were more of them, which meant more hands for braiding. So after some early success in their new enterprise, it became increasingly difficult for the pair to turn a profit, especially with their lives split between work in Eilat and family in the *kfar*, which was over 100 miles to the north. They were also still adjusting to life in the Israeli desert and the ease with which dehydration could sneak up on anyone not judicious about their liquid intake, a judiciousness that it took many AHIJ saints quite some time to cultivate. When Eilat's desert air got too hot and debilitating, the pair simply wouldn't work, they wouldn't even start looking for potential clients until nightfall. It wasn't worth it, they say, even though some of their Ethiopian competitors often worked right through the heat. When the daytime temperature wasn't too unbearable, the couple would try to braid hair all day and night, making the long trip back to Dimona once every couple of weeks to see Ahmahlyah, who was going to school back in the *kfar*.

With an uptick in Israeli-Palestinian violence in 2000, many foreign tourists were dissuaded from visiting Israel altogether, which meant that the couple's hair-braiding operation had fewer clients than ever, and the they eventually decided to abandon the business.[2] The Israeli tourists who continued to vacation in the area from other parts of the country were much less generous, they claim, than the foreigners who had come before them. So, husband and wife packed up and headed back to Dimona, pondering their next move. They had to figure out a way to support themselves. He had always been good with vegan cuisine, having played a small part in the community's slow evolution to veganism, even being something of an inventor in that realm, someone credited (among certain saints) with inventing the formula for a "ginger drink" that is very popular throughout the Kingdom—and sold in many AHIJ-affiliated restaurants around the world.

Eventually, husband and wife left Israel for Northern California and opened one of the community's staple U.S.-based franchises: an entirely vegan "soul food" restaurant. The hair-braiding trade had been tough, and the notion of starting a new restaurant (in a part of America where the AHIJ had relatively few deep institutional roots) would be no less difficult. They had the support of the AHIJ leadership, but that just made things all the more challenging in some ways. Since veganism is such a fundamental component of the AHIJ's communal project, a central element in their bold claims about physical health, many saints around the world go into business making vegan food—first, for their own families and friends, often as caterers for community events and operators of mobile vending trucks, and sometimes, with enough local demand, as proprietors of brick-and-mortar restaurants. Most jurisdictions in the United States are organized around a series of restaurants and grocery stores that serve as economic lifelines for community members in those areas, providing saints with a way to make a living while also giving them (and health-conscious neighbors) access to intricately prepared meat-less cuisine, usually traditional American fare with a nondairy twist, macaroni and "cheese," lasagna, "beet loaf," "vege steaks," tofu salads, and more.

Opening a new restaurant is an ambitious venture under any circum-stance, but it is even more daunting and difficult when negotiating a com-plexly formal and informal relationship with interested partners halfway around the world, in this case, other saints and the AHIJ leadership thousands of miles away in Dimona. After some conflicts about the degree of autonomy they would/should have to run their new California eatery, the two eventually decided to close the operation. As Semhieh tells the story many years later (when she no longer uses her Hebrew name), their business might have survived much longer had they been able to successfully leverage the resources and expertise of other AHIJ saints who have run similar *Soul Veg* franchises, but the couple ended up pushing back against the idea of allowing other saints to help them run their restaurant, mostly out of fear that they might lose control of the business in the push and pull of the Kingdom's commitments to what might be labeled "divine capitalism," an investment in entrepreneur-ialism that privileges the social and spiritual health of the AHIJ commu-nity over any financial bottom line. It is a model of the economy in service (and subservient) to social life, a mode that operationalizes some of the ways in which anthropologist David Graeber critiques a certain fetishiza-tion of "the economic" within traditional economic thinking, a fetishiza-tion that assumes economic relations to have a *sui generis* reality that always controls, outstrips, and over-determines other organizational principles of human life.[3] For the AHIJ, economic activity was sup-posed to be a means to a social end, to a decidedly sociospiritual end. Nothing more.

The AHIJ engage in what the community labels "redemptive enter-prises," part socialist (even kibbutz-like) commitment to communal mutuality and part spiritually-inflected/Yah-focused deployment of a capitalist ethos. It is a difficult balancing act, not least of which because saints realize that their businesses won't last very long if they don't spend time pointedly thinking about profit margins and cash flow. They are supposed to contribute whatever they can afford to the collective pot and are allowed, therefore, to remove (theoretically, at least) whatever it is they need to support their families. "All things in common," saints say.[4] That's their economic philosophy. Of course, the Kingdom's treasury isn't limitless. And the vast majority of their businesses are owned by specific saints, not the community as a whole (or even its leaders), so it takes a lot of work to make sure that they stretch their resources as far as possible—for as many as possible. And everyone is responsible for demonstrating discipline and creativity on that front.

Saints find innovative ways of making money for themselves and the larger community by fostering a marketable skill or valuable service, often more than just one. It could be running a minivan operation like "Divine Samaritan" (to shuttle guests and saints back and forth to Ben Gurion Airport); custom-making the community's distinctive attire or mending those clothes; catering community events; developing hair-care products; offering colon and foot therapies; providing reflexology treatments; giving meticulous manicures and pedicures; designing jewelry; marketing fluoride-free toothpaste; selling groceries; producing, distributing, and performing "Divine Music"; renting cars (a saint opened Dimona's first rental car company, "Global Wheels," in 2010); or taking orders to carve household furniture out of wood. But the point is that saints have to be able to successfully sell their wares or services within the Kingdom and even (optimally) beyond.

From the 1970s to the 1990s, many of the adult men in the community did construction work (always off the books), building homes for traditionally nomadic Bedouin—so that that community could be more easily located by a census-taking and tax-collecting Israeli state. And in at least one instance, they designed and produced a large community center in Jerusalem's Old City for a Palestinian activist's extended family and neighbors. The adult women made much of their money during that same stretch (and still today) cooking, catering, sewing clothes, and engaging in all kinds of seasonal labor throughout Israel, even though a traditionally gendered division of social labor meant that their first priority was always supposed to be taking care of their households and raising their children.

For the saints who produce their own men's and women's underwear "with all natural fibers," entrepreneurialism means identifying a factory that can work with the materials they need, sometimes in Africa or in another part of Israel, coming up with a sustainable and reasonable pricing scheme, and even using an anthropologist's return trip to Philadelphia as a way to ship clothing samples to saints in the United States.

Up until the late-1990s, all of this work was carried out under the cover of darkness. For the majority of their time in Israel, these necessary jobs had to be illicit, cash-only affairs. They were being hired illegally, working for less than Israeli citizens usually demand, and paying no income tax. This was "real-life hustling," as one saint described it. "Hustling for real." (Even now, Zakhah, a thirty-something saint who found the Kingdom during her graduate school stint at Howard University in the 1990s, describes herself as an entrepreneur, raw food chef, mother, wife, bestselling author [of *The Joy of Living Live: A Raw Food Journey*], webmaster, online virtual assistant, and all around "divine hustler.") From 1969 until the 1990s, saints were living in Israel on long-expired "tourist" visas, which meant that they weren't allowed to be in Israel at all, let alone work there. In fact, however, everyone worked—men, women, and children. They worked all the time, which was a dangerous proposition, especially since the government would occasionally mount sting operations to round up these illegal workers and deport them back to the United States.

One major episode occurred in 1986. More than seventy community members were picking, washing and crating oranges for a local Israeli fruit company. The job usually lasted several weeks, and they would spend that time living right next to the orange-packing facility in the middle of the country, a good distance from Dimona. Entire families relocated up north to take advantage of this opportunity, though they had to be careful about how they made the trek to the packing plant (a series of stealthy vehicular caravans across the countryside) and how they negotiated their temporary residency up north, relatively far away from the *kfar* (piling into too-small apartments near the work-site). This was just one of the ways in which saints made money, and they had done this kind of seasonal work many times before, but in the spring of 1986 Israeli forces raided the orange-packing plant and locked up dozens of AHIJ workers for violating the terms of their visas.

In the intertitle and voice-over preamble to a video that the community produced in 1987, part of their attempt to fight back by publicly proclaiming their ongoing persecutions at the hands of the Israeli state, the community pointedly framed those arrests for an international audience, saints and nonsaints:

> On April 17, 1986, a garrison of armed Israeli defense forces swept down on a citrus plantation in a pre-dawn raid that resulted in the arrest of 46 members of the spiritually-centered, peaceful Hebrew Israelite Community. Among the eight men, eleven children and twenty-seven members of the community arrested was the pajama-clad sixty-five-year-old mother of the community, who was denied even a change of clothes. This arrest climaxed an epic struggle between the Israeli Powers and this community, as they had been deported, denied work permits, housing, education and medicine in their effort to establish the Kingdom of Yah, the paradigm of a spiritually-based society of righteous lifestyle, desiring to worship the God of Israel in Peace. The following is actual footage shot by an amateur cameraman depicting the face-off between the awesome Israeli military machine and the unarmed, immovable Hebrew Israelite Community. The anointed spiritual leader of the community, Ben Ammi Ben Israel, declared that this day shall always be remembered because every man, woman, and child of the community displayed extraordinary courage, perseverance, and strength in the face of a formidable, life-threatening power. This day has been proclaimed, now and forever, as "The Day of the Show of Strength."

The footage was shot, edited, and narrated by members of the community, and the Day of the Show of Strength is, like New World Passover, one of the community's most important annual commemorations. Some of the imprisoned saints from the orange-packing plant ended up stuck in jail for months. They "sang hosannas" together for much of that time and refused to eat the "flesh-based" food they were offered during their incarceration. Many saints got sick as a consequence, and they were eventually allowed their vegan meals.

Members of the Kingdom back in Dimona vehemently protested these imprisonments. They enlisted sympathizers and saints in other parts of the world to put pressure on the American and Israeli authorities as well, asking them to make sure that they monitored the Israeli government's rhetoric about removing all the saints from Israel. In April of 1987, the AHIJ started circulating a twelve-page pamphlet, "Answering the Challenge," an open letter addressed to all three branches of the American government, which was produced in response to an even earlier 1985 "conspiracy between the United States and Israeli governments" when the two nations "raided homes, meeting places and work sites of African Hebrew Community members, arresting approximately 20" in an attempt at "the complete and total destruction of the community." The Day of the Show of Strength was less than a year after that raid, on a morning when the IDF had assembled to stop the community's planned protest march up to Jerusalem. They had been denied the necessary permits, but were going to head north in smaller and dispersed groups, each group fewer than the number of people that would constitute an illegal assembly. The IDF meant for them not to leave Dimona that day.

Elders gathered the youngest saints together in the Hilltop Manor, just one day before that anticipated showdown with the Israeli military. All the saints had been tasked with collecting canned goods, gathering extra clothes, and locating other items that might be needed during their planned protest against Israeli forces. Those little ones slept in Hilltop Manor over night and woke up to soldiers, tanks, and horses surrounding the *kfar*.

Ahmahlyah's mother's husband, Shivooel, was one of the people locked up for working in that orange-packing facility, and like several other saints arrested during that sting operation, his prison time ended with deportation to the United States—along with a stern governmental declaration that he would never be allowed back in Israel again.

"We did what we wanted to do," he reminisces these many years later, "because we had God on our side. We have God on our side. So, if they're saying I can't go back, and I've been back more than once, then that lets me know that we really have a God on our side looking out for us. I just left Israel about two weeks ago [in December 2008]. That was the last time. But I am back and forth all the time so that should show you that they can't stop the plan of God. They can't stop God's people."

ELEVEN

Ignorance

A S A SERIES of video excerpts, "The Day of the Show of Strength" is almost completely viewable on YouTube. I hadn't even thought to look for any information about that clash online until I had an initial discussion with my editor, Sharmila Sen, about this AHIJ project. After our conversation, she surfed the web for more information on the community, subsequently hipping me to the fact that they had quite a robust YouTube presence—as do other Hebrew Israelite groups, along with many detractors who spend their time posting challenges to the legitimacy of such groups. This YouTubification is an important part of the AHIJ story, one subset of an expanded universe of cultural stories retold on the web. Other people put up footage of the community's exploits, or provide critical commentary about their beliefs, but the AHIJ also retell their own tales, which is one of the reasons why this book is not just a work *of* ethnography but *about* it, at least in part—a take on the community's collective and individual auto-ethnographic offerings, on their self-portrayals and critical meta-commentary about their own evolving cultural formulations.[1]

Ethnography was never the exclusive property of anthropologists or
sociologists. And it is not only claimed by researchers in other fields, by
journalists, documentarians, and reality TV producers interested in
depicting the relatively less-scripted realities of everyday life. Research
subjects themselves also lay claim to the term, to the method, and very
self-consciously so, with many of its modes, genres, and platforms at their
ready disposal. This doesn't accurately characterize every group that
social scientists observe today, but it is probably the future of us all.[2]

Studying the AHIJ demands not just an examination of previous
anthropological, sociological, and historical accounts produced by
university-based academics, but also a careful look at saints' readings
and assessments of that work, and of their own growing corpus of literature on themselves, the counternarratives they've produced, the archives
they've maintained and circulated. Of course, the AHIJ community is
certainly not in the business of revealing everything. (What community
practices complete transparency, or could even survive such a thing,
were it possible?) Instead, they are very purposeful about what they
choose to divulge—or not.[3] Theirs is an ethnography that is as careful
about keeping secrets as it is about educating the masses and exposing
others to the *truth*. In fact, as an insular and self-protective community,
the AHIJ have more of an inaccessible "backstage" area (off-limits to outsiders, ethnographers included) than some other groups that social scientists might hope to study. They have frustrated many an interested
researcher who has tried to gain something other than a glossy and prepackaged rendition of community members' everyday lives, a rendition
that these researchers would deem relatively shallow and whitewashed,
decidedly thin, little more than rote reiterations of a sanctioned party
line. And part of the AHIJ's sociocultural project (a part not that different from the traditional forms of protectiveness that communities have
always performed/enacted vis-à-vis the cherished secrets that ethnographers most desire to unearth) is predicated on their concerted effort to
control the terms of any ethnographic conversation about themselves, to
steer the ethnographic ship from below, to have some substantive role in
constructing and transmitting their story.[4]

The "power to define" is an attempt to challenge and displace others'
dismissive characterizations and definitions of their community's past

and present exploits. It is not about simply swapping out the word *diet* for *live-it*. Or placing "Divine" in front of anything done to the explicit glory of Yah, which is yet another way saints mark their redefinitions (*Divine* Marriage, *Divine* Music, the Ministry of *Divine* Information, phrases like "it is my divine pleasure to serve you" as rejoinders to expressions of gratitude, and so on). Any attempt at a distinction between works *of* versus *of and about* ethnography is also implicated here. Mostly because there is so much that cannot and will not make it into my ethnographic accounting of the Kingdom. In some ways, this is an ethnography that is not one, if such a rubric demands full disclosure in the name of social science, if it requires producing the fiction of full and complete knowledge. There is so much that I do not share in this book, cannot or simply will not, a plethora of secrets kept, stories not shared, purposefully confounded, for better or worse. A different kind of thinning.

Of course, anthropologists have always been pretty good secret-keepers about certain things. It is hardly controversial to say that ethnographic research has long been powered, to a certain extent, by what cannot or will not be written, from Malinowski's infamously offensive diary to the juicy stories of humor or intrigue or inappropriateness usually saved for academic cocktail parties and university lectures (that is, before the latter entered the domain of online permanency and global accessibility not all that different from formal publication). But many people know that the artscience of ethnography has always pivoted on the inextricable ties between revelation and nondisclosure, between what's said and what's better left unsaid—and for any number of reasons, personal or political. For the AHIJ, it could mean stories about, say, a saint who might also be a closeted Buddhist. Or another who secretly indulges, even just occasionally, in nonvegan fare. Or those who tiptoe on the tightrope between adherence and alienation, between their Jake-selves and their Israelite ones. Some of these secrets might even be "public secrets," at least within the community, inconsistencies that one could readily excavate in any social group, and the ethnographic project means determining which of these would-be inconsistencies and contradictions merit wider exposure.[5]

This is all reminiscent of classic anthropological attempts to access the most secret and sacred forms of communal knowledge, the kinds that are highly guarded, most off-limits to the uninitiated. Even if saints sometimes make it clear what information might fit that bill, it is still up to outside researchers to theorize their own justifiable calculus for parsing these distinctions, a move that often outstrips the ethical configurations of Institutional Review Boards and even formal guildwide regulations. The ethnographic touch it requires is subtler than usually discussed in public, especially since it is almost impossible to protect people's anonymity from other members of their own social network, especially for a community as small and intimate as this one—small, intimate, and emphatically transnational all at the same time.

A community that is as prolific and proactive as the AHIJ (in terms of their concerted effort to spread the word about their cultural initiatives and cosmological claims) is just as thoughtful and focused about what they will not say, about the logic of their ethnographic silences. And part of my job entails finding ways to tell their tale without compromising on issues of integrity—both in terms of what I can reasonably expect saints to assume about the nature of my own scholarly investments and what I expect of myself as a social scientist taking part in ongoing discussions within and beyond the academy. Even when those two ends feel least reconcilable, they must be brought together, somehow. And the patterned ways in which a community writes itself into a partial and guarded view produces the intricate grooves within which (and against which) an outsider-ethnographer situates any derivative telling.

For every YouTubed version of the AHIJ story, either one offered up by saints themselves or by detractors committed to exposing their supposed hypocrisies, there are many tales not relayed, tucked away from broader public view: of young saints leaving the community in a huff, of semipublic squabbles between senior leadership, of the illegal methods used to finance saints' trips back and forth to Israel in the 1970s and 1980s. Some of those stories will make this version of things, but in delicate, somewhat opaque and mostly anonymizing ways, both to respect the privacy of the saints involved and to protect the community from certain kinds of public vulnerability. But even the stories not adamantly told are still noticeable, sometimes partially readable between the lines. Or they'll come out later, when certain readers decry their relative underthematization or outright omission. The ethnographic dance is always about the inter-connected revelations and concealments that mediate the relationships between ethnographers and ethnographic subjects, between ethnographers and readers, between readers and ethnographic subjects—even and especially when the same people can increasingly occupy all three roles. Part of what "everything is ethnography" looks like is constituted by these kinds of nested negotiations, another example of how ethnography becomes a "risky practice" that demands circumspection and self-consciousness—and that need not devolve into the condescending trap that others have cautioned against, a kind of "bad faith" and dehumanizing relationship that finds researchers unwilling to "judge or criticize the communities" they study, which only "destroys intersubjective relations" in the name of saving them.[6]

The question, of course, is not whether to critique or not. But which criticisms and why? Toward what ends? And an ethnography about others' purposeful ethnographies (more and more unavoidable in the twenty-first century) is an attempt to think through these questions in the context of a larger discussion about how ethnographic knowledge is actually culled, the real-time textures of ethnographic practices, encounters that are often, as Laura Bohannan puts it, "disconnected and unordered: small, particular incidents" made to stand-in for larger social sensibilities and cultural understandings.[7]

What definition of *ethnographic time* does this imply? The way we acquire our ethnographic expertise is usually quite unpredictable and jumbled (at its best, an openness to the wonders of "chance," according to anthropologist Michael Taussig).[8] But one of the first things lost in the purposeful translation of ethnographic experiences into written monographs is a rendition of how ethnographic research feels in "real time," what my colleagues in engineering might call a kind of "ethnographic haptography," an accurate portrayal of how ethnographic knowledge bumpily unfolds.[9] This haptography is also about the kinds of things stated and silenced in any ethnographic exchange, the twists and turns of data collection, redundancies and recursivities, patterns and provocative unpredicabilities, an act of induction much less straightforward, orderly, self-certain, and closed-ended than we sometimes admit.

What we do and don't do as ethnographic researchers might productively be embraced, using Giorgio Agamben's formulation, as a combination of knowledge and nonknowledge. Not knowing, an active cultivation of continued ignorance, is vital. It has productive force. It makes all kinds of things possible. "Indeed, articulating a zone of nonknowledge," according to Agamben, "does not mean simply not knowing; it is not only a question of lack or defect. It means, on the contrary, maintaining oneself in the right relationship to ignorance, allowing absence of knowledge to guide and accompany our gestures. . . . The art of living is, in this sense, the capacity to keep ourselves in harmonious relationship with that which escapes us."[10] The art of living (and writing) *ethnographically* in "a zone of nonknowledge" is about cultivating an appreciation, as reader and writer, of the productivities that not-knowing affords, which is what a certain definition of *sincerity* wallows in—zealously. What could be worse than a reader finishing a book, any book, let alone an ethnography, closing the back cover, and imagining full mastery? Each blink, wink, and twitch meticulously distinguished, conjuring the sense of complete knowledge. Calculated modes of nonknowing and constitutive incompleteness are sometimes, for some stories, at least in the long term, much more useful. The point is not to overcome ignorance in some absolute and totalizing way. It is about encouraging a form of knowing that doesn't simply treat mystery as its mortal enemy, as nothing more than a land to be conquered.

TWELVE

YMCA

THURSDAYS MEAN SWIMMING lessons at the local YMCA, classes for young people of any age and skill level. Daddy-duty at the Y is never easy, especially when my wife's out of town. So, I am playing single-parent for a few hours on this particular Thursday, which always makes me more anxious and short-tempered than necessary, tension and fear about my own lack of fatherly skills, I suppose. Or maybe sublimated subconscious recollections of my own (biological and step) fathers' imperfect—though seemingly sincere—parenting efforts. Whatever the reason, all this is just meant to provide a little context, in hopes that it helps explain—at least in part—why I was probably primed to get into a shouting match with a gym patron inside that humid, sticky, and puddle-filled men's locker room.

I was trying, frantically, to get both of my children, a three-year-old and a five-year-old, on and off toilet bowls and into swimsuits before their class, which was set to start in less than five minutes. As often happens, something inconsequential (the prospect of getting my children into the water a few minutes late) felt monumental (like conspicuous evidence of my obvious parental inadequacies), an example of the wild elasticities of meaning-making that make us human.

A heavy-set African American man, white towel hugging his waist, happened to be walking right in front of us as we entered the locker room. I smiled politely, nudging my little ones to move a little faster. The man looked at my youngest, the girl, and shook his head, a silent opening salvo.

"This isn't a place for girls," he said, looking everywhere in the locker room except directly in my direction. "With all these grown men up in here. She shouldn't be in here."

Before we even opened the door to the locker room, only a second or two earlier, I had noticed a brand new glossy blue sign in the small anteroom to the men's lockers. So did my children. "What's that, daddy?" They wanted to know, so I read it aloud. It specifically requested that fathers not to bring their daughters into the men's locker room if said daughters were six years of age or older. My three-year-old was almost four, and she was big for her age, but she could hardly pass for six.

He probably doesn't have kids, I thought, which must have explained why he mistakenly believed that she was over the cutoff age. So, I responded immediately, just to assure him that she wasn't.

"I saw the sign," I said, grinning pleasantly. "She's only three."

"Three?!" he responded, laughing heartily, from his shoulders, as though he had just heard the funniest one-liner. "Three?! He's in here talking about *three*." He was now speaking to some invisible interlocutor in the far corner of the room.

"The sign says six," I said, furrowing my brows. I started the furrow calmly enough, truly reaching for clarification, but my blood pressure jumped to boil as I thought about him invoking me in third person.

"It doesn't matter if she's six or not," he said, still shaking his head. He'd never stopped. "She shouldn't be in here with grown men changing in the first place. That just ain't right. Why would you even want her in here with that?"

The end of this exchange took place over his shoulder as he walked out of the changing area and toward the showers, making his way to the pool. He didn't even break stride. In a few more seconds, he was almost at the exit door. And he wasn't done.

"I know some of these others are perverted like that, but I didn't think we was, too."

"What?!" I yelled back. "What?!"

He didn't respond, so I went on, even louder, as he got to the poolside exit door. "No, I'm not perverted! Thank you!!! I'm not sure who's perverted, but I'm not perverted! And my daughter isn't either." Then I barked at my kids to take off their clothes while I gruffly fished their swimsuits out of a bag and glared, unblinkingly, at the door through which this stranger had just departed. I could marshal enough of my faculties to determine that it wasn't really fair to the children if I followed him, my initial reaction, so after a few steps in that direction, I caught myself and turned back. That's when a twenty-something black man who was changing into basketball shorts a few lockers down chimed in.

"It's OK, It's OK," he assured me, walking passed me and toward the toilet. "You can be in here. It's OK. You can take them right in here." I walked the kids inside the stall, and he closed the stall's door behind us.

Once the kids were changed and ready to make the trek to the pool, the young man escorted us to the door and reiterated that it wasn't a problem for my daughter to be in the men's locker room. He also apologized for the earlier man's insistence.

"She can be here," he said. "It is fine. It isn't a problem. And that there brother, he meant well. He meant well. He did. Some people just don't know how to say things, you know. They don't know how to put stuff. But he meant well."

I tried to smile, still coming down from the heights of my quickened rage. He started to open the door for us as we braced ourselves for the pool area's ungodly humidity.

"Yeah, she can come in here. He was just trying to say that sometimes you have these sex perverts around here and you never know. They'll come in here and you don't know. Like some of these Jews around here. Just go online and you can see it. You can see it. Just do a search for sex offenders on the computer, and you'll see how many they have around here. Go on your computer and you'll see. They have their names and everything. He meant well, but there are a lot of perverts around here. That's all he was saying. And you just gotta be careful."

Without even a goodbye, the second stranger vanished back behind the locker room door.

My little ones had already broken free of my grasp and eased themselves into the water, but I just stood there for a few more minutes. Jews?! I thought. Did he really just single-out Jews as being particularly prone to pedophilic sex crimes? Out of the blue? Could I be on some kind of Ethnographic "Candid Camera"? Academia's version of the MTV show "Punk'd"?

Of course, this second stranger also ostensibly "meant well" with his advice about the potential threat of Jewish sex offenders. And he even challenged me to go online and see the threat myself. Anthropologist Roger Lancaster takes issue with the irrational overreaction that "sex panics" represent in the face of specific data and details about actual sexual crimes committed against the young.[1] And the overestimation of young people's sexual vulnerabilities vis-à-vis pathological predators seems to dovetail perfectly with historical overvaluations of "the Jew" as a primordial social threat—in Sarte's framing, someone cast as an existential Evil instead of just another differently invested and reasonably self-interested social actor like everyone else.[2]

As the children practiced dipping their heads under the water for the next thirty minutes and made motorboat sounds by blowing air out of their mouths at the water's surface, I typed fieldnotes into my Blackberry calendar, writing down everything I could remember from the first stranger's comments and the second one's clarifications before trying to list some questions about what might help to constitute formulations of the sexually deviant Jew: (1) the Jew's ambiguous whiteness? (2) concerns and questions about Jewish men's compromised sexuality/masculinity (what the Boyarins' describe as a kind of tricksterlike ability to switch sexes)?[3] (3) the complicated forms of political affiliation and collaboration that constitute "the Black-Jewish alliance" in the context of such effortless anti-Semitism? And might all of this help to explain why Hebrew Israelite camps perform such hypermasculine public performances on so many sidewalks across urban America—brash, loud, and unapologetically confrontational. Is it an overcompensation for historical and contemporary black skepticisms of Jewry, of Jewish masculinity? Might proclaiming some genealogical link to ancient Israel demand an anticipatory pushback against interpretations of such moves as an embrace of sexual effeminacy? Complex and cathected, does discourse about Jewish sexual depravity translate into a special animus—or fear of it—against the would-be black Jew/Israelite, a fear met with hypermasculine brands of redisciplining?

UnAfrican

"Don't be a sucker," he shouted from our subway car's flickeringly lit corner seat. His unexpected eruption sounded ferocious. Raw and piercing. Bitter and cold. At least to my ears. But maybe that's just because the words had been aimed directly at me, not merely overheard from some kind of "second-order" anthropological distance scrupulously in it, but not of it.

It was my first year in graduate school, and I was commuting from my mother's East New York apartment in Brooklyn, about an hour or so from Columbia. I majored in filmmaking as an undergraduate, which meant that entering any doctoral program in anthropology became a crash-course in all the many social science theories and theorists that I didn't need to master while I was producing 8mm and 16mm films in and around Howard University's campus. Those postbaccalaureate train rides back and forth to Manhattan felt like cramming to catch up, drowning myself in dense prose from scholars I'd never heard of. And even the names I recognized (like Marx and Freud), I didn't really know; I hadn't actually read, not at length, which is why, distracted, I missed more than a few subway stops that academic year, wrestling sentences that refused to relinquish their meanings without a fight.

So, when those five high school students sprinted by me during one evening's train ride, knocking whatever book I was reading out of my hands and onto the floor, I didn't think twice about it. I was so absorbed in what I was half-comprehending, I thought, that I must not have realized just how much space I'd been taking up, probably more than anyone racing through the middle of a mostly empty subway train might have reasonably expected. I didn't even take it personally when those same teenagers sat down at the far end of that subway car, glancing back at me without so much as a halfhearted "sorry" or "excuse me," laughing uncontrollably with one another about something they clearly found hilarious. I just buried my head back in the book as soon as I retrieved it, which is when I heard the aforementioned admonishment: "Don't be a sucker."

A few more train stops came and went without much else happening, at least nothing I can recall now. Several more passengers got on and off, sharing the screechingly silent subterranean space between and around us. At some point, the teens exited, too. And eventually, the stranger who had chosen to chastise me earlier about the perils of suckerdom from the far corner of the train, a guy who looked to be in his late twenties or earlier thirties, rose from his seat and headed toward me.

"Just because you want to extend your mind," I remember him saying, as he leaned over and gestured toward my reading material, his goateed face about a foot from my forehead, a leathery Star of David swinging from his neck, "you don't gotta be soft, man. You don't need to slice nobody up or nothing, but you don't need to be a punk, either."[1]

He then handed me a wrinkled flyer designed by the Israelite Church of Universal Practical Knowledge (ICUPK).[2] My road to Israel and the AHIJ began, in part, on that train car that day, only a few months removed from viewing Marlon Riggs's gripping chronicle of his own death. The ICUPK and its many offshoots are still generally considered "extremist" organizations, rabidly antiwhite and homophobic, even if incapable of actually causing a global race war. And although they share several basic tenets with the AHIJ, the points of divergence between those two brands of Black Hebrewism are equally enlightening. This train ride would be my first up-close-and-personal introduction to the camp, starting me on my extended search for more information about varied Africana commitments to Israelite identity.

I'm not sure how seriously my flyer-dispensing critic took his association with the ICUPK. Seriously enough to proselytize on a late-night IRT train, surely, but I never did see him again, not even when I started to attend some of the ICUPK's nightly classes not too long after that. Still, I can picture this brief exchange on a New York City subway car in what feels like mnemonic Technicolor. I never interviewed him, and I can't remember anything more about what he said to me, but my anthropological journey along the routes of this project got a forceful push from that brief confrontation on a Brooklyn-bound subway train, just a bit of unsolicited advice and a pocket-crumpled handout.

That ICUPK flyer had one simple drawing, an outline of the African continent with a circle around it and a thick diagonal line slashed right through its middle, mimicking the definitive and iconic clarity of a No Smoking sign. The text read, in all caps, YOU ARE NOT AFRICAN. There was also a listing for the time and channel of the ICUPK's weekly public access television shows and references to several scriptures from the King James Bible. It was my first, short lesson in one prominent claim of this particular Hebrew Israelite camp, something that separates them from the AHIJ: their contention about Africa's absolute alterity, about the continent's complete irrelevance to their political and spiritual aspirations.

There might have been a backside to the flyer with even more information. I haven't seen it in years and can't recall. I just remember thinking that the idea seemed so wildly provocative: African Americans are really not descendants of Africans—are not from Africa—at all. That's a hard claim to hawk in most black neighborhoods (no ties to Africa *in any way?*), even for those neighbors who proudly declare themselves to be, say, part Cherokee. And it felt particularly ironic coming from a group infamous for a certain racialized swagger that seemed indebted to many Black Nationalist forebears, the kinds of activists and thinkers who have long demonstrated a clear investment in the historical, mythological, genealogical, and symbolic centrality of The Continent.

Not too long after that train ride, I started to think about conducting a bit of ethnographic research on the ICUPK. They had a lot to say about the AHIJ's exploits in Israel, but none of it positive. They dismissed their emigrationist move as delusional, their trip to Israel useless, the myth-making of a false prophet and his blinded sheep, and it wasn't all that surprising to hear that the ICUPK community was overtly hostile to another Israelite group's assertions about history and cosmological truth. The ICUPK is probably best known for such pointed dismissiveness, for confronting passersby with bullhorns and megaphones on crowded city sidewalks all across America, challenging the legitimacy of every other faith and ideology: Christianity, Islam, Afrocentrism, alternative Black Hebrewisms, and just about anything else that runs counter to their own idiosyncratic and ever-evolving beliefs.

Even before I began my more formal examination of the ICUPK, I witnessed quite a few of their public debates—with black pedestrians, interracial and homosexual couples, Orthodox rabbis, baited foreigners, and anyone else willing to spar with them. Their brand of curbside soap-boxing has long been *de rigueur* for a dynamic "black public sphere," and the ICUPK are following in a well-documented tradition when they take their message straight to the streets. That message (and much of the style with which they disseminate it) reveals some of the shared institutional history that ties the ICUPK and the AHIJ together despite their profound differences. The two groups agree on a few very key points and share some basic positions (though not the AHIJ's most fundamental commitment to veganism and its links to physical health), but one thing stands out most prominently at the policed borders between their beliefs: they have diametrically opposed takes on the place of Africa in their reckonings of Israelite identity.

The ICUPK starts with a premise about the Middle Passage that isn't all that different from what grounds the AHIJ's historical revisionism, a reading of the transatlantic slave trade that is fairly cut-and-dried: African pagans and Arab Muslims sold Hebrew Israelites into chattel slavery to Europeans. Anything else, the ICUPK argues, is a lie, a conspiratorial rewriting of history. The rest of the ICUPK's arguments (about the "lost tribes," about the Bible's true directives, about figures like Socrates and Shakespeare actually being black) stem from that central interpretation

of the transatlantic slave trade, and they are unflinching in their commitment to its paradigmatic importance.

I used to show my classess excerpts from videos of the ICUPK's confrontational street exchanges, much of it footage that ICUPK members
recorded themselves, renditions of their no-nonsense truth-telling about
all things misconstrued as sacred and holy by misled "African" Americans, "so-called Negroes."[3] That entails more than just challenging the
hallowed status of Africa-centered black political philosophies. It also
requires denouncing the "skin-whitening and Toga-dressing" of iconic
Jesus Christ imagery, exposing the demonic nature of the Catholic
Church, dismissing rabbinical Judaism as a complete sham, and brutally
castigating black people for complicity in their own miseducation (for
being duped by erroneous and falsified rewritings of the historical
record).[4] In that sense, my introduction to the ICUPK on that #3 subway
train was exactly right in terms of the group's general evangelizing mode:
confrontational, accusatory, and no-holds-barred personal attacks meant
to startle sleepwalkers from their open-eyed slumber. Stop being such
suckers. You are Israelites, which means you are God's warriors.

"Black people have wooly hair," the ICUPK street-teacher makes clear
after another member reads a description of "the Most High" from the
book of Daniel, a passage about how "the Ancient of days did sit" with
hair "like pure wool." Many of the ICUPK's street teachings emphasize
the body's physical features as signs of celestial chosen-ness. The
"imposter Jews" of Revelations (demonic and even specifically pedophilic in the ICUPK's descriptions of things) don't have wooly hair, they
argue. And the "so-called white man," the "devilish so-called white
man," is "so-called" because the ICUPKers consider Europeans *red,* not
white. They are Edomites, the supposedly jealous and leprous descendants of Jacob's usurped older brother, the "ruddy" Esau. This interpretation of the Jacob and Esau story acts as a counterweight to the Curse of
Ham (the idea that blacks were damned by God with darker skin and
perennial slave status), mirroring the kinds of counterclaiming that has
long animated Afro-Diasporic responses to social marginalization and
racial demonization.

As different as some of their specific claims might be, just about all of these varied Black Israelite groups agree with the AHIJ that the Hebrew Israelites were relatively new arrivals to Central and West Africa when the transatlantic slave trade began, cultural outsiders easily captured for delivery to European slavers. But whereas the AHIJ would still imagine Africa, "Eden," as germane to its transformational and transnational project, the ICUPK and several other Hebrew Israelite camps do not. To them, Africans are evil and irredeemable. They are different peoples. Everyone might be a child of Abraham, but only certain children, even among all of those lumped together as members of the same racial group, are Hebrew Israelites, descendants of Jacob. The others are Nubians, Hamites, Hagarenes, Cushites, and Ishmaelites, but not Israelites. And that difference is paramount. According to the ICUPK, the Middle Passage produced a diasporic community, but not an *African* diasporic community. Their notion of "diaspora" includes communities all through-out the Americas, former slave populations and indigenous groups, but continental Africans are categorically excluded from the fold. To the ICUPK, being a Hebrew Israelite means you are decidedly *not* Jewish (at least not in the way that Ashkenazi Jews are Jewish), but at the very same time, YOU ARE NOT AFRICAN, either. Again, in it, but not of it.

The AHIJ, however, proffer a version of Israelite identity predicated on a sense of history that begins eastward in Eden, continues through the ministry of Yeshua (Jesus), and then reemerges (after a period of African captivity within foreign nations) on the shores of a new New World, a reversal of the transatlantic slave trade led by Ben Ammi. They don't denounce Africa; they reclaim it, a move reinforced by the fact that they got to Israel and changed their official name from the "Original Hebrew Israelite Nation of the Kingdom of Yah" to the "*African* Hebrew Israelites of Jerusalem." Since the AHIJ consider Israel a part of Africa, iconic pictures of the continent throughout the *kfar* and in jurisdictions around the world include a strip on the upper-right corner (a rendering of the landmass that cuts across the Suez Canal). As Sar Ahmadiel says, " 'the Middle East' is a geopolitical term, not a geological one. Israel rests firmly on the African tectonic plate," a point that the text from the African/Edenic Heritage Museum highlights.

Africans might have sold Hebrew Israelites into slavery, but the AHIJ haven't written off the entire continent, especially with Hebrew Israelites still potentially scattered among many African populations: Ethiopian Jews, the Lemba, the Yoruba, the Ashanti, the Igbo.[5] The ICUPK exclude Africa, refuting its symbolic and historical significance. The AHIJ expand Africa, adding a chunk of the Arabian Peninsula and dismissing the Suez Canal as little more than an African land grab predating the Berlin Conference. And for both groups, the AHIJ and the ICUPK— and for their would-be ethnographer—these discrepant readings of Africa have implications for the kinds of Israel and Israelite that can be produced or imagined.

The ICUPK claim to know where the "lost tribes" are located: sprinkled all throughout the Americas.[6] To this very day, some street corners in Brooklyn are consistently draped with placards listing those tribes and their precise locations whenever the ICUPK set up for their megaphoned Bible-readings. However, the AHIJ don't boast nearly as definitive a mapping of how the ancient tribes fit onto a grid of modern nation-states, but many current saints consider themselves the tribe of Judah, if only because the scriptures make clear which tribe will lead the community's return to Israel, laying the groundwork for others to follow, finally establishing the Kingdom of Yah on Earth for all eternity.

FOURTEEN

Empress

2008 AND 2009: I found myself galloping around the island of Jamaica recording mini-DV footage for an ethnographic film about a group of Rastafarians who annually commemorate the murder, torture, and imprisonment of dozens of "bearded men," mostly Rastafari elders, at the hands of Jamaica's citizenry and police force in 1963 (just a year after that nation's Independence from Great Britain), a sociopolitical convulsion euphemized as "the Coral Gardens incident"—and so named for the community in Montego Bay where the violence began.[1] My wife, Deborah, remember, is also an anthropologist, and she was researching the "incident" and its annual commemoration (the latter, in part, a way to publicize Rasta calls for government reparations) as part of a book she was writing about the country's history of violence—from the colonialist butcheries of chattel slavery to their present-day, postcolonial reincarnations in the form of drug wars and bloody garrison politics.[2]

Deb decided to make a film on the subject (enlisting my assistance to coproduce it) only after one of the Rasta elders she interviewed for her book suggested, almost offhandedly, that videotaping her interviewees would be a good way to provide victims (some of whom were in their eighties and nineties by then, many of them poor and living in the remotest parts of the Jamaican "bush") an opportunity to "look into the camera" and describe exactly what they experienced back then, "in their own words," through their own strained voices, before they eventually passed away, the distinctive timbre of their individual stories lost forever. The Rastaman also thought that these same video testimonies could help their reparations cause, and we would eventually be asked to provide local prosecutors with all of the raw footage from our interviews, including sit-downs with several elders who had, in fact, died before we finished the project.

Several of our film shoots entailed following a fledgling effort, spearheaded by a group of Rastafarians outside of Montego Bay, to create a Rasta-themed tourist site that showcased their culture and raised funds to sustain older members of their spiritual community.[3] Rastafari are divided into separate "houses" (something akin to religious "denominations," though, like Israelites, Rasta usually reject the rubric of "religion" altogether), eschewing any overarching central authority figure (other than Haile Salassie, Emperor of Ethiopia from the 1930s to the 1970s and the "returned messiah," according to their faith) in favor of allowing each house its own authority and autonomy. Houses sometimes vary drastically in terms of sanctioned practices and beliefs, some of them clearly frowning on the idea of such Rasta-themed tourism altogether, especially given the spiritual formation's longstanding and often-documented separatist, anticapitalist and antistatist postures.[4] Western politics ("politricks") and economics are abominations to the light and teachings of Jah/God. Still, the Rastafari we met were banking on the potential financial benefits of this kind of ethnotourism, a move to capitalize on the global notoriety of Rasta culture (already successfully marketed by the Jamaican tourist board) and to circulate their vernacular knowledge about health, spirituality, *Ital*-ity (veganism), and an all-around "natural" lifestyle.

Traditionally, Rastafari shunned the trappings of Babylonian modernity, which is part of the reason why some Houses dismissed this project as an unrighteous attempt to commercialize the sacred, a Faustian pact with materialist debasement. Our visits with various Rastafari communities reinforced my appreciation of the uncanny symmetries between

Rastafari and Hebrew Israelites, with the emergence of new (sometimes contested) versions of the AHIJ Kingdom's "redemptive enterprises" often serving as explicit hinges for the articulation of those similarities and connections.

During one visit with a Rastafari contingent in Belmont (outside of Montego Bay), I met a woman with ties to the AHIJ who had just arrived—that very week—from Baltimore, Maryland. She was born in Jamaica but spent the bulk of her life in and around Washington, DC, though she'd recently stopped working in one of the community's mid-Atlantic restaurants to help cultivate stronger ties between Hebrew Israelites and other spiritually conscious Jamaicans, especially Rastafari. She was joined in that effort by a saint (another native Jamaican raised in the United States) who had also come back to expand the AHIJ's business relationships (on health-related ventures) with the Rasta community, which would eventually bear fruit in Fire Light, an AHIJ-affiliated vegan restaurant launched in Kingston two years later. When we met him, however, he had just helped to set up a brand new homeopathic business that provided massage therapies and sauna treatments to interested patrons, and the restaurant seemed a long way off.

After first introducing myself to that Jamerican woman in one Rasta community's mosquito-filled compound in the woods of St. James Parish, I reconnected with her a few days later in Portmore, outside of Kingston, my family and I stopping by on our way to Hellshire, a nearby beach. She was staying with a friend, and the length of that stay (in the country and in that friend's home) had yet to be determined, which meant that she was still living out of unpacked suitcases and handbags.

Greeting my family warmly and welcoming us into her friend's cinderblock home with the offer of mangos and something to drink, she escorted us to the bedroom off the house's front door and spent our entire visit generously sharing stories about her connection to both Jamaica and the AHIJ community. Within fifteen minutes, she had fished a DVD out of her luggage, commandeered her host's main television set, and started playing footage from 2007's New World Passover ceremony. As we watched, she relayed her affection for Ben Ammi, for *"Abba."* She had never been to Israel, but she looked forward to going. "It is so expensive," she said, "but Yah willing."

The DVD's depiction of that annual ceremony's festivities blared loudly from the television's speakers, but she never turned the volume down, spending as much time looking at the footage as she did talking to us, indifferent to what her host might think of the television's unnecessarily high volume. She simply watched her DVD and described the footage to us, almost a kind of play-by-play commentary, its sequences supplying opportunities for her to explain details about NWP and its larger significance to the Kingdom. I told her that I'd been to NWP, which did seem to excite her a bit, but she still toggled back and forth between awe and envy at my good fortune (to have seen NWP up close!) and an assumption that every aspect of the ceremony was still completely new and unknown to me. We were only planning to stop by for a few minutes, so we politely took our leave before the NWP video was done (a second Kingdom-produced DVD already poised to replace it) and promised to keep in touch, either during our next trip to Jamaica or whenever she returned to the United States, whichever came first.

At the end of that short visit, I actually wasn't sure if she was a Rasta or a saint, or some idiosyncratic hybrid of the two. Her hair was dreaded, and she used the titles "Empress" and "Princess" (almost interchangeably) before her name (indications of a Rasta connection), but she had worked in an AHIJ restaurant in Baltimore for years, warmly called Ben Ammi "abba," and memorized every facet of that NWP DVD with an investment and longing that might have rivaled the enthusiasm of any saint on the *kfar*.

The Caribbean has a long history of Black Judaism and is full of Hebrew Israelites today, some of them directly linked to the AHIJ, part of the "West Indian jurisdiction" led by Cohane Michael Levi, a priest, author, saint, and Israelite scholar based in Guyana, South America, someone who grew up in the same sections of Brooklyn that I called home more than thirty years later, those very parts of the borough that would first spark my own interest in studying Hebrew Israelites.

FIFTEEN

Camps

S EVERAL SCHOLARS HAVE written compelling histories of black Jewish/Hebrew groups in America, including many that predate Ben Ammi and the AHIJ by more than half a century. These studies tend to be written with a single-mindedly schematic focus on the beliefs and practices that distinguish these groups, more or less detailed overviews of their stated orthodoxies. Many of those histories start in the late nineteenth century with the founding of the Church of the Living God, the Pillar Ground of Truth for All Nations in Tennessee by F. S. Cherry, a man who preached that white people were intrinsically evil and who predicted Armageddon at the end of the twentieth century (the same prophesy that the ICUPK espoused, the one that landed them—and other Hebrew Israelites like the AHIJ, by association—on the FBI's terrorism watch-list).

William Crowdy started the Church of God and Saints of Christ in Lawrence, Kansas, a few years after Cherry's group began, and he was adamant about African Americans being descendants of the lost tribes of Israel. His group (after several permutations and reconfigurations) continues its work throughout the Americas and other parts of the world, including Africa, with Crowdy's great-grandson now at the helm. Some historians operate under the working assumption that Cherry, Crowdy, and other earlier "black Jewish" pioneers mixed together everything from Christianity to Freemasonry as they literalized an erstwhile metaphorical identification with ancient Israelites, an identification that European missionaries cultivated in their African slaves.[1]

In Harlem, New York, the Commandment Keepers, founded in the early twentieth century by Rabbi Wentworth Arthur Matthew (who claimed to be from Nigeria but was more likely born on the Caribbean island of Saint Kitts, another version of Equiano's supposedly revised autobiographical flourishes), drew from white Jewish traditions as well as black separatist and gnostic ones in their forging of a distinctive black Jewish sensibility. As that African/Edenic Museum guide/curator tried to hammer home during my 2005 tour, Rabbi Josiah Ford, Marcus Garvey's onetime confidant and musical director for the Universal Negro Improvement Association, helped to bring Matthew to Judaism (a feat he also tried to accomplish, less successfully, with Garvey), and Matthew's Commandment Keepers looked to those Ethiopian Jews for inspiration and ancestral legitimacy.[2] Even before Matthew died in the 1970s, the community was already beginning to form factions and offshoots, one of which was founded by Eber ben Yomin (or Yamyam), who was also known as Abba Bivens. His group would become known as the Israelite School—later, the Israelite School of Universal Practical Knowledge, renamed upon Bivens's death by the same individual who helped to develop their peculiar version of the Hebrew language, meant to distinguish it from more "Yiddish-contaminated" contemporary varieties. According to historian Jacob Dorman, Matthew's version of black Judaism was always a bit duplicitous (or at least polyvocal), consisting of a public face and a set of sometimes quite divergent private actions, a tension that might have greased the wheel for the departure of Bivens, who found the inconsistencies troubling. Not necessarily because Bivens intended to take the Commandment Keepers in a completely new direction, but rather because he was simply planning to go public with some of its more esoteric and "hidden transcripts."[3] Depending on who tells the next part of this story, the Israelite School then changed its designation from a *school* to a *church* in the 1980s (to make a case, one argument goes, for tax-exempt status), and then even more splintering occurred, as several members of the community (among them, a clique of priests called "the seven") decided that they didn't agree with certain proposed changes in approach and philosophy that emerged as the derivative ICUPK group continued to evolve.

Disputes over doctrinal changes happen all the time. In one dramatic example many decades after its founding, the ICUPK changed its fundamental position on group membership in the late 1990s.[4] At first, they used patrilineal descent to decide who was allowed to join their ranks. You could only be a real Hebrew Israelite and a member of the ICUPK if your father and your father's father were black (i.e., Israelites). However, they eventually settled on a more open-ended way of deciding such things, declaring that God explicitly forbade such genealogical gate-keeping in the Bible and arguing that the mysterious workings of the Holy Ghost alone best determine belonging, regardless of the lineage or skin color of any prospective member.

At about that same time, several disgruntled Israelites decided to start another competing camp (arguably in response to such drastic kinds of changes in basic assumptions about how to decide who belongs): the Israelite Church of God in Jesus Christ (ICGJC). One leader would call himself "comforter" and rail against the wrongheaded ideas of his former allies. And there are many more offshoots and former ties besides these: the House of David, the House of Israel, and the Twelve Tribes. And more. Still, today, the Black Hebrew Israelite community continues to fissure, much like all groups do. The dividing line between Shia and Sunni Islam or the ever-increasing denominations of Christianity speak to similar fracturing dynamics. For the AHIJ, its latest manifestation is seismic, the 2011 departure of Prince Asiel, once Ben Ammi's closest confidant and the international spokesperson for the community, who would take several saints—and the community's most famous vegan restaurant in Chicago—with him.

But the story of Hebrew Israelite communities isn't just about fission and splintering. There are also continued attempts to bring camps together, to form a grand Kingdom that would unite all Israelite groups under a single banner. For Sar Levi in Philadelphia, such a Kingdom, a very successful one, under which all groups could fall, has already been formed in Dimona, and he wants other Israelite camps to seriously consider submitting to the authority of Ben Ammi and recalibrating their practices to more fully align with the decrees coming from "on high." When Levi's Philadelphia-based camp stopped attacking Ben Ammi and decided to become the newest American jurisdiction of the AHIJ community back in 2005, they lost a lot of their followers. New camps formed and new leaders emerged galvanized by protest against Sar Levi's decision to join ranks with Ben Ammi and the AHIJ. But Levi was determined to follow his spirit, and his spirit told him that this was what the Bible commanded.

When New York–born and Guyana-based saint Cohane Michael visited Philadelphia in the summer of 2012, he and Sar Levi convened an informal meeting with the heads of several Israelite camps in the area. Cohane Michael himself had come out of a New York–based group that wasn't tied to the AHIJ. He had trained with a very different black Israelite community and had spent almost forty years using local radio shows and Shabbat services to cultivate a vibrant Israelite community in Guyana that was distinct from the AHIJ. It was only in the mid-1990s, while Cohane Michael was trying to publish his first book, *Israelites and Jews: The Significant Difference,* when he and the AHIJ saints began to seriously talk. He couldn't find a publisher for his manuscript, and the AHIJ seemed willing to publish his work through their own publishing arm, which had already put out several of Ben Ammi's books. So, he was willing to meet with them and discuss the idea. (This was about the same time that Sar Ahmadiel was first conceptualizing and constructing the African/Edenic Heritage Museum, back when he was stationed in Georgia and Tennessee, hoping to eventually travel with it to several Historically Black Colleges and Universities and to other community institutions across the country, which he spent several years doing before moving to Dimona for good.) After meeting with saints in Washington, DC, Cohane Michael could tell that this group was "serious" about disseminating their knowledge far and wide. He was impressed by their organizational infrastructure—and by the way they treated his manuscript, respecting his reading of the Bible (even where its shadings of things diverged a little from the AHIJ) and helping to edit his book down to a more readable length.

After the book's publication, Cohane Michael formalized his link to the Dimona community and accepted the political and spiritual authority of its leadership—Ben Ammi, the Princes, and the Ministers. But he still kept in touch with various Israelite camps that continued to be unsympathetic to the Kingdom and its saints. He had a long history with them; he respected their efforts, and many of them were still close friends. So, if anyone could talk to these camps, Cohane Michael could. And he was willing to take his time, to use his cultural capital, and make the case.

During the meeting Sar Levi and Cohane Michael convened in 2012, leaders from those other camps listened respectfully, but they still weren't convinced. One thing that did seem to impress them, though, was the amount of development work that the AHIJ was undertaking all around the world, especially in Africa. Sometimes, as many as one-fifth of the adult saints in Dimona are somewhere else on the planet working with other communities of saints, teaching them the newest information about food consumption and preparation, helping them to run community-connected business operations, or actively attempting to bring new members into the Kingdom.

Cohane Michael had just come back from South Africa the month before that meeting, and he was providing the various Israelite leaders with some details about his AHIJ-sponsored trip: how well it was organized; the number of cities they visited; the energy and receptiveness of the South Africans they met. Out of everything they discussed that day, it was the AHIJ's ongoing efforts in Africa that most impressed the skeptics. The Kingdom's work in Africa demonstrated a level of organization that was hard to dismiss, and the other leaders seemed keen to hear more about how the AHIJ pulled off these exploits overseas, their success at finding and organizing Africans willing and able to understand themselves as descendants of the ancient Israelites. Africa might serve as a sticking point for some Israelite camps, the ones that define themselves as categorically distinct from Africans, but the AHIJ's work in Africa might actually go a long way toward bringing other Israelite groups into the fold, an elastic Africa that expands and contracts to fit varying definitions of diasporic and racial collectivity.

SIXTEEN

Liberia

PREPARING TO LEAVE the United States in 1966, and even reflecting on that departure once saints first started landing in Liberia a year later, Ben Ammi and his fellow emigrationists always talked a great deal about "the spirit," about the ultimate power of Spirit, about the irreconcilable differences between spirit-filled bodies and mere flesh. And even today, the AHIJ's cosmological contentions are perched on that same dividing line, especially their central ideas about health and human life, the very ideas that would begin to take on the particularities of their current shape with a second exodus from Liberia to Israel in 1969. But in 1966, before Liberia was even in the conversation (in terms of possible emigration destinations), they were still just trying to find an exit strategy, a way to get from Chicago to just about anywhere else, and they gave "the spirit" all the credit, all the glory, for finally coming up with one.

The paradigmatic shift away from just thinking about leaving to actually doing so was engineered, more accurately, by spirits, both a singular "Spirit," *the* Holy Spirit, and the spirits within individual Israelites, the latter expressed quite clearly in Ben Ammi's third-person (third-people?)

recollections during the 1970s: "And I was thinking about the spirit of Ben Ammi. And I was thinking about the spirit of Niflah, and I was thinking about the spirit of Nasik Hashalom. I was thinking about all these different things, all these different names, but they don't know him by name." Spirits with their own names (and unknown names) guided those Israelites in efforts to recruit travelers for their relocation mission, a mission that was unsure and unsecured, but ordained, they believed, and foretold.

"Because we had no ships," explained Nasik Shaleahk Ben Yehuda, the Kingdom's first Minister of Education, "we had no airplanes or other kinds of vessels, or transportation, or . . . finance[s]. So, everything we did had to be motivated from the word 'spirit.'"

When the Chicago Israelites were leaving, a holy spirit guided them, steeled them for their journey, and hardened them against onslaughts from naysayers and saboteurs. Friends and family members, many of the same folks who doubted their sincerity and sanity to begin with, would openly mock them. In fact, Ben Ammi wouldn't even tell members of his own Israelite community about that visit from Angel Gabriel, until some three weeks after it happened, not sure what they'd think or how they'd respond to such talk. They knew how crazy they *already* looked to people. Why give detractors more ammunition?

Even a few future saints, before they accepted "the truth," thought that Ben Ammi and the others were up to something, working some crazy angle for fun and profit. A few friends and relatives even messed with the new believers. Nasik Gavriel HaGodol relays a memorable tale on just this score. He had been childhood friends with Ben Ammi and was one of the first people Ben Ammi tried to teach. Not too long after joining the black Israelite community in Chicago, Gavriel was invited to a friend's house for dinner. The host wasn't an Israelite but assured Gavriel that the meal being prepared would be completely pork-free, the Israelites' only major dietary restriction back then. However, Gavriel soon found himself being laughed at—right after the meal, right around the dinner table—when his host finally revealed that pork fat had been added to every single dish they'd eaten, just to mock him. This was the kind of hostility that some of Chicago's Israelites faced, even from friends and family, which would make life in Chicago all the more difficult—only intensifying their commitment to leaving.[1]

Black Israelites set up their soapboxes on Maxwell Street, in a Jewish section of the city, and made their case for the true Israelite identity of African Americans. Some people were moved by their teachings, especially because of their "back to Africa" emphasis, one of the most prominent aspects of their street ministry. But other people scoffed at their timing. It was the middle of the civil rights movement, and many African Americans were digging in their heels to fight for inclusion and equality, in the streets and in the courts, not hightailing it out of the country, running off to someplace they'd never been. To some people, that seemed like the cowardly option, a kind of cop-out.

And then there were the deepening fault lines between many members of the old guard in Chicago's Israelite community and the relative newcomers like Ben Ammi and Nasik Gavriel. Many of the elders wanted these adamant emigrationists to slow down. They were being too hasty, not waiting for the appointed time. Some of the elders might have agreed about the agency of "the spirit" in such matters, but they doubted that that spirit was sanctioning any immediate departures. It wasn't yet time, no matter how gung-ho some Israelites (and other African Americans) might be about the prospect. And it would certainly not succeed, not when they weren't yet meant to leave. Many members of the community, people like Rabbi Devine, could not be convinced otherwise. Though Ben Ammi and others tried to win them over, their spirits would not be moved, and the rift between pro- and anti-emigrationist Israelites intensified.

The pro-emigrationists so believed in the workings of the spirit, says Singer, that they packed their suitcases, met at the community's meetinghouse, A-Beta Center, on Passover of 1967, and supposedly waited right there to be raptured, miraculously, back to Africa. They waited and waited, singing and praying, he says, but nothing happened.[2] As the evening wore on, Singer claims, they wallowed in their own dashed hopes, anticipation morphing into frustration. But the spirit was testing them, they soon decided, and the leaders of this fledgling emigrationist movement were determined not to fail. They would work with the spirit to help themselves. They'd meet with other African Americans agitating for repatriations, comparing strategies and forging collaborations. They threw themselves into more research, more prayer, and they eventually decided that Liberia, not Ethiopia, was the most feasible site for their proposed relocation, not least because it was less difficult (and much cheaper) to get to.

When I talk with saints in the Kingdom about those final few months in Chicago, they discuss that Passover in 1967 much differently. Yes, the community met at A-Beta, but it was to celebrate the ancient Israelite exodus out of Egypt, to mark the similarities, the prophetic mirroring, that their emigrationist longings represented, not to imagine being whisked away in some magical whirlwind. They were willing to put in the hard work to prove their commitment to God, their repentance for past disobedience, for the sins of their fathers, sins they had been taught to naturalize and reproduce. The spirit works, but they would work, too. They always knew that. And they met on Passover in 1967 to affirm that need for such collective effort. That was it. Only three weeks later, Ben Ammi, Nasik Gavriel, and Ben Yaacov would do some reconnaissance, heading out on a flight to Liberia in an effort to make sure that that destination could really serve as the community's new home.

In the early nineteenth century, the American Colonization Society and the U.S. government created Liberia, a new nation specifically meant for former African slaves and freedmen. Liberia was established to help solve America's race problem by finding a new home for emancipated slaves whose anger at their past enslavement, many whites believed, would only make them hostile neighbors and difficult citizens in any imaginable future without legalized racial slavery. About 100 years after Liberia's initial founding, Marcus Garvey would agree to help raise funds for the country's cash-strapped Americo-Liberian ruling class in exchange for an open-armed welcome of Universal Negro Improvement Association settlers from the Americas. But some UNIA leaders in the 1920s "frankly could not advise under present conditions" that African Americans make that move. In their opinion, opportunities for gainful employment and infrastructural necessities were woefully underdeveloped.[3] Several decades later, Ben Ammi and his Israelite compatriots would not let such worries stall them.

As soon as the three ambassadors from Chicago's black Israelite community disembarked from their plane in Liberia and headed to Gbatala (part of Liberia's Bong County), they confirmed the major *legal* obstacle to their plans. When the country was first founded any new arrivals would be given land that they could eventually own (after proving their willingness to cultivate that land for a set number of years), but by the time the Israelites were making their move, anyone relocating from America would be ineligible to acquire land in the country for several years. So, new arrivals could not just put their money down and buy a plot of land. Undaunted, Ben Ammi, Nasik Gavriel, and Ben Yaacov were able to convince a couple of American expats, Garveyites who'd been living in Liberia for some twenty years, more than long enough to qualify for land ownership, to serve as their proxies for the purchase. Originally from Cincinnati, James Flemister and his wife (no saints I spoke with in the Kingdom could remember her name) had met members of the Israelite community in Chicago, were impressed by their emigrationist commitments, invited them to visit Liberia, and eventually agreed to buy some land on their behalf.[4] James Flemister served as official owner, but the community would make any and all decisions about how to use the land. When it was legal to do so, Flemister would formally transfer ownership to the Chicago group. He promised not to interfere, and he allowed the community's ambassadors to stay with him during their exploratory visit as they prepared to report back to the Israelites in Chicago.

By all accounts, Ben Ammi, Nasik Gavriel, and Ben Yaacov had a very successful preliminary trip to Liberia, especially given Flemister's willingness to show them around the country and to assist them with their group's relocation. The spirit had moved this African American expat in Liberia, someone who didn't consider himself as Israelite, to facilitate their divine project, their attempt to join him in West Africa. He could understand, as one wire service reported in 1968, why they had gotten "tired of waiting for equal rights in the United States."[5] It was time to leave.

Ben Ammi and the other early emissaries got back to Chicago encouraged by how their fortuitous connections with Flemister had played out, spreading the word among community members about their increasingly more tangible plans, even providing details on the specific stretch of land they would occupy. They told anyone who'd listen. Indeed, even before they got back to Chicago after that Liberia trip, during a short layover in New York City, the men tried to meet with Rabbi Wentworth Matthew, to share their Liberia plans with his Commandment Keeper congregation. But their overtures were rebuffed. "He wouldn't even take the time to meet," Sar Ahmadiel says, rejecting their request right over the phone. But such dismissals didn't dissuade them, even when they came from other black Jews/Israelites. It wouldn't stop their progress. They just kept soapboxing and fundraising up until the first few families left for Liberia several weeks later. Ben Ammi and a few others would take even longer to depart, spending their time in the United States raising money for people's plane tickets, foodstuffs, and the other items—while also actively recruiting more African Americans to the cause, Israelites or not. They were going to a specific place, a section of unfarmed land "in the Liberian jungle." They had Israelites lined up to take the journey, people who had sold their homes, cars, appliances, and anything else they could unload in favor of Sears and Roebuck tents, canned goods, and durable travel clothes.[6] The spirit was leading the way, and they needed to prepare their minds and bodies, their cells and souls, for the challenges ahead.

SEVENTEEN

Visitations

THE AHIJ placed us—me, my wife, and a Jewish-American friend who agreed to come along as an informal research assistant—in one of their fairly spacious guesthouses just outside the AHIJ's "Village of Peace" *(Kibbutz Shomrey Ha Shalom),* the official name of their *kfar* in the Kingdom's capital, Dimona, a growing city developed for newly arrived European immigrants, especially Russians, during the 1950s, and roughly equidistant from Be'er Sheva to its West and the Live Sea farther East.[1]

After finishing a light vegan lunch that several female saints had prepared, carried to the guesthouse, and dutifully served, we sat down with our hosts to discuss an upcoming trek across Israel, which was scheduled to begin the following day. For most American visitors, especially first-timers, saints set up what they call "Sacred Visitations," multiday excursions across the nation that allow AHIJ tour guides ("Divine Guides") to educate foreigners on some of the country's most important landmarks, all interpreted and redefined from the Kingdom's perspective. One saint (or several, if it is a particularly large party with a little more time to spend in the countryside) will be responsible for providing a curated trip through Israel's most famous sites, all with the intended purpose of dispelling "misconceptions" about "the Holy Land" that Western visitors have internalized, saints contend, as a function of European Jewry's hegemonic articulation of the landscape.[2]

Sacred Visitations rewrite the story of Israel by focusing on the African populations already residing there, from those nomadic Bedouin in the arid Negev Desert to holy men in an Ethiopian monastery linked to the Church of the Holy Sepulchre. Guests get a chance to briefly visit with many of the people whose photos are featured in the African/Edenic Heritage Museum, to sit with them, to take their own photos with them, arm in arm, listening to their stories. Our Sacred Visitation was scheduled for the next morning, and we went over the final inkjet copy of our trip's itinerary, which included a stop in Jerusalem, specifically the Old City, meals in Rahat, an opportunity to wade in the Jordan River, and an overnight stay in the city of Tiberias, near the Sea of Galilee. The schedule also included shorter stops in others cities, including Arad, where, not too many hours later, the "Divine Guide and Hermeneutic Scholar" leading our contingent would point out African Muslims in the region who "look like Pookie and Rae-Rae and Big Earl and all those folks you know from back home. They don't ever show you that on CNN," he declared. "Why do you think that is?" But the visit to Arad and our entire Sacred Visitation had yet to begin, and as we discussed specifics, I was wondering if the trip needed to be canceled altogether.

On the television screen behind us, in the corner of that AHIJ guesthouse, muted for much of the time that we discussed the particulars of our journey, was live news coverage of Israel's attempt to forcibly remove Jewish settlers and sympathetic protesters from the Gaza Strip and several small sections of the West Bank. The images were sometimes startlingly brutal and disturbing. At one point, a rabbi, trying to restore calm amidst a group of angry protesters, was pulled from his perch on the roof of an automobile and beaten mercilessly, all right on camera, a helicopter above catching the entire thing (with at least one news station constantly replaying that same short clip of the beating over and over again). Israeli armed forces were being greeted with violent resistance as settlers ignored the government's mandate that they leave the designated areas, choosing to dig in their heels for a fight. We were scheduled to navigate our way around the West Bank on our drive, but the violence looked intense and unpredictable enough, at least as far as I was concerned, to merit reconsidering those plans. Prudence seemed justifiable, and friends back in America had already started emailing me for updates about our whereabouts, especially with American news outlets ramping up their journalistic reports on the conflict.

With removal operations receiving almost nonstop coverage on Israeli TV, the entire body politic seemed to be holding its collective breath. Saints in the AHIJ community took note of the clashes and expressed disappointment about its most obvious performances of brutality, but they also appeared somewhat removed from the entire affair, guaranteeing us that none of this was going to endanger the next day's journey.[3] They would not think about cancelling our trip, offering only smiling reassurances when my research assistant finally broached the topic. Indeed, the AHIJ's general obliviousness to the potential hazards of the road during this politicized situation seemed somewhat bizarre to us, even inappropriate—"reckless," my assistant would say. It was as though saints were watching the entire thing transpire from far away, like we were all back in the United States somewhere, removed, geographically and subjectively, from the material realities of those rocks and bottles, rifle butts and rage-filled exchanges beamed at us through the guesthouse's thirty-two-inch television screen.

Though much of Israel seemed preoccupied with the clash, orange (antiremoval) and blue (proremoval) ribbons tied around car antennae, belt buckles, and shirt-sleeved biceps serving as nonviolent expressions of discrepant civilian feelings about the forced relocation of Jewish settlers, our AHIJ hosts watched images of the conflict with a kind of distant wonder—again, almost as though they weren't right there, in Israel, at all. They had no intention of rescheduling our Sacred Visitation. We would be safe, they promised, even though Gaza was only a short fifty or so kilometers northwest of where we sat to go over the stops on our journey—and though our trip around the West Bank would certainly entail many more checkpoints than usual. As they carefully explained to us, the community's obedience to divine mandates (by returning to their ancient homeland, considered a fulfillment of biblical prophecy, and by reinstituting an Edenic *live-it* ordained by Yah) was part of what would keep them safe, and it was that sense of ultimate (and divine) protection that informed their public fearlessness on a daily basis.

Every evening during that first (and some of my subsequent) visits to Israel, when saints and I would saunter down Dimona's quiet sidewalks late at night, young Israeli preteens innocently playing atop moonlit street corners, saints asked me a version of the same question: why would America's news media choose to portray the region as violent and dangerous when it is actually so peaceful? One saint likened the neighborhood immediately surrounding the *kfar* to media representations of American suburbia circa 1950.[4] "This is 'Leave it to Beaver'," he quipped as we bounded across the parking lot in search of two scoops of vegan ice cream before the community's parlor closed. "We couldn't walk around like this in Chicago or Detroit or anyplace back in America. Not without fearing for our lives," he laughed.

I watched the news coverage of the evacuation for several hours that final night before our trip—only sporadically while saints played cards with us in the early part of the evening and more intently once they'd left us to rest up for the morning. Televisual mediation, even there in that AHIJ guesthouse just outside the *kfar,* appeared to help push the conflict farther and farther from view, making it somehow less proximate than objective measurements of physical distance might have implied.

One of the things that drew me to the AHIJ community in the first place was its fascination and facility with "new media," especially the community's deployment of digital media technology. As their consistent video coverage of New World Passover ceremonies attests (along with their filmed documentation of past clashes with the Israeli state), they are deft mediamakers and autoarchivists, documenting their lives in Israel with meticulous self-consciousness, circulating that material to saints throughout the world, and promoting a powerful form of social intimacy and cohesion between saints across vast distances.

The first AHIJ DVD that I ever received was that forty-five-minute "birthday present" to Nasik Asiel, who was still on good terms with the Kingdom at the time and had just turned sixty-five years old. It consisted of footage from past PBS documentaries about important historical moments in black American history, situating Asiel within the context of his Chicago upbringing. It also included interviews with younger saints in Israel and the United States, people who talked about Nasik Asiel's leadership and his long-standing dedication to the community. It was a very personal piece, edited in Dimona but disseminated to "jurisdictions" throughout the Americas.

I saw a copy of the DVD being dubbed for a saint in Washington, DC. The saint visiting Jamaica (to collaborate with Rastafarians on the creation of that new vegan/*ital* restaurant in Kingston) had already seen it back home in Baltimore before she'd left, and you could tell that this transnationally mobile document assisted in facilitating a sense of community that felt tangible and intimate. Indeed, the video was as much about the production of such global intimacies as it was a tribute to an important elder in the community. As David Graeber argues, economic relations and exchanges were historically just a specialized way of cultivating much more fundamental social relations, another way of producing and reproducing social connectedness (all the more necessary, we might add, when members of these would-be groups are transnationally dispersed).[5]

News coverage of those forced relocations, however, represented the opposite impact of mass-mediated storytelling, producing a response very different from what the community's own media productions generally sanction, creating distance and anonymity over and against the closeness of their physical proximity (to the public skirmishes) and the aforementioned intimacies that their own video offerings appeared formulated to nurture. Saints seemed to be speaking at a safe distance from things, very far away (subjectively) from the pullout and its political fallout. And this was all despite the fact that community members were not invulnerable to the dangers of the region's geopolitical present. Indeed, the AHIJ had had its first victim of a terrorist attack only a few years earlier, while the young man was singing at a *bat mitzvah* in Hadera. Saints mark this event as a turning point for them, a moment when the Israeli media's coverage of the attack led to an outpouring of national sympathy. It was one of the most valuable media stories about the group to date (that and the international reports, years later, about a community member who won the right to represent Israel in Eurovision, a popular singing competition).

Besides the death in Hadera, there were other links between AHIJ saints and the region's central political conflict. During our trip to the Old City that next day as part of our (not-cancelled) Sacred Visitation, we sat and took pictures with an elderly Palestinian activist from the "fifth quarter" (the "African Quarter") inside a recreation center that saints had had a hand in building back when they were still working illegally to make ends meet.[6] During this short stop inside the walled-off city's "Prison Gate" area, a standard part of Sacred Visitations (the afore-mentioned Palestinian activist's younger relatives and friends clearly awaiting our visit and prepared to fetch him as soon as we arrived, having done so many times before), we are regaled with stories highlighting similarities between the plights of Palestinians in contemporary Israel and African Americans in America. The saints nodded their heads with appreciation.

Once our minivan left the Old City, we were told that the trip would not include several usual stops at places where the community consis-tently shops for fruit and vegetables in the occupied territories, their one major concession to the realities of the current political moment. Such a detour (to visit these Palestinian farmers) was deemed "not worth the aggravation" given the country's heightened security measures, but they assured us that had we gone we would have seen their warm and respect-filled friendships with their Palestinian neighbors. All in all, the AHIJ community demonstrates a complex take on the entire Israeli-Palestinian conflict. They are committed to the integrity of the Israeli state (boldly manifested in their recent willingness, about a year before my first visit, to *voluntarily* enlist their high school graduates in the military), but they also identified (in many different ways) with the Palestinian cause—at times comparing it not only with their previous second-class citizenship in the United States but with their own relatively marginalized and vul-nerable status vis-à-vis an Israeli state that they had previously dubbed (throughout the 1970s and 1980s) bitterly racist—in contrast, they would quickly add, to the generosity and acceptance that they have often felt from the Israeli people.

Nevertheless, the AHIJ traditionally stayed outside the fray, chalking this conflict up to merely "religious" differences between Judaism and Islam. Religion, AHIJ saints argue, is the problem. They define their own beliefs and practices as a "way of life" instead of a "religion." Religious differences will always lead to human strife, they claim, which is why they are adamantly antireligion. The central problem with religion, they say, is its compartmentalizing approach to the necessities of spiritual life. It relegates God to one day a week, an optional superstructural flourish atop what's presumed to be secularism's sturdier base. The Israelites I met in Harlem when I was still a graduate student would always stress that the root of the word *religio* is derived from *religare,* to bind or hold back, arguing that such an etymology exposed the ultimate bankruptcy of the idea. Religion is an abomination to the sacred, not its defender. For the AHIJ, no peace can come to the region so long as wars are waged—and holistic divine truths crushed—under by the banner of religious solidarity.[7]

Two years earlier, the AHIJ had launched (with some local fanfare and even a little international news coverage) their *Reverend Martin Luther King Jr.—SCLC—Ben Ammi Conflict Resolution Center and Institute for a New Humanity,* just around the corner from the Ministry of Information inside the *kfar*. This relatively new center demonstrates their growing interest in playing a more substantial role in ongoing attempts to bring peace to the area. The AHIJ's own "settler" practices (their claims about being the legitimate heirs to that land) are deemed problematic in the context of competing Palestinian claims to autochthonous belonging ("How is that really different," anthropologist Saba Mahmood asked, after a talk I'd given at Berkeley, "from the Zionist Israelis?"), but the AHIJ's relatively rich relationships with African Muslims and Palestinian activists (over and against their weaker—though cordial—ties to local Israeli Jews, including Ethiopians whose faces are featured in the traveling museum) hint at the charged and overwrought fault lines and tensions that they are trying to straddle.

EIGHTEEN

Immortality

"Back in the day, Sar [Ahmadiel] couldn't have told us anything," Sar Levi said, gripping the steering wheel, shaking his head, nodding at Ahmadiel, who was riding shotgun, and glancing periodically at me, seated in the backseat, through the rearview mirror. "Man, we'd have been ready to fight this brother. Fight! Physically. We didn't want to hear nothing about what they were doing in Israel or anywhere else. If you'd have told me we'd be where we are now, I would have called you crazy. Impossible."

The three of us have just started a short drive on I-76 in Philadelphia. At this point, I still didn't know Sar Levi very well, but our pasts had crossed before, seven years earlier, during my first trip to Dimona. Sar Levi also just so happened to make his initial visit to the *kfar* that same week. He was still not an official saint back then, still not a full-fledged member of the AHIJ, and he was still somewhat skeptical about affiliating with the Kingdom. The Philadelphia-based Israelite camp that he led, which had been around for over twenty years, was among the most vocal Israelite critics of the AHIJ in the United States, and they had been for a very long time. Sar Levi even admits to the fact that he only accepted Ben Ammi's invitation to visit that year in an effort to gather more ammunition against the Kingdom, to collect more material for his anti-Ben Ammi archive. Now, he was escorting Sar Ahmadiel, one of the community's most important international spokespeople, from the University of Pennsylvania to the Philadelphia jurisdiction's main headquarters in Germantown. His group had gone from a hostile camp to a newly recognized and official AHIJ satellite community within about five years, significantly reconfiguring many central aspects of their beliefs and practices.

We were riding to a Shabbat class on the first floor of a tenement building that served as central location for all the community's activities. It was a meeting hall, a performance space, their business offices, an eatery, a classroom, and the site for Shabbat services. Sar Ahmadiel was just in town for a week, staying at a West Philadelphia bed-and-breakfast, so that he could meet some Penn students and strategize with me about how we might bring the African/Edenic Heritage Museum to campus. I was hoping that the university's Museum of Anthropology and Archeology could exhibit some version of it, and I had started to meet with a few of the museum's curators to gauge their interest in the idea. After a brief tour of the space I had in mind, Ahmadiel was doubtful that the dimensions of the room would work. The museum's many Plexiglas exhibits are bulky, wide-based, and two-sided, which meant that the room's relatively narrow space might prevent visitors from seeing the fronts and backs of all the components—almost no matter how the pieces were configured. But Ahmadiel promised to keep thinking about ways to potentially redesign or scale-down the museum with these spatial specifics in mind.

The next day, during our Shabbat drive, Sar Ahmadiel and I told Sar Levi about this idea of bringing the exhibit to Penn, but the two of them spent most of our travel time simply catching up with one another. This was their first chance to reconnect since collaborating in South Africa several months earlier (cultivating new saints in some of that country's main cities). The too-short week Ahmadiel was spending in Philadelphia would be a whirlwind, including several different events with students at Penn and a short jaunt down to DC to visit some of his family members (relatives who are not in the AHIJ community) before heading back to Israel.

Our conversation during that drive ranged from a brief mention of Eden Roc, the Open Mic night that Sar Levi's son organizes every other Thursday evening, to a discussion about the extent to which Christian televangelist Creflo Dollar's "prosperity gospel" might have been informed by his attendance at AHIJ classes in the Atlanta jurisdiction back in the 1980s. "He was there," Levi assured us. "He would come out. Learn from the saints. And he took some of that with him." But the bulk of our twenty-minute drive pivoted on Sar Levi relaying a very personal story to us, a tale about what happened when he first told his family that he was a "Hebrew Israelite."

He had grown up in a "fairly traditional" African American household, and he wasn't completely sure how they would react to his revelation. Would they think he was nuts? That he just didn't want to be black? He wasn't sure, but he was surprised to see them reacting as though the contention was obvious and self-evident, nothing to make a big deal about. His family even had corroborating evidence that they shared with him, stuff he'd never heard before, about ancestors, going back several generations, who had already been claiming Hebrew or Jewish backgrounds. "It blew my mind," he said. "Why hadn't they told me about any of this? I didn't hear any of it before. But they knew the truth."

Ahmadiel had a somewhat similar story about his grandmother's reception to his revelation. She didn't actually say anything to him when he told her of his Israelite identity, but she just looked at him with what he now appreciates as a kind of "knowing smile." During his two-hour lecture in front of the Philadelphia saints that afternoon, he provided even more details about his relationship to this Ashkenazi Jewish grandmother, someone who he simply understood—and even dismissed—as the "white" part of his family tree. Ahmadiel's recollections of her, of how he'd treated her, these many years later, would help him to rethink some of his earliest commitments to racial reasoning.

"So many things are just distractions," he told the seventy-five or so saints assembled for class that evening in Philadelphia. "Just distractions, distractions from the truth. Race is a distraction. We are unlocking the keys to immortality, not getting trapped in mortal man's foolishness. We have no time for nonsense and foolishness."

A saint seated next to me repeated the word "nonsense" a few more times. "Even living forever," he added, talking to himself as much as anyone else, "don't mean you got time for nonsense."

Several saints reminded me to sign up for Ben Ammi's webcast, "a message of utmost historical and prophetic importance, during which he will share a revelation that promises to be the most significant since his earth-changing vision of 1966." It was scheduled to stream through a link at www.yahkai.com on October 9, 2011 "at 3pm EST (for North America, the Caribbean and South America) and 1500GMT (for Africa and Europe)." It cost $10 to participate and proceeds went to the AHIJ's "Restoration Village projects in Eden-Africa," the Kingdom's ramped up effort to bring their message to the entire continent. I sat in my living room to watch the online program, which emphasized the community's central ethnobiological contention: that veganism can lead to physical immortality in these human bodies. It is a claim that has evolved over many years—and it is still evolving. Yah is slowly divulging more and more details about how to attain immortality, and there will be further revelations to come. Ben Ammi continues to get keys to unlocking the immortal potential of our species.

For the AHIJ, being human, in its fullest sense, means living forever. Mortality itself is dehumanizing. Adam and Eve were supposed to live forever, before they disobeyed and were banished from the "garden eastward in Eden," an exit that mirrors, saints argue, the subsequent transatlantic expulsion of Hebrew Israelites from what they now refer to as "westward in Eden" (West Africa) to the old "New World," another eviction cosmically caused by willful disobedience. This idea of humanity's founding immortality is a vital element in AHIJ orthodoxy, linked to all of their powerful interpretations of the Bible as a spiritual roadmap, a detailed history book, and "an instruction manual for the human body." The Kingdom's understanding of the body is central to its interpretation of many things, including the nature of heaven and hell.

Love Wins, the controversial book by Michigan-based evangelical and megachurch pastor Rob Bell, criticizes Christianity's imagery of hell as a literal lake of fire within which those who have not repented and accepted Jesus Christ will burn for all eternity.[1] Bell objects to this depiction of divine retribution. Instead, he argues (though he sometimes appears to take back that argument during contentious television interviews) that there is no hell at all if by hell we mean a place where the dead are brought back to consciousness to be tormented forever for their sins. The AHIJ wouldn't agree with the bulk of Bell's theology, but they make a similar case against popular characterizations of heaven and hell, especially those that would posit them as actual physical places to which other-worldly figures escort us.

In a very profoundly immediate and material way, the AHIJ believe, heaven and hell are lived right here and now on earth. They are simply a function of the "thoughts" we manifest in the everyday choices we make about how to live. Sometimes, when saints talk about heaven and hell, they'll point to the top of their heads, arguing that the heaven and hell of the Bible are states produced and reproduced in our minds (as a consequence of many things, including the chemistries of our respective brains), states of mind that impact our physical bodies, our social ties, and our entire planet's ecosystem. Our brains' manifestations of hellish ideas in our everyday behaviors are the things that kill us; everything else is just a symptom. Those "Satanic" ideas allow us to destroy the earth's resources with callousness and indifference. Heaven, however, is the translation of "Yah-inspired thoughts" into everyday action, the consequence of willful obedience to God's commands. It seeks to protect and regenerate the earth, with hell being simply its very tangible and terminal opposite.

Earth was meant to last forever. Adam and Eve were, too. Death wasn't a part of humanity's original design, which is why there is nothing fantastical or magical about how and why humans can live forever, saints say. It is how Adam and Even were constructed, something programmed into humanity's very DNA. And the Kingdom feels increasingly vindicated as they interpret growing numbers of mainstream medical scientists slowly backing into the same conclusions about our body's potential capacity for much longer life spans.

I entered the Soul Veg restaurant in Atlanta just as a saint I've never met before was explaining the Kingdom's ideas about immortality to a dreadlocked patron, a twenty-something-year-old black woman, in line ahead of me. I had planned to take my food back to the hotel with me (after a late speaking engagement with some of the University of Pennsylvania's alumni-of-color in the area), but I decided to linger in the restaurant and eavesdrop, a quintessentially ethnographic impropriety.

The saint spent several minutes on the Adam and Eve story, on its commonly superficial and nonsensical interpretations, including the "lie" about Eve eating an actual apple. As the African/Edenic Heritage Museum exhibit makes clear, the "fruit" wasn't a literal fruit (even if it were, there is no "apple" anywhere in the passage), and the book of Genesis should have been translated—from the ancient Hebrew—as "In *a* beginning . . ." not "In *the* beginning . . . ," which potentially changes that story's larger implications quite dramatically. The saint punctuated his discussion with claims about how "alternative" spiritual practices (specifically, "Yoga" and "Buddhism") are attempts to get "part of the way to the truth" that Hebrew Israelites already know, truths about the indivisible links between minds and bodies. And these are all better options, he says, than the "lies and half-truths" of Christianity. The many flyers on tabletops and windowsills throughout the restaurant mark some of the spiritual and cultural eclecticism that he mentions, material advertising "Africa for the Africans" tours "and investments," classes on breathing and spiritual guidance, all-natural hair and scalp crèmes, and many other health products, some of these clearly "redemptive enterprises" launched by saints in the area, others more standard countercultural fare that might be found in almost any Afrocentric or independent bookstore in the country.

I ate my food and listened to the saint's lesson. God tells Adam and Eve that they can eat almost everything in the garden, he says, unpacking the Genesis story in vivid detail. He talks about Adam naming all the animals, about Eve's "feminine power," about God specifically forbidding the two of them to eat from one particular tree. Just one. It was the tree of the knowledge of good and evil "together, at the same time," which is nothing but "confusion," he says. Death emerged as a consequence of disobeying Yah—a death, the saint clarified (for both of us, acknowledging my interest with a nod of his head), human beings didn't necessarily have to experience. He quoted biblical passages verbatim, including the serpent's coy rebuttal to God declaring the certainty of death's ties to disobedience.

"People forget that Adam and Eve still lived a long time after that," he added. "A long time. Why do you think that is?" The question was rhetorical, or at least the dreadlocked woman and I took it that way, staring back at him in silence. "Because the poison only just started. It would take time to work. They lived so long, because they were only starting to destroy their bodies. They were naming animals in the garden, not eating them. As soon as they leave the garden, God tells them that they can start eating meat. That was a death sentence, and people will tell you about some 'new covenant' and the old one is done and that kind of thing, but the 'new covenant' is a death sentence. And that is what it was supposed to be." The trick, he said, the "trap," was "flesh," consuming it, but veganism is key to writing a positive end to that story of "original sin" and reclaiming our immortality.

A month after my trip to Atlanta, Ben Ammi offered a second webcast that would continue to "unveil the formula for physical immortality." In the ads for this follow-up event, there are a series of excerpts from a news story about molecular geneticists trying to reprogram human cells so that the strings of DNA at the ends of chromosomes, telomeres, no longer get shorter over time. This chromosomal shortening is theorized as a cause for cellular deterioration and, ultimately, human death—from aging. If scientists can find a way to counter this process, they might be able to regrow organs and produce cells that survive for hundreds of years, the story notes, maybe even forever.[2] But that's just one scientific theory that the AHIJ reference—that saints bring up in their discussions with one another.

They also invoke a Cambridge scientist who is believed to have isolated a bacterial enzyme that keeps cells "from getting clogged up with the gunk that eventually suffocates them." Without such suffocation, these cells could effectively be immortal, or so the most ambitious and optimistic interpretation of that argument goes. The point in all this, the reason why they reference such articles and studies, is to produce an archive demonstrating that the community's vernacular theories about humanity's capacity for everlasting life (not in some heaven after death, but in our earthy bodies) is finally starting to be treated seriously by medical researchers from prestigious mainstream institutions in many different scientific disciplines. Their ongoing collection and circulation of press clippings and journal articles showcasing science's newest theories about how the body's cells might be reengineered for longer life is an example of what anthropologist Carlo Caduff calls the "boundary concept" of scientific information, a perch at the crossroads between sanctioned and institutionalized scientific thought/practice, on the one hand, and various interested publics with their own agendas and endgames, on the other.[3] Caduff describes how fears of bioterrorism have become not just about policing hazardous/noxious materials but also about making sure that potentially dangerous scientific information doesn't fall into the wrong hands, terrorists' hands. The "circulation of scientific information," he says, is increasingly offered up as a new kind of global threat, but this same circulatory effect (toward health-related goals as opposed to the production of contagious microbial threats by "malicious agents") characterizes the meticulous ways in which saints comb through contemporary scientific findings for corroboration of their claims about immortality's physiological plausibility.

AHIJ commitments to the body's ability to reproduce itself at the cellular level into perpetuity, which grounds their investments in veganism (a recuperation of Adam and Eve's garden-based diet), is an ethnobiological claim that serves as the pivot point for much of what saints do and how they do it. This investment in a literal and physical immortality is also another version of the community's culturally specific rethinking of time itself, expanding human life into infinity and challenging the inevitability of mortality, the assumption that human time eventually runs out.

Anthropology has often framed "the body," material embodiment, as a central site for emergent and contested claims, vernacular and scientific, about the "natural" contours of human identity and social community. From notions of "biological citizenship" and "sensuous scholarship" to calls for a deconstruction of racialized bodies or renewed claims about racial groups having different propensities for certain diseases, anthropological theory has made a point of participating in ongoing debates about the relationship between social differences and physical/"natural" diversity.[4] Popular discussions about the Jewish body's susceptibility to Tay-Sachs disease or to certain forms of cancer or (as at least one Philadelphian argues) to a mappable propensity for pedophilia mirrors talk about Africana predilections for sickle-cell anemia or for salt retention or for congenital laziness. Even though these very links demonstrate the lie of racial reasoning (since any traits invoked or individuals offered as examples always operate at a subracial level, not in ways that are ever coterminous with the wider and more ambitious borders of presumed racial groups), they are still easily proffered as examples of the very categories they problematize.

Race has long been an adamant theory of absolute differences between groups, a theory that has to take what it can get, which is never absoluteness. But even facts that should justify a more universal and antiracial impulse get enlisted, ironically enough, in tales to the contrary. This tragic charade is something like race science's equivalent of what politicians have come to call "swiftboating."[5]

NINETEEN

Jungle

B EN AMMI, ELIYAHU Buie, and the other pro-emigration Israelite leaders shepherded, all in all, some 350 people from Chicago to Guryea, a rural area about 100 miles from Monrovia, Liberia's capital. The year was 1967. Guryea was a remote place isolated from the relatively longer list of amenities that city life in Monrovia would have provided, and saints weren't prepared for what that remoteness would demand from them. They crossed the Atlantic in drips and drabs, and a majority of the first few arrivals were women and children who left a few of the Israelite men, their husbands and fathers, working in the United States to raise more money for the relocation.

Some Israelites made a big deal of leaving, visiting family members and friends to say their goodbyes, ceremoniously marking their official departures with parties and dinners. Others left without a word, more like "thieves in the night," their families and friends caught mostly unaware, sometimes only finding out weeks or even months later, and with little confirmation beyond rumors from the grapevine. But no matter how individuals handled their particular departures, just about everyone who left agreed on one thing. They were embarking on very important work, and it couldn't be entered into lightly. This group represented the vanguard, an opening salvo. Not just the first *Israelites* to leave for Africa, they proclaimed, but also the smallest and sharpest tip of a much mightier sword. They were fashioning the beginnings of a new era, a new age, God willing, when *all* African Americans would eventually see the impossibility of life in the land of their birth and accept the inevitable: that their only chance for survival required finding a new and more appropriate home beyond the belly of the beast, someplace without the same white-sheeted and Jim-Crowed versions of justice.

They knew about the history of European colonization in Africa, of course, and that the continent wasn't beyond racism's ambitious reach. But at least newly formed African countries had started trying to flex their decolonized muscles, and some of those new nations were eager to open their borders for the continent's diaspora. Liberia's President William V. S. Tubman, a vocal supporter of the Israelite émigrés, would be one of the most adamant advocates of Africana repatriation. "All who have black skin are Africans," he said, responding to journalists' specific questions about black Israelites entering his country. "They belong here. Mass immigration is no problem if they tell us they are coming, disperse and assimilate into the community and become good Liberians."[1] If all went well, Ben Ammi and his Chicago group would be preparing Liberia for a much larger American exodus. And Tubman was all for it. As long as these new arrivals would willingly integrate and "become good Liberians," Africa could accommodate them. It had been doing just that, on a smaller scale, for a long time already.[2]

A Quaker businessman, Paul Cuffee, his father a former slave in Massachusetts, had taken fewer than ten black families with him in 1815 when he emigrated to Sierra Leone, a nation established by the British for just such endeavors. The American Colonization Society had only gotten about 100 newly freed slaves to take part in the founding of Liberia about five years later, America's version of the same postemancipation, race-cleansing project.[3] Marcus Garvey's Universal Negro Improvement Association, a century later, might have had a little more bark than bite on the emigrationist front, with probably only a few handfuls of Garveyites ever successfully returning to Africa, including Rabbi Ford's small contingent and the Flemisters (who helped Israelites settle on land in Liberia back in the 1960s). Chicago's Israelites would eventually surpass those numbers, and the first few émigrés worked feverishly to finish their compound in anticipation of the many more arrivals to come.

The earliest groups of black Israelites to reach Liberia back in 1967, ten and fifteen at a time, began the daunting and thankless task of clearing their overgrown plot of land, about 300 acres of dense "bush." A literal and figurative "wilderness," as far as the community was concerned, their settlement was about fifteen miles from the Flemister home, where arrivals would continue to sleep until the grounds were ready for full-time habitation or anything close to it. But this untamed territory would not easily bend to the community's plans.

When AHIJ Princes and other Kingdom elders reflect back on their earliest impressions of Liberia, they invariably mention the ubiquitous smell of rubber (some say "burnt rubber") from Firestone's rubber tree farms. Firestone was one of Liberia's most important economic institutions and largest employers at the time, and had been for decades. Elders also stress the amazing amounts of rainfall they initially withstood. Community members started arriving in the middle of the region's rainy season, and monsoonlike weather only made their land-clearing project that much more difficult. Almost immediately, they fell behind schedule on the compound's construction, which helped to spawn frustration and infighting.

Even with early difficulties hindering their progress, Israelites continued to trickle into Liberia, straight to the Flemister home, including many more male hands for clearing land. But the natural elements persisted in thwarting their best efforts. Days remained less productive than they'd hoped, and the community decided to enlist the help of hired hands, local villagers from surrounding communities who knew the land and were willing to work. The injection of new laborers would help a bit, but it also demanded even larger sums of money from the fundraisers back in Chicago, the donors who had to finance these workers.

Everyone labored all day long, sunup to sundown, chopping trees and poisonous snakes at almost equal rates. Though things still took longer than they anticipated, the community finally started to see some tangible results. They put up their first few tents on newly cleared swaths of land, tents raised several inches from the ground with bamboo or woven mat platforms. Most saints still slept on Flemister's property (the one he lived in, not the one he purchased for these émigrés), but they were able to set up a community center and a house of prayer on their lot, along with designated spaces for cooking and going to the bathroom. The broadest outlines of an institutional world began to take shape as they started to plant food and carve out small patches of land for recreation and relaxation. It was slow-going, but they were making real progress.

This was a hard life, but it was what they wanted, what they'd asked for, and their spirits were high, at least for a while. They were even doing their fellow Africans, their Liberian laborers, a huge service, they believed, paying them more than the sixty-seven cents that employees received from Firestone, the going rate for tapping heavy buckets of sap from rubber trees. In a way, they were already giving back, pitching in, adding to Liberia's national economy. These earliest émigrés could only afford any this, of course, because so many community members were not yet in Liberia. They were still in Chicago, including Ben Ammi, facilitating more departures and sending resources over to the expats— all while fending off ceaseless attacks from Southside naysayers.

Competing Israelite leaders in Chicago ramped up their attempt to dissuade people from joining these "misguided" souls. They predicted that the project would fail. Some even publicly rooted for such an outcome, preached about it, the lines drawn between different Israelite groups (emigrationists versus antiemigrationists) growing more and more volatile. As the contingent in Guryea was focused on that herculean task of building a town for themselves, almost from scratch, their compatriots in Chicago were battling antagonisms from all sides while continuing to raise money. They solicited strangers in their homes, cashed retirement funds and veterans' checks, sold all kinds of merchandise on the street, and kept testifying all across the city about the community's exciting new undertaking in West Africa, telling everyone about their amazing home-to-be in Liberia. Some people who had never thought of joining the Israelites before were moved by the success—or even just the guts—of this small group, by the organized and focused commitment they showed to seeing this "back-to-Africa" impulse through. Ben Ammi and others leaders could always talk. Israelites had long been dynamic speakers. And Ben Ammi, for one, was incredibly charismatic. No one disputed that. But what the group was trying to pull off in Liberia seemed, to some, like so much more than mere rhetoric.

At the same time, Southside residents in a tension-filled Windy City didn't know what might have been lying in wait, just around the corner, for them. Martin Luther King Jr. had already described white Chicagoans as more virulently racist than many of the Southerners he'd previously done battle with in Mississippi and Alabama.[4] Towns like Cicero, on the western edge of Chicago, had served as hothouses for white race riots since the early 1950s, with 1966 producing another spectacularly brutal public moment of white-hot rage against new civil rights challenges to historical racial privileges and the looming prospect of residential deseg-regation. Throughout the 1960s, African Americans and Puerto Ricans were clashing with police as well, sometimes violently, about America's stubborn commitments to the same logic of racial privilege that white residents sensed was already slipping away. Everywhere they turned, Ben Ammi and the emigrationist Israelites found telltale signs that they had to leave the urban powder keg as soon as possible. And they wanted to take as many African Americans with them as they could.

The more Israelites championed African repatriation to their urban neighbors, the more they extended their practical reach and circulated their larger philosophical positions throughout Chicago's black commu-nity. Their brand of back-to-Africa rhetoric came with its own particular truths, a distinctive sense of spirituality, and a very specific rereading of African history. As much as they could, they wanted to make sure that people understood those differences before agreeing to join them over-seas. So, they redoubled their efforts to speak the truth of their mes-sage to anyone who would listen. This street-corner ministering was about moving to Liberia, but it was also about reeducating people on the transatlantic slave trade, on the history of African American crypto-Hebrewisms, and on the Western lies, they argued, that were propagated to extinguish the latter truth's faint but flickering flames.

The community members already in Liberia would also be willing to bear witness to those same beliefs over there, taking time, during their too-few and too-short respites from backbreaking labor, to explain for local Liberians, across differences of culture and language, just what had brought them to this new land in the first place. There was little spare time for leisure, but they took every idle moment they could find to explain their project and to learn more about their newly established homeland, about what necessities could be procured most readily so far away from Monrovia, about the animal threats to be avoided in the wild, and about how best to get around the countryside by foot and (more rarely) by cab. They also had children to educate, which they did, sitting together in the dirt or on makeshift wooden porches (before their proposed schoolhouse would be completed), teaching the youngsters math, reading, writing, and important biblical truths about their own history. They tried to create a radically different life for themselves, refashioning everything they left behind in America, remaking it, only better, less tainted by the symbolic violence of Eurocentrism and the actual violence of white racists—not to mention the self-inflicted injuries of a pathological black culture that all of that violence helped to produce.

TWENTY

Thin

T̲RINH MINH-HA AND Jean-Paul Bourdier's Musee du Quai Branly installation, *The Other Walk,* an exhibit that ran in Paris from 2006 to 2009, starts with a discussion of strolling as one simple gesture in the direction of infinity, a tiny instantiation of the kinds of immortalities intrinsic to daily life. "Walking is an experience of indefiniteness and of infinity," they say, by way of curatorial notes. "With each step forward, one receives the gifts of the universe."[1] This striding—in lockstep with forever—is another way to gloss how one might embrace the peripatetic and sprawling nature of all ethnographic practice, and Trinh-Minh-ha has explicitly declared as much.

During a lecture at the University of Pennsylvania, discussing her 2005 film *Night Passage,* a meditation on death's potential transcendence in the blink of every instant, Minh-ha framed social scientific approaches to knowing as similarly pitched strivings, strides of only a slightly different kind, whether scenic ambles or blinkered sprints, providing something like an artscience of *walking* ethnographically.[2] "Research is a relationship to infinity," she told us. "There is no end to it." We think that our charge as researchers is to organize the chaotic, Minh-ha continued, to bring order to disorder. But the world is not chaotic without our exploits, she said, even if we always impose our forms/frames on its own versions during the process of social analysis, an imposition that always comes with a politic, whether acknowledged or not. Form's functions are multipronged and complex, she offered, even forms as seemingly formless as infinity.

Minh-ha's hypnotic film and iconoclastic postfilm comments summon Alan Klima's work for me.[3] *Ghosts and Numbers,* his 2009 film, tells a story of global economic crisis, new media technology, and microphone-wielding chickens that might best be described as a genre-resistant ethno-horror-comedy; his book, *The Funeral Casino,* is an examination of Thai Buddhist meditation on death that argues (as his film does) against many conventions of ethnographic form, including the double standard in modern ethnographic writing that allows for "scholars" and "theorists" to flit across published pages like specters and spooks, hovering and haunting anywhere that authors deign to slot them, unfettered, disembodied, ethereal (like Klima and Minh-ha are doing right here, right now!), plopped down to do our bidding without nearly as much tethering to situational context as other ethnographic elements ostensibly require. *(Who is this research subject being introduced now? How did we meet her? What does she do for a living? Where is she from? Who is she talking to or playing with or running from when we, the readers, first meet her? And on and on.)* Instead, they move with a nimbleness that our proper ethnographic subjects usually cannot boast, the latter more like mortal and material supplicants to these godlike figures that lord over them, figures traveling through ethnographic time and space like Neo from *The Matrix,* not totally oblivious to physical laws and rules, but restrained by far fewer of them than anyone else.

Ethnographic spacetime is *queer* in that sense, differentially punctuated, odd and uncanny in its many divergent geometries, in its uneven appreciations of time's inertias. And there is a gravitation force, but not all bodies are equally bound by it. That depends on the object in question. Who moves? How far? Where do they go? Maybe to those peripherally perceived "nonplaces" Marc Auge theorizes, homogenously designed as greasy means to other stickier ends, glossy way stations en route to some elsewhere. These are places designed and built to be over-familiar (through heightened homogeneity) and intended as a catapult to other—more bona fide—destinations. But what if all we have left are those nonplaces? Or if *the means* can't be distinguished from the spatial *ends* anymore? Everything seems governed by the same flattening logic, always experienced as utterly temporary and transitional—homes, jobs, relationships, cell phones, iTunes downloads, political scandals. And that's not just because of newfangled vulnerabilities wrought by global economic downturns, and it may only seemingly be backstopped by the Internet's reassuring ubiquity and completeness, its status as a search-able black hole that sucks in everything it touches. If we are all on the move, all the time, even when not ostensibly moving at all, what ethno-graphic stance does such motion demand? What kind of ethnography would do justice to nonplaces?[4] Auge has one answer, calling for an anthropology of supermodernity that would see our everyday lives navi-gating more and more of these nonplaces with their prepackaged, life-less, and self-contained excesses, nonplaces that promote partial and incoherent perceptions of life. Real places do still exist, he claims, and their authenticities sometimes push back against the spectacular distrac-tions and superficialities of nonplaces (supermarkets, airports, and high-ways), but he also wants us to come to terms with the fact that these nonplaces are just as real. They produce such isolation and detachment (reducing people to crowds, passengers, or atomized customers on a cashier's line), he says, that the contemporary world demands a new anthropology of social life. One potential ethnographic response to his cultural diagnosis is "thin description."

Many anthropologists might balk at the seemingly preposterous idea of championing "thin description." Geertz's invocation of ethnographic thickness has just about universal appeal, especially as a way of justifying ethnography's seat at the social scientific table. Geertz states definitively that "ethnography is thick description." Period. And thinness represents an inadequate attempt, its dilution.[5] As Bruce Knauft puts it, "thin eth-nography and floating theory" go together as failures in anthropological effort and vision.[6] It is the problem with the ethnographic exploits of cul-tural studies, some say: its thinness, ethnographically. Or the "bedrock of very thick description," anthropologist George Marcus argued, gets preempted by "a discourse of purpose and commitment within a certain moral economy," a way of fast-forwarding to the political and ethical finish line.[7] "Thin ethnography," William Shaffir contends, "is written by social science academics who care more about whether ideas (and concepts) are new and interesting than whether they are true."[8]

For Geertz, thick description gets us from blinks to winks to fake winks to twitches to anything else that eyelashes coming together might imply, helping us to expose the native's supplest intentions. The anthropologist has a chance to get the joke, which might already be a "burlesqued burlesqued" gesture lost on the more humorless of ethnographic researchers.[9] But there are good reasons, I would argue, to resist, even just momentarily, this fetishization of thickness, this call for ever more obsessively detailed and fine-grained renderings of one's observational prowess. The anthropological assumption has always been that ethnography, careful ethnography, transforms any place, even Auge's ostensible *nonplaces,* into areas that reward close scrutiny with cultural significance. Thick descriptions of would-be nonplaces might attempt to demonstrate their hidden placeness. But is that the point? Going back to Minh-ha's articulation of things, what would a social science of thick description mean if the true object of study is infinity itself? Klima poses a similar question, just differently: What would it mean, ethnographically, to connect the dots between childhood ghost stories, film narration, transgendered mediums, collapse of the Thai baht, lottery tickets, people who sell lottery tickets on the street, lottery sellers' children, fantasies of building homes with lottery winnings, possessed cell phones, globalization, the IMF, rice farming, George Bush, the stock market, flea markets, technology expos, taxi cabs, buildings abandoned before they're even completed, and the many different kinds of people who purchase those aforementioned lottery tickets?[10] What kind of thickness is this? Lewis Carroll and Jorge Luis Borges have given us ways to map the ridiculousness of hyperthickness, and those who don't heed Klima or Minh-ha may be poised to reenact the same misguided meticulousness that Borges and Carroll allegorize.[11]

Thin description would be a way to gallop in the direction of Agamben's "zones of nonknowledge," to plunge into the nonknowledge of ethnographic nonplaces. And ethnographic field-sites having always been just such nonplaces, only temporary sojourns on the way to some elsewhere, no matter how long the stay or heightened the attention. (Labeling the airports nonplaces might simply distract us from that fact.) But it isn't that easy, is it? "Perhaps," Agamben says, "a nonknowledge does not exist at all; perhaps only its gestures exist." Then thin description is one such gesture, a nonknowing that disentangles the ethnographer's *will to know everything* from an interconnected *will to disclose everything*. And although we recognize that every divulgence is partial, animated and energized by its constitutive concealments, thin description is soaked in purposeful cover-ups, nonrevelations, and calculated glosses. At its best, it privileges them, unabashedly.

One of the biggest problems with ethnography is that its totalizing ethos is so seductive—and so susceptible to trafficking in what Walter Benjamin dismisses, simply and stunningly, as "information," a dehumanizing and debasing form of knowledge that supplants the social and epistemological fullness of storytelling. Stories aren't about the circulation of facts; they privilege the cultivation of community. Storytelling, like David Graeber's humbled economics (as told through his tale of "social currencies") is about reproducing social groups first and foremost. Anything else is a cart pulling horses.

If thick description imagines itself able to amass more and more factual information in service to stories about cultural difference, "thin description" doesn't fall into the trap of conceptualizing its task as providing complete and total knowledge—readers finishing monographs, putting them down, and walking away with the self-satisfied belief that they've mastered some previously opaque *other*. Ethnographers themselves can hardly boast such mastery. As anthropologist Michael Jackson persuasively argues, their approach is valuable "not because ethnographic methods guarantee certain knowledge of others but because ethnographic fieldwork brings us into direct dialogue *with* others."[12] Thin description values that dialogue, acknowledging a way of knowing that privileges continued nonknowing, even as just a stride or two away from the ambition of anthropological totalism.[13] So, there are secrets you keep. That you treat very preciously. Names of research subjects you share but many more you do not. There is information veiled for the sake of story. For the sake of much more.

The value of thin description also pivots on the changing demographics of anthropological practice itself, an institutionalized anthropology that consists of "outsiders within" who don't just critically rebuke the Western anthropologist with a kind of "reversed gaze" but also disproportionally use ethnography less as a way to understand some distant *other* than as a vehicle for seeking out faraway selves.[14] Anthropology has always included this ethos, but what counts as *self* and *other* is the question. For instance, I have always been committed to the idea of conducting anthropological research in the United States, working on issues of identity and community, social difference and cultural conflict, in urban America, specifically poor "ghetto" neighborhoods like Harlem, New York.[15] As a graduate student, the interest forced me to negotiate departmental hallways and stairwells rife with cautions from senior faculty members who felt that I was setting myself up for a long life of unemployment if I followed through with my decision to study an American city under the auspices of anthropology.

"You should go to Japan. Or India," one professor suggested, genuine concern further wrinkling an already weathered face. "Study there. That way, you have a better chance of getting a job. You can always do something here later on in your career."

That unsolicited bit of professional advice during my very first semester of graduate school has always stuck with me. In subsequent years, more students and faculty members would pile on their own caveats, similar recommendations that I seriously consider conducting my dissertation research abroad, suggestions couched in terms of "marketability" and disciplinary "legibility." Part of the problem, of course, is that the United States is often seen as sociological territory, unless the study is on Native American populations, which were traditionally considered more properly anthropological subjects. But the other problem here is that anthropologists usually study themselves more *indirectly*. That's also why researching in Africa or the West Indies would have been deemed safer bets for me. I could have had my cake and eaten it, too. Anthropologists get at similarity through an emphasis on difference. It is the foundational irony that powers the entire discipline. But even in those scenarios, what's lost on nobody is the fact that my choice (of Ghana or Senegal or Jamaica or Guyana) doesn't just have traditional anthropological implications. It is also assumed to be predicated on a self-identification, either because of my familial ties to the Caribbean, or because of Africa's symbolic place in the African American imagination (the ICUPK's critiques notwithstanding). But either way, it is less an attempt to fling oneself away from oneself (culturally and existentially speaking) than an effort to expand one's sense of self through a connection to others, especially those complicatedly linked through the notion of diaspora.[16]

At least one geographer based in Canada claims that little of my work has ever been truly ethnographic at all. That it was always ethnographically *thin*. Not his grandfather's anthropology. At another moment, in an earlier time, such an accusation might have merited defensiveness, a detailed articulation of my indisputable thickness. (Something like, "Oh yeah, well, this is what you don't understand about how I'm deftly dancing atop those razor-thin but jagged lines between the singularity of individuals and the racialized cultural groupings that they purportedly represent. It is so thick, in fact, you just can't see around it 'cuz you're too busy being corny and staring straight ahead.")[17] But I wonder if such a posture still makes sense these days, in the era of expanding field-sites, of cannibalistic nonplaces, of flat ontologies and natures that purportedly theorize themselves. Especially when trying to write about a group like the African Hebrew Israelites of Jerusalem, cultural translation doesn't seem like the only point. But if the ethnographic question is still some version of "what do the drums say, Booker?" (as political scientist Adolph Reed mockingly phrased the merely translational and lackey role played by many black scholars in the American academy), then anthropologists might do well to answer that call with subterfuge and misdirection—tricksters discombobulating folk messages for the sake of romantic notions of revolution, only pretending to be well-meaning translators for Empire.[18] "Drums, what drums?" one of them might say. "I'm not a musician myself, but I will tell you one thing. You should think about getting back on those ships you came in on and never coming back. Tell the king there is no land down here. Forget you even saw it. We'd all be better off." In one sense, and only one, thin description is another way of saying just that.

TWENTY-ONE

Carrel

I FIRST HEARD ABOUT Alexis Carrel from Rofeh Yehoshuah, one of the Kingdom's main healers, a man in his late thirties who helps run the *kfar*'s birthing clinic and health center, *Beyt Chaym* (House of Life).[1] He also runs a "redemptive reflexology," "holy spinal alignment," and massage business, "where you can fully experience the power of the ancient art of the laying-on of the *Hands of Life*." I was scheduled to conduct an interview with him and then I wanted to see if he had time to give me another guided tour of the *kfar*'s health facilities. Yehoshuah was running late for our appointment, still consulting with a saint in the middle of the *kfar*, an impromptu follow-up on a previous diagnosis and treatment plan. I waited to the side so that we could head back to the House of Life together. The rofeh wanted to get a quick update about this saint's recent health-related challenges, and he was pleased to hear that things were going well. The man was feeling "100 percent better" than he did a few weeks earlier, no longer bed-ridden or convulsing in pain. The two men hugged, lightly bumping chests three times (a standard Kingdom greeting between men), and then parted ways, Yehoshuah promising to check back again at least once more that week before walking over to greet me.

"We've had over a 1,000 births in Israel," he declared proudly as we made our way to his office. "Babies born right here in the community. No hospitals. No medical doctors. No drugs." He gave me a few Kingdom-produced pamphlets to skim, emphasizing the fact that much of what he was saying could be found in those materials, and in much more detail, including specifics about how they approach pregnancies and the inescapable connections between mind and body that any mother must value if she wants a healthy child. Full health, real health, he stressed, begins with that indisputable connection.

"Western medicine doesn't want to cure people," he said. "It isn't designed that way. Sickness and death are big business. What's their incentive to make people healthy? To make people whole?"

When we arrived at the House of Life, newspaper clippings covered every tabletop, along with books about various allopathic and homeo-pathic medical practices and techniques. There were multiple copies of all the pieces, so he made sure that I took some of them with me, including a few recent magazine articles and newspaper stories related to new med-ical findings about the body's plasticity vis-à-vis environmental stimuli, several printouts of online articles highlighting innovative scientific techniques for detecting and fighting cancers, a glossy health magazines that members of the AHIJ helped to produce in Ghana, and a lot more. But we spent the bulk of our time talking about his particular journey to the Kingdom—and about the early twentieth-century medical experi-ments performed by Carrel, an infamous French medical scientist.

The *rofeh* was born in the United States but had left for South America in his early twenties, an alternative to medical school, his initial plan. Before long, he was apprenticing with a "natural healer" in Guyana and learning all of this elder's knowledge about the medicinal powers of dif-ferent plants and herbs.

"He had that understanding," the rofeh said. "He knew the land. He studied it. He didn't have full knowledge of the Kingdom, but he recognized the healing powers of nature, natural remedies. So, people would come to him when they got really sick, when nobody else could help them."

He told me the story of one particular elderly Guyanese man whose wife had brought him to see this rofeh's mentor and teacher after doctors at a nearby hospital had discharged him.

"They told her that there was nothing else they could do," Yehoshuah said. "They had written him off really. So, they were telling her, basically, telling her that he had to go into a kind of hospice care, palliative treatment. He was so far gone, so sick and frail. The doctors told her that he didn't have much time left."

So, the two of them, Yehoshuah and his mentor, put the old man on a completely vegan diet. The healer knew about the powers of veganism. His daughter was actually in the Kingdom, even though he hadn't completely committed to the idea himself. "But he did understand the killing power of meat, the destructive power of flesh," the rofeh added.

This sick man's wife considered their intervention a miracle. Within a few weeks, her husband was walking again, talking, sitting upright, looking and feeling much stronger. Color had returned to his face, purposefulness to his movements. Pretty soon, he was finally able to move around normally, without any physical discomfort. Locals were astonished.

"To the people who knew him," the rofeh said, "it really was amazing. Even to me, to see this man standing on his own two feet, walking, moving around. He was on his deathbed, and now it was like he was back to life again. The doctors gave up on him, but it was as simple as giving him the right things to eat, food that wouldn't continue to kill him, getting him to exercise. That simple."

The story had an inspirational middle, but its ending was tragic—instructively so. The man became so confident and complacent with his newfound vitality and strength that he started to get lax about continuing to follow-through with the lifestyle changes that had made such a difference, the regimen that made his rejuvenation possible, specifically the meatless diet they put him on. It wasn't long before he went back to eating chicken and beef, even drinking alcohol.

"So, you know what happened," the rofeh said, shaking his head. "He went right back to where he was before. He got sick again. Couldn't walk, nothing. Worse than before. And fast. And he ended up dying, all because he didn't keep doing what got him there, what got him healed and whole again."

Rofeh Yehoshuah described the body as a perfectly designed vessel, one with super abilities, gifts most of us can't even tap into today. "They'd call it superhuman," he said, "but it is how we were created to be." That's when he asked me if I'd heard about Dr. Alexis Carrel's "immortal chicken heart," which I hadn't. He immediately started rummaging through his stacks of papers, searching for something on Carrel that he'd photocopied a long time ago. He couldn't find it, but I promised him that I'd look Carrel up online as soon as I got to a computer, so he decided to give me the story in broad strokes and in his own words.

The rofeh regularly provides visitors to the kfar with lectures on the health benefits of veganism, raw/live foods, periodic enemas, and the importance of emerging scientific research in cellular biology. He does this almost every week, sometimes several times a week, even more than once a day, often using the "immortal chicken heart" as a memorable example of scientific scaffolding for the Kingdom's biological claims.

The "immortal chicken heart" is a reference to one of the many medical experiments conducted by French physiologist and Nobel Prize winner Alexis Carrel. Carrel was an eccentric medical doctor who was famous for his tabloidized experiments and later rebuked for his cozy ties to the Nazis during World War II. But long before that, starting in 1912, Carrel claimed that he was able to keep the cells of an excised chicken heart regenerating indefinitely—outside of any bodily host— inside his black-walled laboratory. The only thing that his lab technicians needed to do, he claimed, was periodically clean that heart, removing its waste products, leaving the perfusion pumps (built by aviator, inventor, and fellow Nazi-sympathizer Charles Lindbergh) to provide the necessary conditions for this modest form of organ-specific immortality. Using Lindbergh's machines and his own carefully designed suturing procedures, Carrel was believed to have expertly removed that heart and kept it alive, continuing to beat and grow in plasma, for over three decades, longer than the life span of an actual chicken.

Carrel and Lindbergh spent much of their adult lives and their decades-long collaboration explicitly looking for a way to prove that human immortality was possible.[2] And the chicken heart Carrel had used to demonstrate this point was only his most "successful" search for the keys to everlasting life. His career was also littered with all kinds of

Frankensteinian attempts to place, say, one dog's kidneys into another's body, or to transplant organs across species. These procedures always ended in failure, as the new hosts' immune systems eventually interpreted the foreign organ as a threat, fighting against it, but the "immortal chicken heart" didn't have a breathing host, only an elaborate storage device that would act as surrogate, a much more controlled physical environment. And for years, Carrel would trumpet the success of his still-beating chicken heart, which only "died," it was claimed, because an absentminded office assistant failed to replenish the nutrients one fateful morning—some three decades into the experiment.[3]

Explicitly invoking Carrel as a kind of experimental forefather (despite his ties with the Nazi regime and his unwavering commitments to Aryan supremacy), the AHIJ argue that their Ben Ammi-decreed vegan lifestyle is the key to cell-regenerating eternal life here on earth in ways that Carrel's more convoluted experiments only glimpsed.[4] If a chicken's heart can live much longer than usual with careful precautions taken about how it is fed, cleaned, and stored, how much longer can human beings live with the same purposeful care and attention paid to their diets and social surroundings?

The rofeh has spoken to many outsiders about the community's intricate health beliefs, and he has several things he usually emphasizes. The first time we had an extended conversation, he made a point of talking to me about casein, a protein precipitated from milk, one of the basic elements in cheese and other dairy products, which he describes as possibly the single most important carcinogen in our entire diet, citing medical studies from Europe, the United States, and all over the world to bolster this claim, including *The China Study*, a summary of several research experiments that argue for a definitive causal link between meat-eating and various human diseases, including diabetes, heart disease, and cancer.[5] The human body is only fallible, Yehoshuah explains, only mortal, as a function of its divergence from God's Edenic laws, laws given to Adam and Eve about how humans were supposed to eat for all eternity. But if meat can catalyze cellular death, veganism can cure the incurable, beating back diseases such as cancer and diabetes by rebuilding healthy cells and making it impossible for cancerous ones to colonize their human hosts.

What's the lifespan of the earth? Human bodies are composed of the same material, which is why eternal life, saints argue, shouldn't seem so farfetched. Of course, the AHIJ's spiritual beliefs didn't always flow so fundamentally out of commitments to veganism. Their road to an Edenic live-it began, in many ways, with rules against eating pork, and spurred by a young Israelite from Chicago (with a notorious sweet tooth for ice cream), Ben Ammi, who would help the community develop a more holistic dietary approach—and far more ambitious claims about the links between eating and eternal life.[6]

TWENTY-TWO

Orientalism

AFROCENTRISM OFTEN GETS attacked for its romantically revisionist racial narratives and its sexist social proscriptions, for its attempts to recast canonical versions of history as purposeful distortions in service to "Eurocentric" (the AHIJ would say "Euro-Gentile") ideological and political goals.[1] Most of this debate is organized around questions of ancient Egypt's racial composition (were they "black" or not?) and framed in terms of the extent to which ancient Egyptian (read: African) mysteries served as fundamental building blocks for subsequent Greek (read: European) philosophies—and, therefore, as the very foundation for Western civilization, a Western civilization that has long defined its modern promises and practices in firm opposition to so-called "primitive" African cultures.[2]

Ben Ammi and several other black Israelites in 1960s Chicago wired more traditional Afrocentric claims to their own distinct reckoning of identity.[3] However, Afrocentricity has a canon, and the AHIJ is not usually considered a part of it. Even still, the AHIJ demonstrates a debt to larger Afrocentric attempts to make sense of global racial hierarchies, attempts based on a sustained critique of popular and scholarly assumptions about contemporary geopolitical conflicts and the histories that explain them.

One reason Ben Ammi and the African Hebrew Israelites are often omitted from common definitions of Afrocentrism is simple. They look to Israelites of yore as their role models and progenitors, not to their supposed Egyptian captors, the latter usually lauded and lionized in Afrocentric circles as justification for race-pride and for major historical reassessments. But there are interesting parallels between black Israelite revisionisms and the ones that Afrocentrists adopt, even as black Israelites also display peculiar eccentricities that highlight their ideological difference from more standard articulations of Afrocentrism and its discontents.

Senegalese anthropologist Cheikh Anta Diop's *Civilization or Barbarism: An Authentic Anthropology* and South Carolinian historian Chancellor Williams's *The Destruction of Black Civilization* are both classics in the Afrocentric paradigm.[4] They provide interpretations of the ancient past that are vastly different from most people's versions of "mainstream" history. Williams's book is organized as an ambitious 6,000-year saga of racial struggles and skirmishes from ancient Egypt to contemporary Ghana. His point is to make a case for the historical depth of "White supremacy" and its single-minded preoccupation with black/African annihilation. Diop dramatizes a different portion of the same story, specifically highlighting the scholastic cover-ups that keep Williams's interpretation of the historical record hidden from general audiences, cover-ups not all that different from the ones exposed by the African/Edenic Heritage Museum—many of them, exactly the same.

George G. M. James's *Stolen Legacy* is probably the classic among classics in the "Egyptology" branch of Afrocentrism, laying out a case for the aforementioned argument that those thoughtful ancient Greeks weren't so thoughtful after all (i.e., that they actually stole their most impressive ideas from even older Egyptian inventions). James considers this particularly important because of the equally controversial contention that bygone Egyptians were culturally linked to sub-Saharan Africans and racially "black" by contemporary standards, which explains, he says, why European scholars wanted to conceal this portion of antiquity's story in the first place. According to James, Aristotle studied under African teachers. He then simply pretended to rightfully own the massive volumes found in Alexandria, volumes only housed there, James argues, thanks to Alexander's earlier plundering of Egypt. Of course, if the Egyptians were phenotypically "black" and Moses could pass for one of them, the race/color of the ancient Israelites are also implicated in this discussion—and again, in ways that are explicitly written into AHIJ representations of the past.

Martin Bernal, a specialist in Chinese political history, revisited and extended this argument in a multivolume study on the "Afroasiatic roots of Western civilization."[5] Bernal maintained that an "Ancient Model" for understanding the relationship between Egypt and Greece recognized the latter's debts to the former (just as James contends), but that such a position was replaced by an "Aryan Model" more aligned with Western racist assumptions. Bernal would push back against a few of the particular claims made by earlier Afrocentric scholars, but his work bolstered their basic contention: Northern Africa had been robbed of its proper place history, analytically removed from the rest of that continent. Classicists dismissed Bernal as an untrained amateur, an illegitimate "armchair archeologist," but many contemporary Afrocentric scholars still find a lot of value in Bernal's critique.[6] The AHIJ's community library includes copies of all of these books, and the authors' arguments are referenced in the traveling museum exhibit and its curators' comments to audiences.

Afrocentrism is the intellectual wing of a larger political and social project, and theorist Molefi Kete Asante is its most often-cited academic proponent. He is one of the most significant academic champions of Afrocentrism in the world, and much of his scholarly output over the years has been framed around clarifying Africa's contributions to the world of big ideas. His books represent powerful anchor points for the field of Afrocentrism, arguments for the concept's contours and fuel for debates about how we should reconfigure the African continent's insides and outsides, its cultural and conceptual geography.

Asante conceptualizes Afrocentrism as a response to the subjective biases of European thinkers, biases that are passed off, he emphasizes, as impartial and objective. (One could have heard this same claim in Ben

Ammi's Chicago of the 1960s, even from Ben Ammi himself.) Afrocentrism is offered as a corrective to this cloaked Eurocentrism, this "situated knowledge" that pretends to be universal and noncontingent, an epistemological "nonplace" (in Auge's terms) that objectively shuttles us off to other wished-for analytical destinations. Asante doesn't argue that Afrocentrism is any more universal and transcendent. "There is no anti-place," he declares, not even for the Afrocentrist.[7] Afrocentrism is unmistakably situated. It speaks from someplace, a culturally specific locale. However, it is better positioned, Asante maintains, from its particularistic perch, to deal with any questions about Africa or Africans, questions that Eurocentrism's self-interested claims can only ever dismissively and inadequately address.

In Asante's hands, Afrocentrism calls attention to the inescapable situatedness of all knowledge, which amounts to something like a version of feminist "standpoint theory," or even a kind of racialized poststructuralism.[8] Afrocentrism isn't objective; it simply represents a more appropriately subjective place from which to theorize African history, culture, and possibility. For Asante, centrism entails "the groundedness of observation and behavior in one's own historical experiences."[9] It does not matter if one is studying facts from the historical record, processes of psychological development, theories of political practice, or anthropologies of cultural difference. Afrocentrism is supposed to provide a non-Eurocentric point of entry into any of those domains, which can't help but produce profoundly different findings. Curators for the African/Edenic Heritage Museum start their tours with the exact same contention, with talk about the need for a new African history from an African perspective, for a complete change of thought, "a paradigm-shift in everyday thinking" about the continent, says Sar Ahmadiel.

Asante's invocation of "historical experiences" is especially significant, because it justifies his attempt to use ancient Africa, specifically ancient Egypt ("Kemet"), as a fulcrum for the origin story that grounds all of African difference. Although Asante's first two book-length treatments of Afrocentricity give relatively short shrift to the role of ancient Egypt in discussions of Afrocentrism, his first exhaustive engagement with the philosophical underpinnings of Afrocentric thought spends a great deal of time "interpreting the Kemetic record" in an effort to demonstrate the distinctive place of ancient Africa vis-à-vis Eurocentric theories of life and death, biology and sociality, political life and its supernatural/divine correlates. This is AHIJ territory, and the similarities are worth flagging.

African sensibilities (exemplified by "Ma'at") and European ones are depicted as radically, even irreconcilably, different. "Ma'at in the Kemetic tradition," Asante writes, "is predicated on our appreciation of the concept of order, measure, limit and form, that is, form in the sense of order and justice."[10] It is "the cumulative appearance of the divine properties."[11] Asante goes on to argue, explicitly invoking George James, that the Greeks subsequently tried to redeploy (and replace) Ma'at as a basis for their own impoverished (because more secularized) attempt at mathematics.[12]

As far as Asante is concerned, mathematics is Ma'at with the spirit and soul ripped out of it. Indeed, Afrocentrism is as mystical and soulful as it is empirical, and that, declares Asante, is extremely important to remember. His forays into Egyptian thought emphasize the centrality of spirituality to any authentic approach to Afrocentric thought, which is why Asante spends quite a bit of time explicating the constitutive significance of "soul" for the Afrocentric project. It is a "concrete motive force" that "activates research" and grounds the validity and appropriateness of knowledge claims. This investment in the unavoidable fusion of reason with soulfulness, pragmatism with romanticism, hard-nosed realism with what political scientist Richard Iton might call "the black fantastic" also grounds black Israelite claims today—and the most interesting ways of parsing them.[13] However, Asante's commitments to these themes of divinity, spirituality, and soulfulness also help to explain what he excludes from his conceptualization of African/Kemetic situatedness (as foreign to its fundamental nature) and why.

What is Africa to Asante? Near Eastern Studies scholar Sherman Jackson argues that Asante misguidedly attempts to disqualify Islam and its alternative spiritualities from any fundamental role in constituting Africa.[14] Jackson calls Asante a "Black Orientalist," borrowing from Palestinian literary theorist Edward Said's Foucault-inspired and "deconstructionist" formulation, which argues that Western representations of other cultures tell us much more about the West's preoccupations than about anything else.

Jackson grounds his accusation in three interconnected points.[15] First, he considers Asante's characterization of Muslim societies generally racist; second, he believes that Asante casts Islam as just another institutional form of white racism, no better or worse than Christianity; and third, he argues that Asante defines Islam as categorically alien to any Kemetic version of Africa. According to Jackson, Asante's "authentic African self" cannot be Muslim—even though, Jackson points out, relishing the irony, one of Asante's most-cherished theoretical interlocutors is Cheikh Anta Diop, a Muslim.

Jackson quotes Asante to damn him. "Adoption of Islam," Asante writes, "is as contradictory to the Diasporan Afrocentricity as Christianity has been."[16] So this isn't just about Africa; it is about Africa's diaspora. And Islam is discounted on both fronts. Asante portrays Arab Muslims in Africa as little more than invaders, Jackson says, carpetbaggers who don't really belong. If anything, Jackson claims, Asante relegates Arabs and Islam to the role of cancer, a poisonous contagion on African life.[17] Their incursions into the continent marked the beginning of the end for Africa's Kemetic traditions and political autonomy. "Indeed, [Asante] seems to intimate," Jackson writes, "had it not been for Arab Muslims, the Europeans might have encountered a thriving, powerful civilization in Africa that they would not have been able to dominate."[18]

Asante falls into this "Orientalist" trap, says Jackson, because he projects American racial circumstances onto an African canvas, making anachronistic claims based on fears of late-twentieth-century windmills in supposed need of toppling. Asante's Afrocentrism, Jackson maintains, suffers from a kind of Americocentrism, the philosopher's location in America, the centrality of American sensibilities in his conceptualization of Africa, uncritically and unknowingly, biasing his read of the continent.[19]

In the same way that Asante can condemn Islam for its historical role in the subjugation of African peoples/culture, Judaism and Christianity function as threateningly extrinsic elements as well—with no necessary and constitutive relationship to Africa. According to Jackson's reading of Asante, all of these groups ARE NOT AFRICANS! In a context where ancient Egypt is privileged and Judaism is little more than complicit in clearing ground for transatlantic slavery's ideological justifications and practical machineries (in the guise of Jewish slave traders), the black Israelites represent a different articulation of this ongoing attempt to recast Africa as more than simply Europe's dark lack. However, given his ostensible dismissal of Islam, some versions of Afrocentric thought might not approve of the black Israelite denunciations (ICUPK) or reconfigurations (AHIJ) of Africa—the former dismissed as a kind of self-hatred, the latter as a bizarre usurpation of African autonomy under a Hebraic banner.

But I don't need to couch this entire discussion in hypotheticals, in what some Afrocentricities *might* say about black Israelites. The AHIJ have already started their own investigations and were already rummaging through scholarly backstages long before I got interested in theirs. And they keep good archives, which just happen to include a series of exchanges between the AHIJ's Minister of Information, Sar Ahmadiel, and Professor Asante. The earliest set of correspondences started with Sar Ahmadiel registering "great disappointment" in an otherwise "quite enlightening" 1992 *Temple Review* article.[20] Ahmadiel points out the article's "failure to relate/include Israel and its surrounding areas within the scope of what is commonly called 'Africa.'" He also notes "one significant 'ancient, dusky river' which failed to make your roll call of rivers the African has known." The Jordan River.

A couple of months later, Asante's handwritten response arrived. Addressed to "My Dear Brother," the short note thanked Ahmadiel for his critique—and for an article he'd included summarizing the AHIJ's Eleventh Annual Holy Jerusalem Writers Conference, which had taken place in September 1991 in Dimona and focused on a global reassessment of "the Bible and Bible Lands." The article, coauthored by two saints, was more like an extended press release and summarized conference speakers' presentations. "Thank you for your corrective piece," Asante wrote, "I have seen the point you have made with dignity and power. Thanks."

A different conference, this one at Temple University in 2000, would spark a less amicable exchange. Asante was coordinating the Twelfth Annual Cheikh Anta Diop Conference, "The Afrocentric Study of

African Phenomena: Challenging the Traditions." A call for abstracts was sent to

> scholars who are committed to the advancement of African American Studies (Africology) as a discipline rather than as an aggregation of subjects about African people and who are determined to underscore the classical foundations of the discipline with serious interrogations of ancient and contemporary Africa, Caribbean and American realities . . . dealing with the Afrocentric paradigm, theories of location and dislocation, Pan Africanism, Afrocentricity, methods of Afrocentric research, and the application of cosmological, axiological, epistemological, and aesthetic/technological modes of inquiry.

Ahmadiel had just seen Asante in April at a New York African Studies Association conference and wrote to express interest in attending the Temple conference that coming October. He proposed using the African/Edenic Heritage Museum as the centerpiece of his presentation. "Relative to your theme," he wrote, "I intend to deal with some specific and critical differences which appear in Biblical traditions when viewed from the African Hebrew perspective." Asante was brief in response this time as well. "It is good to hear from you. Unfortunately the theme of the Diop conference is on Afrocentricity and this is quite different from what you do. I believe that there will be other venues as we go through the year. Thanks for your interest in Diop."

Two days later, Ahmadiel wrote back, registering his "great disappointment at having been dismissed so casually from involvement in the Diop conference and at having 'what we do' disassociated from 'Afrocentricity.'" Ahmadiel mentioned Prince Asiel meeting with Diop in Dakar in 1977 and then asked Asante to explain what disqualified the AHIJ from the conference. "Why is it," Ahmadiel wrote, "that members of 'African American' academia generally tend to dismiss us? Are they frightened by our suggestion to 'cross the Suez Canal' in our reclamation of Africa? That's right in line with your conference theme . . . maybe 'challenging traditions' should begin 'in-house'!"

In his reply to Ahmadiel's letter, Asante expressed "regret that you misunderstood the nature of the Cheikh Anta Diop Conference and took my response in the wrong manner." Admitting that he had waited a few months to respond so that he could do so "in a spirit that would be becoming an African," Asante then went on to say that he didn't want any religious groups, "Muslims, Yoruba, or Christians," to use the conference as a venue for promulgating their beliefs. "We are trying to refine our understanding of the African world," he ended, "through as much science as possible."

Ahmadiel began his immediate email reply to Asante on that very point. "I'd be less than African," he wrote, "in not saying that I am insulted: Do you think we sit around all day reading Bibles? . . . That we don't have a body of scientifically-verifiable evidence to back up our claims?" Ahmadiel reiterated—several times—that the AHIJ are not *religious*. "We DESPISE religion!" And he ended with a question: "Isn't the detachment and compartmentalization of spirituality—as something unrelated to every aspect of our daily life—about as Eurocentric a concept as they come? I know that you are not telling me that Afrocentricity is disconnected from the Creator. But I KNOW that Diop recognized the role of spirituality." And as laid out in his Kemet discussion highlighted above, Asante did, too. His subsequent response to Ahmadiel was mostly a string of Egyptian (Kemetan?) references, "Hotep, Djed, Seneb Heheh!," ending with what some might mistake for a typed-out chuckle.

Given the complicated historical connections, conflicts, and strained alliances between African Americans and Ashkenazi Jews, all fanned by the flames of mutual accusation (charges of antiblack racism versus charges of black anti-Semitism), Asante is also negotiating a political landscape that already presupposes serious African American skepticism vis-à-vis the Jewish community.[21] Indeed, the rich work of a figure such a Lewis Gordon, whose "black existentialist" philosophizing provides a careful articulation of such reasonable skepticisms and an argument for how they might potentially be overcome, pivots on the idea that any ostensible dissonance and irreconcilability between blackness and Jewishness can and should be met with a swift and potent phenomenological-existential rebuttal.[22]

All of this mutual skepticism coincides, of course, with other philosophical and historical links between Judaism/Jewry and Afrocentrism.
For instance, Ethiopianist Edward Blyden's late-nineteenth-century
investments in learning Hebrew while studying with Christian missionaries in West Africa, all financed by his church back in the Virgin Islands
and interpreted by some saints as his reclamation of an Israelite identity
inherited from his parents, Nigerian Igbo. The Igbo are one of the contemporary African ethnic groups most often cited as demonstrating clear
cultural links to ancient Hebraic practices and beliefs. There were also
the early-twentieth-century Jewish American anthropologists, figures
like Franz Boas and Melville Herskovits, who proved quite valuable to
Afrocentrists in terms of providing empirical evidence for claims of West
African cultural unities and continuities with the African Diaspora.[23]
Marcus Garvey's conceptual debts to Judaism, specifically Zionism,
have been well documented, and the earliest black practitioners of
Freemasonry in the eighteenth century, central to discussions about
African American investments in the symbolic significance of ancient
Egypt, actually identified more with ancient Hebrews than with their
Egyptians masters.[24]

If the ICUPK would throw out the baby with the bathwater by the late
1990s, dismissing Islamic and pagan Africa for their "unbiblical" beliefs,
and the AHIJ would add Israel and the rest of the Arabian Peninsula to
an expanded African/Edenic homeland, black Israelites in mid-1960s
Chicago were still simply interested in Africa's potential status as a literal
place of residence, a new world that could nurture their ancient and dor-
mant spirits back to life. Besides, Africa had some very real geopolitical
specificity in the 1960s, which wasn't reducible to talk of biblical Edens
and ancient Egyptians, including the reality of several newly postcolonial nation-states, the history of "black Atlantic" conversations and collaborations against imperialism, and the renewed calls for a Pan-African
unity that began to look like a political project with real teeth after the
response to Italy's invasion of Ethiopia some thirty years earlier.[25]
African Americans had long been other than provincial, their global
interests in the middle of the twentieth century fueled by the rhetorical
heft of the antiwar movement, championed and promoted by the likes of
Malcolm X, and fanned by the revolutionary and aspirational zeal of all

types of internationalists, including communists and socialists of various stripes.[26] "As with the Jew," literary critic Alaine Locke put it in the 1920s, "persecution is making the Negro international."[27] And with the help of television's growing popularity, the Africana world got even smaller than ever in the 1960s. This meant that leaving for Africa—for good!—felt as plausible as it ever had to many African Americans frustrated with their country's continued racial exclusions. Black Israelites in Chicago helped to push that plausibility into practical action.

TWENTY-THREE

Digital

AT THE START of this millennium, a group of AHIJ emissaries approached a successful African American entrepreneur with a business proposition. The Philadelphia-based businessman knew little about the lives of these individuals or about the transnational group that they represented, but he was intrigued by the ambitiousness of their pitch. The terms of the proposal would change radically over time (from a request for hands-off venture capital to more collaborative configurations of cross-Atlantic partnership to a final scenario that found the American businessman and his family playing a decidedly leading role in the entire endeavor). But the idea itself, the "redemptive enterprise" suggested, was clear and fixed.

The AHIJ wanted help procuring the rights to sell and lease an invention that imperceptibly and automatically shortens television programs, allowing networks and cable outlets to add even more minutes of advertising time to daily broadcasts. This relatively new apparatus did not delete entire scenes or large contiguous sequences from shows, one traditional (and fairly conspicuous) technique that networks already use to "reformat" theatrical motion pictures so that they fit television's conventional scheduling requirements. The technology was also far more sophisticated than earlier inventions that attempted to squeeze films into advertisement-punctuated time slots by speeding up certain sections, another simple (though sometimes distractingly noticeable) way to decrease a show's overall running time.

The AHIJ emissaries were pushing for the proprietary acquisition of a newfangled mechanical device based on advanced digital technology, and they walked their potential business partner through the specifics, providing details about the machine they coveted, which works at the unit of the frame, digitizing material and intermittently eliminating single "redundant" frames that function as duplicates to the human eye, making the deletions nearly imperceptible. There are enough "redundant" frames in the rebroadcast of an average feature-length motion picture or football game to open up space for additional commercial spots—and without any substantive impact on narrative content or temporal flow. The machine would offer a way to profit on media outlets' predictable interest in subtler ways of squeezing more advertising revenue out of every standard hour of commercial television, selling a way to game the media system itself (by hyperexploiting its dependence on advertisers). In some ways, these men's lives back in Dimona help to explain a few of the reasons why they might be interested in this bit of technology and motivated to capitalize on a media industry's cultural logic in ways that interface with their own reworkings of time.

I invoke this short rendition of a tale about one business arrangement organized around a piece of media equipment that precisely manipulates time (by appearing not to do so) as a way to discuss how such new technologies reframe and reformat traditional (predigital?) formulations of transnational and/or diasporic community—and of cultural representations. Similar to the difference in scale between, say, a *scene* and the individual *frames* that combine to animate it, a difference most easily (even automatically) exploitable by digital technologies like the above-mentioned gizmo designed to intricately trim programs without noticeably impacting storylines or frustrating the visual senses, this story helps us to continue a conversation about reconfigurations of (punctuated) ethnographic time and (expanding) ethnographic space through a discussion of what might be called "digital life."

In some ways, all I want to highlight here is a simple claim that "the diasporic" and "the ethnographic" have, in a sense, already gone "digital." Of course, this digitalization is disproportionately distributed. Even as arguments are made about "digital diasporas" not being simplistic extensions of race-based digital divides, "the digital" can still have ethnocentric inflections when uncritically presumed to be a kind of universal reality.[1]

The AHIJ saints who approached that would-be financier in 2002 were emissaries from a group that provides just one example of what a notion of "digital diaspora" helps to capture. Digital and "new media" technologies supply the glue that keeps their deterritorialized spiritual community together, a community that spans four continents and continues to successfully persuade new members to join its ranks all around the world.

And it is not just happenstance that the AHIJ would gravitate to new technological innovations predicated on reframed temporalities. Their own time travel (including "exodus" from a Babylonian America, sojourn in the "wilderness" of Liberia, and eventual resettlement in "the promised land," a modern state of Israel regeographized as "Northeast Africa") is based on a refashioned (and punctuated) sense of temporal possibility, on a contemporary retelling of that Old Testament story in a decidedly New World way. And the ethnographic gambit itself is implicated in such moves. AHIJ saints are constantly traveling transnationally, and it is their implementation of the newest media technology (online radio shows, community-maintained websites, YouTube uploads, the circulation of community-produced digital-film content) that provides some of most powerful mechanisms for cultivating forms of commonality and mutual investment that have allowed this emigrationist community to survive for more than forty years—and to pose a challenge for conventional ethnographic efforts.

Such AHIJ exploits offer a series of frames for thinking through how the digital overdetermines ethnographic practice in the contemporary moment, and this is an invocation of the *frame* both in the sense of context (a way of framing relevant issues) and the notion of a singular impression/image captured in time (as in the presentation of a framed painting or the relative irreducibility of a film/video still). But this is not meant to imply a kind of taxidermy, an unchanging and lifeless simulation of inert and frozen realities. As many scholars have argued, countertemporalities are always (to use anthropologist Michael Taussig's term) "nervous" with movement and agitation, recursive organizing principles that offer non-linear logics of diachronic possibility—nonlinearity being one version of the digital's most fundamental difference.[2]

Kara Keeling argues that such nonlinearity (in the form of assumptions about differential access to "nonchronological" temporalities) has long determined Africana exclusions from modern Western subject-hood, the latter (especially in the writings of Hegel) mapped neatly onto a purportedly linear trajectory called "progress."[3] Keeling's point is that the Africana exception is increasingly becoming the global rule, providing angst and existential nervousness for Western subjects through the rise of digital culture's nonlinear insecurities. (An inevitable March of Progress seems so much more secure and reassuring.) My invocation of the *frame* intends to channel Keeling's point while also providing a productive unit/metaphor for marking what Brian Axel calls (in his conceptualization of diaspora) "disparate temporalities (anteriorities, presents, futurities), displacements, and subjects."[4] Each of these frames represents a different scale of analysis, distinct styles, angles, and emphases. Different voices and views, genres and constitutive "gaps."[5] I offer them as variously pitched building blocks for an ethnographic montage that provides a quick look at some of the linkages and overlaps constituting diasporic and ethnographic realities today, demonstrations of artscientific practices, quantum anthropologies, thin descriptions that might spy "the immensity that is accommodated within the instant."[6] Call it the social science of strategic superficiality, an adamantly everyday ethnography (conducted every moment of every day), which is only one way to approach an inquiry into immortality, which would mean trying to do a bit of justice to what might be efficiently glossed as "the ethnographic impossible."

TWENTY-FOUR

Children

I MET ORIYAHU, A teenage saint who was born and raised in the *kfar*, within a few days of my second visit to Dimona. The meeting was brief, but I had already read quite a bit about him before I'd arrived. In 2004, he became the first AHIJ high school graduate drafted into the Israeli Defense Force. More than sixty other teenage saints were slated to join him very soon, and many had already reported to the draft office in the nearby city of Be'er Sheva, a grand demonstration of the group's commitment to the Israeli state and appreciation of their newly conferred status as "permanent residents," which was made official in 2003.[1] Permanent residency meant a different kind of relationship to the rest of Israel, starting with the fact that it allowed saints to earn their livings legally and on the books, as opposed to hustling for underground gigs, the very real threat of deportation always lurking just around the corner. This was part of a longer process of regularizing their relationship to the Israeli workforce that first began in 1993 (with help from many quarters, including lobbying efforts by members of the U.S. Congress). Unlike Israeli citizens, permanent residents aren't necessarily required to serve in the military, but they can volunteer to do so, which the AHIJ community has done.

Oriyahu was the "test case" (as news reports described it), but dozens of other teenagers from the community had already received their "draft letters" by the time I first arrived in Dimona. These young AHIJ saints, all born in Israel, the Second and Third Generations (as they are called), represent incredibly important cohorts. They were born without many of the inherited cultural assumptions and dysfunctions borne of an earlier life in America, the very dysfunctions that their parents had been trying to unlearn. Instead, these youngsters have spent their entire lives without "consuming flesh." They have known nothing but the strictures and mandates, beliefs and philosophies, of the Kingdom. By those standards, saints argue, they are relatively unsoiled by the pathologies of Euro-Gentile culture, and they are an example of what the community's divine and redemptive practices can produce in term of bright eyes, sharp minds, and healthy bodies.

Even though the community's veganism is meant to clear the way for eternal life, some community members will concede that many of the elderly saints' bodies have been so damaged by previous practices (including years of meat-eating, drinking, and smoking prior to their life in the Kingdom) that they have little hope of actually living forever. Some of those elders have already died. Or they might occasionally go to the States for cataract surgery or to consult with specialists about other illnesses associated with old age. Physical immortality may not be their fate, but if the community can get some of these patriarchs to live for, say, 125 years, maybe even 150, then the rest of the world, they argue, would have to take notice.[2]

But these young people, if they diligently and lovingly obey Yah's commandments, have much more of a shot at immortal life. They should certainly live much longer than 150 years, which is why several saints felt that it was worth pointing out to me, during walks around the *kfar,* that you could often see twenty-something-year-old saints playing on monkey bars with preteens. If they are expected to live so much longer, then that means having more time to be children. The entire developmental process is primed for recalibration, saints say, and their Israel-born young

Three daughters of the Kingdom sharing good times. *(Photograph by Crowned Sister Cattriellah eshet Rockameem.)*

people are central to that process, to the project of "extending adolescence," reconfiguring the human life cycle to accommodate longer life spans. And many of the stories told about children born in the *kfar*, touching or slanderous, are often some of the most memorable renderings of the AHIJ's complex relationship to the Israeli state. Just a few months after my second visit to southern Israel, the *Jerusalem Post* ran an article, "Distrust in Dimona," claiming that Israel's National Insurance Institute (NII) had placed an undercover agent inside the AHIJ community in an attempt to investigate rumors about saints filing fraudulent state-benefit claims worth millions of dollars. The FBI and the U.S. State Department were also said to be actively collaborating with the NII on this investigation.

When the AHIJ were finally given their "permanent residency," it also meant that saints were newly eligible to file for NII benefits. According to the article, "Israeli authorities" expressed quite a bit of concern about the fact "that they couldn't gauge the community's exact population, as estimates range from 2,000 to 4,000. Even now, while the adults who have received permanent resident status have identity numbers, the community's size is impossible to determine. The children are born within the community, without the use of hospitals or conventional medicine—and, of more concern to the NII, with no official birth certificates. Authorities have no accurate way of registering newborn babies or deaths."[3] The community's relative impenetrability to the state's prying eyes is consistently deemed one of its more threatening features in news stories and investigative reports. Indeed, calls to make them full citizens are at least partially predicated on the idea that such a move might finally create a kind of social transparency more amenable to bureaucratic inspection.

The article even mentions allegations that Ben Ammi has encouraged AHIJ women to register the same children with NII officials under different names—so that the community could receive multiple benefits, speculations and accusations fueled by the group's relative secrecy and opacity. The community is on guard against such negative press, and the Ministry of Information is charged with helping to disseminate counternarratives of AHIJ's successes, which is why some detractors might dismiss their media productions as little more than propaganda, the community putting its best foot forward and hiding any sign of warts. One of the interesting things about those AHIJ productions, however, is that they are clearly pitched to two very distinct sets of viewers: (1) saints already in the kingdom (in the Dimona *kfar* and all around the world) as well as (2) curious outsiders interested in learning more about the community's beliefs and everyday lives. The way their media productions negotiate the differences between those two audiences pivots on a fine-grained appreciation of the flexible cultural and personal ties that can both bind people together and cordon them off from one another.

The Divine Ministry of Information's Audio Visual Truth Center produced a forty-minute documentary about (and for) its Second Generation saints in 2010, a documentary that describes this group as "heroes" and thumbs its nose at naysayers who predicted that these young people would leave the community in droves as soon as they came of age. The point of this video, "The Second Generation of the Kingdom of Yah," is to celebrate the fact that such a mass exodus never materialized. "These children had no need to stay," the narrator explains, speaking to those detractors, to older saints, and to that Second Generation all at the same time. "Saints, behold the uncompromising and unconquerable Second Generation. . . . These children had no need to stay. What caused them to stay? Only a mighty spirit kept them here. You have to understand what we are saying! They had to look into their parents' faces to get something that could not be explained. We were running because those forces were after us. This is real, not a movie. They stayed and did not abandon us. Second Generation, we will not let anyone forget your generation who has grown up in this land!" For the rest of the documentary, members of the Second Generation, some born in Liberia, others in Israel, talk about what it has meant for them to live their entire lives (or just about) in the Kingdom, reflecting on the early difficulties of West Africa and their eventual "blessings" in "Northeast Africa," Israel.

On furlough from the Israeli military for that portion of the summer when we met, which entailed nothing more than a handshake and some small talk, Oriyahu, one of those young people who did not "abandon" his community, sported an IDF-mandated buzz cut, which made him the first and only AHIJ male I'd met with a completely shaved head, a fairly jarring sight in the *kfar*. Saints believe that God proscribes the shaving of facial hair. However, with this new military service, young saints are being integrated into the larger Israeli society like never before, which means finding ways to obey divine commands while also adhering to military ones. For example, the community's rule against wearing artificial fibers bumps up against the fact that Israeli military uniforms have traditionally been made out of both natural and synthetic fabric. So AHIJ saints doing military service have special uniforms made for them. They also are entitled to vegan meals, and the military tries to accommodate other community practices as well, like their weekly Shabbat fasts.

One serious question that the community must address, however, has to do with whether or not they can safely and independently develop the next generation—a Fifth Generation—of saints without being able to monitor their high school graduates as stringently as they have in the past. Integration into the military and its demand that soldiers live well beyond the *kfar*'s borders introduces some powerful changes into the everyday lives of this intimate and insular community. Is it a Faustian pact?

In an open letter published online in 2011, Prince Asiel flagged the community's new military voluntarism as one of the reasons why he was deciding to speak out about problems within the Kingdom after some forty years by Ammi's side—and as the community's most recognizable public face. Asiel sees this newly instituted military service as a real threat, a self-destructive concession to outside interests that will potentially weaken the community by assimilating saints into the rest of Israeli society. He questions the decision. Given such emergent porousness between younger saints and the rest of Israel, will the Hebrew Israelites continue to live self-sufficiently in the Negev? Will their emigrationist success endure? On their terms? And make no mistake about it; the group can boast some real successes, especially in the area of health and nutrition.

It was one of the first things the community healer Rofeh Yehoshuah shared with me in 2006, but many other saints also made sure that I knew about the study. At the end of the 1990s, a team of American physicians from Vanderbilt University and Meharry Medical College, including a biological family member of one of the saints, a "friend to the community," traveled to Israel and tested many of the AHIJ's seniors for hypertension, diabetes and other diseases known to disproportionately plague African Americans in the United States. The community's elderly saints were much healthier than their American counterparts, with few incidents of the aforementioned diseases, especially when compared with health figures for African Americans. Saints invoke this study all the time.[4] They also offer tales of septuagenarians who regularly run Israeli marathons or take part in other nationwide sporting events, all possible because they have followed the "instruction manual" that God provided in Genesis, an instruction manual that explains how His people should properly take care of their bodies for optimal performance. But it is the young saints, the Second, Third, and even Fourth Generations, "not ordinary children," who have been following those divine instructions for the bulk of their lives and should be able to embody—literally—the truths that the Kingdom espouses. For the AHIJ in the early twenty-first century, a great deal rides on what that lifelong obedience means for the kinds of bodies and spirits their emigrationist project has actually produced.

TWENTY-FIVE

Eden

Despite all the determined effort, their Liberian experiment seemed only to get worse by the day. Life was harder than many of the migrants had imagined, much harder, and things weren't easing up as the weeks dragged on. The early settlers had their work cut out for them, a lot to juggle and still not nearly enough help, even with the newly enlisted local recruits. But there were other issues. For one thing, a small portion of the earliest émigrés weren't actually Israelites at all. It was just a tiny minority, but that still came with some costs. The community's "back-to-Africa" rhetoric convinced a few sympathetic African Americans to join them on the journey, even those sojourners who weren't necessarily sold, at least not fully, on the idea of being Israelites, and some of these emigrants became increasingly less willing to abide by decisions from the camp's Israelite leaders, especially when those decisions used the "Spirit" or biblical exegesis as justification. This would produce some very real tensions around rules and regulations within the early settler colony.

More pressing, however, were financial issues. Since they still didn't actually live in the unfinished campsite, members had to commute back and forth from the Flemister house daily. The time needed to make this trek and the precious amount of money paid for gas took its toll on the community. Even with the remittances brought over from America with new arrivals, community members were having an increasingly difficult time making ends meet. They had to pay for everything (transportation, food, supplies), and although a few men and women had found employment in Monrovia, many more had not—and the latter would need to be buoyed by the former (who were relatively far away in the capital). A few settlers resented having to pick up slack for others, especially since some émigrés didn't appear to be working as hard as others, not really carrying their weight. People got more and more competitive over resources.

Still gathering souls in Chicago, Ben Ammi received an urgent telegram in 1967 describing what amounted to a kind of civil war taking place within the Liberian camp. He immediately left for West Africa in an attempt to fix things, to help keep the peace (and ensure that the core of the group's Liberian contingent stayed together). When he arrived, he couldn't deny just how much they were struggling—or that some Israelites seemed almost inconsolably disheartened by their Sisyphean attempt to clear land that wouldn't be tamed and to feed themselves and their loved ones with so little food to go around. People were weak, sick, and diseased. Many of their Sears Roebuck tents were just about destroyed by the elements, dry-rotted and almost useless. The kids were covered with sores and mosquito bites, the same mosquitoes that kept infecting community members with malaria and other debilitating illnesses. Ben Ammi reunited with his wife and young children, who he'd sent ahead to Liberia, and they were no better off than anyone else. It was a depressing sight. He could see the big picture, and it didn't look promising. The community had money problems, health problems, and morale problems. A few people had begun to secretly hoard food, others had to fend off accusations of hoarding, and all of this translated into bitter disputes, including disagreements about who should be officially responsible for the community's funds, for distributing resources and determining purchasing priorities. They had begun to split into two major factions, and everyone was armed with something—guns, bats, machetes, knives—in preparation for what seemed like the inevitability of an all-out battle.

When Ben Ammi arrived, he came with money, a new injection of funds. That helped, a little. The lion's share of cash went to Elder Yaacov Greer, who was overseeing those Liberian workers. The laborers had to get paid, but Ben Ammi had to do a lot of wrangling to defuse debates within the camp about how every dime was to be spent. People were on edge, frustrated. Even with these newly distributed resources, some members of the camp remained skeptical, angry. Several complained about Greer having control over the camp's coffers. Some wanted to move from the Flemister's place to their camp-in-the-making, even though it wasn't finished. Almost everybody seemed to gripe about something.

To appease the most disgruntled and frustrated settlers, Ben Ammi and the other elders agreed to let some people move to the compound. Those who wanted to remain with the Flemister's did. There was still tension, but this helped a bit. They effectively split the camp in two, and a major revolution, a potentially serious conflagration, had been averted.

Ben Ammi got back to the United States and worked even more feverishly to raise money and stir new souls, only this time he realized that he would have to make his own more permanent move to Liberia sooner than he'd anticipated. The community needed his leadership, his insight. He shouldered a great deal of responsibility for their current struggles. The Angel Gabriel had come to him. He had helped to convince so many people to leave. It was time for him to follow his own call. He would spend a little more time in the United States, only as long as he absolutely needed to be there, before moving completely to Liberia, hunkering down with his Israelite brothers and sisters in their new West African home. He didn't know how long they would stay there, how long they could survive, or how Yah would eventually make a way for them, but he was determined to believe, to trust in the Spirit. He would not doubt Yah's power. Losing faith would be the worst thing they could do, he said. Even if they had little power over anything else—Liberian laws, obstinate co-emigrationists, the elements—they had control over what they would believe. And he would help them to keep faith in Yah's divine wisdom until its fullness was revealed.

By the summer of 2007, some of Yah's plan for these saints had become clear. In a different part of West Africa/Eden, Retired Major Courage

Quashigah, Ghana's Minister of Health, was championing the slogan "creating wealth through health." According to the World Health Organization, treating malaria and other relatively preventable diseases costs African nations billions of dollars a year. "Imagine if we could save just 40 percent of this money," Quashigah said, "allowing it to be freed up for investment in other productive enterprises."[1] Ghana could not experience real economic success, he emphasized, without making sure its citizens, especially its children, were physically fit—exercising and eating right. "Research has proven," he added, "that the quality of nutrition children are exposed to from the fetal stage to the first five years of their lives contribute to their IQ levels in the future." Ghana needed to supplement its traditional medical services with a more holistic approach to health-care, he argued, holistic approaches that included a new appreciation for how much "hygienic, sanitized environments and healthy lifestyles produce health." He was offering up a "multi-sectoral" model of health-care in Ghana, a model that included paving roads, providing cleaner water, building more parks, and growing/distributing better food, especially fruits and vegetables. His Ministry would also soon be collaborating with the country's Ministry of Education to make sure that Ghanaian students were more "health literate."

This was an expansive and ambitious plan, and many of Quashigah's "creating wealth through health" initiatives were sparked, to a significant degree, by his experiences with the AHIJ. Any saint could tell you that. Two years earlier, Quashigah had visited the Dimona *kfar* to get a better sense of how the Kingdom was approaching health issues. He had already heard about their veganism (from a contingent of saints living in Ghana), and he wanted to find out more about what they were doing and how they were cultivating healthy lifestyles.

The first thing Quashigah learned was that saints are supposed to take everything into account when considering the health of their physical bodies, and he was given a crash course in how the community operationalizes healthful living: a flesh-free diet, focused and purposeful breathing, a positive mind-set, good personal hygiene, periodic rest and relaxation (for saints, particularly on the Shabbat), avoiding fluoride, "Divine Childbirthing" (with specific instructions for "prenatal and postnatal care based upon Hebraic cultural and Biblical law"), safety from the threat of physical violence, and a general appreciation of the impact that larger environmental factors have on people's physical and spiritual well-being. The AHIJ's hardships in Liberia, a time before they were even called the African Hebrew Israelites of Jerusalem, provided direct and indisputable evidence of the environment's influence on human health. Those early adversities in Liberia were not empty ordeals, saints argue. They planted the seeds of an evolving investment in the connections between physical health and environmental context. Liberia provided brutal examples of how much physical and spiritual welfare were impossible to achieve without a functional relationship to one's natural surroundings. It was a lesson saints would not soon forget—and that they'd build upon for the next forty years. By the time Quashigah arrived in the Village of Peace, the community had taken over 25 years to codify its post-Liberian philosophy of biology into "the Dimona System" of preventive health care, exporting that model to interested jurisdictions in South Africa, the Congo, and Benin.[2]

One of the first manifestations of the Kingdom's collaboration with Ghana would be touted in a special issue of *Health Foresight!: The Most Authentic Health Magazine* ("Your FREE copy, strictly not for sale" printed on its cover). The magazine aimed at getting Ghanaians to think more proactively about "regenerative health and nutrition." Reducing their program to its most basic elements in a two-page spread, the publication delineated the community's basic contention that food, water, exercise, and rest are medicinal, the most important weapons humans have in the battle against diseases, even cancer and AIDS, though the magazine's editors are also careful to provide the requisite disclaimers about their recommendations not being a substitute for seeking the advice of actual medical practitioners.

And many saints do consult conventional medical doctors, particularly for troubling ailments that they haven't been able to treat otherwise. Elders especially, whose bodies have been ravaged and contaminated by life in America before they left for Liberia, would see a specialist in the United States in conjunction with their embrace of a rofeh's more holistic treatments. Such saints don't deny the power of "Western medicine," rejecting only its generally retroactive logic, which is why saints try to teach themselves (and anyone else who will listen) how to avoid a

surgeon's scalpel. Ben Ammi has often acknowledged the mastery possessed by surgeons, but he highlights a commensurate appreciation for
masters who can teach people how to avoid surgeons altogether. *An ounce
of prevention is worth a pound of cure.* All the Kingdom is doing, its
members contend, is taking that age-old adage seriously—and pushing
the rest of Eden/Africa and the world to do the same.

TWENTY-SIX

Disciplining

ABIR HA COHANE (Ahbir the Priest) has started writing a book that outlines his approach to Edenic energy exercises and African/ Edenic Hebrew Israelite martial artistry. Besides being one of the Kingdom's priests, Cohane Ahbir is a rofeh (healer), and runs the kfar's Academy of Life Discipline, which teaches a form of spiritual-physical exercise techniques founded on "original prophetic writings in the Holy Bible." The Philosophy of Divine Martial-Arts Discipline is based on several key principles: the fundamental worship and glory of Yah; the rejection of violence except in self-defense, especially "in defense of the Kingdom of Yah"; and an approach to physical training, even sparring, that is good-natured and collaborative, not vicious or competitive. The point of this physical regimen is to strengthen and regenerate the human body in service to the AHIJ goal of conquering physical degeneration and death. The very need for martial arts, Ahbir makes clear, is also a function of the ancient patriarchs' disobedience to Yah, their breaking of the covenant, and Ahbir excitedly anticipates a point in the future when there will be little demand for much of his ministry at all. Even when he isn't giving classes in martial arts, the academy is training saints on the cultivation of "correct breathing" and explaining the many links between his program of bodily conditioning and the community's belief in Ben Ammi as Messiah. Bodies that are properly attuned, Cohane Ahbir says, are better able to recognize Ammi's divine anointing.

Cohane Ahbir's manuscript will focus on three themes, all subjects that he plans to further develop with a little editorial assistance from saints who have already published their own writing—and from at least one curious anthropologist. He and I spent some time discussing the format of his project. He wants to begin with a detailed section about the history of African American success in the martial arts, from Grandmaster Ronald Duncan, an ex-marine who many people consider "the father of American Ninjitsu," to Billy Blanks, a six-time tae kwon do world champion and recent infomercial mainstay. Many of these fighters are people that Ahbir knows or once knew. He fought them or trained with them in the past. Even the people he doesn't know personally are filed away in his mental Rolodex with an amazing level of biographical detail about their fighting styles, their training histories, and their championships, all of which he can recall and invoke with machinelike speed.

His book will also attempt to tell a more overarching story about martial arts, a story that includes necessary discussions of China and Japan while also providing space for analyses of Congo-Brazilian capoeira and Zulu stick-fighting forms found in West Africa and the West Indies. Listening to Ahbir talk, one is convinced that he could narrate all of the important eras of world history with martial arts as his sole organizing principle. He has spent the last few decades collecting articles about the African presence in early Asia and the history of martial arts in ancient Assyria and Egypt, material that he will use to ground a case for Hebrew Israelite/Judaic forms predating and informing more well-known genres such as kung fu, judo, and karate do. As often as not, the ancients used staffs not to offset limps, he says, not because they were feeble, but to wield as weapons in battle. "We read the Bible," he says, "and don't even remember that these folks were warriors."

Cohane Ahbir breaks down his manuscript's entire structure as we sit together in the *kfar*'s health and fitness center. He has just finished an exercise class with a few saints, and there is even talk that I might get a massage or reflexology treatment later on that day. My first. (A monthly full body massage is mandatory for all adult saints.) But he has another appointment scheduled, and we get preoccupied spending most of our time talking about his life before the Kingdom as a member of the Black Berets in Bermuda, an anticolonialist organization modeled on the Black Panthers, a group that championed "armed struggle" and worked in local public schools. The Black Berets were committed to circulating banned Nation of Islam literature on the island, and they were infamous for violent and unrelenting militancy throughout the 1960s and 1970s.

Ottiwell Simmons Jr. (Ahbir's Jake name) was the son of Ottiwell Simmons Sr., an important political activist in Bermuda and the president of the Bermuda Industrial Union, and Ahbir was also a founding member of the Berets, one of the members who had to flee that country in 1973 (disguised as a woman) not too long after the group was implicated by Scotland Yard in the murder of two white storeowners in Bermuda's capital city.[1] When Ahbir arrived in the United States, still in his late teens, he immediately ran afoul of the law, including almost getting shot during an attempted jewelry store break-in. Before he left Bermuda, Ahbir had started to develop a real love for martial arts, a skill also valorized by and valuable to the militant Black Berets. Before leaving Bermuda, he also became a founding member of one of the nation's first jujitsu schools. When he arrived in upstate New York, Cohane Ahbir started training with his first karate and judo teacher, Sensei Hidehiko "Hidy" Ochiai, a Japanese instructor who moved to upstate New York in the early 1960s and began working with Ahbir almost as soon as the young man arrived. Ahbir received his first- and second-degree black belts in karate and judo with Sensei Ochiai, competing professionally in sparring matches, forms, and weapons displays through the 1980s. His Japanese teacher treated him with respect, he says, a fact he waxes nostalgic about even today, which inspired Ahbir to begin redisciplining himself under Ochiai's tutelage, and he started thinking about his body in very different ways. At that point, he would not have been able to anticipate that so many years later he'd be considering his martial arts training as another way to reach Yah and spiritual righteousness. The book that Ahbir is currently writing is thus meant to plot his path from a secularist investment in the physical powers of the martial arts to a more fundamental appreciation of its role in the spiritual and physical regeneration of the African Hebrew Israelite community.

"We do everything different," Cohane Ahbir assures me. "It is the same, but it's different. Like weight training. Out there in the world, their approach is unnatural. It is unhealthy. It makes you look unnatural. Not only that, but they are using all kinds of self-destructive drugs to make themselves even more unnatural. Either to get bigger or to numb the pain because they are overdoing it. So, these guys are dying young. They are actually killing themselves. We lift weights—and do all of our divine Edenic exercising—to heal our bodies and to support everlasting life. That's it. So, we aren't trying to rip ligaments or tear our muscles. We are trying to keep this body prepared for hundreds more years of life on this planet."

The Divine Life-Discipline and Holystic Health Sanctuary is Ahbir's main "redemptive enterprise." He teaches and administers "Edenic Energy Exercises, Messianexercises, Positive Energy Touch Therapy, African Judean Martial Arts, African Judean Power Walking, Adamic Breathing, Meditation, Fit-for-Life Calisthenics, Iridology, Holystic Life Style Techniques, Holystic Healing and Nutrition." A framed certificate from a prestigious Israeli massage institute is only the newest plaque lining his gym's much-adorned walls.

After talking about his business exploits, Cohane Ahbir reiterates what the Kingdom requires of saints in terms of Edenic workouts. It means exercising "to the point of sweating" at least three times a week. Saints should be walking, jogging, or running local trails on a consistent basis, taking part in competitive sporting events, visiting the community's health center for breathing and stretching exercises, or for sauna, Jacuzzi and massage treatments. A few times a year, they should also purify their bodies of any toxins in the House of Life's colon-cleansing facility. In his notes for the book, Cohane Ahbir articulates the community's basic philosophy about physical exercise as spiritual or sacred activity quite succinctly:

> We consider exercise our moral responsibility to Yah/God. . . .
> Regenerative exercise is a community obligation not a social option.
> The Holy Concern is a term we use for our exercise program. We

call it the Holy Concern because we realize that Yah/God cared for us so much that in the beginning we had perfect health, a disease-free world, no death! We were in a sanctified environment. As we travel this path of redemption, returning back unto the way of Yah/God, we are concerned about being Holy once again to return to the High Holy state of Genesis.

But there isn't really a need for self-defense in the *kfar* saints will tell you. Even the ones who have never been to Dimona boast about the community's safety. *"People don't lock their doors on the kfar."* The peace they wish to usher into the world begins, they say, with the relative tranquility and security of their everyday lives in the Village of Peace. Cohane Ahbir is part of the Kingdom's security force, one of the men tasked with walking through the village after dark, mostly to ensure that youngsters are behaving themselves and that outsiders don't come in and make trouble, which rarely happens anyway.

Rabbi and psychologist Israel Gerber's 1977 account of the community in Dimona begins its conclusion with a discussion of a 1972 clash between community members and three Israelite men who had been recently kicked out of the group.[2] One of those three unwelcomed men was killed in a scuffle (falling on his own axe, Ben Ammi told the press), and Israeli authorities convicted five members of the community for that murder. Their sentences were relatively light, however, and the controversial incident would serve as the last widely publicized scandal about violence within the Dimona group. Everything since has been gossip, allegations in news reports, and the guilt-by-association that found them lumped in with more openly hostile Israelite camps in the United States during the months and years leading up to Y2K. Or they have been confused with the notorious Hebrew Israelite Nation based in Florida that was eventually linked to a string of violent murders—and whose Messiah, Yahweh Ben Yahweh, was imprisoned for several years before finally being released from prison and dying of cancer.[3]

TWENTY-SEVEN

Zimreeyah

WE WERE ON our honeymoon in Portugal when I heard that recording artists Whitney Houston and Bobby Brown had taken some of their family members and friends on a trip to visit the AHIJ's Kingdom of Yah in Dimona.[1] It became international news, which is how we found out about it, via CNN reports on our hotel's television set. I remember seeing their photo-op with Ariel Sharon and learning that they were staying with "a group of African Americans originally from the United States." Those other Hebrew Israelites (ICUPKers) in Harlem had already piqued my interest in this competing group of Israelites, so I focused on that short news story, which was probably rebroadcast something like eight or nine times during a two- or three-day stretch. I wouldn't get many more details about that Houston-Brown trip until I visited Dimona myself several years later.

Houston had gone for a couple of reasons. First of all, she'd been officially invited to the *kfar* in 2000 when she met a few saints at the Million Family March in Washington, DC, a follow-up to the Million Man March called by Nation of Islam leader Louis Farrakhan in 1995. She had brought along a close family member to Dimona, someone who was very sick, and she wanted to see if the AHIJ's healthy lifestyle might provide the recipe for her relative's full recovery. She had heard good things about the community's approach to health and figured it was worth a shot. Arriving to much fanfare (in the *kfar* and throughout the country), Houston received a Hebrew name from Ben Ammi (*Zimreeyah*, which they translate as "I sing for Yah"), and was immediately considered a kind of honorary saint, a would-be "sister" in the Kingdom. Ben Ammi fondly called her "Yah's Songstress." That's one of the reasons why, when she died so suddenly and tragically, discovered in a hotel bathtub during 2012's Grammy weekend, saints were devastated by the loss. They had always wanted Houston to return, to continue talking with them and learning from them. She might have visited—that first time— with someone else's health at stake, but saints believed that they could help her, too. With a history of substance abuse and the very public loss of her vocal virtuosity, Houston was just the kind of tragic figure that Yah's mercy and love could redeem and revive—as a testament to His power and grace. But she would never get to the *kfar* again.

During an interview with *The Insider,* a television news magazine in the United States, Whitney's goddaughter, Brandi Burnside, recounted the last conversation that she had had with her godmother—on the very day of the pop superstar's death. According to Burnside, earlier that morning Houston had brought up, out of nowhere, the idea of going back to Israel. And immediately. Burnside relayed their conversation, at least partially: "'You and Max' (my husband), Krissy, she said Krissy, my sister, and uncle Rae, she mentioned Rae, within the next two weeks, we need to get into the river. Her exact words were, 'We need to get into the Holy Water so that nothing can harm us or touch us for our new journey.' And I didn't know that she was going to say that. And I knew how special Israel was to her, because she had shared with me a long time ago, when she had went with her husband, how great the experience was. And she told me that if we go in the river and there's a cut on my body that it'll heal the moment that we get into that river. And the fact that she said that we have to go soon, it bothers me thinking about it, because she's not here."

It isn't lost on the AHIJ community that Houston was calling for a return to Israel, actively talking about doing so, of going back and bathing "in the river," on her last day alive, and seemingly out of the blue. "We have to go to Israel real soon," Burnside claims she said. Houston allegedly believed that the entire family had to take the trip, and they needed to do it "real soon." They had to get in that "Holy Water." It would repair their scarred bodies. Help to heal their open sores. It was clear that Houston's visit to Israel almost ten years before had had a major impact on the pop icon, and the physical healing that Houston's goddaughter says she emphasized is easily read as a proxy for whatever emotional and psychological wounds also needed treatment.

As is the case with most Americans who visit the community, Whitney Houston, Bobby Brown, their family, friends, and entourage all went out with saints on a Sacred Visitation, which, for them, included constant battles with the paparazzi, even a bit of pushing and shoving to keep prying cameras at bay. I watched a couple of hours of raw footage from that trip back in the Ministry of Information on the *kfar,* and there were many more hours of mini-DV tapes lining the MOI's walls. The community tried to document much of Houston's sacred visitation, which included standard stops in the Old City's "fifth quarter," "its African quarter," and a stint in the Jordan River, which for Houston and her crew entailed wading, singing, and even some baptizing in the water.

News of her death reverberated throughout the *kfar.* Not surprising in a community full of talented singers ("Divine Music" being a central emphasis in the Kingdom), saints appreciated Whitney Houston's vocal talents, especially in her younger days. That she had been given a divine gift was beyond dispute, even if she had seemingly squandered it over the years (with her bad decisions, especially a highly publicized drug addiction). After her Dimona trip, some saints would continue to pray for her and hope that her spirit might be moved, radically shaken, by the truth of their message. They had accepted her as an extended daughter to "Abba" Ben Ammi, and certainly as a friend to the community. And that came with responsibilities on their part—or at least some Divine well-wishing.

The Hebrew Israelites are very good at cultivating such friendships. High profile celebrities and entertainers—as well as national and international politicians and dignitaries from the United States, the West

Indies, and Africa—visit the *kfar* on a consistent basis. I have yet to spend a single night in the *kfar* without some major African delegation representing the ministries of tourism or education or agriculture in Ghana, Senegal, Benin, or South Africa sleeping in a guesthouse not too far away. Indeed, the story of the group's fight to stay in Israel from the 1970s to the 1990s can't be told without some discussion of the investments the AHIJ have always made in leveraging associations with "friends" outside of Israel, most especially members of the Congressional Black Caucus. Developing these relationships entailed several visits from important American political figures, visits that would have been incomplete, of course, without requisite Sacred Visitations through which saints could teach their high-profile guests how to understand the AHIJ's take on Israel.

Americans unaffiliated with the Kingdom have long played a key role in the community's story. In the early 1980s, Bayard Rustin, an important civil rights figure and former confidant of Martin Luther King Jr., led a delegation of African American leaders (from the NAACP, the National Council of Negro Women, the National Urban League, and other organizations) on an eleven-day fact-finding mission in Israel. The goal of their brief inquiry was twofold: to investigate saints' allegations that the Israeli government was waging a racist war against them and to propose some strategy for how that government might more productively relate to the AHIJ community going forward. The Israeli government allowed the delegation into the country (allegedly out of concern that these accusations of racism were gaining traction in the United States, creating unnecessary and unwarranted bad press), and they were willing to consider any recommendations that the committee might make about how they should deal with this group of American expats, a community that arrived in Israel in 1969 proclaiming that they were the true Israelites of Revelation, that European Jews were imposters, and that the latter should take their leave of the place at once.

By the time Rustin and his delegation had arrived in 1981, the community had already softened this exclusivist position, though some people questioned their sincerity, including Rustin.

"Israel must determine," Rustin said, "whether Ben Ami Carter still believes what he originally said—that he and his group will inherit the earth and that the Jews are imposters in Israel. If that is the case, the Black Hebrews are indigestible. If, on the other hand, as his current public statements indicate, he has changed his tune, the group is digestible."[2]

The delegation met with saints in Dimona and Arad, interviewed former saints who were estranged from the community, talked to Israeli officials, and sat down with the U.S. ambassador. The committee found "no official racism in Israel," but their report warned that the Israeli government "risks being perceived as racist no matter what" if they don't re-evaluate their immigration-screening procedures at Israeli airports, which included pulling blacks out of lines and subjecting them to more elaborate forms of interrogation than other visitors (in an attempt to keep more African Americans from illegally settling with the community). Some of these harassed blacks were, in Rustin's words, "bona fide Christian pilgrims," and delegates warned that "such behavior encourages anti-Israel propaganda and creates conflict between American Jews and American blacks."[3] At the same time, the delegation explicitly recommended that Israel ban any more Black Hebrews from relocating to southern Israel, but it wasn't necessarily clear how the Israeli state was supposed to respond to the report's somewhat contradictory message: be more diligent about keeping saints in America from joining the community in Dimona, but don't subject black visitors to any heightened scrutiny (so as not to appear racist). The committee also proposed that saints be encouraged to live all throughout Israel, not just in "an isolated *moshav*," a self-contained agrarian settlement, which had been suggested by Israeli's Glass Commission in 1973 (as a way to most productively give the community legal status within Israel).[4]

When I originally read about Rustin leading this American delegation to Israel in the early 1980s, I imagined that he was also a "friend" of the community, but I was quickly disabused of that conclusion. Rustin, saints told me, was out to get them. He had even upstaged the committee's formal report by declaring that his conscience wouldn't allow him to keep silent about his distrust of Ben Carter. "Carter is a dictator," he said, "and dictators don't have the same moral standards as democratic leaders."[5] Rustin compared Carter (and he seemed to pointedly called him "Ben Carter" more often than the "Ben Ami Carter" that other delegates used) to Hitler and Stalin, recounting claims from former saints that he'd confiscated their passports, seized their bank accounts, stopped them from leaving the community, and separated family members from one another as punishment for any disobedience. Rustin's characterization, not the delegation's report, made headlines that day, and the writers of that report, including Rustin, were soon compelled to draft a "letter to the editor" more than two weeks later voicing their chagrin that "*The Jerusalem Post*, Israel's major English language publication[,] would permit a personal expression to overshadow an important jointly prepared report." They disassociated their report from Rustin's personal comments, and emphasized their support of that report's less inflammatory findings.[6]

The community has had many well-placed American "friends," but Rustin was not one of them, which at least a few saints readily chalk up to his homosexuality. How could he hear their message when he had strayed that far from Yah's truth? Of course, he would be hostile to it. In another version of Afrocentrism's traditionalist assumptions, the AHIJ consider homosexuality an abomination—further example of Western culture's toxic impact on Yah's people. But even Rustin signed that letter and the report, which provided some cover and support for the community's continued existence and protection in Israel.

As some saints were publicly renouncing their U.S. citizenship and symbolically destroying their passports in the face of continued threats of deportation throughout the 1980s, other saints working and living abroad were able to cultivate even more American connections for the community's long-term goals. In the 1990s, work with the Congressional Black Caucus and other elected officials produced more than one million dollars in American funding to construct a school building specifically allocated to children in the *kfar*.[7] It would be part of the larger Israeli school system and staffed by Israeli teachers (as well as co-instructors from the community), but it only taught the community's youth, a far cry from the days when saints would educate their young in the crowded living rooms of their absorption center apartments and courtyards.[8]

Nasik Asiel long served as a public face for the African Hebrew Israelites of Jerusalem all around the world, and many of the dignitaries and politicians were first contacted and introduced to the community by

Ben Ammi (center) with local Dimona politician Benni Beton and Israeli Prime
Minister Benjamin Netanyahu at the AHIJ's Village of Peace in 2008.
(Photograph by Crowned Sister Cattriellah eshet Rockameem.)

him. It was a job that often allowed him access to some of the most powerful and important social spaces in the world, parlaying such entrée into
very real gains for the saints back in Dimona: Senator Carolyn Mosley
Braun hosting Nasik Asiel in a Senate Dining Room; politicians regularly eating at his Soul Veg East restaurant in Chicago; several members
of Congress and Illinois state representatives from Chicago making several trips to the *kfar* throughout the early 2000s.

Whitney Houston wasn't a politician, but she was another example of
just how far and wide the AHIJ's global footprint and social influence
actually extended, and saints who watched the live broadcast of her
funeral in Newark, New Jersey, took note of the Kingdom's unmistakable
thrice-repeated *HalleluYah* chant (recited by Patricia Houston, Whitney's
sister-in-law) to open the ceremony, interpreting that as another sign of
the AHIJ's lasting influence on the life of this international icon.

TWENTY-EIGHT

Sincere

T HE TERM "ETHNOGRAPHY" is used to define both a literary genre
(descriptive social scientific writings that attempt to capture groups'
cultural beliefs and practices) and an approach to producing those
written accounts (collecting data through methodical observations and
face-to-face interactions over an extended period of time). Anthropology's
emphasis on ethnography is still considered one of its most distinctive
features, and an ambitiously holistic (holystic?) intervention. Even in an
age when human genomics and the statistical analysis of massive data
sets are popularly considered, in many circles, far more compellingly
"scientific" and "objective" techniques for analyzing social life, potential
Holy Grails of analysis, ethnographic research and writing continue to
occupy, somewhat stubbornly, a central place in anthropology's investigative toolkit, the only way to construct those thick descriptions.

Anthropology is far from the only field with a stake in the definition
and future of ethnography. The term morphs—in big and small ways—
as it travels across traditional disciplinary dividing lines, and even
well beyond the academy, into embedded journalisms or documentary

filmmaking of various kinds.[1] And one of the biggest challenges facing this ubiquitous ethnography is "globalization," a shrinking of our planet caused by the expansion of our technological capacities to traverse it, virtually and vehicularly. Emphasizing this notion leads to a concomitant expanding of traditional ethnographic field-sites, once considered siloed and decidedly nonglobal bastions of vanishing primitivity that need protection from contaminations and assimilations wrought by contact with the Western world. That "salvage" mentality has been replaced by one that foregrounds appreciation of (and engagement with) the global contexts and processes impacting everything and everyone on the planet, without exception, and ethnography is constantly being retooled to allow for this rather radical change in framing and focus.[2]

So much about ethnographic writing, now as well as then, can seem like a gestaltlike portrait irreducible to the many observations and interviews that constitute it. There is the perennial question of its placement on the arts and humanities versus sciences continuum, which has major implications for how ethnographies are written and read, with an art-science answer probably not satisfying most skeptics in the least. Cultural anthropologists conduct ethnographic research to explain the "strange" lives of distant social communities to colleagues (the "science") and to wider audiences (at least partially an "art"). In the past, degrees of strangeness were measured in distances of time and space. The subjects lived many, many miles away, in remote areas, preferably only accessible by the most treacherous of paths, the journey itself proof of an anthropologist's authority. And these researched communities represented a primitivity that was atavistic, from another time, indications of a civilized world's barbarian and savage pasts.[3]

There was also a call to render such communities in their totality. Ethnographies covered every aspect of society, the mapping of a culture's complete geography. To make a society's strangeness more familiar to readers meant situating everyday actions in their widest social contexts (though rarely wide enough to glimpse much of European colonialism), connecting dots between special rituals and quotidian group proscriptions, between biopsychological needs and sociostructural ones. It meant the clean, linear predictabilities of kinship charts. This was even the case once anthropologists began to focus more specifically on certain slivers of larger cultural worlds, contextualizing just one theme—say, dance or religion or economics or childrearing—instead of giving everything equal billing. Offering ethnography as an ensemble of cultural actors and actions, each ethnographer would choose its star, its lead, situated in a wider context, of course, but with varying configurations and theoretical constellations. That was part of a related desire, from some anthropological quarters, to challenge earlier attempts at easy cross-cultural transparency, dreams of totalizable knowledge doing more harm than good, counterproductively providing an unhealthy sense of full access and understanding. But what kind of science would *not* try to provide full and complete answers, as complete as can be mustered? *Now you know everything we know right now.* But that *everything* is always partial and subject to change, a fact that the authorial voice of ethnographic monographs often drowns out in seemingly timeless pronouncements.[4] But we know that there is always the other trap, in the other direction, the "formalistic fallacy," emphasizing the seductiveness of writing over the substance of what's known. And that's even before anyone throws out the idea of simply keeping certain ethnographic things secret, inaccessible, opaque. But we want to know. We're built that way. Who has the luxury to bathe in nonknowledge anyway, Agamben's poetic suggestion notwithstanding? And we want a "systematic" approach to things, which should be different from the meanderings of everyday life, no?

Since the 1990s, I have been conducting fieldwork and interviews, collecting videos and written material, visiting saints in America and beyond. It started in Brooklyn and Harlem, New York, mostly with the ICUPK and other U.S.-based offshoots of that particular camp. Then, since about 2004, I began to look at other groups of black Israelites and black Jews, in places like Chicago and Durham, Los Angeles and Atlanta, London and Durban, Washington, DC, and Kingston—and, of course, in the modern state of Israel, especially the Negev, where many saints from the AHIJ are based, and not just in Dimona, but also in the towns of Arad and Mitzpe Ramon, and scattered throughout the rest of the country.

I've interviewed over 250 people for this project, some of them contemporary members of one Israelite group or another, some of them former Israelites who have moved on to another faith, or to no faith at all. Some people have changed affiliations from one Israelite/Hebrew community to another—from Jew to Israelite, from Israelite to Jew. Some interviews lasted barely an hour, quick and dirty attempts to find out how people came to their current position inside (or outside) the fold. Others went on for three or more hours, taking place over several days or weeks, life histories captured to provide a sense of how people communicate and situate their social identities. These interviews were conducted with everyone from young adults to senior citizens. They took place in people's homes, over the phone, at community centers, schools, my office, and anywhere else people felt comfortable, including those quieter hotel hallways in American Anthropological Association meetings.

Interviews are obviously important, but "deep hanging out" is really ethnography's bread-and-butter, what a colleague of mine in a southern English department mockingly described as "you drinking some beer on the corner with folks." There was no beer drinking with *saints* (just a swig of their own processed and bottled plum wine after a vegan dinner in Philadelphia), but the gist of his characterization still works. I spent time in Israelite classes, visiting subjects' homes, touring their jobs, and shadowing them in neighborhoods throughout the world.

All the while, I have been constantly negotiating reasonable skepticism from some saints, especially the ones I don't know that well, which means the vast majority of them, skepticism about my ultimate intentions, about the sincerity of my motives. This question of sincerity, in my opinion, is a fairly understated theme in contemporary anthropological circles. Sincerity conjures up images of self-conscious subjects capable of willfully (or unwittingly) misrepresenting themselves and their true inner feelings. It is predicated on the possibility of dark human interiors, interiorities that might house ulterior motives, something not accurately or honestly expressed to the outside world. Psychoanalysts provide ample evidence for the fact that such imagined interiorities are never simply self-transparent or straightforwardly accessible either. And postmodernists have done a compelling theoretical number on the many pitfalls endemic to all depth-based models of human subjectivity, including the classic ones offered up by psychoanalysts. But what is most compelling about our ordinary notion of sincerity is that it smuggles an inescapable doubt and uncertainty into every social interaction, a doubt grounded in the distinction between purportedly latent and manifest individual objectives. Some call for a "politics of recognition" that values authentic cultural differences; sincerity recognizes the irredeemable misrecognitions that constitute and confound all social interactions, even those cultivated by ethnographers in the field.

Authenticity and authenticity tests are about shooing such doubt away, pretending that we can find foolproof techniques for distinguishing sincerity from insincerity, the genuine article from social fakery and misrepresentation. But no matter how sophisticated our authenticity tests, no matter how elaborate our analytical strategies, the slippage between what we see and what we can trust, between what is obvious or self-evident and what must be taken on faith about other people (based on partial and ever-changing shreds of evidence), always remains.[5]

The question of sincerity has always been paramount in the Israelite community, even as early as the 1960s. For many detractors, that was the first issue of concern. Men like Ben Ammi and Shaleahk Ben Yehuda must have been running some kind of scam, some "religious" con, soliciting donations from people with this talk about black folk being descendants of ancient Israelites. They couldn't be serious. Insincerity became a central frame for delegitimation. Civil rights activist Bayard Rustin, for one, seemed to offer up a two-pronged critique in just these terms after his 1980s mission to Israel: that Ben Carter was just a thug pretending to be a spiritually motivated figure (named Ben Ammi), and that he was also simply making believe that the community had changed its position on Europeans being "imposter Jews." Many, like Rustin, could barely contain their skepticisms about the earnestness of Ammi's spiritual project.

But even worse, maybe these folks were serious. Once the community really began to organize for life away from America in 1966, their sincerity looked a little more testable, more measureable, but also more potentially incomprehensible and bizarre. This would have been a particularly elaborate ruse for con artists looking to trick black people out of their savings, especially if they were planning on living in Liberia with everyone else as part of the scam. The emigrationist preparations began to silence some of that concern about insincerity—only to raise questions about their actual sanity.

The sincerity of the ethnographer is also at stake—and increasingly verifiable as ethnographic research morphs into publishable material. But before publication, sincerity demands vetting. For the ICUPK, they felt the power of Yah was more potent than any potential espionage I might have been performing in their nightly classes. How could I hear the truth of what they were saying, with books they asked me to bring back from my own school's library, and not eventually come to accept their claims as well? Likewise, for some of the AHIJ saints, skepticism (about me) was tempered by their faith in Yah's divine and preordained plans. I might have imagined that mere curiosity brought me to Dimona that first time in 2005, but just because I believed that to be true didn't make it so. More likely was the idea that Yah had guided me to my scholarly interests, to this vanguard community, to His chosen people and their truth. To my destiny. Whatever I believed about my anthropological mission might very well be irrelevant. Spirit had guided me there, and it was just vanity and ignorance to think otherwise. At least one saint in Philadelphia asked me how I couldn't interpret all of my previous life experiences as preparation for the AHIJ's truth: my Seventh-Day Adventist upbringing and its reverence for the Sabbath, my favorite childhood uncle owning the only vegan store I knew of in Brooklyn, my childhood in a Canarsie neighborhood predominantly populated by Jews, many of my earliest friends teaching me Hebrew (because they had to learn it) or inviting me to Seders and Bar Mitzvahs. This was all the divine unfurling of fate, some saints offered, even if only Cohane Michael would consistently ask me, point-blank, what I actually *believed* about the AHIJ truths I was documenting, interrogating me about whether my interests went beyond merely academic concerns.[6] For the anthropologist who hasn't already "gone native," it is mandatory, however, to keep such thoughts at bay, considering my past less as a preplanned pathway to the Hebrew Israelites than as a subconscious driving force behind my scholarly interests, an early priming academics would more likely chalk up to the contingencies of history than designs of the Most High.

One of the first things an anthropologist starts to ponder in the field, while those ethnographic subjects are determining his or her sincerity, is the sincerity, in turn, of his ethnographic interlocutors and the stories they share. Maybe they just don't want to divulge secret information. Or they are trying to say what they think they're supposed to. Whatever the reasons, ethnographers rely on long-term immersion because it is believed to provide tools for determining the difference between cultural winks, twitches, and nods, as Clifford Geertz put it, to recognize when subjects simply get things wrong and when they are actively trying to stop the ethnographic outsider from getting them right.

Potential insincerities crowd the ethnographic encounter at every turn, in every project, from the very beginning. No one was there to disprove Ammi's claims, no third party to verify his anointing. Or that angelic visitation. The success of his future shepherding would serve, for some, as retroactive proof, the judging of a tree by its fruits. How could he not be anointed given his success at bringing so many of Yah's people to the Holy Land, despite so many obstacles? Naysayers consider that a flimsy hook for hanging millennialist claims, about as flimsy as the superficiality of ethnographic storytelling, the thinness of anecdotes and vignettes. It might be sincere, who knows, but it isn't the stuff of science.

TWENTY-NINE

Casein

T HE KINGDOM TRAINS its scholars at the School of the Prophets, producing specialists in statesmanship, diplomacy, history, the priesthood, preventive medicine, nutrition, and more. Founded by Prince Shaleahk Ben Yehuda in 1975, the school has recently started an online extension, the Institute of Regenerative Truth, which aims to "acknowledge the Creator in all things, seek the ancient truths once hidden, clarify our responsibility to the planet and each other, and promote spirituality through culture."[1] The school's dean, Ahtur Khazriel, launched IRT as a way to bring the *kfar*'s instructors, its "master teachers," to the many saints living outside of Israel. The IRT is "dedicated to the development of the Yah-mind (truth centered spirituality)" in its students. Though the human mind has been destroyed by centuries of cultural depravity, saints maintain that it can be rewired; it can regenerate, as long as people make the disciplined choice to live their everyday lives in accordance with God's laws. The school teaches those laws, and their contemporary implications for questions of environmental justice, dietary habits, governmental policies, and entrepreneurial decision making.

The School of the Prophets represents the community's most important institutional mechanism for developing knowledge and expertise in
all fields. Priests answer their priestly calling, in part, by studying with
instructors inside the IRT's building on the *kfar*. Teachers and community scholars—the ones who curate the African/Edenic Heritage Museum
or lead Sacred Visitations across the Israeli countryside or draft press
releases for Kingdom events—all learn (and later teach) bits of their crafts
based on the readings, discussions, and exams there. Midwives in the
House of Life get training in how to birth newborns (per biblical directives) and counsel their temporarily quarantined mothers. And all of
these graduates frame their efforts most tightly around questions of Yah-
mandated regulations about nutrition and health, mandates that have yet
to be fully revealed or understood. But the more the Kingdom shows
deference to Yah's will by incorporating newly uncovered truths into
their daily routines, the sooner Yah will disclose "the final keys to
unlocking physical immortality." And every road leads back to that most
proximate finish line: an articulation and refinement of the singular
importance of policing bodily practices, starting with a careful parsing
of what and when to eat.

The scholars and priests of the AHIJ spend most of their time
preaching and teaching not just about the history of the ancient patriarchs, which goes without saying, but also about the increasing hazards
of meat-eating, along with more fine-grained discussions about raw
versus cooked foods, the best and worst kinds of vegetable oils, and the
mounds of "purposeful misinformation" circulating about what items
count as healthy in the first place. Sacred Visitation tour guides organize
their multiday excursions with a calculated sense of how much food and
beverage to take for their charges, structuring the trip so that they have
plenty of time to stop at community-affiliated homes or eateries along the
way, all while making sure to leave the requisite length of time for properly digesting food before and after drinking anything. Saints wait one
hour after eating meals to drink in an effort to make sure that "nutrients
make it into the body before being diluted," as one saint first explained
to me. This health message is central to the community's larger cosmological and spiritual goals, but it is also somewhat detachable from those
concerns. Saints consider their health mission one of the Kingdom's

most important, practical, and immediate interventions. Even if you don't buy their claims about the body's capacity for physical immortality, their argument that death is itself a form of "dehumanization" (an unnatural warping of Yah's original design), they challenge you to find fault with the practical benefits of their health-related mandates.

Everything from mad cow disease to high blood pressure is deployed as fodder to justify claims about the benefits of a plant-based, casein-free diet. Their *holystic* approach to health is the cornerstone of their entire project, the link between two interconnected units of analysis: the collective body of the Kingdom and the specific bodies of individual saints. Drawing on the work of fellow anthropologist Mary Douglas, Merrill Singer stressed this interconnectedness when he worked with the community in the 1970s. Conducting his research just as the House of Life was first being created, he caught the earliest codifications of AHIJ health mandates. Singer argued that the vulnerabilities of any individual saint's body—to sickness, disease, and death—were linked to the potential social dangers faced by the group as a whole, dangers predicated on their relatively vulnerable existence in an overly hostile and antagonistic world.[2] According to Singer, any uptick in public discourse about the community's external threats (from an Israeli government trying to deport them or from rival black Israelite groups disparaging their efforts) coincided with ramped up requests for saints to be increasingly vigilant about their health regimes, about maintaining their commitments to eating and exercising in accordance with Yah's desires and the community's expectations.

The evolution of AHIJ health commitments over the past four decades shows changing articulations of care and rigor in their reading of the individual body's physical weaknesses and of the social body's (the Kingdom's) external threats. From a ban on pork and cigarettes in the late 1960s, which still allowed saints in Liberia to sell ice cream and hamburgers for a living, to the slow unfolding of veganism as one of the central planks in their reparation of the covenant with Yah, a covenant that Adam, Eve, and the ancient Israelites all broke. They take their Edenic charge over the planet and its wildlife very seriously, which translates into an environmentalist ethos and a commitment to protecting the planet from the most destructive byproducts of modern technology unleashed with little consideration of its impact on the earth. This has also meant an ever-more sophisticated and granular meticulousness vis-à-vis scientifically mediated claims about the body and its susceptibility to pollutants of all kinds. A mixture of biblical literalism and "science studies," the AHIJ health program represents an evolving and nuanced winnowing of their Edenic live-it's particularities.

At their weekly Shabbat classes in West Philadelphia, dozens of members of the Philadelphia jurisdiction spend the bulk of their afternoons analyzing the latest science headlines from around the world, new discoveries about the oils used in McDonald's french fries, or reports about new vaccines that show promise in allowing the human body to more effectively fight off cancer cells. The latter is usually invoked both to mock science's attempted circumvention of the more "natural" vegan solution to cancerous cellular growths and to comb through modern scientific research for any small kernel of actual truth about the human cell's immortality, truth spied between the more explicit lines of these studies. The saints spend every Shabbat discussing new scientific theories about, say, the impact of sleep on daily productivity, or on the ways in which video games and other new media technology rewire human brains (for the worse), or on the tumor-causing dangers of cell phone radiation, a concern that prompted Ben Ammi to call for a daily limit on the number of minutes saints spend using such devices. Any given Saturday, you can find saints all over the world getting together to ponder the relative effectiveness of different vitamin supplements or the latest evidence about the conspiratorial ways in which milk, meat, and juice lobbyists misrepresent the nutritional values of their products. The eldest priest in the Philadelphia jurisdiction spends fifteen minutes one Shabbat driving home the point that raw vegetables are healthier for the human body than cooked ones. Veganism is meant to eventually clear the way for an all-live/raw diet, he reminds them. Nothing cooked.

Each Shabbat afternoon, a priest recaps discussions from past weeks and presents new information, often playfully quizzing saints on the health-related lessons they should have already incorporated into their daily routines from previous sessions. Should they be using nutritional yeast or not? Why does the community advocate cold-pressed oils? What techniques are saints supposed to use to help them metabolize certain nutrients and why? All of this is offered up in fine-grained detail—in the cool, calculated register of logically reasoned argumentation (always with a joke or two thrown in to point out most people's ignorance on such important matters). Citations are from the American Medical Association and *Science* magazine. Recommendations are always linked to what most people would label "hard evidence." The goal: to produce an extremely health-literate community that can spread the message to the rest of Philadelphia.

The scientific findings are looped into Edenic mandates, newly understood and corroborated, and always keyed to the community's central contention: that Yah's plan is immortality, for the planet and its inhabitants, the second a material extension of the first—both sentient, living, and communicating entities. One saint talks about a *Natural History* article examining the claim that plants might actually be said to have brains. (Yet another potential example of Vicky Kirby's thoughtful/ thinking natural world?) A few saints had already read the piece, and they found a lot of value in it, summarizing its main point me: that plants possess receptors similar to the kinds found in human nervous systems and respond to external stimuli in ways that seem to imply quite complex mechanisms for processing environmental forces. Saints mine these articles for valuable data. And they link that data to earlier discussions they've had about plants' leaves folding up when abusive people enter a room or withering and dying whenever they are given microwaved water as nourishment. The human body and these plants, they argue, are, in essence, at a certain level, the same thing. It isn't happenstance that human beings and the soil of the earth have the same number of minerals, a fact that Ben Ammi often emphasizes: "102 minerals in the earth, and the same amount in our bodies." And so veganism stands up to reason, saints maintain, even without any biblical verification, which they get from Genesis 1:29. Plants are from the same earth that contains all of the minerals that our human bodies need.[3] It all comes from the same source, which is why veganism is far from a fad, they argue. It is the natural order of things. So-called "evolution," they'd argue, is the physicalization of Yah's curse, nothing but a slow degeneration. But it is also potentially reversible with a renewed commitment to eating properly. Veganism is in harmony with the Creator's will and moves his people from transience (deathability) to absolute life. Without the correct complement of minerals in the right proportion, we will surely die, "make transition," which is why, Ben Ammi emphasizes, the Hebrew word for the first man is *Adam* and for the soil, the earth, out of which that man sprang, *adama*. This is all more proof that the biblical tale of Adam's birth from a combination of spirit and soil is quite literally true. It is verification of the Torah's wisdom, a Torah that guides their reconfigurations of contemporary social practices and life cycles: birth (with time for the sequestering and postpartum caretaking of women as well as special diets for both the mother-to-be and the breast-feeding new mother), marriage (specific guidelines and timetables for courting and counseling), and even death (a rather ungodly result of human disobedience and not very ritualistically expressed in the public sphere as a consequence). These are bodies that must be attuned to the divine spirit that first enlivened them if their cells will ever have a chance to turn on completely.

THIRTY

Prodigal

O NE TWENTY-YEAR-OLD SAINT in the community, "a son," as elders would say, tells the moving story of his relationship with an older brother, a skinnier and taller twenty-something who has recently left the *kfar* and moved into an apartment in Tel Aviv with the Israeli mother of his newborn child. She isn't a member of the Kingdom, and the two of them didn't get married, which helps explain why the brothers' relationship has gotten more complicated. This decision to leave the community effectively meant that the older brother was no longer in the Kingdom, not fully. Breaking Yah's covenant meant being a potentially negative influence on other young saints, his brother included. He represented one example of just what so many naysayers had long predicted: a member of the Second Generation who didn't stay—who was opting out.

The younger brother is a relatively quiet, disciplined, and tender-hearted saint who is respected and trusted in the *kfar*. The older sibling, who seems (at times) to share some of that same quietness, might have fallen into some nondivine habits (like drinking beer and smoking ciga-rettes) even before he stopped being a full-fledged saint. Though he has moved away (to "Hell Aviv," as some saints have renamed it), he is still in cell-phone contact and easy bus-riding distance, still trying to maintain relationships with some of his friends and family members in the *kfar.* The question of his insider versus outsider status is complicated, but his connection to the AHIJ still overdetermines his relationship to other Israelis, regardless of whether or not he has actually chosen to leave.

Saints often relate the story of one of their young sons killed in a terrorist act in 2000. At the time, however, he was also not fully in the community. He'd been born in the House of Life on the *kfar,* and the community in Israel was all he'd ever known, but he'd decided to try his hand at leaving and playing music with a band that did weddings and bar mitzvahs all around Israel. At the time he was killed, his ties with the community were a bit strained. He maintained some links with his family and closest friends, but he was not necessarily a saint in good standing. Even still, his death represented an opportunity for other Israelis to commiserate with the AHIJ, to empathize with them over their mutual vulnerabilities in an era of suicide bombings. To hear some saints talk about the death many years later, it stands as one of the watershed moments in the Kingdom's history, the loss placing a larger Israeli society more firmly in their corner as fellow sojourners.

Besides that tale of Whitney Houston's trip to Dimona in 2003, the only other recent international news story about the Kingdom (aside from this 2000 bombing) was based on reports of a saint who was representing Israel in Eurovision, a trans-European music competition. Since the community has always had a strong tradition of training saints to play and sing music, Divine Music, their dozens of recorded CDs (of individual vocalists and groups) always available for purchase at local events and online, it is no surprise that they have developed quite a bit of musical talent. But what struck me about the articles in the *New York Times* and other venues that colleagues and friends forwarded my way, was the name of the saint: Eddie Butler. He was never referred to by a Hebrew name; it was always his Jake name, Eddie Butler, which saints never use on the *kfar,* even if they do, grudgingly, in other contexts. For instance, saints who have to travel internationally use the non-Hebrew names found on their U.S. passports, but that's because official government agencies require it. So, it seemed strange to me that "Eddie Butler" would not be stressing to journalists that they use his Hebrew name, clarifying this point for their articles about the show. At the subsequent New World Passover ceremony, he actually performed some songs in the *kfar*, his celebrity status creating a buzz throughout Dimona, and he was certainly not referred to as Eddie Butler.

For that 2006 Eurovision competition, Butler sang (in English and Hebrew) a song called "Together We Are One." He sported no facial hair and wore a white two-piece suit with a collar-less white shirt—and none of the mandatory visible fringes and blue tassels on the edges of his suit jacket. He had already launched an international pop music career, and he had clearly gotten support from saints for this recent Eurovision run, an early video for his Eurovision song even including a gospel choir singing behind him that consisted almost exclusively of saints from the *kfar*. Seven years earlier, he and several other young sons in the Kingdom had submitted an entry to the Eurovision contest as the group Eden. They didn't make it into the competition, but he has been singing, as a solo act, all around Israel and Europe ever since.

During the press conference for his 2006 Eurovision appearance, Butler was also talking about going through a formal conversion process, converting to Judaism, which might only further complicate his relationship to the Kingdom. Of course, one of the things to stress in all this might be that individuals are always complicated members of their communities in one way or another. Depending on the particulars, those complications can get them killed, expelled, mocked, or simply disregarded.[1] That is part of what makes cultural anthropology—and its obsession with social/cultural *groups*—so tricky. We often oversell this idea that individuals stand in for their communities—or for discrete subsections of those communities—in other than idiosyncratic and particular ways. We almost never know totally what to do with the specifics of these walking and talking repositories of cultural knowhow.

Back in 2006, Butler seemed to have a precarious relationship to this community, which emphatically stopped any talk of a groupwide conversion process back in 1969, as soon as Ben Ammi brought the final few saints to Israel from Liberia, considering it a concession to the assumption that they weren't already who they claimed to be, descendants of the ancient Israelites. Judaism couldn't work for them, Ben Ammi made clear. It recognizes none of the Kingdom's claims, starting with the very anointing of Ben Ammi.

But there is also something representative, I think, about the twoness of an Eddie Butler. His complicated connections to the community—in it, but potentially not recognized as such, at least not from certain angles. It is a twoness that every person manifests. For many saints, it is more than just the differential deployment of Hebrew *and* Jewish names. Other AHIJ members also have complex *personal* relationships to Judaism, not just Sar Ahmadiel and the grandmother he pushed away during childhood. Even Oriyahu, the Kingdom's first military inductee, stands in for that twoness, in a very different way. He is also a Butler, Oriyahu Butler, Eddie's younger cousin, and his induction into the Israeli military was expedited as a function of the fact that he was already an Israeli citizen, the son of a biracial Jewish mother whose own mother was a Dutch Holocaust survivor.[2] So, he is a Second Generationer with even more of an opportunity to leave. Yet he hasn't done so, unlike the young son who left the Kingdom to move in with an Israeli girlfriend and child in Tel Aviv. Like several other young saints who came before him (including, for a stretch, Eddie Butler, whose Hebrew name is Eitan), he decided to see what kind of life he might live beyond the strict regulations of the *kfar*. But instead of going to Atlanta or Chicago, he relocated to another part of Israel, the only country he's ever known, and part of his new life, far from the community, but not so far, consists of cathected and moving conversations with a younger brother still in the Kingdom who cares about him. And who deftly wields a video camera.

One of the features of the current ethnographic moment is that most research subjects are also citizen-ethnographers, purposeful describers of their own lives. As much as social scientists tend to critique the Heisenbergian quality of participant-observation, the unavoidable ways in which participation affects our objects of study, the fact is that even if the ethnographer isn't there to meddle, research subjects are messing up the classic ethnographic model (with its dividing line between researcher and researched) themselves by conducting their own studies, an important point that isn't in any way resolved by the fact that academic ethnographers might still fold such "vernacular" and "emic" renderings into their own accounts.

So I was first introduced to the story of one young saint's prodigal brother through a powerful forty-minute ethnographic film, a film that the younger brother shot, narrated, and edited. As his business card reveals, "videographer/editor" is his "redemptive enterprise," and he went to Israel's Sapir College to improve on the filmmaking skills he first developed during shoots on the *kfar* for the Ministry of Information. The 2007 film about his brother, Katriel, "The Prodigal Son," is a project that he completed to graduate from Sapir.

The movie starts with the filmmaker talking about growing up in the *kfar* and loving his life in the Kingdom, even showcasing several events from a New World Passover ceremony. He explains what NWP is and uses that footage to segue into a discussion about Katriel, fretting over that brother's decision to leave the Kingdom about six years earlier. The film quickly moves from shots of the *kfar* to images of his older brother's new apartment in Tel Aviv, Katriel's girlfriend, Linah, voicing frustration about his unwillingness to give her enough money for their child's food. The story includes a series of scenes depicting the couple negotiating with one another about how to best care for their newborn—and for one another.

This is a one of those tales about the Kingdom that is sometimes most difficult to see. It isn't something that the community celebrates in its own literature, and the young filmmaker does a careful job trying to articulate his love for a brother who has left a community (and, at least partially, a family) that he, himself, cannot imagine forsaking. Their mothers (they are half-brothers in this polygynous society) and father weigh-in on the matter while washing dishes, preparing sandwiches, cutting oranges, or assembling the community's all-natural footwear (hand-crocheted cotton "Eco-shoes"), which the brothers' father designs and distributes. The family can only hope that "the truth" Katriel learned as a child will eventually bring him back home, and they leave open the possibility that it just might.

"Katriel, I know he got out and did a lot of foolish things," their father says. "He's probably still doing some foolish things now, but he's still my son, you know. And when he decides he wants to come back, I'm gonna welcome him."

THIRTY-ONE

Esau

ALTHOUGH OTHERS MIGHT have been confused about how to define them, the Israelites leaving for Liberia in 1967 were very sure about what made them different from Jews. They had spent many hours in Chicago clarifying that distinction, and using it as a way to galvanize community members for their departure. The elders talked at length about it, used biblical passages to explain things, and framed the entirety of their nationalist project around that singular distinction. Jews, including black Jews, they argued, practiced a religion. Black Israelites embraced their true nationality, their actual heritage.[1]

"Israelites are the descendants of Abraham, Isaac, and Jacob," Ben Ammi would explain, "the seed of the promise, and Jews are people who adopt Judaism . . . Sammy Davis Jr. is a black Jew who just adopted Judaism, and that's his religion . . . But I'm talking about Israelites, the descendants of the Biblical Israelites."[2]

Journalists might have confused the two, and sometimes still do, calling self-professed Israelites Jews, but it was one of the first things those Israelites wanted people to understand.

"We never said that we were Jews like that," Shaleahk Ben Yehuda argued, "and we didn't convert to Judaism according to their doctrine of Halakhah. We didn't go through any conversion."

This purported difference between Jews and Israelites, conversion and descent, was something of an odd peculiarity for interested parties in the United States during the latter half of the 1960s, but it would have the profoundest consequences for the AHIJ community once they finally left America. When they made their way to Israel, policing the distinction would be their main worry—and of gnawing concern to the Israeli state.

The early black Israelites in Chicago were often labeled all kinds of things. To some, they were simply black Jews, their adamant protestations notwithstanding. To others, they were more like unorthodox Christians, especially given their embrace of the New Testament and the messianic role of *Yeshua*/Jesus. When they first arrived in Liberia in 1967, the local press called them Muslims, ostensibly because of the way they dressed, which seemed akin to what journalists thought of as Islamic or Arabic attire. But the black Israelites were unambiguous about what made them Israelites and about how they differed from all of those other groups.

For the black Israelite communities in Chicago during the 1960s, the story of their genealogical identity—and its existential significance— begins in Genesis with the birth of Abraham and Rebekah's twins, Jacob and Esau. After Noah's family replenished a flood-ravaged earth, Terah, Abraham's father, leaves Ur to relocate his kin in Canaan, a trip that Abraham must finish for him. Along the way, Abraham is duly tested by God (with the famous command to kill his beloved son, Isaac) and passes. Isaac is spared and grows up to give birth to Jacob, whom God renames Israel, forefather of His "chosen people." Abraham is the father of many nations, only one of which is Israel, founded by his grandson Jacob.

For the black Israelites leaving Chicago, the sons of Abraham and Isaac tell a foundational story about the specifics of their identity, one that counters earlier invocations of Noah's fatherhood as the moment when racial groups emerged. In the "Curse of Ham" version of Old Testament hermeneutics, a favorite of Christian slave masters in the antebellum South and long cited by Catholics and Protestants traveling the Atlantic since at least the fifteenth century, a drunken Noah's naked body is glimpsed by a disrespectful son, which gets that son rebuked with a curse darkening his offspring's skin, physically distinguishing them for easy enslavement. According to historian Winthrop Jordan and others, the Curse of Ham's links to black enslavement (and to Christian theories of racial genesis) were passed on from rabbis to Catholic scholars and priests, a theory of transmission that others dispute (and even dismiss as anti-Semitic).[3]

Israelites read things differently, starting with the premise that Noah and his sons were already "black" by modern standards. The creation of racial differences meant the emergence not of the world's first dark-skinned peoples but of its first "white"-skinned ones, the product of leprosy (as some Black Hebrew Israelite camps interpret things).[4] Abraham's other son, Isaac's brother from another mother, Ishmael, is considered the founding father of Islam. And one of Isaac's wives, Rebekah, would birth two more nations, Edomites and Israelites, the progeny of two brothers, Esau and Jacob, who would look, according to Israelites, racially different from one another. Colin Kidd makes the important point that the Bible mostly "tells us very little about the racial appearance of the figures and groups who feature within it."[5] So little, in fact, that it leaves the interpretive barn door wide open, he says, for readers to project their own racial ideas all over its relatively color mute pages.[6] The Bible does, however, describe rivalries between nations, and the King James Bible's description of Esau, Isaac's favorite son, as "red" and "hairy" becomes a visible distinction that grounds claims to Israelite racial difference—and to the fundamental links between race and nation.[7]

Esau starts to emerge from the womb first, destined for his father's inheritance, but Jacob clenches his twin brother's foot from behind, a move that would speak volumes about the nature of their relationship and how it was destined to unfurl, presaging the fact that Jacob eventually persuades his older brother to sell him the family birthright for some bread and lentils. When Jacob makes his demand, Esau, faint and close to death, has little choice. Jacob and Rebekah then conspire to trick an almost-blind Isaac into further blessing Jacob, instead of his intended

recipient, Esau, creating an elaborate scheme to fool the family patri-
arch, complete with costumes and Rebekah's flavorsome cooking. Isaac
doesn't suspect a thing, though he knows that the son standing before
him and preparing to receive a blessing sounds more like Jacob. He
blesses Jacob (thinking it is Esau) with a kiss anyway. "Let people serve
thee," he declares, "and nations bow down to thee: be lord over thy
brethren, and let thy mother's sons bow down to thee: cursed be everyone
that curseth thee, and blessed be he that blesseth thee."[8] No sooner has
Isaac bestowed his blessing on Jacob than Esau returns from a hunt to
witness the trick's denouement. The jig is up, but the damage has already
been done, and Isaac can't undo the blessing he has been tricked into
bestowing upon the wrong son. Jacob then flees for his life after hearing
his mother tell him that Esau is mad enough to kill him.[9]

The story of Jacob and Esau is pivotal to many Black Hebrew Israelite
discussions about their history and identity. The "hairy" and "red" Esau
and the smooth-skinned (non-red) Jacob are progenitors, they maintain,
of the white and black races respectively. They are brothers—twins, no
less—but they are also forefathers of different nations, kinship ties not
nearly strong enough to keep a family together that God would rip
asunder. According to many (if not most) Hebrew Israelites, European
Jews are Edomites, Esau's offspring, passing themselves off as Israelites,
"imposters" pretending to be Jacob's seed (or duped into believing as
much)—in effect, reversing the ruse pulled off by Jacob himself, imper-
sonating Jacob's people like Jacob impersonated Esau, returning the
favor from so long ago. It is this "imposter Jew" rhetoric that Bayard
Rustin highlighted in his discussion about whether or not Ben Ammi
and the community were "digestible," supposing that they may still
believe such things even if, by 1981, Ben Ammi had already started to
claim otherwise.

Speaking to the 1944 graduating class of Talladega College in Alabama,
W. E. B. Du Bois used the story of Jacob and Esau as an object lesson.[10]
A Marx-inspired attack on capitalist exploitation the world over, Du
Bois's commencement address paints a "very unfavorable" picture of
Jacob, not Esau, an impression that Du Bois claims to have held since

first hearing the story as a child in Sunday school. For Du Bois, the story of Jacob and Esau is the story of "spiritual descent." It exposes "the poison of the Jacobean idea" that stealing, lying, and cheating for nation, empire, and personal wealth are to be applauded. Jacob is actually more like the forefather of greedy tyrants, slave-masters, and imperialists from all around the world, Du Bois declares, but especially for "the white world of Europe and America," people "who owned the birthright of the masses by fraud and murder." Why, Du Bois asks, do we make a hero out of a man like Jacob, a cold and calculating usurper willing to lie, cheat, and steal, "whether his cause was just or unjust." This lionizing of Jacobean tactics, argues Du Bois, created space for transatlantic chattel slavery, for the decimation of aboriginal people in the old New World, and for the callous exploitation of industrial workers across the globe.

Although Du Bois saves most of his venom for Jacob, he does realize that "neither was perfect, but of the two, Esau had the elements which lead more naturally and directly to the salvation of man; while Jacob, with all his crafty planning and cold sacrifice, held in his soul the things that are about to ruin mankind: exaggerated national patriotism, individual profit, the despising of men who are not the darlings of our particular God, and the consequent lying and stealing and killing to monopolize power."[11]

THIRTY-TWO

Soul

BEN AMMI'S FULL-TIME presence in Liberia by 1968 helped to boost morale, but everyone continued to feel the financial pinch, very tangible difficulties that resulted from the lack of resources. Several men in the community were, like Ben Ammi, veterans of the American military, so they had some basic training in survival skills, but this wasn't supposed to feel like the throes of combat. If anything, Liberia was envisioned as an escape from the horrors of Babylonian warfare, from the humiliations and brutalities of American racism. It was supposed to be a glorious new start. Instead, they had exchanged a metaphorical wilderness for a literal one, and it wasn't necessarily clear that they had traded up.

On top of that, everything was so much more difficult with children in the mix. Adults might be able to tough it out on their own, some of them, but they would almost break down and cry when they thought of the pain and suffering their little ones were going through. Unable to take it anymore, a few more community members chose to sever ties with the camp and pick up work in nearby factories. One gave up his Hebrew name and took a job with Liberia's top pineapple exporter, leaving with an invention he'd crafted that spaced seeds for planting.[1] Still others began their humbled journeys all the way back home, back to America, defeated and denied, inconsolably frustrated by the slow pace of improvements in what was supposed to be an African refuge.

For those who stayed, soul music would be a small lifeline, specifically the exploits of a traveling R&B group, the Soul Messengers. One of the Israelite émigrés was Charles Hezekiah Blackwell, who, along with some of his family members, was an early supporter of Ben Ammi. He would also be the person that Bayard Rustin quoted, over a decade later, as unabashedly committed to the idea that European Jews were imposters, even after Ben Ammi had publicly disavowed such views.

Blackwell had been a bass player for the Metrotones, a studio band for one of Chicago's most successful musical families, the Leaners, and during the mid-1960s, before Ben Ammi and the community left for Liberia, Blackwell's group had played back-up for a string of major dance hits.[2] Hezekiah, Thomas "Yehuda" Whitfield, and John "Shavat" Boyd made up the core of the Soul Messengers, a group that, out of a desire to help the Liberian contingent stay afloat, would start playing music in Monrovia, eventually touring other parts of Africa and Europe and sending a portion of their profits back to the camp. The "all things in common" credo that grounds the Kingdom's Redemptive Entrepreneurialism started with saints moving to Liberia, and the Soul Messengers were an early example of that ethos, becoming one of the community's most important means of financial support. The money they contributed was sorely needed, but it was not nearly enough.

Saints would learn to say that this was about more than just community finances. Yah was preparing them to think of pooling resources as a divine mandate. He was also cultivating the Kingdom's reliance on music as an invaluable gift, something to be cherished and treated with care, transforming it into what saints would eventually call Divine Music. That long-term goal would get institutionalized in 1996 with the founding of the Lion of Judah Messianic Musicians' Hall of Fame and Institute "for the Continued Research and Development of Messianic Sound." A pamphlet announcing the launch included a discussion of "Kingdom

Sound," which is "composed with the objective of returning mankind to a rejuvenated awareness of the spirit and to the true worship of God." In his 1982 book *God, the Black Man and Truth*, Ben Ammi had already described music as "a series of thought waves that cause men to think and do right or wrong, wise things or foolish things."[3] There is a "musical sound that can destroy the mind," he warned, and Kingdom Sound was an answer to that threat. It was, according to the 1996 launch, a way for "the priestly musician" to demonstrate "a manner of prayer and praise of the Creator." Using Hebrew, "the original Holy tongue," and "tap[ping] into the music of the great King David," Kingdom Sound would be "an integral part of the Universal Corrective Force that establishes a new musical concept to cycle sound back unto God," a divine extension of the musical virtuosity the early saints like Blackwell took with them to West Africa. Eddie/Eitan Butler's Eurovision opportunities blossomed from the kernels of that same commitment. As do all the many CDs that saints have produced over the years, acts like the Sons of the Kingdom, Zehorah, Shadaiyah, Anavyah, and (most famously) the New Jerusalem Fire Choir—CDs all produced and manufactured by *kfar*-based Redemptive Enterprises such as Royal Kingdom Productions, King Conga Productions, and Positive Music Works Records.

Several of the Soul Messengers' original tunes were re-mastered and rereleased in 2008 by a Chicago-based company specializing in "dragging brilliant recordings, films, and photography out of unwarranted obscurity."[4] The liner notes for that 2008 CD, *Soul Messages from Dimona*, explain the significance of the group's Liberian experience in the late 1960s through Hezekiah's recollections:

> His army experience had prepared him for settlement life, and his leadership was crucial to building Guryea's foundation. On the outskirts of the campsite, the unrest amongst the bush people that would lead to the revolution in 1980 was already growing, though this had surprisingly little effect on the unassuming settlers. Humbled by their new African home, they had none of the arrogance of the Americo-Liberians, which granted them accelerated acceptance in the bush.

Even if they did find some modicum of "acceptance in the bush," or simply local laborers appreciative of a few more economic opportunities than usual, it still wasn't enough. And in 1968, the Liberian government, headed by those same "arrogance"-filled Americo-Liberians, felt compelled to step in.

Press coverage of the Chicago Israelites was national news in Liberia back in 1967. By some accounts, those same news stories were what first informed several Liberian government officials that the group had even arrived. After hearing reports of how difficult a time the community was having in their unfinished compound, government emissaries inspected the camp and were flabbergasted by how poorly these Americans seemed to be doing. Their homes looked wretched and unfinished. Their children seemed malnourished and imperiled. They were having undocumented dealings with locals in the nearby "bush," some of whom would later take part in coups and countercoups (starting in the 1980s) predicated on the excesses/injustices of Americo-Liberian governance and ongoing neocolonial exploitation. According to some Israelites, this fledgling alliance between these new arrivals and the country's underserved peasantry more than anything else made Liberian officials even more troubled. It was probably a combination of all these factors that spurred the government into immediate action, and they made very public plans to intervene.

Given President Tubman's public advocacy for the struggling Americans, local officials would try to help as best they could—with expertise, supplies, financial assistance—but their biggest concern had to do with the community's relative isolation, just them and their workers/neighbors out there in "the bush." Members of the government were especially disappointed by this, the Americans' lack of integration. Tubman's excitement about diasporic relocation to Liberia had always been predicated on assimilation.

With those issues as a backdrop, negotiations began. Ben Ammi and the community refused to accept the government's offer. The state was going to waive a two-year probationary period for immigrants to gain citizenship if they would agree to disperse, to spread out across the country. Though the Israelites sometimes still talked about Liberian citizenship as their ultimate goal, especially when fielding questions from the American media, they were adamant about not becoming *cultural* Liberians. They were Israelites, and maintaining that identity meant keeping themselves a close-knit and insular community. That might have been plausible, some government officials thought, if these Israelites were thriving. It wouldn't be the best option, but they couldn't begrudge them their insularity if it came with genuine social success. But as Liberian politicians and bureaucrats assessed things, the American expats were barely holding on, and someone needed to make sure they didn't die out there, which would have been a scandal of international proportions, embarrassing and disheartening for everyone involved. To avoid that, the decision was made that these Americans would be provided with more governmental assistance and actively monitored until their situation showed real improvement. For less sympathetic members of the Liberian elite, this might have been the time to toss all of them, potential political troublemakers, right out of the country. But Tubman and his allies, still hoping that the group might eventually blend into the larger Liberian population, would win the day.

Though their lives were tough in Liberia during the late 1960s, the community also believed that the international media was mischaracterizing their situation. So, they made public pronouncements describing reports of their starvation and suffering as overblown and exaggerated. "Oranges are a penny," they'd tell journalists, "and bushels of bananas are a quarter."[5] At those prices, how could they be doing all that badly?

Back in Chicago, Rabbi Devine and the old guard Israelites who had tried to convince these folks not to leave in the first place felt vindicated by the news reports—and would offer up a version of "I told you so" to any reporters soliciting comments on the matter. Some of the returnees to Chicago provided even more pointed tales of disease and destitution in the camp, and media coverage oscillated between two poles: stories about how poorly the community was doing and others highlighting their bold creation of an amazingly holistic lifestyle, but the latter narratives were also sprinkled with comments about the unbelievable difficulties that their everyday lives entailed.

Despite such adversities, at sundown every Friday, the *shofar* (horn) would blow to mark the start of Shabbat within that Liberian group (that *shofar*, saints would remind me, being yet another manifestation of ancient Israel's deep appreciation of music's sacred character), and they wanted to believe that each week they continued to press on, to obey Yah's laws, to stay the course, they were cleansing themselves of more and more American muck, being rebuilt, recharged, and regenerated by the ordeals of Liberian life. They would continue to submit to Yah, follow His commandments, and listen to the Spirit. Those who returned to the United States, they said, must have left America for the wrong reasons in the first place. They weren't ready. They weren't chosen. God was sifting, separating wheat from chaff. And those who trusted God were being prepared for the next stage of their divinely predetermined journey.

THIRTY-THREE

Laughing

CAROLYN ROUSE KEEPS reminding me to think more seriously about the ethnographic significance of humor, most recently at an American Anthropological Association conference. We were on a panel together, and she spent some of her time talking about ethnographies that made her laugh, productively and profoundly, even while treating dreadful and tragic subjects. Her point resonated with many of the people in that room. The very idea made some audience members smile.

Anthropologists, she argued, shouldn't underestimate how much humanity's existential difference is constituted, at least in part, by our uncanny ability to find the smallest, incongruous comedic pathway through even the most horrific situations, a capacity hinted at and colloquialized in the vernacular adage about "laughing to keep from crying." But this is not just laughter as a form of repression and strategic amnesia, although that clearly gets bundled into what the phrase implies. The laughter Rouse was talking about also indicates a kind of vulnerable and vernacular pleasure that ethnographic accounts can document, a pleasure that pivots on people's stubborn recognition of their own continued worth despite external threats of devaluation and marginalization. Even because of such threats. Antaeus, the Libyan giant of Greek mythology, epitomized one version of this paradoxical endowment. In battles, he only got stronger each time his opponents slammed his body into the earth.

An argument for the anthropological value of humor demands that ethnographies not only "break your heart," a differently compelling proposition.[1] Ethnographic work might also actively solicit a kind of compassionate and empathetic guffaw at the many ways in which people hold fast to a robust sense of self, fending off a dehumanizing slide into the anguished and pathological embrace of one-dimensional victimhood. The social exchanges at ethnography's core are justification for rethinking the implications of research based on cultivating intimate relationships with people, individuals who are never just victims or victimizers. This process is only vulgarized with apolitical euphemisms about "building rapport," a phrase that walks right up to the outer edges of a discussion about ethnographic sincerity and insincerity but refuses to go further. What is this "rapport," which anthropologist George Marcus famously marked as "complicity," and what are its implications for "everyday ethnography," an ethnography conducted every single day, not magically cordoned off into neat packages of time and space—a well-partitioned year in, say, West Sumatra or West Harlem?[2]

Anthropology continues to be a fiendishly self-reflexive discipline, a trait only heightened and refined in the 1980s and 1990s, back when anthropologists and their critics laid bare some of the rhetorical strategies that produce certain kinds of textual plausibility. Even though those critical gestures sought to engage all of the ethnographic experience, the finished monograph (maybe a too-easy and reified prey) was the thing most often pedestalized for subsequent toppling in those discussions— over and against a more sustained set of conversations about the quotidian, affect-laden and ethical demands of working the intimate hinges of all ethnographic encounters. Of course, "the field" was constantly invoked and theorized, its messiness sometimes flattened out and papered over, though a different kind of flattening than we might advocate for. Anthropology has done a lot of thinking about the politics of cultural representation, and that ongoing thoughtfulness continues to push the traditional limits of our writerly genre in productive, challenging, and sometimes wonderfully frustrating ways. But I want to offer up what I've been calling "ethnographic sincerity" to suggest the epistemological and political importance of focusing an analytical eye on potential problems that accrue from underappreciating the substantive relationships forged between anthropologists and those they anthropologize—relationships that are only more complicated for "everyday ethnography," an "everything is ethnography" mode that doesn't find much solid ground for standing outside of an expanding and digitized field.

It has become *de rigueur* to invoke the politics (not to mention the ethics) of participant-observation, anthropology's quintessential methodological gesture, its inadequacies and mystifications almost too ripe for justifiable picking, especially given common stereotypes (fair or not) about the discipline's traditional unwillingness to formally and systematically train students in ethnographic methods. Even as recently as the 1990s, when I was still in graduate school (and getting advised against the idea of conducting ethnographic research anywhere in America), would-be cultural anthropologists were still being taught to envision fieldwork as a kind of trial by fire, a rite of passage you didn't prepare for so much as simply endure, by the seat of your pants. Certainly, we registered for mandated courses that required us to write research proposals delineating our approach to ethnographic fieldwork and linking our immersion in a particular geographical locale to a larger set of anthropological questions and concerns, but we didn't really operationalize things much more than that. And how could we? At least that's how a version of the argument went. Each student plops down in such a distinctive political, cultural, and social world, making the experience of fieldwork an unpredictable cocktail, which only becomes more capricious when combined with the idiosyncrasies and psychologies of all the individuals involved, dissertators conducting their research and research subjects enlisted to take part.[3] Fieldwork is often considered a kind of hazing process, one with a discrete structure to it: a beginning (of culture shock and discomfort), a middle (of normalization and that aforementioned "rapport-building"), and a definitive end (of saying good-byes, packing up gear, and heading back home). There was something reassuring about ethnographic research conceptualized in this way, as time outside of time—and on a strict timetable (as laid out in grant proposals). One year. Maybe two. Light always already hardwired into the end of that ethnographic tunnel.[4]

These days, when students ask me to parse the difference between urban anthropologies and urban sociologies, which they still sometimes do, I often begin my answer with a claim about discrepancies between how these two social sciences frame the ethnographic project itself, our respective assumptions about, say, *methodological rigor* and *validity*. We can both "do" ethnography, but the differences are sometimes striking. And we occasionally see that quite conspicuously in the disparity between sociological appendices (that take us through a step-by-step unfurling of methodological maneuvers) and an arguable anthropological privileging of textual offerings that can sometimes make the methodological back-stage (the specific *whos, how manys,* and *for how longs*) a little more murky, a technique for both enthroning "theory" and maybe even protesting, at least orthogonally, genuflections to the presumed superiority of bench sciences and their representational conventions.

We can see that same disciplinary difference, more or less explicitly, on just about every single page of most ethnographies. It might sound unnecessarily provocative, even ludicrous in its overstating of the matter—laughably so—but I want to believe that some of these disciplinary dissimilarities stem from the fact that anthropology is (potentially, at least) a more hopeful (or, even better, hope-filled) disciplinary formation than sociology, using "hope" in ways that lean lightly upon Vincent Crapanzano's attempt to proffer that term as a powerful analytical rubric for reimagining ethnographic possibility, even if many reasonable anthropologists might reject it.[5]

In distinguishing desire from hope, while conceding their ongoing and sloppy (if somewhat understandable) conflation in the scholarly literature, Crapanazano notes social theory's relative underappreciation of *hope.* It is too cagey, protean, ephemeral, and autonomous to be domesticated into the kinds of claims that provide anthropological theorists with a modicum of certainty or predictability. "In its worldly manifestations," he writes, "[hope] may be quite specific, edging on desire, as when a lawyer hopes to win a case or a father hopes to have a daughter. Or it may be open-ended, lacking final definition, vague . . . and subject to chance."[6] Its expansiveness is an asset that, for some, only muddies the ethnographic waters. And then there is the inescapably seductive danger of "false hope," against which Crapanzano calculates true hope as a fusion of realism with "social change, progress, and even revolution."

My take on sincerity's ethnographic significance would jerry-rig questions of realism and methodological possibility to Crapanzano's ambitious reclamation of hope as an invaluable anthropological rubric. It is a version of this hope that allows, I would argue, for that laughter-in-the-face-of-calamity that Rouse demands. We are talking about the importance and inescapable ordinariness of affect, something central to an ethnographic praxis that is always funny and traumatic, extraordinary and mundane. It emphasizes some of how anthropologists and their informants embody an equally affect-saturated subjecthood during the ethnographic (especially the "everyday ethnographic") encounter.

"The politics of ordinary affect," writes Kathleen Stewart, "can be anything from a split second when police decide to shoot someone because he's black and standing in a dark doorway and has something in his hands, to a moment when someone falls in love with someone else who's just come into view. Obviously, the differences matter. The politics of any surge depends on where it might go. What happens."[7] Indeed, "what happens" (or doesn't) in the "split second" when ethnographic sparks start flying, the very sparks that ignite the intersubjective collisions that produce "data" for a discipline that might best define its divergence from other forms of social scientific research (at least in their overly scientist iterations) as a way of "marking time" between a transparent version of ethnographic research and an alternative black box of feedback loops, inter/subjective contaminations, thinking natures, thinned-out descriptions, flattened field-sites, a not-so-mere chance, and artscience? This is an anthropology that no longer just flies headlong into the delusional fantasy of political self-evidence and clarity. Instead, it tries to heed Virginia Dominguez's call to rescue anthropology from a creeping hopelessness by paying particular "attention to the presence or absence of love and affection in our scholarship—at all stages in the production of our scholarship."[8]

My too-quick leaps (of faith?) from humor to hope to affect to love are, in part, attempts at flagging a conceptual distinction between sincerity and authenticity, two related lenses for spotting "the real" and its varying implications. In a way, the "writing culture" moment proffered "authenticity" as a Trojan horse for falsified renditions of ethnographic authority, and its privileging of ethnographic authority-making (by critiquing it) necessitates that we ask ourselves "what happens" when we move our discussion of realism's stakes from authenticity to its "cognate ideal," as Lionel Trilling put it, sincerity.[9] What do we gain, and what do we lose? Why? How might the shift offer a drastically newfangled commitment to ethnographic work itself? And all of this is especially important to think about for a few reasons. First, there is something about the distance between sincerity and insincerity (not to mention sincerity and authenticity) that always separates a good joke from a bad one, which means that an ethnographic approach intending to value laughter (even among seemingly more urgent sobs and screams) might gain from parsing those differences very carefully (the very call of thick description). And second, it is impossible to do research on the AHIJ and not recognize that even the most sacred spaces allow for a sense of humor (saints always willing and able to offer up a joke about the ridiculousness of contemporary cultural assumptions) and that many nonsaints who first hear about the AHIJ's atypical beliefs are prone to laugh at their antics. In both instances, everybody is laughing (again, to keep from crying)—and mostly about different aspects of the very same thing.

THIRTY-FOUR

Occulted

Paschal Beverly Randolph was a self-educated African American born in Manhattan in 1825.[1] He was raised on a patch of what was then a teeming, soot-filled slum known as "Five Points," a neighborhood where several of the city's most dangerous and sometimes bloody streets intersected. A tragedy far from unusual for the time period, Randolph's mother died of cholera when he was only six years old, during the epidemic of 1831, and the tale of his father, of "the Virginia Randolphs," seems to have been made up, by Randolph himself, out of little more than wishful dreams.

Despite humble and poverty-stricken beginnings, by 1855 Randolph was a world-renowned transatlantic sex magician and spirit medium who practiced alchemy, numerology, and various forms of astral-projection. He was also a proto-anthropologist of the first order. His mid-nineteenth-century research trips throughout Western Europe, North Africa, and other parts of the Ottoman Empire netted him powerful fetish objects, potent talismans: magic mirrors that he magnetized for clairvoyance (to gaze into the future and the past) by carefully ejaculating on their surfaces; hashish that he ingested to free himself from earlier "slavery" under the negatively "vampiric" powers of spirit mediumship; and a variety of crystals, magnets and newly learned meditative techniques that allowed practiced men to engage in sexual intercourse for extraordinary amounts of time, techniques he sold through the mail as part of his "sex science" system—and for approximately $5 a secret.

As a medium, Randolph channeled historical figures such as Benjamin Franklin, John Adams, Martin Luther, and Socrates to aid in the abolitionist cause, using these long-dead spirits to rail against the injustices of racial slavery and female disenfranchisement.[2] Even after Randolph denounced his earlier commitments to spiritualism (which, he claimed, evacuated his soul and individual subjectivity, replacing them with "uncontrollably foreign forces") and began the occultist search he would bequeath to the likes of Madame Blavatsky, of Theosophical Society fame, his continued use of magic/mediumship as a civil and political tool in debates about the future of the nation-state, law, and governance were clear examples of the extent to which "the public sphere" was soaked through and through with more than just finely sifted rationalities.[3] As literary theorist Russ Castronovo argues, nineteenth-century America's pseudoscientific and unapologetically illogical politicking (the kind that Randolph exemplified) was actually aligned with political philospher Jürgen Habermas's own definitions of civic engagement, its privileging of disembodied and passively immaterial citizen-subjects, "human beings pure and simple," as Habermas put it, without any trace of the social baggage that physical embodiment produces: sexuality, gender, race, class, ethnicity, religion.[4] A politics, in a sense, without the flesh or the spirit. Habermas's public sphere was always what Castronovo labels an "occult public sphere," demanding that participants embrace a form of humanity stripped of everything that gives social intercourse its specificity and value, bereft of everything that makes human beings human.[5]

As others have pointed out, the common caricatures we proffer of Habermas and the forms of sociality that he conceived as being birthed from a thoroughly modern public sphere are complicated models of political possibility.[6] We readily invoke a Habermas who glimpsed the emergence of a modern public sphere in European coffeehouses about a century before Randolph first journeyed there, a public sphere supposedly enabled by capital and ordered by principles of rationality and reasoned debate. Habermas envisioned a civil conversation hostile to status-based authorities, immune to unfalsifiable claims, purged of groundlessly unexamined or superstitious beliefs, and disentangled from parochial biases of various kinds. Of course, many scholars have argued that irrationality and exclusionism (far more pronounced than Habermas recognized) has long informed the public sphere as a discursive and political space, but Castronovo's wrinkle also emphasizes the degree to which Habermas himself constructs a public sphere that sneaks occultlike properties and priorities through the back doors of those very same eighteenth-century coffeehouses.

Randolph followed famous clairvoyants and spiritualists, such as Andrew Jackson Davis and John Murray Spear, people who combined mesmerism and Swedenborgianism into a spiritualist praxis complete with séances, automatic writing, spirit channeling, crystal gazing, and other techniques for communicating with the deceased. At the time, these techniques also included spirit photography, the practice of documenting and capturing communiqués between the living and the dead in pictures.

The process of communicating with dead spirits (whether photographed or not) was considered, according to cultural historian Jeffrey Sconce, a kind of spiritual telegraphy—the telegraph, back then, a new and seemingly magical device allowing Americans to talk with one another across vast geographical distances.[7] And the deployment of science (electricity, magnetism, physics, biology, etc.) served as backbone to the new mass media undergirding claims for spritualism's legitimacy. It took photography only about ten years to hitch a ride unto the spiritualist bandwagon, and by the mid-1880s, photography was being institutionalized as a genre of transparently self-evidential fact in legal proceedings even as spiritualists used the same photochemical principles to capture the ephemeral movement of spirits and their smoky auras.[8] And this distinction was always couched as a difference between fact and fiction, science and hucksterism, (false) hopes and in/sincerities hanging in the balance: spiritual photographers reduced to insincere frauds preying on the naïve hopefulness of the living's "cruel optimisms."[9]

The history of photography has long wended its way around this difference between iconic/indexical properties and more fancifully artifi-
cial/rhetorical ones. Theorist Roland Barthes offered up one of the most
interesting musings on the inextricable linkages between photography
and magic—even as he further canonizes the medium's claim to self-
evidential and transparent "proofing," of authenticating "what was
there" over and against the constructedness of artistic "representation."[10]
Barthes distinguishes the "studium" (obvious and conspicuous aspects
of what any photograph objectively captures, including cultural contexts
informing and surrounding the subject matter depicted in the image)
from the more romantic and subjective (and individualized) "punctum"
of a photographic image, a wounding and pricking of the viewer by that
invisible and repressed subject of all photographs: death itself. This is a
punctum that emerges, unpredictably, from portions of the photographs
themselves, as though a product of their own volition in tandem with the
idiosyncratic sensibilities of specific viewers. And again, according to
Barthes, all photographs are spirit photographs. No matter what they
ostensibly depict (the embrace of lovers, a tractor in a field, children
playing soccer), they are really just showing us death, the dead, ourselves as always already dead. Little more than pictorial archives of our
own existential impermanence. An entire Marlon Riggs film in every
snapshot.

And Barthes wants to have it both ways: photographs as magical and
"private" readings (looking at a photo, he says, is always a personal
viewing) as well as a factual authentication of what was—that which has
been. Even though his assessment still traffics, partially, in some realist
assumptions, it is that same indexical realism that allows the photographic image to signal our own pending doom. We are already looking
at a ghost, seeing death, spying a reminder of our own too-soon demise.
No matter what the studium of the picture showcases, we are always
simply watching our own obliteration, something like that time-traveling
guinea pig in Chris Marker's 1963 film *La Jetee,* the one who, as a child,
witnesses himself getting killed as an adult—an image he can never get
out of his head, even before he finally deciphers its true meaning. He is
the poster child for Kara Keeling's nonlinear malaise. And this marking
of death is a fact as self-contained as the sixteenth-century double-ledger

bookkeeping that Mary Poovey characterizes as equally a function of discursive force and self-delusion—not just simplistically self-evident and indisputably numerical truths about an economic world of hard and fast material items existing beyond the bounds of its carefully scribbled-on pages.[11]

Randolph doesn't seem to have been an avid practitioner of spirit photography, but he did consider his sperm-soaked magic mirrors "a sensitive surface upon which the attendant dead could, can and do, temporarily photograph whatever they choose to." If talking to the dead was explicitly considered telegraphy, even Randolph's magic mirrors could be understood as would-be photographic surfaces for the mechanical reproduction of spiritual realms, spaces where an occultist proto-anthropologist conjured up a disembodied other, seeing through that other's eyes, speaking with its voice.

Photographs also provide a suggestive example for parsing the analytical space between authenticity and sincerity. For most people (other than Barthes, perhaps), it would seem odd and illogical to call a photograph sincere or insincere. They might consider the photographer or the photographed subject sincere or insincere, but the inanimate photos themselves are less obviously capable of such self-conscious subterfuge. If anything, the sincerities of the people involved (photographers, photographed subjects, and even third-parties sizing up the finished products) are assumed to authenticate or de-authenticate the photograph: in the case of "spirit photographs," either as genuine reflections of spiritual communication (spirits leaving their photographic likenesses on a rickety séance table) or as purposeful effects of a camera operator tampering with the film for monetary gain or public notoriety.

Though obviously connected in some fundamental ways, the in/authenticity of the photograph and the in/sincerity of the photographer translate into a cavernous divide. When Paschal, for one, turns his back on spiritualism (or a version of it) in the 1850s, it is precisely because he wants to defend himself from the inanimate nature of mere photographs, from being spiritually and subjectively evacuated, rendered nonconscious, left empty and open for another agential being (from another

dimension) to control. In fact, he claims to have spent much of the first
half of his entire life under the thumb of hostile spiritual entities, a
somatic automaton unable to refuse the commands of powerful aliens
from other spheres.[12] As a response to that spiritual enslavement, his
form of occultism emphasized the active and purposeful use of magic
forces (as opposed to just mediumship/self-thingification). Randolph
justified renunciation of his prior spiritualist practices by maintaining
that he didn't want to be reduced to a receptacle for others' subjectivities,
a different version of Peter Schwenger's tear-filled thing, just a photograph-
esque reflection of another's reality.[13]

Randolph was far too proactive for that. He spent the Civil War, for
example, agitating for abolition, even if he sometimes seemed to flinch at
more radical stances on the matter held by the likes of Frederick Douglass
and William Lloyd Garrison, both duly impressed by Randolph's intel-
lect and rhetorical abilities. The Civil War, of course, saw a major uptick
in spirit photography, because people wanted to speak to dead relatives—
especially those soldiers killed in battle. And they also just wanted to *see*
them, to take one last look at their fallen fathers, husbands, and sons.[14]
The end of the Civil War was also a watershed moment for Randolph.
He used the era's newfound potential (and racial optimism) to segue
from spiritualism to more mundane (and this-worldly) exploits (prior to
his subsequent occultist turn), moving to New Orleans and teaching
newly freed slaves how to read and write—that is, until wealthy Creoles
drummed him out of town for his odd Christianity, a version still steeped
in Randolph's desire to fend off external forces threatening to deny him
sovereignty.

Many anthropologists call for a more relevant anthropology, for a
renewed guildwide investment in the political implications of our efforts,
and for a greater appreciation of what can happen when cultural research
and political activism meet. To achieve this (and to deploy it most
humanely), we should also think about the many ways in which the political potential of anthropological engagements necessitates more than just
a form of Habermasian reductionism, more than abstracted and disembodied (fleshless) figures haunting ethnographic field-sites. Any longing
for a postracial, asexual, and ambitiously universal ethnographic researcher
privileges an apparition that further occults the entire anthropological

project. It pretends that the ethnographer can be a kind of ghost in the cultural machine, floating at some remove from the fray, except as the proponent of research-based sociopolitical claims.

This is hardly the stuff of what I'd call everyday ethnography. Our investments in ethnographic research and writing shouldn't fall prey to that brand of occultist (which Randolph would call "spiritualist") evacuation—and no matter how popular such aspirations have become in the age of a reactionary postracialism and an abundance of female prime ministers. Not to mention America's first black president.

Paschal Randolph's public sphere is still an "occult public sphere," but it fights for a sloppy and irreducibly somatic existence over an abstract and dematerial emptiness of any kind. It demands to be taken seriously and laughed at, productively, in the selfsame instant. We need a notion of anthropology that is committed to the detritus of ethnographic practice, and that constructs a scholarly endeavor that will not finesse its interpersonal manipulations and machinations with antiquated and nonreflexive rhetoric about "rapport" as some kind of mystical mind-melding, ethnographic angels communicating without the noises and distractions caused by physical embodiment, noises and distractions like race, sexuality, and gender.[15] This would be the beginning of a radically engaged (in every sense of the term) everyday ethnography disconnected from the reifications and dehumanizations that sometimes pass for politics all along the ideological spectrum. It could be an anthropology that better facilitates cultural critique and collaborative action by way of the empathetic connections that sharing a laugh, even in the face of certain death, implies—let alone a laugh that some might not be able to suppress when hearing about the seemingly bizarre idea of making death itself far less certain to begin with.

THIRTY-FIVE

Order

THE POLITICAL STRUCTURE of the African Hebrew Israelites of Jerusalem begins with Ben Ammi at the top. As messiah, his edicts carry absolute authority. The Kingdom is far from a democracy, and Ben Ammi has preached (at New World Passover ceremonics and on many other special occasions) about the evil presuppositions of democracy. "Western democracy is marked by a relentless hostility towards Divine authority," writes Ben Ammi, "and without respect to that authority as a means of ensuring law and order, society is bound to fall apart."[1] At a time when everyone seems to publicly laud the value of democratic life, even those who might secretly try to subvert it, Ben Ammi and the saints are not shy about demonizing democracy for authorizing the masses, an ungodly legion, in their attempt to rule the day at the expense of Yah's clear, explicit, and top-down laws.

Ben Ammi makes decisions about AHIJ rules and goals through prayer to the Most High and in consultation with his council of Twelve Princes. The council is one of Ben Ammi's most important political creations, part of a 1973 project to streamline the Kingdom's political system by formally incorporating other elders (including, according to some scholars, potential competitors for leadership) into key authority positions within the community, positions that answer to Ben Ammi.[2] The Princes help translate Ben Ammi's pronouncements and precepts into specific policy mandates that community members follow: from foundational truths about the particularities of their vegan practices (explaining, say, the required number of "live days" per week and reinforcing the importance of praying in Hebrew before every meal) to recent attempts at lower cell phone use among saints out of fear for how radiation might impact the chemistry of the brain, which is ground-zero for the physiologico-spiritual production of heavenly or hellish realities.

Princes cover different specific domains within the community and have distinct titles, with Ben Ammi serving as the Prince of Peace, *Nasik HaShalom*. Nasik Asiel was "international ambassador" for the Kingdom until 2010. Prince Immanuel is a "national spokesperson" (one of three) and "director of international affairs" for the African Hebrew Development Agency (AHDA), their Israel-based NGO. Prince Rahm Ben-Yehuda is head of the Atlanta jurisdiction. And so on. Each of the Princes is a member of the "Holy Council of Elders," and some of the oldest Princes are also "Founding Members," such as Prince Gavriel HaGadol and the late Prince Shaleahk Ben Yehuda, who also started the School of the Prophets. The Council confers with Ben Ammi about important issues, providing advice and publicly championing new Kingdom policies.

The next level in the AHIJ hierarchy consists of Ministers *(Sareem)*, with each of them assigned to different Divine Ministries: Information, Education and Dedication, Distribution (tending to social welfare needs), Building and Maintenance, Transportation, Health, Performing Arts, Economics, Sports and Recreation, Agriculture, and Security. Once Ben Ammi and his twelve Princes decide on a new policy or revisions to an old one, Ministers must implement these directives, perhaps having to explain the details to saints throughout the Kingdom, as happened after the recent decision to have community members use cold-pressed oils exclusively for their increased nutritional value. Using less heat during the oil-making process means a lower yield overall (hence, a more expensive product), explains Sar Yadiel, Minister of Divine Agriculture, but it is much healthier for the body. All of this means training saints to tell the difference (with taste and touch) in an unregulated world where fake cold-pressed oils abound. The Ministers help to get this information out to the rest of the community while also thinking about how to operationalize those mandates into terms that saints can realistically incorporate into their daily routines. On average, Ministers aren't quite as old as Princes, but they are still relative elders in the community, saints who have a track record of discipline, Divine intelligence, and obedience to Yah.

When it comes to explicitly spiritual affairs, the *Cohaneem,* the Prophetic Priests, are trained in the School of the Prophets to preside over such matters.[3] Everyone can pray and ask Yah for assistance, and all of the community's cultural mandates are expressions of their spiritual commitments, but only priests lead Shabbat services, counsel saints preparing for Divine Marriage or beginning sacred unions, officiate at wedding ceremonies, perform circumcisions, read to expectant mothers during their final moments of pregnancy, and help saints to fully understand and internalize the biblically inspired wisdom of Ben Ammi, whose books demonstrate his reading of the Bible in ways that priests elaborate upon and extend.

The Princes, Ministers, and Priests are all exclusively men. And combined with the community's transnational/diasporic polygyny (male saints often having two or more wives, with some of those wives based in different jurisdictions around the world for many months of the year), the Kingdom recognizes how its gender politics look to outsiders, especially to African American women.[4] "The Sisters can have a hard time with that," one Brother on the *kfar* explains. "But we send them to the sisters, our sisters, in the Kingdom, and they can show them better than I can." Women are responsible, above all else, for taking care of their husbands, children, and households, "sister-wives" pooling resources and energy in that effort.[5] Women must do other things as well, especially to help sustain the household; everyone has a hustle, but those tasks begin after their most sacred duty to family is fulfilled. The Kingdom's "traditional"/patriarchal position on gender roles means that women cook meals, wash clothes, and keep households clean. They are also asked to teach younger sisters how to improve their own household

Members of the Prophetic Priesthood presiding over a collective prayer at the annual "Marriage of the Lamb" ceremony. *(Photograph by Crowned Sister Cattriellah eshet Rockameem.)*

skills. This, saints contend, is "the Adamic family," which necessitates a particular version of Eve, domestically minded even though diasporically mobile—responsible for taking care of "the home," even if the places she might calls home are in different parts of the world during different parts of the year.

After cofacilitating daily Brain Seminars in South Africa during the summer of 2012, one sister from Dimona, Sister Aturah, a summa cum laude graduate of the School of the Prophets, spent her mornings and evenings showing a local saint from Durban how to prepare different kinds of vegan dishes and drinks that they then used to feed the Dimona delegation those several weeks. The lessons would take place in the mornings, and the successful dishes would be wrapped up for bag lunches or distributed to the group of saints staying in different rooms of the South African woman's home. Female saints model a form of Divine Womanhood meant to counter stereotypical versions of black femininity in the United States, which is a part of the Kingdom's "holystic" approach to the eco-system: everything is interconnected, nothing is innocent or irrelevant. This is why one of Ben Ammi's writings (always sprinkled with excerpts from news stories and press releases—along with Bible passages) would feature an entire verse from the song "Independent Women," by platinum-selling recording group Destiny's Child, the verse that ends "Cause I'm my number one priority, no falling in love, no commitment from me." Given "soaring divorce rates" among African Americans, Ben Ammi asks, what should we make of "the new, feminine separatist vision where men are summoned only for specific needs so women do not have to care for them"?[6]

A Divine government, one that is "governed by men and women who are governed by God," functions without internal opposition.[7] It is not "a house divided against itself." Female saints are asked to submit to their husbands as part of their submission to Yah, a version of matrimonial relations not unfamiliar to many evangelical Christians. In the Kingdom, husbands have a responsibility to listen to and consult with their wives, to always respect and invite their counsel, but men make the final decisions. This reinvigorated Israelite masculinity (in the wake of longstanding discussions about African American men being emasculated in the United States) is another manifestation of the Kingdom's close-quartered relationship to an Afrocentrism that has long attempted to recuperate an African patriarchy supposedly dethroned by slavery and its aftermath.[8]

The functional unit of authority within the AHIJ is the patriarchal family, which usually covers several households—and can even cut across continents. In a scenario that is not at all atypical, one Minister's wife spent over nine months away from the *kfar* last year, away from her husband and family, helping to manage a Soul Veg restaurant in the United States. Other women spend similar amounts of time as consultants for saints in places like Ghana or Benin, where communities are trying to establish new small-scale clothing factories or health and fitness centers. Or a saint might court another wife in another part of the world without assuming that that woman—often a successful professional in her own right who must be wooed into polygamous marriage and the Kingdom simultaneously—will relocate to Dimona full-time. What saints are trying to cultivate, in a sense, is women with the skills and abilities to be "Independent" (in that Destiny's Child kind of way), but who choose not to be. A refrain often heard when explaining the role of AHIJ women is that "a woman can be anything . . . except a man."

The next category of formal social authority within the Kingdom, the first with female saints among its ranks, consists of community members who are charged with assisting Ministers in their efforts to put Ben Ammi's messianic edicts into daily practice—and to troubleshoot any unforeseen snags that might produce. Crowned Brothers and Sisters represent the front line of AHIJ's governmental bureaucracy, leaders closest to the ground and responsible for translations of divine truths into practical deeds and appropriate microdecisions. They help the Council of Princes and the Ministers oversee the everyday lives of the saints, "counseling, teaching and setting examples of unity and harmony." These saints do have quite a bit of authority and status among the rank and file, often running key operations or handling important, long-term assignments. For instance, the community's head public relations person (and primary Hebrew-language spokesperson), is a Crowned Sister with the authority to decide the terms upon which outsiders interface with saints on the *kfar,* helping to determine what representations of the Kingdom get captured and circulated.

"Men and Women of Valor," "Brothers and Sisters on the Move," and "Senior Brothers and Sisters" represent three additional categories ("orders") for active saints, categories formally deputizing them to assist in any efforts sanctioned by the Princes, Ministers, or Crowned Brothers and Sisters. "Men and Women of Valor" and "Brothers and Sisters on the Move" are merit-based orders, and although not sanctioned leadership, they are often the first places Ben Ammi will go to fill such positions.

The "Chosen First Fruit" consists of a cadre of younger adults who are said to "represent the first harvest of the *new world* order." They include members of the Second Generation and those that came later, saints born in Liberia or Israel or who were extremely young during the 1967 emigration. The "Chosen First Fruit" might be tapped at a moment's notice to help carry out all kinds of projects, large or small, reflecting the point that everyone has a role, or a potential role, in the Kingdom's organizational structure. Even teenage saints are members of the "Youth on the Move" and tasked with preparing themselves for a lifetime of service and obedience to Yah, to Ben Ammi, to their elders, and to the entire AHIJ community. Being a formal member of any of these groups is an important public recognition that has to be earned—and that can also be revoked.

If someone in a leadership position errs or engages in some activity that is deemed particularly inappropriate or unbecoming of his post, Ben Ammi might choose to place that person on "sabbatical" or strip him of his formal title, publicly marking him as censured. The person is supposed to reflect on whatever he did—or didn't do—to warrant a reprimand. The sabbatical is considered an "early intervention," an opportunity to "get it together." Several of the Ministers I know best have been in some way disciplined—publicly or otherwise—at least once during the past eight years, which means that they lose their more regular access to Ben Ammi and are unable to carry out the full duties of their office. Whenever this happens, other saints may have to step up their workloads for indefinite periods of time—the exact length, determined by Ben Ammi. In more serious situations, a Minister or Prince will be "set down," forbidden from standing before the saints in any teaching or counseling capacity whatsoever. Or they can even be removed from their posts altogether.

Prince Asiel's very public split with the community in 2011 began with a "sabbatical" he received in 2010. As Asiel describes things, he didn't even know that he was being reprimanded. He just quickly began to realize that his phone calls to Ben Ammi from overseas, the United States and West Africa, were no longer being answered or returned. He says that he spent many months trying to reach Ben Ammi, and at some point those unsuccessful attempts turned into a serious concern about what Asiel describes (to other "friends of the community" in Chicago and across America) as Ben Ammi's warping of the Kingdom's original vision, an original vision, he says, that they had all collectively initiated with their departure from Chicago.

By early 2011, Asiel was finally ready to make a public issue out of his sabbatical, calling for transparency and accountability within the AHIJ community. And he was doing this not just for himself, he said, but for all of his Brothers and Sisters in Dimona whom he described as living in relative fear and physical danger as a function of Ben Ammi's tight reign. Asiel narrates a tale of Ben Ammi ruling despotically, which he describes as one of the community's central problems. Ben Ammi shuts people out of the fold with impunity, he says, even a Prince who has served with him for over forty years. And these unilateral decisions, according to Asiel, go unchallenged.

Asiel's version of the Kingdom's actual political structure also places a large wedge between Ben Ammi and the Council of Princes, alleging that Ben Ammi actually removed the Princes as advisors quite some time ago. According to Asiel, Ben Ammi rules without their formal counsel at all. "We hadn't met in over fifteen years," he declared in an interview on one Chicago-based public-access show in October, 2011.[9] No matter what decisions are made, and no matter how potentially destructive to the community, Asiel says that Ben Ammi is able to rule with an iron fist and to the detriment of saints' well-being—even allegedly stopping the Israeli authorities from removing asbestos roofing panels from homes in the *kfar*, asbestos that has been banned in Israel for decades and that Asiel claims has been hurting and even killing saints for years. Asiel says that he wants to know why Ben Ammi stopped the removal, and why he has turned down several relocation sites that have allegedly been offered to the community as larger and more appropriate spaces for their growing Kingdom. Other saints reject Asiel's claim, touting Restoration Village (over 6,000 acres of land earmarked for them to build, according to AHIJ literature, "a full range of tourist attractions, an international health and wellness center, state-of-the-art sports facilities, over 300 housing units, extensive bio-organic agricultural development, a variety of cottage industries and much, much more" in Ghan Mamsheet National Park) as just such a space.[10] Asiel even talks obliquely about the supposed complicity—by nonaction—of several high-ranking saints in a case of alleged pedophilia within the community, a case currently winding its way through the Israeli court system.

Asiel admits that there are "rumors circulating" inside the *kfar* about his mishandling of Kingdom funds, but "no official charges" have ever been brought against him, and he wants to know why. His theory is that the rumors are an excuse to justify a move (his "sabbatical") that would otherwise have been unintelligible to saints given Asiel's long history with the Kingdom. At the same time, the deposed prince says that he doesn't want to reproduce "Cain and Abel's story," to be another public example of "Black men not agreeing among themselves." Think of the very public differences between Martin Luther King Jr. and Malcolm X, he says.

Asiel says, emphatically, that he doesn't want to elevate himself above Ben Ammi, that this was never his intention, even though he is sure that others have tried to convince Ben Ammi of just that. Still, he criticizes Ben Ammi for forgetting "that the people are the leaders, not him." He was chosen by acclamation of the people, Asiel says, a fairly serious affront to the notion of Ben Ammi's divine anointing—and a nod to democracy's potential value (another battleground—of political philosophy—on which this dispute is playing out). Asiel also maintains that he isn't "calling for followers" or declaring his separation from the Kingdom. "I'll always be a Hebrew Israelite," he says. "Nobody can take that away from me." Instead, he's asking for "open justice and transparency" so that the people know what decisions are being made on their behalf. He calls himself "the repairer" and says that he simply wants Kingdom reforms. "We didn't understand that democracy didn't mean anarchy," he reflects. "It means transparency."

And why, Asiel asks, would Ben Ammi allow the Kingdom's young people to enlist in the Israeli Army? The decision should have been brought to saints beforehand, he adds. Instead, he contends that Ben Ammi made that call on his own. "We went to Israel as peacekeepers," Asiel says. "Blessed are the peacemakers. To give them a gun at seventeen that could kill a man has traumatized the entire community. This isn't a personal thing between me and Ben Ammi. This is about the future of the Kingdom, and we must remove the fear associated with disagreeing with your brother. The children are suffering. The people are suffering. We need justice, due process, a constitution ratified by the people. That's all I'm saying to Ben Ammi, but he won't listen to me. He won't hear me. The Bible says that the sun must not set if two angry brothers don't sit and discuss their dispute. Or a third party should resolve it. It is in the interest of humanity." Asiel made these comments on a public-access television show in Chicago during Yom Kippur in

Youth of the AHIJ serving in the Israel Defense Forces in May 2010 participate in
the New World Passover youth parade in which they received a special tribute.
(Photograph by Crowned Sister Cattriellah eshet Rockameem.)

2011. He wanted to make his case to anyone who would listen, even if
Ben Ammi would not respond to his overtures.[11]

One recurring critique of the AHIJ, especially from other Israelite
camps, is their supposed deification of Ben Ammi, a critique that saints
dismiss as grossly inaccurate (even as Asiel seems to imply that such a
deification has, in fact, evolved over time). Members of the Kingdom call
Ben Ammi *abba* (father), and they have fewer opportunities to interact
with him than they do with other Princes.[12] That is true, saints admit.
Getting anointed by Yah makes Ben Ammi a sacred figure, someone who
merits being kept away from the profane, quotidian, and mundane
aspects of everyday life. Someone who must be protected from those who
would seek to "prevent the rise of the messiah". He is their messiah,
his face adorning community homes and businesses all over the world.
But he is not, they argue, Yah. He is Yah's anointed. Detractors call
this double-talk and semantics, but saints argue that Ben Ammi's

spiritual importance does not make him the God of Israel, just God's vessel, which is why he is loved, trusted, and worthy of being followed without hesitation.

One saint in the Philadelphia chapter, a relatively new member of the community who became increasingly estranged from his wife as he became more and more involved in the Kingdom, eventually getting a divorce, uses an occupational metaphor to explain things. "When people ask me about Ben Ammi," he tells me, across a stack of vegan pancakes at an all-you-can-eat vegan brunch in the extension's main facility, "I say to them, 'You have a boss at your job, right? Do you follow him? Do you listen to him? Do you do what he tells you do to? Why? Because he is in charge. He's the boss. It's the same thing. You don't think your boss on your job is God, but he doesn't have to be God to merit respect and obedience.' Some people can get it that way."

THIRTY-SIX

Genesis

S AINTS RESIDING IN Israel during the 1970s and 1980s lived lives fraught with all kinds of vulnerabilities. These were lives rife with elaborate and sometimes illegal schemes for financing members' clandestine return to Israel whenever some of them were periodically rounded up and deported, sent back to the United States by the Israeli government, which was an everyday fear within the *kfar*. Nasik Asiel and Sar Ahmadiel were both defendants in different American lawsuits brought against them for alleged criminal activities, crimes in service to attempts at bringing (or returning) saints to Israel from America as often as possible.

Ahmadiel fled to Israel in the early 1970s and avoided prosecution in the United States for over two decades before eventually going back to have those charges, effectively, dismissed as part of an elaborate plea-deal involving several more fugitive AHIJ members. According to Ahmadiel, the judge who presided over the case recognized his sincerity and acknowledged that everything he'd done was simply about ensuring the community's survival, not an expression of individualistic greed.

Ahmadiel maintains that even the FBI agent who met him at a New York City airport and escorted him to prison for a single night (before his meeting with the aforementioned judge) admitted, as did the lead prosecutor, that had they been in a similar situation ("black and oppressed"), they would have considered doing the same thing.

In the 1980s, a grand jury in Washington DC brought sixty-nine indictments against Nasik Asiel and eight other members of the AHIJ community (all of whom served as their own defense attorneys in court) "for conspiring to conduct the affairs of an enterprise through a pattern of racketeering activity."[1] The RICO (Racketeer-Influenced and Corrupt Organizations) laws had already been used to prosecute other religious groups, including other black Israelites, most famously, Yahweh Ben Yahweh's Florida-based community.[2] Asiel and his codefendants were charged with engaging in "shopping sprees" (opening checking accounts with fake IDs and paying for merchandise by writing checks that accounts linked to those IDs couldn't cover), stealing blank paper stock from airlines to produce counterfeit plane tickets, and attempting to attain welfare and social security benefits using fraudulent personal data. Nasik Asiel would serve five years in prison for a conviction, though the case was reversed on appeal because of the lower court's decision to discharge a juror (several weeks into the jury's deliberations) who informed the judge that he was unable to agree with the rest of the jurors' decision to convict. The appellate court ruled that Nasik Asiel and his codefendants had been denied their right to a unanimous decision. The lower court couldn't just replace a juror because he wouldn't go along with the rest of the jury.[3]

The community in Dimona has come a long way since then, partially evidenced in a million-dollar school building (exclusively for young saints in the Kingdom!) facilitated and financed by the U.S. Congress, testament to the fact that the AHIJ's public outreach efforts entailed cultivating more than just celebrity visits from the likes of Whitney Houston or purely symbolic photo-ops with African American politicians. And the days of saints being expelled from Israel for trying to find work are long gone. Members are also less interested in convincing more African Americans to move to Israel on a permanent basis (which community leaders agreed to stop promoting in exchange for a "normalization" of their relations with the Israeli state). Instead, the Kingdom's top priority seems to be mounting its own ambitious development projects throughout Eden (contemporary Africa).[4] And all of that development work is centered on a concerted effort to export their conceptualization of the human body's physiology and the notions of personhood, nationhood, and geopolitics that flow from it—anti-neocolonialist registers, for instance, framed by a discussion of African bodies being regenerated, holistically, through an Edenic veganism that is expected to revitalize the continent from within—economically, culturally, and spiritually.[5] Saints talk about the human body's seemingly superhuman potential as a way to wire nationality and spirituality to reimagined senses of diasporic and global community. Their ethnobiological contentions are part of a larger discourse about how bodies are made meaningful and powerful in the Kingdom. What need is there for USAID if Africans/Israelites would just follow Yah's commands? Environmental and economic revitalization would surely follow.

There are many points of entry into saints' rhetoric about bodies and embodiment, rhetoric with implications for mortality and membership. For instance, there is a complex calculus that determines which bodies are even "Hebrew Israelite" bodies in the first place—as opposed to, say, Ishmaelite or Edomite bodies. Bayard Rustin's distrust of Ben Ammi and the Kingdom stemmed from the community's articulation of authentic identity through the prism of "imposter Jews" whose very bodies (including pale skin supposedly ill-suited to the severe North African sun) gave them away. And remember the ICUPK Hebrew Israelites in New York City and their attempt to turn over a new leaf in the new millennium by rereckoning belonging, transforming their members from strict genealogists (who read patrilineality as the definitive and unyielding basis for authentic group membership) to advocates of an adamant antigenealogic. The latter was an emergent belief that the real prerequisite for Hebrew Israelite identity was not a black father, or any epidermal evidence of Blackness at all, only the readiness to hear and accept "Yah's message," regardless of an individual's social background, family tree, and physical features. That transformation, which took place at the end of the 1990s, may seem like a radical recalibration, a rerendering of identity for the once-in-a-lifetime *fin de siècle*, but it is also the very stuff that typical revisions are made of, paradigms ripped out at their roots as much as daintily pruned. Where previously the ICUPK espoused a precise racial and genealogical organizing principle for group acceptance, they subsequently decided to eschew any explicit determinations of membership based on racial logics. They reread Titus 3:9, which admonishes people to avoid "foolish questions, and genealogies," and an entirely new Israelite was born. That move from genealogy to antigenealogy already expresses the competing ways that many spiritual and religious groups mine the body's implications for belonging. Either its history and materiality determines one's legitimacy, or bodies are unreadable and spiritually unintelligible except as a function of their performances of faith and acceptance.[6]

In any discussion of Israelites and their valuations/revaluations of physical bodies, especially still-mortal bodies, it also makes sense to recall the case of the AHIJ's first victim of terrorism, the young musician killed in 2000 while playing with a band on Israel's northwest coast. The body, even and especially the deceased body, has real productive force. In fact, before that tragedy, the community decried how poorly they were being treated in Israel with public declarations about the forced burial of their dead in "a toxic waste dump." What, they asked, could be more inhumane than that? (In 1999, local officials began allowing saints to use a Dimona cemetery designated for non-Jews.)

This discussion of death, of the dead body and its implications, provides suggestive scaffolding for a different examination of Black Hebraic definitions of "the body," the "Adamic body," which the Kingdom labels "the Genesis Form." This is their explicit critique of evolutionary biology, reframed as the "devolution/degeneration of man," and starts with Adam's intended, hardwired immortality, an Adam, remember, who isn't the first person on Earth: "In *a* beginning . . ." not "In *the* beginning . . ." That's one of the same places where Paschal Randolph anchors his argument in an ambitious and iconoclastic rereading of both Genesis and the archeological record.[7] A proponent of polygenesis—the belief that different human groups have different origin stories (that all genealogical roads do *not* lead back to Adam and Eve)—Randolph offered a peculiar brand of abolitionism that did not defend African humanity by using the Bible to turn everyone on the planet into distant relatives, a common rhetorical move in abolitionist circles. Instead, he argued that Adam was just one progenitor among many, father of one set of peoples on Earth, which is the quintessentially AHIJ position on such matters. Relatedly, Randolph and the Kingdom are also in sync when it comes to interpreting "the apple" and "the serpent" from that tale. Randolph writes:

> The word translated "serpent" is "the Nachash," and it has at least forty meanings *besides* that of "serpent," and does not then mean a literal, spiteful, fanged, crawling snake, but a *snakish,* cunning thing. No snake ever yet talked either English or Hebrew, and never will. Eve's tempter was just such as one as in these days tempt other Eves, viz.: a snake on two legs, college-bred, and broad-clothed. It was a man! The word is a proper name, chosen for its fitness of application to Eve's human tempter, just as we do in these days. It means a "seducer," a "corruptor," and, on the supposition that the whole cosmological account is a record of real events, and not a mere tradition, legend or myth, it is clear that the Nachash was nothing more than a man of a different race from Adam, who succeeded in making Eve his victim, in some way that disagreed with her and her husband. This something given or administered to her, could not have been a material thing, or a fruit of any kind, but was some sort of knowledge that the couple had not previously possessed [emphasis in original].[8]

Much of Randolph's reading of this story, a corrective to what he dismisses as the long tradition of "accepting Rabbinical nonsense and blasphemy, for sacred wisdom and truth," rests close to the AHIJ's rereading of Genesis (not to mention their disregard for standard Rabbinical customs and traditions).[9] "Contemporary science declares [that] the existence of mankind extends millions of years prior to Adam," Ben Ammi writes in *Everlasting Life.* "However, if there were those that preceded this new Adam, God's objective was that Adam reflect the intervention of God's presence in the affairs of man." God brings "order" to "the chaos and confusion" of the Earth by breathing life into new kinds of human beings, giving them a new knowledge, creating a new world to

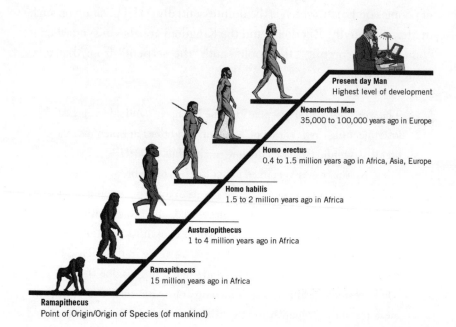

Present day Man
Highest level of development

Neanderthal Man
35,000 to 100,000 years ago in Europe

Homo erectus
0.4 to 1.5 million years ago in Africa, Asia, Europe

Homo habilis
1.5 to 2 million years ago in Africa

Australopithecus
1 to 4 million years ago in Africa

Ramapithecus
15 million years ago in Africa

Ramapithecus
Point of Origin/Origin of Species (of mankind)

The Evolution Paradigm that depicts one generally accepted path of modern man's "evolutionary development." The AHIJ do not subscribe to the theory of evolution, regarding it as an unfounded and deceptive construct. In this paradigm, material transformation is the focal point, leading man away from his true development, based upon biological, ecological, and social measures. However, the Kingdom's interpretation of Genesis leaves them also at odds with typical creationist glosses found in Christianity and Judaism. *(Designed by by Yaheerah eshet Sgan Ahdeev and Sapeer Ben Israel.)*

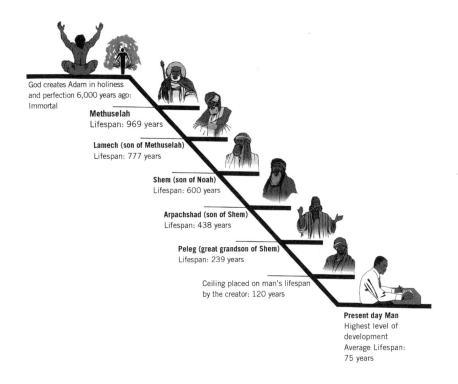

God creates Adam in holiness and perfection 6,000 years ago: Immortal

Methuselah
Lifespan: 969 years

Lamech (son of Methuselah)
Lifespan: 777 years

Shem (son of Noah)
Lifespan: 600 years

Arpachshad (son of Shem)
Lifespan: 438 years

Peleg (great grandson of Shem)
Lifespan: 239 years

Ceiling placed on man's lifespan by the creator: 120 years

Present day Man
Highest level of development
Average Lifespan: 75 years

The Genesis Paradigm that shows the AHIJ's version of humanity's degeneration or "devolution." What has been widely considered to be "progress" in the modern world is deemed to be quite the opposite, which saints maintain has been marked by a correlative decline in any number of areas (tangible and intangible), and in sharp contrast to their objective of physical immortality, by the declining lifespan of humanity. *(Designed by by Yaheerah eshet Sgan Ahdeev and Sapeer Ben Israel.)*

replace the old one. But the old world inhabitants tricked His new creations into disobeying their Creator. In Ben Ammi's *An Imitation of Life,* he even translates the "trees" of the Garden "as individuals, with tongues for talking and knowledge for consumption."[10] Just as Randolph maintained, the fruit, in the Kingdom's interpretation of things, represents the knowledge that people internalize and put into practice, the thoughts and beliefs that inform their everyday actions. Cohane Michael Ben Levi often preaches on the absurdity of the idea that God would give humans "the knowledge of good and evil." That "only confuses you," he argues. "God is not the God of confusion." A serpent of a man confused Eve by mixing lies with the truth and perpetuating the chaos that Adam and Eve were supposed to counteract.

Even with these interesting resonances, many important discrepancies between the Kingdom's Adam and Randolph's are hard to reconcile, at least completely.[11] For example, Randolph presages Ben Ammi's emphasis on Adam's link to the earth, to the soil (Ben Ammi's "102 minerals"), but for Randolph that link "signifies 'redness,' 'red earth,' 'red-men'; so does 'Edom,'" a connection that the AHIJ's reading would hardly highlight, Esau's redness, instead, setting him apart from Jacob and his offspring. Saints agree that Adam's birth was just "a" beginning for one group of people on earth, not for everyone, but they spend much less time parsing those pre-Adamic differences than emphasizing the post-Adamic ones.

Randolph also asserts "that Time moves in cycles, and that each has its own peculiar order of intellectual beings,"[12] which explains, he says, the difference between distinctive species of humans from varied epochs. Randolph even hints that Adam's story might be read, by some, from other epochs, not just his own, as God simply saying to himself "Let us create other men in another and better moral mould than those who now exist." Randolph offers this interpretation in quotes and purports to take it away almost immediately, but it is, in effect, the AHIJ's reading of things. Adam was to be a model of how humanity could and should live, a model for people then and now. If Darwinian evolution is the story of mammals morphing from apes to humans, the Genesis paradigm is a theory about how Israelites degenerated from Adamic immortals to sad mimics of Euro-gentile "development," an aping of the kind of cultural and social knowledge (the untruthful kind) that will only destroy its adherents. Instead of heaven on earth, Adam's body became a fleshy hell, a form of incarceration for which death is the ultimate and seemingly omnipotent warden. Eve is a key figure in this story, but Adam gets top billing, a patriarchal framing of things that many detractors find most troubling of all.[13]

THIRTY-SEVEN

Insincerities

S INCERITY IS A category of inescapable doubt that is only retroac-
tively coated with certainty, a self-delusional reading of other people's insides and intentions.[1] It also flags our fears of betrayal, of the
powers of dissimulation. It marks some of the uneasiness and confusion
that constitutes the ethnographic axis linking informants and anthropologist, their backstages and frontstages digitally fused in increasingly
permanent ways. To spend a lot of time on the changing terms of ethnographic relationships is potentially dismissed as a quietist act, an example
of reflexivity used as an excuse for political inactivity. What manner of
irresponsibility and self-aggrandizement would allow an anthropologist
to obsess over the intersubjective discomforts and disconnections hovering beneath the surface of ethnographic exchanges when human rights
activists are still putting the pieces back together in Darfur? Or given the
hyper-violence of Mexico? Or of Jamaica? Or of America? I want to make
a case for the anthropological social critic whose engagement with the
world begins by treating other subjects/informants as fully embodied
and affective interlocutors, even when the larger social and political

stakes of the fieldwork we conduct seem so urgent. Anything else, I think, risks operationalizing and institutionalizing a form of political engagement within the discipline of anthropology that would already be cut off at the experiential knees.

Anthropologist Saba Mahmood argues that shallow definitions of political legitimacy (i.e., Western conceptions of feminine politics mobilized as a universalist analytic for understanding Muslim women's commitments to Islam) deprive others of true agency by dismissing their choices as the product of something close to brainwashing, of ideological beliefs operating at cross-purposes with true material interests.[2] Of course, this is the classic ethnographic move, challenging the swagger of those who would offer their peculiar cultural predilections as universal facts from some precultural nonplace. To be a critical citizen of a shrinking global world is to heed this call, to deconstruct cultural mandates that dress their peculiarities in nature's too-tight clothing.[3] However, deconstruction alone will not deliver us from evil. We can win the polite public debates about "race" and demand it be labeled a social construction (and the AAA's current traveling exhibit on the social construction of race does quite a bit to further popularize that position), but race continues to function as it always has—only the stronger, some might argue, for the constructionist double-talk its least sincere adherents can deploy.

Anthropologist Karen Fields goes so far as to argue that anthropologists have double standards when it comes to race, challenging the rationality of what she calls "racecraft" (the mystical and erroneous belief that race is simply biology) while allowing "witchcraft" its cultural/rational legitimacy and value as a narrative of causal plausibility.[4] According to Fields, this profound contradiction is at the core of the anthropological project. As others have made abundantly clear, some using Stephan Palmié's provocations as their lightning rod, race (and its mobilization/recuperation in contemporary genomics) does not simply function analogously to witchcraft.[5] Just one point of profound difference: race is actually being used by many Western scientists and medical doctors today as a material reality that allows them to feel like they can more efficiently diagnose sick patients, exposing some of racial deconstruction's political and practical insufficiencies.[6] These are the same doctors who would likely balk at the idea of their patient getting a second opinion from a self-proclaimed witch doctor.

Unlike discourses of "authenticity," which seem to close off critiques of identity politics at the limits of deconstruction, "sincerity" provides a way of asking how decidedly deconstructed identities continue to structure people's lives and life chances, powerfully and unfairly, even after the emperor's nakedness has been flashed all across the Internet. There is something to be said for shifting the ethnographic discussion from authenticity to sincerity, not as a plea for more truly sincere ethnographers. Our sincerities probably do us (and all of our many ethnographic *thems*) as much harm as good. The point is to ask what culling socio-cultural knowledge through immersion-based participant-observation might leave in its wake, especially in an everyday ethnographic moment that might not include a wake, any time away from "the field"—*after* the anthropological deal is done. The traditional model of ethnographic research always left something out, something called "home," but those remainders are now inseparable from the ethnographic experience itself. They also demand that we see our subjects as more than just informants, more than just too-narrowly conceptualized "political" actors. Even the ethnographic recognition of an uncanny emic humor is no smoking gun, because it is also encompasses a kind of nervous joke-making, a laughing to keep from talking—or to hide the awkward silences. But it is a start.

Lanita Jacobs-Huey writes about African American stand-up comics and their response to 9/11 as a powerful distillation of what "laughing to keep from crying" means in a contemporary American context.[7] It may demand that anthropologists become comedians themselves, or that they study religious believers, as ethnographers Marla Frederick or Andre Key might recommend, from within, as a believer, and not just from some distant point of respectful exteriority, curiosity, and secular alienation.[8] Roxanne Varzi unfurls an Iranian landscape that is very personal and intimate even as it attempts to write about the abstract and pragmatic possibilities of a future Islamic democracy.[9] These scholars are offering up a critical and engaged anthropology that is much more than ideological cant and cross-cultural hubris. For them, the personal is political—not a personalized way out of the fray, but the only legitimate space from which to fire off substantive salvos. And it doesn't allow for going "home."

To talk about the politics of ethnographic writing in terms of authenticity alone (or to only theorize the *writing*) doesn't do justice to the ethnographic project. It runs the risk of vulgarizing the ethnographic encounter itself, concocting an occulted exchange that denies coevalness and mutuality in ways that extend common critiques of anthropology's traditional positioning, a kind of vampirism that would deny the cathected ethnographic moment its due. If we're not careful, it can reduce the people we work with—sometimes even as political allies—into objects no less inert for their ventriloquized place-holding of certain beliefs, politics, and interests. An attempt to remember the significance of laughter, love, hope, and the everydayness of affect is an important intervention, a differently animated ghosting of the ethnographic machine.

This is not just a roundabout way to say that "building rapport" is a euphemism for lying and misrepresentation, for dissimulation and insincerity. The stakes of sincerity rely on more than just exposing Malinowskian monographs for their bracketed-out xenophobias.[10] Clearly, sincerity is a multipronged aspect of Derek Freeman's revisitation of Margaret Mead's work in Samoa. His criticism of Mead's findings and the scholarly challenges to his critiques are good reminders of the secrets, subterfuges and suppressions (what Diane Nelson calls "duplicities") that function as inescapable scaffolding for any ethnographic edifice.[11] But that isn't why sincerity is key. David Stoll's controversial exposure of Guatemalan activist Rigoberta Menchú's autobiographical embellishments pivot on some of the same vulnerable ground, as do the infamous accusations against anthropologist Napoleon Chagnon's supposedly unethical activities and complicities in South America and the exposure of Project Camelot's cold-war conspiracies.[12] All of these are moments when purported sincerities (of everyone involved, including whistleblowers and revisionists) are clearly at stake. But an emphasis on sincerity is also about recognizing that the others see us coming and confound us—with the very same tools we use to comprehend them.

The space of ethnographic encounters is a Rilesian "inside-out" world where researchers find research subjects already researching themselves (even using similar terms of analysis: holism/holysm, social constructionism, sabbaticals, evolutionism, cellular regeneration)—and researching their would-be researchers, too.[13]

THIRTY-EIGHT

Sumerians

I N NOVEMBER 2008, Nasik Gavriel and his first wife, Aturah Rofah Karaliah, were surprised to learn that saints had organized a huge gala in the *kfar*'s Hilltop Manor in celebration of the couple's fiftieth wedding anniversary. The room's walls and windows were intricately draped in billowed rolls of dark blue and gold cloth, giving the entire event an aura of regality. Singers from all around the Kingdom, Israel and abroad, danced together and serenaded the pair—in English and Hebrew—with both Divine Music Selections and karaoke'd American tunes like "Stand by Me" and "What a Wonderful World." Several of the couple's adult children and grandchildren, members of the Second and Third generations, gave moving testimonials about having previously coveted life beyond the *kfar,* even plotting their departure, only to be convinced by their parents' loving spirits to stay on the straight and narrow path, to keep their eyes focused on Yah. Saints prepared an elaborate meal, and Prince Gavriel's other wives, guests of honor, laughed and joked with the couple all night.

An emcee helped to set the mood by providing guests with some backstory about how the couple first met, reading passages from *The Impregnable People,* Prince Gavriel's published autobiographical recounting of the community's early years, which includes rich details about the first time its author laid eyes on an eighteen-year-old "Shirley Johnson," his future wife, at a Chicago dance party in the 1950s. It was love at first sight, he wrote, at least for him. She was still in another relationship at the time, with a boyfriend off fighting in Korea, so she was torn. The emcee and crowd shared a lot of laughs at the twists and turns of this early love triangle, and at the typical rendering of a Prince's former escapades out in "the world" as Archie Butler, before his life in the Kingdom began.

Prince Gavriel's book is canonical within the community, the most famous history of the AHIJ ever written by an insider or an outsider, and this 2008 anniversary party wasn't the first time that book—or other published offerings by saints in the community, most especially Ben Ammi—had been used this way, publicly read and incorporated into social activities. Many saints have already gone through that entire book several times. Even those who haven't read the book from cover to cover are given bits and pieces of it in cultural events just like this one, its value as a chronicling of community history is called on to help animate and contextualize contemporary social ties. In fact, many saints, younger and older, those who experienced it all firsthand and those who did not, actually tell a story of the community's history that is quite decidedly filtered through books like this one. They've told and retold that same story so many times that their very phrasings are sometimes amazingly similar, the elements they emphasize as handles for moving the tale along almost identical. Collective memory is a constantly reproduced thing, and different saints from different eras tell the early story of the community in ways that resonate with one another through a collective reliance on texts like Gavriel's.[1]

The story of how this band of émigrés learned to survive in the jungles of Liberia—before eventually making it to Israel—is a major component of Gavriel's book, a rendition of how they began to recalibrate their lives and lifestyles for fuller obedience to Yah's laws. The community was more of a work-in-progress back then, and its members spent much of their time self-consciously ridding themselves of their former American vices, the ones they already knew about and the many more that would sooner or later become apparent once Yah opened their eyes to His fuller plan. As saints reminisce on things now (and the way Gavriel described them then), negotiating everyday life in Liberia would be the hardest thing that any of these expats had ever done. They would begin, in earnest, producing radically new "technologies of the self," newfangled ways of eating, speaking, playing, washing, brushing teeth (without fluoride), and living meant to replace the many "foreign" and self-destructive practices that they had cultivated in America.[2]

There was so much they had to relearn—and learn anew. Most of the folks who left for Guryea didn't know the first thing about building their own homes from scratch, cooking food sans four-burner stoves, or preserving meat (which most of them still ate back then) and other perishable items without the comfort of reliable, electric refrigeration—all skills they needed to cultivate on the tree-filled, rain-soaked, and government-subsidized land they occupied in Liberia. Saints wax poetic about the steep learning curve that obedience to Yah entailed. It is the central thesis of Gavriel's book.

During their Sabbath services and whenever they had time to talk, the neo-Liberians reminded one another that this was divine justice—that their ancestors had brought Yah's condemnation upon them by brazenly disobeying His word. They deserved His censure, His curse. Liberia had to be hard, at least at first, but blessings were prophesied to all those who didn't turn back. It would take a lot to prove themselves worthy, to have their lives made whole. But it would be worth it. Until then, existence would be grueling and their daily lives full of ordeals.

The women picked, cleaned, and cooked rice in large black kettles, the same vats of rice that inevitably hid small rocks and pebbles lying in wait to chip people's teeth. Whenever trunks and crates of new supplies did arrive from the United States, community members often didn't have enough money to pay the duty on them, which meant that those same items, necessary or not, couldn't be used for weeks or months. Every once in a while, locals would steal from the camp or get into confrontations with the émigrés, periodically raising tensions between native Liberians and the country's American newcomers (contrary to the conflictless version of things at least one rereleased Soul Messengers CD emphasized). Each new day brought unexpected trials and adversities, new threats to endure, unexpected dangers to be averted, and more life-sustaining schemes to hatch.

Along with the Soul Messengers' national and international music tours, there were several other ventures that the community launched to raise money. Hana's Afro-Diner in Gbatala served home-cooked meals with a decidedly African American flair, an example of the community's pre-vegan commitment to selling soul food. Elder Yaacov Greer and his wife transformed some of the camp's trees into chairs and clothes hangers in their own small factorylike set-up, supposedly the only hangers being produced in all of Liberia at the time.[3] With every passing week, Yah gave the Israelites more insights into which cultural practices needed to be changed, which ancient law next needed to be integrated into their daily lives. They started to wear all-natural fibers, giving up polyesters for cottons and silks. They adamantly promoted the idea of eating off the land, even if their own relatively meager crop yields couldn't support that initiative as abundantly as they would have liked.

These changes recast the community, moved it more in line with "the natural order." With every new set of cultural expectations, each step in the right direction, Yah seemed to provide a minor miracle, a new opportunity. Firestone would end up donating money and vehicles to their efforts. A Liberian media mogul loaned them movies so that they could set up a business screening them throughout the country. Just as they seemed to get to the end of their collective rope, they found a new way of extending those same frayed ends even farther into the future.

When Ben Ammi or one of the Liberian elders got sick, they simply tried to push on, maintaining a focus and purpose that they hoped would serve as a model for others. The spirit was more powerful than flesh, they kept reminding themselves, and so they would not let their spirits be broken. Everyone learned to work through chronic pain, even discovering some local remedies for alleviating it. If life in Chicago had been difficult, life in Liberia seemed, to some, even more brutal and unforgiving. They would be forced to work harder than many of them had ever worked before—and with mostly minor successes to show for it. They seemed to barely tread water.

After the Soul Messengers, one of the community's most ambitious entrepreneurial projects found them selling ice cream in a Monrovian restaurant they called Mr. C's Misadah Tovah ("Mr. C's Good Restaurant"). Ben Ammi had long had a sweet tooth, and ice cream was one of his favorite pleasures. They would experiment with different kinds of ice cream, and different ways to make and market their product to the local population. (Once the Kingdom went vegan, the community's chefs would go back to the drawing board to develop a vegan ice cream that satisfied Ben Ammi's discerning palate. It took several attempts, but they finally found a recipe that Ben Ammi approved of, and it is now being mass-produced and marketed throughout Israel, in all the AHIJ jurisdictions and beyond.)

Along with ice cream, Mr. C's sold burgers, fried chicken, and all the conventional staples of "soul food" cooking, dishes that saints would also learn to make without any meat. Like the pre-Israelite band that Abraham's father led out of Sumer and into Ur, a group that would have undoubtedly carried its Sumerian cultural traits along with it, the Israelites that left Chicago were thoroughly American, and it would take a long time for them to feel like they were successfully letting go of that Babylonian imprint.[4] At least the babies would be born without this same handicap, they thought, except insofar as they might emulate the Americanisms that their parents didn't fully shed.

It was precisely that connection to a past in America that community members attempted to leverage for whatever financial opportunities could be finagled. They would continue manufacturing their own ice cream, procuring more locations for their business ventures, and selling their wares all over Liberia. They gained a small foothold in Monrovia by using their own cultural strengths (some of the very things that exemplified the community's Babylonian captivity) to carve out the semblance of a bearable social existence. Although they had found a reasonable daily routine in their new home (not perfect, but organized and predictable, a system that made the best of a very difficult situation), by 1968, almost three-quarters of the Israelite émigrés had returned to the United States, unable and unwilling to hazard the physical and mental hardships of "bare life" in the Liberian jungle, mostly beyond the bounds of the nation-state and left to fend for themselves on the dangerous outskirts of that nation's legitimate body politic—asked to disperse and potentially

forsake their divine Israelite mission as the price of a ticket to full acceptance into the Liberian fold.[5]

The Liberian contingent continued to experience marked changes in
outlook and cultural expectations in 1967 and 1968, changes that often
meant codifying new ways of being that were modeled after new ways of
reading the Torah. Besides the move to natural fibers and the acceptance
of hard manual labor, they also actively reconfigured their approach to
family life. Even back in Chicago, there had been talk of polygyny, of
men having more than one wife. A few may have actually practiced it,
secretly and unofficially, within the confines of their own insular and
ghettoized neighborhoods (maybe even without those "wives" even
knowing), but the men would ramp up their efforts to institutionalize
polygyny once they arrived in Liberia, and several of the women in the
camp, including some of the newest recruits, were skeptical about that
portion of the Israelite message and reluctant to accept positions as
"plural wives."

It would take a lot of convincing, and not before more than a few
women considered that arrangement a deal-breaker and left the community altogether. Even Prince Gavriel's and Ben Ammi's wives took some
persuading, the latter organizing a few formal and public acts of protest
against this newly explicit mandate quite early on. The women continued
to reject polygyny, saints say, until the men could prove to them that it
wasn't just a ruse for womanizing, until they came to believe that it was
the truly most effective and divinely ordained way to build a strong and
integrated social community. "A brother will often look for a second
wife," one saint explained, "who is a little older. Maybe she hasn't found
a partner and she's getting older. The idea is that she shouldn't be left to
fend for herself all alone. That just wouldn't work . . . It isn't just trying
to get the next young thing."

With all of the financial pressures and cultural changes that impacted
the community in Liberia, there was a clear need for stability, and Ben
Ammi's presence was a calming and reassuring force. Nevertheless, it
wasn't at all a foregone conclusion to everyone that he should be anything close to a singular leader for this group. Ben Ammi was loved and
respected, but there was still grumbling from some quarters about how
he could justify singling himself out as leader. The visit from Angel

Gabriel was important, of course, but other community members had taught "the truth" for many more years. Elder Yaacov Greer, for one, had been given the mathematical key to deciphering the specific year of their departure. So, he surely had some claims to authority, as did other elders with more history in the movement, which all translated into potential leadership disputes that the community had to address, leadership ambiguities that would stay somewhat unresolved, by most accounts, until 1973, when Ben Ammi—with the help of soon-to-be *Prince* Shaleahk—created an organizational structure that designated certain elders Princes and Ministers with their own distinct domains of authority.

THIRTY-NINE

Munir

Brothers Jonathan and Daniel Boyarin, an anthropologist and a historian respectively, characterize some versions of "the Jew" as a kind of trickster, a sex-changing counterpuncher who deconstructs and discombobulates conventional orderings of time and space.[1] This is a trickster whose skills are invaluably "sharp practices in a time of colonial domination."[2] And the trickster's sharpest practice, they argue, is guile and deception, which they offer as an emphatic rejection of martyrdom, a practice with its own too-easy concessions to the straightforward sense of time that an inevitable, inescapable, and sacrificial death presupposes. The trickster doesn't wait for time's many inherent punctuations to emerge; he concocts his own. He is a liar, but a particular kind of liar: one that actually conjures his social world into existence.

In another twining of Jewish and African diasporas, it might be pointed out that literary critic Henry Louis Gates Jr. calls these kinds of "sharp practices" forms of "signifyin(g)," which is what a transatlantic, shape-shifting monkey does to save its own skin "in a time of colonial domination."[3] For a group of Israelites who reject both Jewishness as well as conventional forms of African American identity, it might seem like a stretch to invoke some gender-bending trickster figure at all, even given the complex genealogical work that Gates does to link the signifyin(g) monkey to African forebears like Esu-Elegba. But there is something about the trickster that still works as a way to talk about how saints tell stories, the playfulness of those stories, even and especially in the most dire and tragic of circumstances.

The trickster is a master of what poet and literary critic Kevin Young describes as the Louisianan folk practice of "storying"—again, a kind of lying. But not the lying of "writers from Jayson Blair to Margaret Seltzer to James Frey," he specifies, "in a manner lately called 'truthiness.' For where these faux journalists and worse seem to exhibit imagination, they in fact mark the failure of it. They bend the truth, instead of taking it apart to explore or expand it—*or does it explode?*"[4] This is another version of documentary filmmaker Marlon Riggs's master metaphor, Louisianan gumbo, a slow-cooking of every single ingredient until they merge into something else entirely, exploding on the tongue.[5]

Is the trickster an accurate rendition of the Black Jew? Or his cousin, the Hebrew Israelite? If so, exactly what kinds of tricksters are these? It is postcolonial philosopher Frantz Fanon's famous example of racial recognition framed just a little bit differently, "Look mom, a Negro Jew? An African Israelite?" Philosopher Lewis Gordon's intellectual project might be characterized, at least in part, as a sophisticated instantiation of just such a reformulation of things.[6]

Cohane Ohmahn Ben Eliazer has been labeled a kind of bad-faith trickster by many saints, criticized and ostracized for putting out negative reports about the AHIJ, airing dirty laundry in public, and blatantly misrepresenting the Kingdom. Cohane Ohmahn argues that he must speak out, that it is his duty, because so many saints in the community don't fully know what is going on in their midst and under their name, even as he also claims that many saints know good and well what's happening but have decided to be complicit with what he describes as a massive cover-up.

Ohmahn says that he has been writing letters to Ben Ammi for the past twelve years, letters that allegedly have gone unanswered and acknowledged, which is why he started to put some of those same letters on the Internet in 2009. (Again, this move from backstage to frontstage happens easily in a digital age, and even without bringing any anthropologists into the equation.) Ohmahn also accuses the AHIJ of being disingenuous when they contend that his very public agitation efforts are making it more difficult for a sabbaticalized Prince Asiel to have his issues and concerns fully addressed by the Kingdom. There are procedures in place to deal with legitimate concerns between and among community members, but one saint sent a strident letter (not an official document from the Kingdom, nor authorized by Ben Ammi) to Munir Muhammad, host of a Chicago-based public-access television show on which Ohmahn appeared as a guest in 2011, placing the ostracized Priest and Prince in the same problematic box: "These people [ostensibly Ohmahn and a few of his collaborators] are being used to make that process [of having his grievances heard within the Kingdom] unavailable to Asiel."[7]

Ohmahn threatens to have much more "dirt" on the community, and he says that he is only waiting for the right time to disclose it. "I'm getting ready to open up the X-Files," he says, boasting about the fact that he can't be silenced by authorities in the Kingdom no matter how much they might want to do so. "We got magic jacks and cell phones and social media," he says, smiling at Munir Muhammad. In a digital age, if he wants the world to know, it will know. When he wants to expose the Kingdom, there is no way he can be stopped. And saints shouldn't act, he reiterates, like they don't have the information he's been asking community leaders to address.

His biggest concern is about an alleged case of pedophilia in the *kfar*. That accusation is often one of the first to come up whenever I give lectures about the AHIJ to other Black Hebrew or Black Jewish audiences in the United States. They usually try to be respectful and polite, but they want to know why I haven't said anything about it yet? Do I even know? Am I part of the cover up?

Ohmahn is on a one-man mission to get this issue publicly acknowledged in Dimona, which means that he isn't shy about telling people what he says he's seen, what he knows. He talks of one young saint, already enrolled in the military, who was supposedly "disarmed" because he was still dealing with the trauma of his own childhood molestation.

And he wasn't dealing with it well, Ohmahn implies. He describes this alleged pedophilia as an "abomination" without a cure, an abomination that he says the Kingdom allowed to continue since the mid-1980s when, he claims, saints first learned of the problem. "If this is in our community and nobody is standing up," he says, "I'm not afraid." The saint taken into custody by the Israeli police for these alleged crimes was at one time, according to Ohmahn, a "deputy minister," but he supposedly "wasn't operating alone." And when this all came to a head, he maintains, the saints who should have "stepped up" and dealt with this issue "disappeared when it was time to confront this."

As Ohmahn sees it, Prince Asiel, Ben Ammi, and the other elders who led the movement out of America brought in all kinds of people, individuals with all types of "baggage." And this person, he says, left America with his problem. "An airplane ride didn't change him." And when the ministers found out, he says, they wanted to sweep it under the rug. To do damage control. Other brothers, like him, were saying that they had to tell all the saints about these allegations. According to Ohmahn, a saint who finally decided to tell his own wife about the issue was almost thrown out of the Kingdom on the spot when AHIJ ministers found out. They didn't want the truth to get out, he declares. They wanted to pretend it didn't happen, or just look the other way. "You gotta root out the wickedness," he declares. "Even the Catholic Church is investigating [its own pedophilia cases]. Truth can't hurt the Kingdom."

FORTY

Brochure

I CONSIDER MYSELF A pretty committed ethnographic filmmaker, but
I have never given any serious thought to the idea of making a film
about the African Hebrew Israelites of Jerusalem. That's partly because
they make films about themselves that already crackle with such wonderful ethnographicness, films about their newly constructed facility in
Benin (a much more elaborate version of the Dimona *kfar*), about the
workings of their organic farms, about the Day of the Show of Strength,
about a half-brother who has left the community but continues to be
thought about and prayed for by the family members he's left behind.
The films that they are planning to make in the future—a documentary
based on footage from Whitney Houston's 2002 Sacred Visitation, a
DVD version of the African/Edenic Heritage Museum—represent more
fascinating iterations of the community's cultural beliefs and social practices, their expanding archives. Some anthropologists might call these
offerings "thin," but they are thin in the way that an "everyday ethnography" would have to be, an ethnography undertaken as the modality
through which life is lived. And there are other people who make films

about them, too. Just about every time I've visited the community in Israel, a film crew from somewhere else—South Africa, London, California, New York—has just left the *kfar,* or is about to arrive, or is on a Sacred Visitation. And many of their films, in part or whole, are available online.

Just using community-produced footage alone, borrowing the Ministry of Information's impressive amount of visual material, photographs, and video footage, which many outside productions do, filmmakers can come up with amazing pieces. But the issue isn't simply that there are too many filmic cooks in the kitchen. Plenty of people are writing about the Kingdom, too. And from many different angles: historical analysis, ethnography, autoethnography, philology, scriptural exegesis, journalistic exposé.

Tellingly, the other thing that I almost never do is show any AHIJ footage during my lectures about the research, either the minuscule amount of footage that I took when I first started visiting Dimona, or any of the many clips that are readily available online, or excerpts from the hours and hours of visual material that the Ministry of Information and other saints have generously shared with me over the years.[1] I tend not to screen AHIJ footage in any academic contexts, and I can't help but think about those two visual hesitations (not filming the AHIJ and not showing footage of them during presentations) as connected. I want to avoid the particular kinds of easy fetishism that watching the community can sometimes entail. Allowing people to view footage is almost too easy, too deceptive in its efforts at clarifying and demystifying this fascinating group.[2] And it takes work to figure out how one might tell a different kind of story with the images, different from the classic version of representation that anthropologists have always provided or from the self-portraits that the community crafts on its own. The latter offerings are often the most interesting; "ethnicity inc." meets "ethnography inc." in a global touristic marketplace where one of the best ways of generating profits is by selling experiential access to one's cultural particularity, like those Rastafari in Jamaica dismissed by detractors for offering tourists a kind of "Rasta Disney" experience.[3] Places as diverse as Harlem, New Orleans, Paris, Lisbon, and Bangkok (not to mention the Chinatowns, Little Italys, and Little Africas of the world) have long been industries in the productions of self-commodification. And often, the frameworks of classic ethnographic portraiture become the scaffolding for these commercialized forays.

For the African Hebrew Israelites of Jerusalem, such place-marketing means glossy ethnographic pamphlets that serve as snapshots of their overall cultural world, complete with pithy summaries of their fundamental beliefs, organizational structure, and holiday observances—not to mention scriptural references, a chart of Israeli currency's exchange rates, a village map, a glossary, a list of local attractions, and much more, including dozens of photographs of smiling saints and community guests. A mixture of ethnographic reportage and hotel guidebook, the community offerings can frame their cultural and social lifestyle in ways that don't diverge too far from traditional anthropological renditions of things, a one-stop shop for descriptions of the AHIJ's most important practices and beliefs. And although it might appear, to some, again, as far too thin and truncated an articulation to pass ethnographic muster (relegating viewers to the community's carefully choreographed center stage), it does quite explicitly and self-consciously provide basic facts about almost anything a person would want to know—anything, that is, short of gossip about frictions within the community or even actual recipes to go along with the photos of their most popular vegan fare (the latter, at least, made up for by the *The Soul Vegetarian Cookbook* that highlights many signature dishes from the Kingdom's restaurants).[4]

This is the entry for New World Passover in a section of the Kingdom's booklet on National Observances and Cultural Events:

> In accordance with the prophetic return of the Children of Israel (Jeremiah 23:7–8) annually, in May, members of our community commemorate the historic exodus of the vanguard group which left the shores of America in May of 1967. This "family reunion" features two days of feasting, sports activities and entertainment. Aside from marking an event of great historical significance, it is one of our most festive and fun-filled events. This is a time when many family members, friends, and political, social, and religious associates journey from abroad to partake of this holy and sacred season of joy and gladness.[5]

The booklet describes many other important events, including Coming-in Ceremonies (when young saints formally make the transition to adulthood), the *Roche Ha Ahm* Affair (an annual royal banquet and party for the AHIJ leadership and guests), and the Holy Jerusalem Writers' Conference (which I have still yet to attend, though I have made a kind of annual ritual out of promising to do so). The booklet makes a clear distinction between those aforementioned events and "National Holy Days," which consist of the ceremonies explicitly hallowed by Yah in the Old Testament.

This same brochure takes time to explain the difference between entertainment and true "Inner-Attainment," which is how saints redefine those singing and dancing performances that the Kingdom has become best known for. It even includes an opening quote from Ben Ammi about "divine culture," which he describes as "the perpetual trademark that secures the identity of a righteous people and secures the existence of our eternal, living Yah." (What could be more anthropological than trying to define "culture"?) It is quite decidedly learned, Ben Ammi says, which is why it can be unlearned, and it must be actively passed on to future generations. The entire booklet is an elaboration on this definition, an attempt to showcase how the community puts "divine culture" into practice, a culture that it is their charge to share with others. They would call fulfilling that charge their "divine privilege," because it is preordained by God, which is part of the reason why the "redemptive enterprise" that would pitch their *kfar* as a respite for weary souls, saints or not, is a perfect example of the community's positive outlook, their assurance of ultimate success—smiles on almost every photographed face in the brochure.

The AHIJ public relations office (in consultation with the Ministry of Information) decides what to include and what to leave out of all official documents, and this particular brochure includes a discussion of the City of Peace, a previous name for what the Kingdom now calls "Restoration Village," which is supposed to one day supplement the current *kfar,* providing more amenities for saints and their guests in Ghana. There are references to many different facets of their lives and philosophy, classic anthropological domains, but there is most notably no discussion at all of death and dying and any attending rituals, of how mortality is dealt

Members of the Israel-African Ambassadors Group from Ethiopia, Nigeria, Kenya, the Democratic Republic of Congo, Angola, and Ghana on a tour of the African Hebrew Israelites' "Village of Peace" led by Sar Ahmadiel in 2010. *(Photograph by Crowned Sister Cattriellah eshet Rockameem.)*

with within the community. Since the transcendence of death is their reason for being, there is little need to make a fetish out of it—unless one considers it fetishized in its palpable absence. For the AHIJ, death is not a part of life, and its relevance to any discussion of their social world is summarily rejected. "We have been tricked to believe," writes Ben Ammi in the introduction to his book *Everlasting Life,* "by western religious leaders, scientists, health specialists, movie and television moguls, and the media that death is ordinary and acceptable. It's perfectly all right to do anything, believe anything, and live recklessly."[6] Death is the best justification, they argue, for continued disobedience in the guise of "a fairy tale" about reuniting human beings with their Creator—once their physical bodies are no more. The most destructive lie ever told.

"The deception that death is the inevitable cessation of physical activities," Ben Ammi writes in *The Resurrection: From Judgment to Post Judgment,* "has been/is being promulgated to blind you to the fact that death (and the components that cause death) can be/must be overcome."[7] And death is first overcome by the sheer readiness to will it away, to ignore its existence in an otherwise holystic description of life "on high" in Dimona. The community's makes their case about death's ultimate hollowness all the time, in books, lectures, classes, Shabbat services, everywhere, but not in this glossy brochure. In fact, there isn't even any explicit mention of veganism as a cure for cancer, or of the Kingdom's immortalist endgame. And maybe most interestingly of all, this overview of (and introduction to) the AHIJ community, only produced a couple of years ago, is already outdated, which means that it still contains several smiling photos of Prince Asiel throughout, as well as triumphant details about the *kfar's* Prince Asiel Center for International Studies, started in his honor back in 1986.

FORTY-ONE

Rabbi

RABBI CAPERS FUNNYE heads a congregation of Black Jews in Chicago that includes several former saints from the AHIJ community, even a few of its earliest members and their offspring, most notably Moishe Buie, a former "deputy leader" from Chicago (and son of Elder Eliyahu Buie) who was sometimes quoted by the press as a spokesperson for the first few émigrés.[1] "We want to be Liberians," he declared to *The Liberian Age,* "we don't want to be Americans. We are in Africa to stay, and there is no turning back."[2] Moishe Buie lives in Chicago, and he is a teacher in Rabbi Funnye's congregation, capping off a metamorphosis, of sorts, a transformation from Hebrew Israelite to Black Jew.

Rabbi Funnye's spiritual path took a similar course. He first studied under Rabbi Devine, one of the staunch opponents of African emigration within the Chicago community back in the 1960s, and then transitioned to the more orthodox beliefs of Brooklyn-based Rabbi Levi Ben Levy, the person who would eventually ordain Funnye in 1985. Even though that original ordination wasn't necessarily considered legitimate by all of Ashkenazi Jewish America, Rabbi Funnye currently sits on the Chicago Board of Rabbis and is recognized by boards of rabbis in contemporary Israel, a fact that speaks to an increasingly successful attempt to make his efforts compatible with more conventional forms of Judaism.[3]

The synagogue itself was founded in 1918 by a rabbi from Bombay, and first served Mizrahi and Sephardic Jews from Iraq and Iran (Persia). That founding rabbi, Horace Hasan, would not have identified as a Hebrew Israelite, but an East Indian Jew on the Southside of Chicago was readily swooped up into the racial logic of an American society that could most easily absorb him and his brown-skinned congregation into an African American neighborhood.[4]

Today, Funnye doesn't mince words about his lack of patience for some slivers of the Hebrew Israelite community, calling a few of the more sartorially flamboyant and publicly confrontational camps (such as the ICUPK) "Power Rangers." He tries to keep tabs on what they are doing, but their projects, he says, are fundamentally different from his own. Some of them, irreconcilably so.

The first time I visited Funnye, a young member of the temple, one of his Hebrew-language students, was putting the finishing touches on a book manuscript she had written, a memoir about the challenges of being a twenty-something black Jew in Chicago. "You have to deal with all of the racism from other Jews," she said, editing her work on a laptop at Funnye's desk, "and the mocking from members of the black community, the anti-Semitism. You get both."[5] Her book was available for purchase from Amazon within the month.

During that same visit, Rabbi Funnye gave me a tour of the building that houses their spiritual community, Beth Shalom B'nai Zaken Ethiopian Hebrew Congregation (House of Peace for the Children of the Ancient Ethiopian Hebrews), and it became clear that along with Rabbi Horace Hasan, the group traced its roots back to other early twentieth-century Black Jewish figures like Rabbi Abihu Ben Reuben and Rabbi Wentworth A. Matthew. Their actual building—located on South Kedzie Avenue—was previously occupied by Lithuanian Jews, and they rent out space upstairs to the city, which runs a public daycare facility there. The synagogue includes a performance and cafeteria area that houses a wall-mounted exhibit documenting the history of global racism and the transatlantic slave trade, an exhibit that felt strikingly similar to the African/Edenic Heritage Museum's curatorial project.

Moshe Buie teaches weekly classes after Shabbat services that critique Western cultural assumptions in ways that also resonate with AHIJ contentions. After one Shabbat service during Hanukah (a service that consisted of Torah readings in Hebrew and English and ended with a resounding rendition of all three verses of "Lift Every Voice and Sing," the "Negro National Anthem"), Buie's lecture deconstructed the holiday of Christmas, discussing how Puritans in the American colonies considered it a pagan affair and persecuted anyone who practiced it. He even read a 1980s op-ed from a Nation of Islam newspaper that made a case for the twelve reindeer representing cloaked homages to fiendish and even satanic principles. Although I couldn't imagine Rabbi Funnye endorsing this reading of iconic Christmas imagery (his performance of Judaic subjectivity being much more ecumenical than most), this interpretation does reflect historical and ongoing institutional and interpersonal links (the op-ed author and Buie used to be friends) between some Black Jews and other African American religious and political institutions, especially in a place like Chicago. Buie ended the session by showing attendees his newest collection of laminated articles from newspapers and magazines in different parts of the world, articles that profile historical and contemporary Black Jewish leaders and their congregations. Those same laminated articles would be on sale later that evening during a musical concert put on by children in the congregation.

During the start of a different year's Hanukkah festivities, several older members of that Chicago congregation were wrapping gifts. Those preparations represented one of the more straightforward differences between Beth Shalom and the Kingdom; the latter doesn't observe Hanukkah at all, which was established by rabbinical Jews well after the holidays specifically referenced in Torah, such as Yom Kippur. There are many overlaps and ambiguities that produce seemingly porous boundaries between various Hebrew Israelite/Jewish groups, but some distinctions, like this one, are hard and fast. If the ICUPK believe Africans and Israelites to be radically different peoples with discrete diasporas, and the AHIJ consider Israelites a subset of the larger African/Edenic world, Funnye is part of a tradition of Black Jews who feel that being African and Jewish aren't identical or mutually exclusive groups. They simply represent different versions of a global faith. Rabbi Funnye and most of the members of his synagogue feel more than comfortable calling themselves "Black Jews," even though they concede that the designation does not sit well with every single congregant:

> Today, many of us prefer the terms "Hebrew" or "Israelite" for the following reasons: (a) These are the terms used in the Torah (Holy Scroll) to refer to the "children of Israel," (b) these terms do not wrongly associate Jewishness with whiteness [which is the prevalent misconception of the term], (c) they avoid the changing nomenclatures of terms like Negro, Black, and now African-American.[6]

Funnye says that some members of his congregation, the former saints, still hold incredible amounts of animosity toward Ben Ammi and the AHIJ community. One woman saw him in Chicago several years ago and just screamed "murderer, murderer" with mounting intensity until he was out of earshot. Moishe Buie would describe Ben Ammi's 1973 "restructuring" of the community's political hierarchy as a form of patricide, the protégé cutting his mentor out of the community. And then there are the members without any autobiographical links to the group who are just puzzled by their practices. "I hear they don't even do anything on the Shabbat," said one elder. "They just rest. That's it. All day. No service or anything. Is that true?"

Beth Shalom offers a specific kind of syncretism, a version of Jewishness that they liken to "modern Orthodox" Judaism but "with clear conservative and African-American influences." Funnye has used the term "Conservadox." Men and women sit separately in the sanctuary and during Saturday afternoon classes in another part of the building—though one could almost see Funnye doing away with such gender segregation completely if such a move didn't offend more traditional members of his congregation or of the larger Jewish community. (He is also a vocal advocate for the ordination of women.)

Members don't eat pork, catfish, or other animals specifically banned in Leviticus, but they don't demand the strict separation of milk and meat products, even if some members follow such practices anyway.

They clearly aren't vegan, and their project is very differently pitched from the AHIJ's program in terms of its aspirational links to more atypical notions of physical and spiritual health—and to conventional forms of Judaism.

Even though Beth Shalom and the AHIJ each challenge prevailing assumptions about the Europeanness of Jewry, they take on that task in distinct ways. Both groups, for instance, look to Africa and are often noted in the press for their Africa-inspired garb and their inclusion of Djembe drumming in rituals and performances. For Beth Shalom, Ethiopia is symbolically central, an extension of that long history of Ethiopianism within African American spiritual and political communities; however, for the AHIJ, Ethiopia is just one example among many others, and doesn't nearly stand in for the whole. Funnye's ongoing work to gain Jewish recognition for members of the Igbo and the Lemba communities also demonstrates this position, but Ethiopia occupies a more pivotal position within Beth Shalom's historical and genealogical consciousness.

If Ben Ammi and his followers make an argument for reinterpreting the Bible in service to a plant-based diet that might rejuvenate the human species and allow our cells to function much longer, even forever, actively positing a conspiracy at the center of Africa's elision from discussions of the ancient Hebrews, Funnye (if not the entirety of his eclectic congregation) seems less interested in fighting about how one reckons "real Jews" and more invested in producing a model for living that does justice to African American cultural particularities in ways that can still accommodate the norms of Judaism as customarily conceived.

One would be hard-pressed to find a religion that isn't the product of syncretism, a religion not practiced as a localized variation on more global themes, and Funnye can make this case quite powerfully. The African American cultural traditions of his congregation, he argues, are no less legitimate than the realities that cultivated the emergence of, say, Yiddish as a complex, creolized, and situational example of a specific Jewish subject practicing Judaism in a particular social environment. There is no "antiplace" of religious practice that is untethered to social and cultural contexts, and Funnye maintains that traditional African and African American rituals and practices are as legitimate an accessory for expressing the faith as anything coming out of Europe.

Funnye has never visited the *kfar*, according to Sar Ahmadiel, even though he has made several trips to Israel and throughout Africa. He does hear news about the Kingdom, and he met with Prince Asiel at Soul Vegetarian East in Chicago not too long after Asiel's sabbatical turned into a more permanent expulsion. He even went to the Israeli Embassy during the Day of the Show of Strength in 1985 to lobby on the AHIJ's behalf, but he is less interested in forging alliances with Hebrew Israelite groups that reject mainstream Judaism than he is in making sure that blacks who identify themselves as Jews are embraced on just those terms, even going so far as to lead the Pan-African Jewish Alliance, which is specifically charged with that goal—and with building coalitions among Africana Jews around the world. One of his major projects on that score is to facilitate the formal conversion to Judaism for thousands of Igbos in Nigeria. With a history of this kind of international work, Funnye has long been a pretty recognizable figure in Chicago's mainstream Jewish community—and that was well before his cousin, Michelle, became First Lady of the United States.

FORTY-TWO

Hebrews

O NE OF THE ways in which some African Americans talk about "Black Jews" (to disparage them) is as an example of black people trying to deny their blackness, even as a demonstration of internalized racism; like the joke about African Americans trying to claim Cherokee ancestors in their family trees. Though such things aren't always a laughing matter, except in that *to-keep-from-crying* kind of way. Leo Felton, the biracial neo-Nazi skinhead who had to pretend to be from southern Italy so that his white supremacist friends would let him conspire with them to blow up Jewish monuments in New England, is just one illustration of such purportedly internalized racisms. Felton considered himself a sincere advocate for a brand of white identity that wasn't, he claimed, about blood or genes at all. It was also a brand that would have banished him on the spot had those neo-Nazis uncovered his secret.[1]

Despite his concerted efforts to connect spiritualism with antiracist activism during the mid-nineteenth century, Paschal Randolph would adamantly deny being African or African American at several different points over his lifetime, attempting to pass for any number of other things—including, possibly, Palestinian and/or Turkish—even if only as a ploy to make his mail-order "sex magic" business more marketable to whites in a racist society. And none of that race-based pragmatism even comes close to accounting for his polygenesis arguments (placing blacks outside the Adamic family) or his willingness to refer to Africans as "the thick-lipped Negro of the 'Stupid' Tribe."[2]

Links between blacks and Jews are not simply predicated on this theme of self-loathing. There are also tales of covetous longing, simple admiration, and reasonable confusion. Stories of W. E. B Du Bois being mistaken for Jewish during stints in Europe and of black nationalists, before and after Marcus Garvey, celebrating and even studying the political and social moves of Jews as a model for Africana nationalisms—that is, when they weren't (like Equiano) already making the case for the genetic links between Africans and ancient Jews.

Instead of a mutual embrace, for a group like the ICUPK, investment in Hebrew Israelite identity demands a double denigration/denial. They don't want to be African, but they don't want to be Jewish, either. For the ICUPK's institutional forerunners (many of whom didn't mind the moniker "Jew"), if some of them "could have been white," Tudor Parfitt believes, talking to a group of my students at the University of Pennsylvania, "they quite possibly would have chosen to do so."[3] Not every reader of that history might agree, but any serious discussion about the would-be contradictions and incommensurabilities of Blackness and Jewishness is perched atop the entrenched logics of race and racism.

Eliza Slavet revisits Sigmund Freud's complicated allegiance to Jewishness as a way of talking about two related questions: how is "the Jew" biologized, and why did Freud and his new psychoanalytical science have such a hard time negotiating "the Jewish question"?[4] Freud toggled back and forth between an emphasis on the foundational importance of early childhood trauma for the development of adult subjectivity (as theorist of the Oedipal complex) and a sneaking suspicion that past psychological traumas get re-remembered and physically inherited through the body/blood of offspring. The founding of Judaism (in Freud's retelling of that portion of the Torah) is only possible if not only do the sins of fathers get passed on to sons, but also if the memories of fathers' actions enter sons' minds through some kind of material and physical link, some kind of fatherly version of an umbilical cord. Judaism transmitted genetically and mnemonically. It is the stories you were told before you were born that made you Jewish, stories encoded in the body. Not just, say, priests in the next room reading scriptures to delivering mothers in the AHIJ's House of Life. For this Freud, Jewishness is constituted by stories automatically inherited, even those stories that are more like "storying," lies told to keep a people alive (like the lie, argues Freud, of Torah's Moses even being Jewish at all).[5]

This discussion of what makes a Jew a Jew gets played with over and over again. Is it religion? Blood? Ancestry? And is the determination most legitimately made patrilineally? Matrilineally? All of these disputes animate the Hebrew Israelite project, even as adherents choose to define their rendering of Israelite selfhood in contradistinction to the version of Jewry generally considered most representative and acceptable. But what makes a Jew a Jew isn't just genealogy, and the 2000 decision by the ICUPK to reject their previous claim that any authentic Hebrew Israelite had to have an Israelite (that is, Africana) father, replacing that contention with a more voluntaristic version of things (all that matters is that you feel the spirit and obey), is one example of how these ideas change. Some Israelites and Jews cast a quite specific net around such categories. Others take a more inclusive, or even phenomenological approach.[6] What people say and do count above and beyond what they allegedly *are* before they say or do anything in the first place.[7]

The African Hebrew Israelites of Jerusalem have also embraced a marked change in their understandings of racialism's importance to their revitalization project. When they left Chicago, they would have been described as unapologetic racial essentialists, at least that's how Sar Ahmadiel recaps that history to saints in Philadelphia during a Shabbat class in 2012. "We thought it was all about race," he explained. "And we didn't realize that race is a social construction. We didn't know it wasn't real. We believed the hype." They spent so much time obsessing about race, he says, that they didn't realize it was getting in the way of their human mission, their divine calling. "It isn't about race," Ahmadiel told them. "It was never about race, but we had to go through all that to get to where we are now. It's all a process."

Ahmadiel tells me afterward that he was testing out a version of an argument he was planning to make at an international conference on African Jewry in South Africa later that year when he asked the Philadelphia saints, "Who was the first Hebrew?" After some discussion about whether it was Eber or Abraham, Ahmadiel gets to his real question: "What made the first Hebrew a Hebrew?" The congregation blurted out some comments, but they mostly just waited for his answer. "It wasn't biology or genealogy," he said. "It wasn't who his mother was or who is father was. It had nothing to do with blood or genetics or any of those things!" What made the first Hebrew a Hebrew was being "willing to submit, to submit to Yah."[8] That's what makes you a Hebrew, Ahmadiel declared, fully submitting to Yah's will, to have that kind of relationship with the Creator, to do His will. He is careful to distinguish between a blind commitment to racial tribalism and a valid critique of societal racism. Saints rail against various forms of racism in America and Israel, while also offering an expanding message that makes global—and not just narrowly nationalist—claims.

I would get to hear Ahmadiel make that argument, in a more elaborately framed paper presentation at the South African conference he had mentioned, a gathering organized around terminology like "African *Jewry*," which was the first thing he critiqued during that conference, held at the University of Kwazulu-Natal in Pietermaritzburg. Genetic tests can't decide this identity, he said. It isn't reducible to the memories of ancestors or the blood in people's veins. It is a gift that comes from one's decision to follow Yah. Any other discussion, he ended, is a distraction from that one elegant and irrefutable truth. Yah recognized His people because they chose to recognize and follow Him. And then the story began. To reduce that bond to some genetic marker or biological trait, he told that international gathering of scholars, religious practitioners, and rabbis, is to confuse the profane with the divine, the flesh with the spirit.[9] He then gave participants a guided tour of the South Africa-based version of the African/Edenic Heritage Museum, which saints had driven to the conference from Durban (after it arrived from Port Elizabeth only a few days earlier) on a flatbed truck.

FORTY-THREE

Zombie

POSTRACIAL. THAT'S THE term Americans use to describe our contemporary moment, or at least aspirations for it. We are obsessed with getting passed discussions of our racial past and with deconstructing the social identities of all comers, relentlessly exposing their artificial and political coordinates. Even the Kingdom's public recantations of earlier commitments to hyperracial versions of group belonging (a recantation process already underway, remember, in the early 1980s when Bayard Rustin voiced skepticism about Ammi's sincerity on the matter) can be read as presaging postracialism's sprawling ubiquities. But a composite examination of Hebrews and Blacks Jews and Israelites and Hebrew Israelites and African Jews can help to highlight something like the other side of this current postracial fetish, an off-ramp carrying us to a place where racial deconstruction is less a solid finish line than an anxious starting block. It continues to remind us that race is still understood by many as one of the world's fundamental constitutive categories, inextricably central to future understandings of how "biopolitics," "nanopolitics," and "necropolitics" differently constrain and configure people's hopes, dreams, and nightmares—the stories they tell themselves about who they are and aren't, even who they ought to be. This is a biopolitics that uses phenotype (skin color, hair texture, facial features, etc.) as final arbiter of hierarchical difference, categorizing and codifying bodies along a supposedly self-evident continuum of social merit and value.[1] It is a nanopolitics that mines the human genome for invisible racial solidities and causal absolutes, for submolecular answers to visual social inequalities (or, alternatively, for a cellular answer to "the fountain of youth").[2] The necropolitical impulse to control and determine life's ultimate death, consolidating claims on social control and sovereignty, might help Americans to better explain the new "peculiar institution" and its dark-hued tint—not to mention the AHIJ's commitment to death's deconstruction (not just race's). In each of these instances, race becomes a powerful and necessary frame for thinking "the body in pain," a Riggsian body preparing for its material demise.[3] Or labeling such death the ultimate social construction.[4]

Individuals like Leo Felton, Paschal Randolph, Sar Ahmadiel Ben Yehuda, Kara Keeling, Funnye Capers, Trinh Minh-ha, Vicky Kirby, Lewis Gordon, and Ben Ammi remind us—in very different ways, admittedly—to be a little more critical of all this postrace talk, skeptical even, challenging academia's current (if tenuous) racialist détente, an attempt at multiracial peace born of collective agreements among scholars about the need to transcend racial essentialisms at all costs, a supposedly high-grounded response to Afrocentric excesses, white supremacist machinations, and the sometimes less visible signs of inferential or everyday racisms. Of course, each one of these variously scaled frameworks (Afrocentrisms, white supremacies, anti-Semitisms, internalized racisms, subconscious biases) sanction distinctive analytical scaffolding, different causal arguments, for social critique or even transformation. Collapsing these very different commitments to racial ideology can allow an essentializing ethos to remain safely ensconced within adamantly antiessentialist projects—political projects most likely to falter at the nexus where abstract antiessentialisms meet the particularities of everyday living, a place—or nonplace—not too far away from the expanding digital field-sites that ground everyday ethnographies, erstwhile *means* (plane rides, a more and more elaborate online world, cell phones, satellite

TVs, traveling museums, etc.) that have become inextricable from the traditional sweet spot of anthropological *ends* (the cultural stuff conventionally deemed most worthy of ethnographic attention). And anthropological tricksterism would support splashing around in those muddied waters of racial reasoning as opposed to just sifting and sanitizing them into clean and discretely deconstructed jugs.

If an anti-Jacobean Du Bois proved all too easily prophetic about the twentieth century and its foundational color lines, the beginnings of this newest century have spawned divergent pronouncements about potentially race-absent tomorrows yelled from atop towering skyscrapers of racist yesterdays and todays. Clearly, the Jim Crowed categories of black victims and white victimizers hardly seem up to the task of wringing complete social sense out of our "browning" American present. But what best helps us to understand the differences within similarity that cloud our analytical engagements with the everyday realities and surrealities of racial reasoning? More than ever, we need to create new ways of understanding the social facts that underpin race (as belief system, as common sense, as pseudopatriotism, as interpersonal shortcut, as biological mythmaking) and what those underpinnings forewarn about the possible futures of social difference around the world.

This is not a zero-sum game, of course, where race's importance comes at the expense of any serious engagement with class, sexuality, religion, nationality, or gender. Their mutual articulation seems clear. But we also recognize that a discussion of race (even a focus on black Israelites/Jews that hovers too long on the subject) is like playing with fire, something that might possibly work for a "Black Studies" angle on things, but both African studies and Jewish studies tend to organize their heuristic projects very differently—often with these particular kinds of discussions about race hardly as central or sustained.

And the AHIJ's revamped and redefined rubric of "death" seems operative in this moment of purportedly postracial enlightenment, or at least race fatigue, which is really just another way of trying to transcend race. To kill it, to banish it from polite social discourse, is a different take on "social death."[5] In fact, I would go so far as to say that "race" (as an analytical category) is not alive, not anymore. We have murdered it, "socially-constructed" it to death. But things are hardly ever that easy. Instead, the bludgeoned beast has risen from its grave. Continues to haunt us. It is the bogeyman in our collective social closet, make-believe but all the more frightening for its irreality, its ghostly intangibility. Invocations of race nothing more than the suspicious spectral remains captured in spirit photographs. The dead's last gasp. We can't destroy racial reasoning with human genomes or social constructionism because, in some very fundamental ways, we killed race long ago, and its death is part of what plagues us today, keeps us all up at night. We can't find the corpse, and there still seem to be sightings everywhere—of both its waking life and its strangely uncanny demise. Racism, of course, is another matter. And it can do its thing whether "race," its enabling premise, has a heartbeat or not. If anything, the death of race, helps to give racism its strongest alibi.

There's physical immortality, which the AHIJ champion; there's eternal damnation/salvation, which people operationalize differently all around the world; and then there's something else entirely, a different version of avoiding death: the zombie. That is what we can boast of now, a zombified notion of race, one that we constantly put to work, much like Zora Neale Hurston describes things in her ethnography of Haitian voo-doo.[6] Zombies are our slaves, she says, and they do all the labor we ourselves would never want to do. These walking and working dead are not just commodity fetishes (in the Marxist sense); they are a commodified form of death itself, slaving away for the masters who fear their very own Frankensteinian fiends, masters who would feebly wish their creations off into illusory oblivion—that is, had they not already grown dependent on them for the production of so much surplus value.[7]

The task, then, is not to find out why and how race's telltale heart continues to beat. That may already be conceding far too much. Instead, we might need to trade in deconstruction for exorcism, for an analytic of the séance, something more in Pascal Randolph's bailiwick, a starting point that imagines the dead to have agency—even if only as the sacred sacrifices we make to the gods of collective social reproduction. There is an interior to the thingness of the corpse, an animation still, and wres-tling with the realities of race in a self-consciously post–Du Boisian and post-postracial world entails taking that interiority seriously. It means talking with the dead, channeling them, and not sorely underestimating their social influences. The dead provide for the living—and not just through their wills. They allow us to use them in our causes, to invoke them as allies in battle. Even the idea of not-dying, of physical immortality, must necessarily stand on the graves of those who died with the covenant to Yah unrepaired. They lift us up in their animate stillness, ashes to ashes. Some of these dead also walk, talk, struggle, and strain. When they do, they chain us to the scene of our past crimes.

If we've killed race, but it still moves, real analysis might take more than social deconstruction—the analytical equivalent of feebly petitioning the living-dead corpse that chokes us with one pathetic final plea: "But you're dead. You're supposed to be dead. You're not real. This can't be—ugh."

To escape the clutches of our own cultural creations, we need new incantations, new charms and southern amulets, new spells for countering the powerful magics of pseudoscience and social constructionism. Or maybe old weapons, retooled. Veganism. Or a reracialized and repronounced Jesus Christ. Or the careful parsing of Jews versus Israelites. The unearthing of new scrolls for archiving. These are ways of imagining what couldn't possibly be as already here—and right now. Including a racist world without any racists.[8] Without race.

Ethnography, at its best, is a small attempt to create this alternative magic, to provide various paths along a variegated and mystical roadway, alternative tactics for breaking death's ironclad chokehold.[9] This counterspell will demand all the writerly weapons at our disposal—coloring, tracing, drawing, poetry, fiction, collage, memoir, journalism, essay, research report, jeremiad, philosophical treatise, plagiarism, and even the thinnest of anecdotes—to cobble together a rendering of place, power, and history that can take race (and death!) seriously without accepting them at face value.

Race is not real in any already-disproven nineteenth-century way, but that only makes it more difficult to deny. We are trapped in a circular maze. We've even sealed ourselves into it. There is no outside, no categorical difference between nature and culture to faithfully rely upon.[10] No thick response that answers the most important questions. In such a context, the simplest versions of deconstruction aren't enough, the ones that only deconstruct in one direction, waving magic wands that reveal culture beneath every invocation of "nature," race being one of the most called-upon test cases. But our critical goal is not simply to expose race's enabling fictions; we must also find ways to rewrite them—with new plot twists and heroes and dramatic narrative cliffhangers. New kinds of *storying* about the nature of life and death, yarns we weave as though our future depends on it, even as though they've already happened—a different timescale altogether. This requires teasing out fiction's productivity, finding where its power lies, and determining what keeps bringing our dead things back to palpable life, dead and alive at the exact same time, in the very same instant. The living dead trapped in an everyday hell of their own making.[11] That is a special kind of conjuring—contradictory, paradoxical, self-deconstructed—and arguably quite necessary in a world where flesh-eating zombies play peekaboo with race and recirculate the kernels of their own undoing with every new escape from their coffins. Zombies who fool us into thinking they can still die live the strangest kinds of lives.

FORTY-FOUR

MLK

ONCE THE NOVELTY and euphoria of physical emigration finally wore off and the abiding difficulties of their hardscrabble existence in Liberia wore on, the truly daunting nature of the community's venture became joltingly clear. There was no denying the herculean task before them. This would take relentless effort, single-minded focus, and an unyielding faith in Yah's prophetic plan.

Everyday brought new challenges, unforeseen emergencies, life-and-death decisions. Migrants continued to battle diseases. They staggered from debilitating snakebites, succumbed to bizarre accidents. Generator fuel exploded, burning more than a few of the men. One child fell down a well, careening to her tragic death. They could thankfully proclaim that there weren't more actual deaths those first few years, but community members would sometimes feel like they were always on the verge of dying—fatigued, feverish, nauseous, frail. Death seemed to be stalking, even if more often just to mock them than to drag more saints immediately away.

Despite all of their inventive entrepreneurial efforts, the community rarely had any excess funds, which meant pouring just about all of the resources they could find into the project of keeping everyone alive, alert, and healthy. They still couldn't always grow enough food, and they continued to find it difficult negotiating their camp's prohibitive distance from Monrovian amenities. All of this conspired to make that stint in Liberia quite harrowing, seemingly impossible, and their emigrationist experiment seemed doomed to fail by the spring of 1968.

To make matters worse, that Passover they received another divine sign, this one quite worrisome, maybe even damning. Freedom of life outside of Babylon gave them the ability to revisit some sacred practices of Israelite ancestors, practices meticulously documented in the Torah. A close reading of rules and regulations from those five books and the rest of the Bible would serve as the bedrock for their revamped cultural repertoire, their post-American reclamation of a long-lost history and culture. In Liberia, this meant recuperating the practice of animal sacrifice. Yah had asked as much of their forefathers; why would their directives be any different. After a great deal of effort, they located and purchased a goat for the ceremony, no small feat given their meager resources. But just before the sacrifice was scheduled to take place, the kid somehow got tangled up in its rope and strangled to death. This was a horrible omen, they thought, and probably meant that God was unhappy with the community, angered by the infighting and defections. Ben Ammi could hardly diminish a growing sense of panic spiraling its way through the camp. They put a lot of stock into the symbolic importance of that sacrifice, as squeamish as a few of the community members (urbanites, remember) might have been, but now even that effort ended with a setback. The community would need their faith renewed. They'd need another sign. And Ben Ammi would get one—in fact, he'd get two.

After more prayer and meditation, the same process he used in 1966 when he was visited by Gabriel, Ben Ammi received a clear interpretation of that strangled goat's significance. Yah was making a point about the end of animal sacrifice, assuring the community that He didn't need them to perform such rituals anymore. They had proven their willingness to do so, even though it was far from what their lives back in America had prepared them for. They passed that test, and what God actually wanted was simply continued obedience, full and unflinching submission to His will, more than the slitting of a goat's throat. It had been the disobedience of Adam, Eve, and the ancient Israelites that necessitated animal sacrifice as a kind of compensation. Actually, humans were supposed to protect other creatures, not kill them. That was their Edenic charge, and given their return to Eden, their attempt to repair a broken spiritual covenant with Yah, such sacrifice would no longer be necessary. Moreover, although a few members had been vegan back in Chicago, the end of animal sacrifice also began to usher in a return of that original Edenic diet, veganism, which would soon become formally constitutive of the community's overall project, a goat's death clearing space for the possibility of future biological immortality.

And then God sent another message to Ben Ammi—from a different messenger.

In April of that year, Martin Luther King Jr. gave a rousing speech in Memphis during what would turn out to be his final public appearance, just one day before he was killed on the balcony of a Tennessee motel room. In the now-famous speech, one King had given before, he described his own spiritually inspired dream in a way that resonated with this small community of American ex-pats barely surviving in Liberia: "I just want to do God's will," King preached. "And He's allowed me to go up to the mountain. And I've looked over, and I've seen the Promised Land. I may not get there with you, but I want you to know tonight that we as a people will get to the Promised Land."

Hearing these words, a group of seemingly separatist and arguably Afrocentric black expats invoked an assimilationist Civil Rights icon to justify their next major move.

King was certainly a messiah. That couldn't be denied. He may not have known all of the truth, but he was clearly chosen to help liberate God's people. He would not get to the Promised Land with them, as King himself had accurately predicted, but neither did Moses. Or Abraham's father. But that didn't matter. Yah had anointed King just as he had Ben Ammi, and others before them, including Yeshua. For the AHIJ, the difference between Christian fetishizations of Jesus Christ and their appreciation of Yeshua's messianic role pivots on the fact that they don't single out Yeshua for godlike exceptionalism. He is to be respected, thanked, loved, and embraced, but not because he is the *only* messiah.

They accept no definitive article singularity for Yeshua.[1] He is part of a long list of figures who have been used by Yah to better the lives of His people: Harriet Tubman, William Blyden, Malcolm X, William Crowdy, Marcus Garvey, and others. They each focused their energies on the liberation of Yah's people. They devoted their entire lives to that cause. As Yeshua had. According to the AHIJ's "black midrash," Yeshua wasn't even immaculately conceived. If anything, it was an out-of-wedlock birth, a fact covered up by distracting talk of divine insemination. He was born in sin, as we all are, and that makes his anointing all the more powerful, they argue, even more exemplary of Yah's grace. A regular man with foibles and even some larger vices, Martin Luther King Jr. fit squarely within the same mold, imperfect but perfectly pitched to help do Yah's bidding.

Hearing King's inspiring and Amen-accented declaration from the news reports they listened to in Liberia, Ben Ammi interpreted King's last public statement, one messiah to another, as prophesy—as another bit of divine intervention.

Why did God put those particular words in King's mouth on that fateful day? The "Promised Land" was Israel, especially for African Americans claiming to be descendants of ancient Hebrew Israelites. So what were they doing in West Africa? Of course, they could not survive there. Of course, some of them would get disillusioned and head back to America. Liberia was not where their diasporic origin story began.

Saints will say that they always considered Liberia a temporary sojourn, a staging area for the community as God sifted wheat from chaff, tested their mettle and resolve, preparing them for the greater rewards that awaited them in the Holy Land. However, many scholars who have researched the community argue that they had initially intended to stay in Liberia, only changing plans once they realized how difficult their lives would be in a Liberian compound that they had such a hard time completing. Ben Ammi says that they always knew they would leave; they just didn't know when God would judge them ready. King's speech and the goat's presacrificial death both signaled that it was finally time for them to complete their journey, time for them to enter a new world that was once their people's old home. So, in 1969, the remaining 100 or so black Israelites emigrated again—this time, from West Africa to the modern state of Israel. "Northeastern Africa."

Hezekiah (Prince Heskiyahoo) was pulled from the Soul Messengers to help ready the community for its pending move. He and Ben Ammi left a month after King's assassination to conduct some early reconnaissance in Israel. Ben Ammi returned to Liberia after a few weeks, but Prince Heskiyahoo stayed in Israel for a year, improving his Hebrew, learning Israeli culture, and paving the way for the community's subsequent arrival. So, they prepared the people for a second departure, but there was still the matter of how they would get there. They had no extra cash lying around to purchase plane tickets, and they hadn't yet gotten resourceful enough to counterfeit their own. Ben Ammi admits, playfully, over forty years later, that he didn't necessarily discount the possibility of everyone walking the entire distance, which seemed like the only way they could possibly afford the trip. But Yah would find a way; they just had to keep the faith (and risk prison time whenever some of their illicit funding tactics were discovered). In the meantime, they would all need to learn more about their future home, about the "law of return" that allowed any Jew on the planet the privilege of joining that new and controversial nation.[2]

News about this imminent trip spread throughout the community, and people began to ready themselves for another daring journey. This time, there was no Flemister to facilitate their transition. No prepurchased land to anchor them. But it was the appointed hour, and if they were obedient, Yah would make a way—though they would surely have to be careful about letting the Liberian government in on their plans (or the Israelis, for that matter).[3]

As the days passed and Prince Heskiyahoo continued to prepare their way, the community began to feel more and more emboldened by the challenge ahead, excited about the prospect of completing their appointed journey, of making it back home to Israel. What they didn't yet know, at least not fully, though they had some inkling, was that their initial difficulties in Israel would rival anything Liberia had thrown their way. In fact, the trials of Liberia were a good run-up to their future confrontations in an Israeli absorption center, the new roadblocks poised to thwart their efforts at living in ways they deemed fit and holy. The community, however, would prove quite stubborn about the charge of fulfilling Yah's prophesy and bringing His Kingdom to earth, and they continued to trust the Spirit to steady their strides into the unknown.

Whenever I give lectures about the Kingdom, attendees often ask me what I think will happen once Ben Ammi dies. Sometimes, they'll say, "*if* Ben Ammi dies"—to hold out hope, or to be respectful, or even just to poke a little fun, lips buttoned together in a mischievous grin. I don't have a real answer, except to say that their story will change, as stories always do, a little or a lot. It changes as I tell it. But I suspect that saints' mornings will continue to start off with a glass of room temperature water. Then maybe some fenugreek and molasses. Or kelp. And they already know that past messiahs didn't complete the journeys with their charges, so it wouldn't necessarily mean the end of their world if he were to die of "natural" causes at, say, 150 or 175. Yah will decide. But as the digital field expands, warping and reworking time and space for every single one of us, recognized ethnographers or not, I can't help but think that many interested readers would be able to find an answer to that question well before I ever got a chance to share mine.

FORTY-FIVE

Seconds

I WASN'T QUITE SURE if it was more my preoccupation or theirs, but when I first started visiting the community and talking to saints in 2005, I felt like I heard that number, and the phrase, several times: 45 seconds. 45 seconds. "The 45 seconds." Almost a kind of mantra. It was a reference to the exact length of Ben Ammi's visitation from Angel Gabriel back in 1966. The point of saints' reiterations of that phrase was to marvel at the brevity, the ephemerality, of Ben Ammi's celestial dialogue. It was *only* . . . 45 seconds. That's all. A short exchange, but look at how profound its consequences. And how could such an exceptional moment prove otherwise?

I remembered sitting and talking to saints in the *kfar* about it, the 45 seconds, broad smiles extending across their faces. Smiles that seemed to say, look at the lives we are living, all the way over here in the land of the Bible, and because of something that didn't even last a full minute.

I've been holding that number in my head since then, but when I go through my fieldnotes several years later (starting, most systematically, in June 2010) and read the books authored by Ben Ammi himself, his

"Resurrection Series" writings, I don't see it. Not once. For a couple of weeks, I didn't find a single mention, and I started to think that maybe I'd made it all up, the phrasing, its importance, the toothy smiles I recalled it bringing to those saints in the *kfar*. The saying didn't seem to show up anywhere except in my head, my mind's eye, a flash that began to feel like little more than rhetorical ornamentation of my own making. Every scholarly and "official" community retelling of their decision to leave America in 1967 seemed to omit any reference to the number, the 45 seconds, which means that I was more than halfway through my field-notes and nothing, not a single allusion to the 45. It wasn't in my notes about the young saint's 2006 NWP performance in the *kfar*'s parking lot. It didn't seem to show up in any of the glossy pamphlets and brochures that the community had produced. And it wasn't in Prince Gabriel's classic book-length portrait of their emigration experience. How could that be? How had I lost it?

And then, poring frantically through more and more material, I eventually realized that it wasn't even a conversation between Ben Ammi and Gabriel in the first place. It wasn't a *voice* that Ben Ammi had heard at all. Talking to one of the community's early chroniclers, Morris Lounds, in the 1970s, Ben Ammi explained the visitation in some detail, even hinting at why visitors to the *kfar* many years later would see a humorously misleading parking lot version of things put on by one young son:

> The plan [to leave America] came to me by a vision . . . There was
> no voice, but in relating it to other men, you would have to say that
> a voice spoke unto me. But He didn't talk to me, because He has no
> voice like that. It was revealed in the spirit, and as it came into my
> mind. I believed this was the word of God, that the father had
> spoken to me.[1]

So, not even a voice, not as Ben Ammi describes it here, despite the loud-speakered pronouncements interspersed throughout that young saint's NWP performance. And no explicit invocation of Gabriel to speak of either, at least not in the version of things that Lounds solicits. Ben Ammi didn't seem to mention it one time, and in just about all of the work written about that portion in the community's history, about their decision to leave America, there are vague references to Ben Ammi getting a "prophetic vision," often to help explain how quickly he went from being a relatively young upstart in the movement to one of its most important prophets. There are reports of the group's pragmatic search for plausible exit strategies and relocation destinations. But no 45 seconds. Not even in anthropologist Merrill Singer's account, which includes mention of another elder in the community, Yaacov Greer, who, after a series of meditative Torah readings in 1966, determined the exact year of their future departure from Chicago, a vision that demanded he spend time "figuring it out mathematically."[2] It was preordained in the scriptures, Greer determined: 1967. But even in Singer's telling, the only relevant characterization of anything close to "the 45 seconds" is his mention of Ben Ammi's "divine revelation" confirming Greer's earlier calculation. That's the extent of it. No talk of Angel Gabriel. No allusion to any conversation. Certainly not one that was specifically 45 seconds long. For a few weeks, I convinced myself that I must have made the number up, imagined it, or just grossly inflated its importance to the community.

It was psychologist Israel Gerber's reading of that moment in the community's history, of their build-up to the 1967 exodus, which offered absolutely no mention whatsoever of any mathematical calculations or divine dispensations or angelic visitations or anything else nearly so esoteric and preternatural, just a calculated and sober "trial-and-error" process of arriving at the notion of emigration to Liberia instead of Ethiopia after careful library research and an expedited fact-finding mission. No mysticism to speak of.[3]

For a few weeks, I resigned myself to the idea that I had concocted that little temporal factoid about Gabriel's visitation, those vanishing 45 seconds. I must not have heard saints reverently invoking that unit of time in their own descriptions of Ben Ammi's early years of leadership. Or simply misheard something else that sounded like it.

More time passed without an archival confirmation of the event, and I fully accepted that I had just dreamed it all up, for who knows what reason, and fooled myself into believing otherwise. Where did I hear it?

Maybe another spiritual community I'd read about? A television show? I accepted my mistake and began to think about other parts of the community's story (their battle with nature in Liberia, the early clashes with the Israeli government) until, thankfully, I finally started to see some references to "the 45 seconds" in one of my most raggedy (and hard-to-decipher) field-notebooks. Admittedly, not all that many times, not nearly as often as I would have thought, but a few. I outlined them, excitedly, with a black Sharpie and dog-eared the pages. In one instance, a forty-something year old saint invoked it when she was serving me lunch, half of a watermelon, in one of the community's guesthouses. Another saint had talked about it, with what I called "awe and satisfaction," during an evening sitting together in the *kfar*'s main square. Finally, I found a parenthetical reference to it in one of Ben Ammi's most recent writings, an unelaborated upon invocation: "Our prophetic mandate does not lead us to seek social integration with our oppressors, but to evince in a very convincing manner that Yah lives. From the coming of the vision (the "45-Seconds"), our history constitutes the observably relevant evidence that Yah lives."[4]

And the reference was in quotation-marks, too. That was important. It meant that there was a history and thingness to the phrase. I hadn't singlehandedly crafted my own odd fetish out of one saint's throwaway comment. The added punctuation implied that this was, in fact, something of a codified and reified idea, this 45 seconds. I hadn't completely conjured it. There was even a video, "The 45 Seconds to Glory," which I eventually found during a particularly desperate and diligent search through my archives.

Of course, most of the saints in the community today, the people I've gotten a chance to know, including and especially members of the Second and Third Generations, weren't in Chicago in February 1966 when that 45-second visitation took place. Many of them weren't around for any of the exodus story. They only came to the Kingdom, to the truth, after the group had already set up residence in Liberia. Or they arrived during those difficult early years in Israel—through the missionizing of Prince Asiel or the testifying of other Israelites. Nevertheless, saints all know the story—in part, from sifting through some of the very same accounts that I've examined. Or through hearing tales about "the exodus" relayed to them by teachers, fathers, mothers, priests, ministers, or princes in the Kingdom many, many times before. Legends of Liberia.

And the tales get altered with each new telling, in big or small ways. Inflections change. Some things are emphasized anew, some deemphasized or omitted altogether, as with all stories of history, mythology, or anything else. For the AHIJ, some of those narrative silences ostensibly include early prophecies about a kind of apocalyptic judgment day predicted for 1977. According to some academic accounts, there might even have been a prediction of Armageddon before that—in 1970.[5]

There were even scholarly references to the community's alleged belief in reincarnation back in the 1970s. More than one early researcher flags its central importance to their cosmological claims. The notion seems, from a perch in the early twenty-first century, just a bit hard to believe, or something the community evolved out of. Or maybe a literalization of the merely metaphorical, a misreading of (1) the early elders' densely figurative language, (2) their general fondness for speaking in the third-person, and (3) a collective propensity back then for discussing differently named versions of themselves as though each were a separate individual. Going through transcripts of interviews with elders during the 1960s and early 1970s, they do seem to be talking about themselves as other selves (in other times) entirely—for instance, Ben Ammi's description of when he was "baptized" by Shaleahk Ben Yehuda, his "messenger," who he says was once called "John," and of reconnecting with Shaleahk "again" in America, as they once had been "a long time ago." This does seem nestled very close to talk of past lives (and reborn souls), but it might also be read as another active short-circuiting of that dividing line between the literal and the metaphoric, strong analogies with greater aspirations, spiritual restorations that double, in a flash, as surrogates for physical resurrection.[6]

Ben Ammi has another exchange with sociologist Morris Lounds that demonstrates these multivalent tendencies, this highlighting of many identities, many names, and many different subject positions for the self-same human body at varying points in time. Just like there are many "Hebrew Israelite" groups, not all of them on friendly terms, there are, arguably, countless examples of a certain slipperiness to Israelite invocations of the past, and especially of the messiah's past:

Lounds: What were you doing before A-Beta [Hebrew Israel Culture Center]?[7] And would you want to give me a biography of yourself, not a biography of yourself . . .

Ben Ammi (interrupting): Morris, that's quite a question. What was I doing? I was in many places doing many things, and yet I was every-place, and I was doing everything. Won't be able to define it like that. You see, I was in school, but I wasn't in school for learning. And I worked on jobs, but not for income and salaries. And I've been in many areas, doing many different things. But I guess I could just sum it up and say that I was searching and looking for the people, and waiting on the appointed time through which to guide them into a new era. I didn't have where I could go back into a childhood and say this is my life and whatnot. There was a young man, for example, by the name of Gerson Parker, normal child raised in the Ghettoes of America. Normal ghetto family. Relief and all the other non-benefits of the uncivilized civilized society. Raised up on the near Northside, grade school at Edward Jenner, high school at Washburn Trade School. . . . So raised up, went into the army, came out of the Army, went to a job in Howard Foundry. He said, one day—'what is all this great mystery about these great, great, great black people in America'. . . . Then one day he was sitting in the midst of another group of men. One called Carter. One called Daniel Ben Yaakov, a Brother Johnson. They were all sitting and they wanted to get together and they wanted to leave America. . . . So they came and they listened and they got involved in time. I was thinking about him that they call by many names. I was thinking about Gerson, Gerson Parker. And I was thinking about the spirit of Ben Carter. And I was thinking about the spirit of Ben Ammi. And I was thinking about the spirit of Niflah, and I was thinking about the spirit of Nasik Hashalom. I was thinking about all these different things, all these different names, but they don't know him by name.[8]

These are the many names of Ben Ammi, his many appellations, what sounds like many selves, a confusing assortment of designations. And I would also just point out that were we to let his words continue even longer, when he begins to talk about the community's decision to emigrate, there is still no mention of "the 45 seconds," egregiously absent

here, too. He includes many other nuanced recollections, but nothing
about Gabriel or those divine "45 seconds." These interesting absences
and presences, emphases and omissions, are all part of why "the 45
seconds" is so important, so valuable to think with. It makes bliplike
appearances and disappearances, undeniably central, foundational, and
fundamental, but more often than not simply ignored, left out, forgotten,
at least in the majority of recaps, then and now. I heard "the 45 seconds"
and latched onto its presumably unnecessary exactness; its superfluous
specificity. "The 45 seconds." Not 44 or 46. But at the same time, it also
seemed to imply a kind of shorthanded approximation, something with
only the pretense of precision. Closer to *about* 45 seconds, which means
it could have been more or less, each second not ostensibly accounted for,
not meticulously measured. For anyone who studies seemingly marginal
of exotic social, spiritual, or political groups, such precise imprecision
isn't unheard of. It might even be fairly standard, maybe mandatory. I
certainly couldn't stop thinking about the temporal weight of it, and
maybe that's the goal: to provide a pinpoint for emergent fixations, a
focus for contemplation—the sharper, the better. Tiny ontologies that
Weltanschauung's dangle from. And when it comes to those variously
pitched invocations of "45 seconds," there is no ambiguity about the play
of divinity in the affair. Little doubt about the complex temporality that
such divine messaging suggests. 45 seconds. A relatively thin slice of
time, at least for ethnography. 1, 2, 3, 4, 5, 6, 7, 8, 9, 10, 11, 12, 13, 14, 15, 16,
17, 18, 19, 20, 21, 22, 23, 24, 25, 26, 27, 28, 29, 30, 31, 32, 33, 34, 35, 36, 37,
38, 39, 40, 41, 42, 43, 44. 45. Each second, a flash. Each flash, an independent instant of revelation—in turn, embraced and denied.

Notes

ONE ▪ PASSOVER

1. One of my undergraduate courses, "Spiritual Communication," specifically focuses on the ways in which various societies differently conceptualize and operationalize an assumed human capacity to speak to sentient beings other than human ones, such as angels, gods, demons, fairies, saints, and the dead. Although particulars differ from culture to culture, sanctioned and socially shared assumption about humanity's ability to contact such entities (for example, through prayer) is almost universal. On another (somewhat related) point, the idea of glossalia, or "speaking in tongues," as other anthropologists have pointed out, is an evocative metaphor for the ways in which all ethnographic stories unfold: by invoking varied voices in an effort to move the narrative along. This book attempts to play with some of those suggestive symmetries.

2. *Thin Description* is an extended meditation on this posited and policed difference: Jew versus Israelite. For one explicit articulation of that distinction (by a priest with ties to the African Hebrew Israelites of Jerusalem), see Cohane Michael Ben Levi, *Israelites and Jews: The Significant Difference* (Levitical Communication, 1997). For a very differently framed parsing of the "ancient Israelites" versus "Jews" distinction (found in the discourse of Israeli archaeologists), see Nadia Abu-El-Haj,

Facts on the Ground: Archaeological Practice and Territorial Self-Fashioning in Israeli Society (Chicago: University of Chicago Press, 2001). Many people have written about such nomenclatural and categorical debates within Jewry. Some of them get invoked later on in this book (linked to other aspects of their arguments). For now, let me just add that anthropologist Netta Van Vliet has recently penned a provocative dissertation about the *self-differential* "Israeli-Jew" subject that pivots on tensions between and among religion, culture, nation, race, sexuality, and gender in ways that articulate powerfully with the Israelite versus Jew discussion as theorized by (and through) the African Hebrew Israelites of Jerusalem.

3. The quotation marks (around "nuclear research facility") are usually placed there by the folks who remark on this point. What they want to argue is that "research" is a euphemism for "bomb-making," which the Israeli government hasn't officially confirmed or denied.

4. Many anthropologists have written about how centrifugal tendencies (that could potentially pull societies apart) are mocked, managed, performed, and controlled during public rituals that help to bind communities together, rituals that involve unleashing the necessary safety valve of sanctioned and ephemeral "liminality," making unacceptable or unintelligible identities and actions permissible for a particular stretch of time as a way of shoring up social categories of authority and hierarchical value within a given group. For work from one foundational anthropological voice in these discussions, see Victor Turner, *The Ritual Process: Structure and Anti-Structure* (Berlin: Walter De Gruyter , 1969), and *Dramas, Fields, and Metaphors: Symbolic Action in Human Society* (Ithaca, NY: Cornell University Press, 1974).

5. For discussions about diasporic homecomings, see Fran Markowitz and Anders H Stefansson, eds, *Homecomings: Unsettling Paths of Return* (Lanham, MD: Lexington Books, 2004), 183–198, including a specific examination of the AHIJ group. And for a valuable overview of African American "encounters" with Judaism/Hebrewism, see Yvonne Chireau and Nathaniel Deutsch, eds., *Black Zion: African American Religious Encounters with Judaism* (Oxford: Oxford University Press, 2000), especially the chapter by Ethan Michaeli, which speaks to some of the ways in which saints conceptualize their "exodus" from Chicago. Also, for an overview of the community's structure and sensibility, see Martina Konighofer, *The New Ship of Zion: Dynamic Diaspora Dimensions of the African Hebrew Israelites of Jerusalem* (Berlin: LIT Verlag, 2008). Also, for a synthetic overview of global black Judaisms (and historical debates about their very possibility), see Tudor Parfitt, *Black Jews in Africa and the Americas* (Cambridge, MA: Harvard University Press, 2012). And for a rendition of the AHIJ's story that casts a critical eye most pointedly on its gendered political and spiritual investments, see Emily Raboteau, *Searching for Zion: The Quest for Home in the African Diaspora* (New York: Atlantic Monthly Press, 2012), 48–58.

6. For an unpacking of this notion of a "black midrash," see Walter Isaac, "Locating Afro-American Judaism: A Critique of White Normativity," in *A Companion to African American Studies,* eds. Lewis R. Gordon and Jane Anna Gordon (Malden, MA: Blackwell Publishing, 2006), 512–542. In his dissertation research, Isaac, a student of philosopher Lewis Gordon, head of Temple University's Center for Afro-Jewish

Studies, critiques the ontological presuppositions that ground what he calls "the Jews Studies project." He is also someone who grew up in an African American family whose members self-identified as Hebrews, Israelites, and Jews. On a separate issue, let me just note that I will use Hebrew Bible/Christian Scriptures, Old Testament/New Testament, and Torah interchangeably throughout this book, mostly because the AHIJ (and other Hebrew Israelites) use all of these terms—and all of these scriptures. Some Black Jewish groups (and a few Hebrew Israelite camps) eschew the New Testament, but they are a relative minority within this diverse community.

7. These short descriptions (in quotations marks) of NWP come from several pamphlets and other literature produced by the AHIJ community for the express purpose of explaining their beliefs and practices to interested outsiders.

8. Other anthropologists have also studied the AHIJ community, and some of them have attended NWP ceremonies. Their work will come up throughout this book. Some of the anthropologists whose offerings have been particularly useful are Fran Markowitz, who has not written a book on the subject but has penned a series of important articles, including "Blood, Soul, Race, and Suffering: Full-Bodied Ethnography and Expressions of Jewish Belonging," *Anthropology and Humanism* 31(1): 41–56; "Creating Coalitions and Causing Conflicts: Confronting Race and Gender Through Partnered Ethnography," *Ethnos* 67(2): 201–222; and, with Sara Helman and Dafna Shir-Vertesh, "Soul Citizenship: The Black Hebrews and the State of Israel," *American Anthropologist* 105(2): 302–312. Works specifically on the AHIJ include Morris Lounds Jr., *Israel's Black Hebrews: Black Americans in Search of Identity* (New York: Roman and Littlefield, 1983) as well as Merrill Singer's articles (several of which come up later in this book) and his 1979 dissertation, "Saints of the Kingdom: Group Emergence, Individual Affiliation, and Social Change among the Black Hebrews of Israel" (PhD diss, University of Utah).

9. For instance, Zev Chavet, "Obama's Rabbi," *New York Times*, April 2, 2009, http://www.nytimes.com/2009/04/05/magazine/05rabbi-t.html?pagewanted=all.

10. The blue cords are worn on saints' garments per God's command to Moses in Numbers 15; 38–41: "Speak unto the Children of Israel, and bid them that they make them fringes in the borders of their garments throughout their generations, and that they put upon the fringe of the borders a ribband of blue; And it shall be unto you for a fringe, that ye may look upon it, and remember all the commandments of the LORD, and do them; and that ye see not after your own heart and your own eyes, after which ye use to go a whoring: That ye may remember, and do all my commandments, and be holy unto your God. I am the LORD your God, which brought you out of the land of Egypt, to be your God: I am the LORD your God." The "ribband of blue" worn by saints serves a mnemonic function similar to the one performed by *tefillin* for Jews, though the AHIJ read *tefillin* as the literalization of a biblical metaphor from Deuteronomy 6:8: "And thou shalt bind them for a sign upon thine hand, and they shall be as frontlets between thine eyes." According to the AHIJ, this is meant as a command to make sure that one's deeds ("sign upon thine hand") and thoughts ("frontlets between thine eyes") are guided by the teachings of God. (This is also a fairly standard rabbinic interpretation.) I am using the King James Version

of the Bible, which is the version that most saints in the Kingdom use. The Kingdom also sees Ezekiel's prophesy concerning "law in our inward parts" to mean that the fringes and cords no longer need to be seen by saints themselves. It is more of a way to identify oneself to outsiders.

11. Priscilla Wald, "American Studies and the Politics of Life," *American Quarterly*, 64(2), 190.

12. The idea that such confusion is purposefully sown is a function of the belief that many people do not want the AHIJ's truths circulating far and wide—that certain people have a vested interested in keeping humans in the dark about Yah's divine mandates.

13. The Dead Sea gets its name from the lack of fish and other life that inhabit its waters. They have a difficult time thriving because of the extremely high salt levels in the water, which is why it is also sometimes called the Salt Sea. Of course, it is probably lost on no one that the AHIJ engage in a kind of counter-semantics that is similar to practices found in many other communities, most obviously (to those working with the African Diaspora) the Rastafari who think quite seriously about the literal meaning of morphemes as they rewrite the English language in their Dread Talk (also called a "livalect"). Some of their most famous lexical interventions: "understand" is replaced with "overstand" (or "innerstand"), "I" is substituted for "me" as either the subject or the object of a sentence, and "downpression" is used as a more accurate-sounding proxy for "oppression."

14. Of course, other spiritual and religious communities, including Christian Scientists, Seventh Day Adventists, and many others, champion mind and body connections. And one cannot begin to talk about religions that focus on mind/body links without thinking about Asian religions. This book will try to demonstrate a bit of what makes the AHIJ's theorized links between minds and bodies different from some of these other groups.

15. The story of the African Hebrew Israelites proffers many interesting links to canonized versions of Jewish history. And I'll underthematize most of them. Even still, every once in a while, I'll mark particularly interesting parallels, sometimes in endnotes and sometimes in the main text. For example, this playful recasting of newness and oldness could be interestingly linked to Theodor Herzl's notion of *altneuland,* the "old new land," the title of one of his Zionist utopian novels. Other readers will find many more points of convergence that are not as explicitly marked, some of which I'm probably not even aware of.

16. Anthony Wallace, "Revitalization Movements," *American Anthropologist* 58(2) (1956): 264–281.

17. For a discussion about "acoustemology" and the importance of sonic ethnographies listening carefully to communities' social worlds, see Steven Feld, "Doing Anthropology in Sound: A Conversation with Don Brenneis," *American Ethnologist* 31 (4): 461–474. The AHIJ most likely borrowed their usage of the term "saint" from earlier black Hebrew movements in early twentieth-century America, movements that were often described as "Christian-influenced" or syncretic forms of Judaism.

18. Any ethnography is an attempt to follow a moving target, and this one is no different. The AHIJ are constantly refining their beliefs, their practices, and their terminology.

When I started working on this book, the communities outside of Israel were all called "extensions." Before that, they seem to have been called "missions." One saint in South Africa (driving me to the airport in Pietermaritzburg in 2012) talked about his life in the Kingdom by specifically marking that terminological switch. "I've been in the community for over ten years," he said. "I joined in 2001. We were still called extensions back then. We were an extension here."

19. One of the difficult things about this project is dealing with the sometimes-hostile views that other Black Jews/Hebrews/Israelites have about the AHIJ community. Members of these other groups are often very knowledgeable about the Kingdom— and very invested. These other groups come up as part of the sprawling context for any discussion of the AHIJ.

20. For example, Steven Thrasher, "Black Hebrew Israelites: New York's Most Obnoxious Prophets." *The Village Voice,* March 30, 2011.

21. For a magisterial offering on the subject of black Jews, Hebrews, and Israelites (and the terms, as we will see, make a difference), see James E. Landing, *Black Judaism: Story of an American Movement* (Durham, NC: Carolina Academic Press, 2002), especially for its treatment of African American groups in the United States.

22. For just two incredibly clear and powerful articulations of cultural unthinkability vis-à-vis the African diaspora, see Michel-Rolph Trouillot, *Silencing the Past: Power and the Production of History* (Boston: Beacon Press, 1995) and Susan Buck-Morss, *Hegel, Haiti, and Universal History* (Pittsburgh: University of Pittsburgh Press, 2009).

TWO ▪ INTRODUCTIONS

1. Many thinkers have made versions of this point. Here are just two very different anthropological examples: Kamari Maxine Clarke, *Mapping Yoruba Networks: Power and Agency in the Making of Transnational Communities* (Durham, NC: Duke University Press, 2004) shows how a South Carolina community relies on (and redeploys) scholarly evidence in their American reconstruction of Yoruba culture and cosmology. For an example of how a reliance on archival validation serves as a trap in the context of indigenous Australian identity claims, see Elizabeth Povinelli, *The Cunning of Recognition: Indigenous Alterities and the Making of Australian Multiculturalism* (Durham, NC: Duke University Press, 2002).

2. One way to represent the difference between "black Jews" and "Hebrew Israelites" is to emphasize that black Jews tend to recognize conventional Judaism, its institutions and canon, as valid and authoritative. Hebrew Israelites usually discount much of what is taken for granted as constitutive of standard/mainstream forms of Judaism, anything that is not directly traceable to the Torah. For Hebrew Israelites, all of the Jewish teachings that come after the Old Testament are irrelevant and invalid. And for many Hebrew Israelite groups, European Jews aren't legitimate Jews at all.

3. One of my colleagues has a fascinating discussion of how the "science" of physiognomy was used to help Victorian Brits detect Jews (and others) by sight. See Sharrona Pearl, *About Faces: Physiognomy in Nineteenth-Century Britain* (Cambridge, MA: Harvard University Press, 2010).

4. I put "the Middle East" in quotation marks here because the AHIJ reject that category/designation outright as a kind of conspiratorial fiction.

5. For one of the most often-cited versions of the anthropological critique against simply testing vernacular claims against some ostensibly objective archival source, see David Scott, "This Event, That Memory: Notes on the Anthropology of African Diasporas in the New World," *Diaspora: A Journal of Transnational Studies* 1 (3) (Winter 1991): 261–284.

6. A few well-known book-length examples within these debates/discussions are Yosef A. A. ben-Jochannan, *We the Black Jews: Volumes I & II* (Baltimore: Black Classic Press, 1993); Rudolph Windsor, *From Babylon to Timbuktu: A History of Ancient Black Races Including the Black Hebrews* (Chicago: Lushena Books, 1969); J. J. Williams, *Hebrewisms of West Africa: From Nile to Niger with the Jews* (New York: Biblio and Tannen, 1930). For a recent iteration of other entries from both sides of this debate, see Tudor Parfitt, *Black Jews in Africa and the Americas* (Cambridge, MA: Harvard University Press, 2012).

7. Sometimes authors blend these critiques. For a discussion of the AHIJ that might be said to combine psychopathological readings with skepticism about the group's sincerity, see Israel J Gerber, *The Heritage Seekers: Black Jews in Search of Identity* (New York: Jonathan David Publishers, 1977).

8. Annelise Riles, *The Network Inside Out* (Ann Arbor: University of Michigan Press, 2000), explains how these analytical overlaps between researchers and subjects wreak havoc on traditional anthropological assumptions about how to confirm the validity of ethnographic findings.

9. Clifford Geertz, *The Interpretation of Cultures* (New York: Basic Books, 1973), 7. Also, see Gilbert Ryle, *Collected Papers, Volume 2: Collected Essays 1929–1968* (New York: Routledge, 2009), 479–510.

10. There are a lot of useful takes on the philosophy, practice, and presentation of ethnographic research. John Van Maanen, *Representation in Ethnography* (Thousand Oaks, CA: Sage, 1995), offers the tripartitie schema of "realist," "confessional," and "impressionistic" efforts. Kamari Maxine Clarke distinguishes between expressive and instrumental ethnographic efforts (personal communication), while Rebecca Hardin and Kamari Maxine Clarke, eds., *Transforming Ethnographic Knowledge* (Madison: University of Wisconsin Press, 2012), help chart recent changes in ethnographic practices. Also, D. Soyini Madison, *Critical Ethnography: Method, Ethics, and Performance* (Thousand Oaks, CA: Sage, 2012), zeroes in on the ethical implications of participant observation. Moreover, there have been several intriguing recuperations of thin description across the social sciences and humanities. For a discussion of "close reading" as its methodological cross-cousin, see Heather Love, "Close Reading and Thin Description," *Public Culture* 25 (3) (forthcoming). For a communication scholar's articulation of "thin description" as a way to privilege the very communicability of social gestures across time and space (and to deemphasize the specificity of would-be intentions behind behaviors or of any supposedly clarifying contexts of reception), see McKenzie Wark, *Telesthesia: Communication, Culture, and Class* (Cambridge: Polity Press, 2012). For an argument about how social scientific calls for "richness" demand both thick and thin descriptions, see Wayne H. Brekhus, John F. Galliher, and Jaber F. Gubrium, "The Need for Thin Description," *Qualitative*

Inquiry 11 (6) (2005), 861–879. Whereas Ryle would use the camera's images as a way to flag what thin descriptions cannot capture, Heather Love points out that Douglas Bruster, *Shakespeare and the Question of Culture: Early Modern Literary and the Culture Turn* (New York: Palgrave MacMillan, 2003), argues for thin description as a kind of "deep focus" image. It might even represent a version of the optical unconscious, something that allows readers more uncanny ways of seeing. What we will save for another time is a discussion about the potential links between 'thin description' and what philosopher Tommie Shelby champions as 'thin' identity. Tommie Shelby, *We Who Are Dark: The Philosophical Foundations of Black Solidarity* (Cambridge, MA: Harvard University Press, 2005). Such links might be said to traipse through the work of scholars as diverse as Orlando Patterson, Paul Gilroy, and Luce Irigaray.

11. For a discussion of (a) ethnographic anxieties about the incompleteness of anthropological knowledge and (b) a privileging of ethnography as "making a connection to others in a partial manner," see Marilyn Strathern, *Partial Connections,* updated ed. (Walnut Creek, CA: AltaMira Press, 2004), 27. This idea of partial connections between researchers and subjects is preferable, I would argue, to the fantasy of researchers fully inhabiting/entering/embodying their subjects, a fantasy that might be fanned by thick description's ostensible interpretive finality.

12. See Daniel Frampton, *Filmosophy* (New York: Wallflower Press, 2006), for an articulation of film's distinctive value as a particular way of knowing and theorizing the world. I also find D. N. Rodowick's offerings on the specificities of visual media, including the differences between filmic and digital image-making, extremely helpful in these discussions; for example, see *The Virtual Life of Film* (Cambridge, MA: Harvard University Press, 2007) and *Reading the Figural, or, Philosophy After the New Media* (Durham, NC: Duke University Press, 2001).

13. This point came up during a discussion of law professor and filmmaker Regina Austin's analysis of "sentencing videos," which tend to traffic in reactionary cultural stereotypes of poverty to draw sympathy from viewers as opposed to making larger claims about the structural contexts for criminality.

14. See Sarah Pink, *The Future of Visual Anthropology: Engaging the Senses* (New York: Routledge, 2006), 7. For an articulation of the "unphotographable difference between a twitch and a wink," see Ryle, *Collected Papers,* 496.

15. See Ian Bogost, *Alien Phenomenology, or What It's Like to Be a Thing* (Minneapolis: University of Minnesota Press, 2012), 12. He also argues that "there is no hierarchy of being" that would privilege human subjectivity—or any other scale/unit of analysis—over all others (22). This antihumanist (or, at least, nonanthrocentric) position seems in opposition to the very idea of anthropology, at least the version most anthropologists might espouse.

16. Bogost actually wants to move away from "the two-dimensional plane of flat ontology" to "the point of tiny ontology," which he describes as "a dense mass of everything contained entirely—even as it's spread about haphazardly like a mess or organized logically like a network." Bogost, *Alien Phenomenology,* 21–22.

17. Christopher Johnson, *Microstyle: The Art of Writing Little* (New York: Norton, 2011) argues that discursive brevity or thinness has become the new normal in an age of tweets and texts. He argues that being able to write less has become so much more important. That is not exactly the point of "thin description," but it does speak to a

certain call for cultivated rhetorical slightness that might be a perfect vehicle for the "tiny ontologies" espoused by Bogost.

18. For a discussion of how a shoe might be imbued with the essence of its wearer (based on physical contact/connection between the two), see James Frazer, *The Golden Bough: A Study in Magic and Religion* (New York: MacMillan, 1951). Of course, anthropologists aren't the only ones who talk about "stepping into other people's shoes" as a way to represent empathy and connection, which helps to hint at how the discussion of anthropological occulting might have implications for relatedness far beyond the discipline.

19. For a discussion about how all languages (including mathematics) use tropes in ways that compromise their claims to universality or neutrality, see Donna J. Haraway, *Modest_Witness@Second_Millenium.FemaleMan©_Meets_OncoMouse™: Feminism and Technoscience* (New York: Routledge, 1997).

20. Just to be clear, so-called "native anthropologists" don't corner the market on the energizing viscosity of thinness. It isn't another way to prioritize the overall browning of anthropology/anthropologists, though some might read it that way. Simply put, in place of a thick description that might posit (as Claude Levi-Strauss once put it) "I is another," what about an unabashedly thinned anthropology that attempts to see "the other" as fully and completely human through one's own eyes—not as a vessel for fantasies of epistemological astral projection? For the aforementioned Levi-Straus sign formulation, see Anand Pandian, "The Time of Anthropology," *Cultural Anthropology* 24: 4 (November 2012): 551. The piece also notes that the articulation is found in Levi Strauss's discussion of Rousseau, *Structural Anthropology,* vol. 2 (London: Allen Lane, 1976). And there is another potential irony here: that the structure of this book seems to literalize the longing for astral projection that it rejects. But I want to believe that exposing such flights of fancy might actually go a long way toward potentially domesticating them.

21. The AHIJ went from privileging the term "nation" when they first left the United States to anchoring their collective project to the notion of a "kingdom," which is only one of the reasons why a discussion of race, religiosity, and nation is potentially useful. For a framing of the inextricable interconnections between and among these three categories, see Henry Goldschmidt and Elizabeth McAlister, *Race, Nation, and Religion in the Americas* (Oxford: Oxford University Press, 2004).

22. Karen Brodkin, *How Jews Became White Folks and What That Says About Race in America* (New Brunswick, NJ: Rutgers University Press, 1998). For a discussion of how the "lost tribes" became black in various Western scholarly and popular traditions, see Tudor Parfitt, *Black Jews in Africa and the Americas.*

23. For some of those contemporaneous vegan stories, see Etta M. Madden and Martha L Finch, eds., *Eating in Eden: Food and American Utopias* (Lincoln: University of Nebraska Press, 2006).

24. Paul Gilroy, *The Black Atlantic: Modernity and Double Consciousness* (Cambridge, MA: Harvard University Press, 1993). For an ethnographic treatment of ongoing and decidedly two-way Black Atlantic flows, see J. Lorand Matory, *Black Atlantic Religions: Tradition, Transnationalism, and Matriarchy in the Afro-Brazilian Candomblé* (Princeton, NJ: Princeton University Press, 2005).

25. Their search for the correct language and name of the God of the Hebrews has led them to what survived all along: *hallelu-Yah* (meaning "Praise Yah"). It can also be used, saints maintain, in conjunction with other names and attributes—for example, *Yahwah* (the Eternal), *Yah Yahwah, Yah Yaacov* (the God of Jacob), *Yahwah Ts-vah-ote* (the Lord of Hosts or Armies, signifying the warring side of the Creator). Cymatics also has implications for the Kingdom's investment in what they call Divine Music.

26. Every time I give a talk, I hear interesting arguments for how the AHIJ are just like other groups. The several I list here are just the ones that seem to come up most often. One of my former students, Eliana Ritts, did an amazing ethnographic film and undergraduate thesis on the Kaifeng Jews in China. For an overview of the Jewish presence in China, see M. Avrum Ehrlich, ed., *The Jewish-Chinese Nexus: A Meeting of Civilizations* (New York: Routledge, 2008). See also Yulia Egorova, *Jews and India: History, Image, Perceptions* (New York: Routledge, 2006) and Tudor Parfitt and Emanuela Semi, *Jews and India: Perceptions and Image* (New York: RoutledgeCurzon, 2002). Also, for a discussion of the Overcomer movement (another group of American expats that left Chicago for Israel long before the AHIJ), see Jane Fletcher Geniesse, *American Priestess: The Extraordinary Story of Anna Spafford and the American Colony in Jerusalem* (New York: Doubleday, 2008), 27. We remember that the stakes are high when we think about Nazism and the Holocaust, but contests over identity have always helped to fuel our most savage cultural conflicts, including bloody battles contingent on the Bible as final arbiter and ultimate archive. We forget—or downplay—the fact that Rwanda's genocide, for instance, was predicated, at least in part, on Hutus labeling Tutsis Hamitic and Semitic and then using that claim to justify mass slaughter. Tudor Parfitt, *Black Jews in Africa and the Americas,* 130.

THREE ▪ ARTSCIENCE

1. Marlon Riggs, *Black Is, Black Ain't* (San Francisco: California Newsreel, 1994) and *Tongues Untied: Black Men Loving Black Men* (San Francisco: Frameline, 1998).

2. Ralph Waldo Emerson, *The Complete Works of Ralph Waldo Emerson: Miscellanies,* vol. 2 (Boston: Houghton Mifflin, 1903), 430. The fuller citation, a celebration of death as but a portion of life's inevitable rebirth, reads as follows: "In these times we see the defects of our old theology; its inferiority to our habit of thoughts. Men go up and down; Science is popularized; the irresistible democracy—shall I call it?—of chemistry, of vegetation, which recomposes for new life every decomposing particle,—the race never dying, the individual never spared,—have impressed on the mind of the age the futility of these old arts of preserving. We give our earth to earth." I first found this Emersonian take on mortality in John Durham Peters, *Speaking into the Air: A History of the Idea of Communication* (Durham, NC: Duke University Press, 1999).

3. Several books written by Ben Ammi tackle this subject head on, including, *Everlasting Life: From Thought to Reality* (Washington, DC: Communicators Press, 1994) and *Physical Immortality: Conquering Death* (Washington, DC: Communicators Press, 2010), the latter not too far afield from an earlier (and differently

pitched) version of a similar project (arguing for the scientific plausibility of eternal life), Leonard Orr, *Physical Immortality: The Science of Everlasting Life* (Berkeley: Celestial Arts, 1982). Orr grounds his discussion in the claim that everlasting life starts with a true knowledge of God's name, which is also a basic principle of Ben Ammi's formulation.

4. There are many useful pieces on autoethnography, one that seems particularly relevant here (given the critical focus on race and gender/sexuality), is Irma McClaurin, "Theorizing a Black Feminist Self in Anthropology: Toward an Autoethnographic Approach," in *Black Feminist Anthropology: Theory, Politics, Praxis, and Poetics,* ed. Irma McClaurin (Rutgers University Press, 2001), 49–76.

5. Siddhartha Mukherjee, *The Emperor of All Maladies: A Biography of Cancer* (New York: Scribner, 2010), 37.

6. Lynne Littmann, *In Her Own Time: The Final Fieldwork of Barbara Myerhoff* (Santa Monica, CA: Direct Cinema Limited, 1985).

7. James Clifford and George E. Marcus, eds., *Writing Culture: The Poetics and Politics of Ethnography* (Berkeley, CA: University of California Press, 1986).

8. For a description of Anthroman, see John L. Jackson, Jr., *Real Black: Adventures in Racial Sincerity* (Chicago: University of Chicago Press, 2005), especially "Real Fictions," 1–33.

9. James Clifford and George Marcus, eds., *Writing Culture: The Poetics and Politics of Ethnography* (Berkeley, CA: University of California Press, 1986). Although the volume did include Mary Louise Pratt among its contributors, there were many critiques of its omissions. For some of those early critiques, see Ruth Behar, "Women Writing Culture: Another Telling of the Story of American Anthropology," *Critique of Anthropology* 13(4): 307–325; Faye Harrison, "Anthropology as an Agent of Transformation: Introductory Comments and Queries," in *Decolonizing Anthropology: Moving Further Toward Liberation* (Washington, DC: American Anthropological Association, 1991); bell hooks, *Yearning: Race, Gender, and Cultural Politics* (Boston: South End Press), and Frances Mascia-Lees, Patricia Sharpe, and Colleen Ballerino Cohen, "The Postmodernist Turn in Anthropology: Cautions from a Feminist Perspective," *Signs* 15(1) (1989): 7–33.

10. Anna Grimshaw, "The Bellwether Ewe: Recent Developments in Ethnographic Filmmaking and the Aesthetics of Anthropological Inquiry," *Cultural Anthropology* 26(2) (2011): 263–286.

11. Clifford Geertz, *The Interpretation of Cultures* (New York: Basic, 1973)

12. "Guidelines for Evaluation of Ethnographic Visual Media," *American Anthropologist* 104(2002): 305–306.

13. Thomas Csordas, *Body/Meaning/Healing* (New York: Palgrave, 2002). This notion of preobjectivity flags a way of being that is undifferentiated from the world in a manner reminiscent of what anthropologist Vicky Kirby claims—and, arguably, a differently pitched version of Bogost's flatter ontology.

14. John Durham Peters, *Speaking into the Air.* I can't help but read Peters as in productive conversation with the poetic and philosophical moves found in Elizabeth Alexander, *The Black Interior: Essays* (New York: Graywolf Press, 2004), which provides breathtakingly expansive examples of the aesthetic implications of racially

inflected connections and communities, connections that constitute African American life and culture in other than simply atomized, essentialized, and individualistic ways.

15. Roland Barthes, *Camera Lucida* (New York: Farrar, Straus and Giroux, 1981).

16. Greg Urban, *Metaculture: How Culture Moves Through the World* (Minneapolis: University of Minnesota Press, 2001).

17. There are so many books penned with the hopes of defining ethnography and its newest possibilities that I hesitate to list any of them. Here are a few more of the ones that I have found particularly useful over the years and have also assigned in classes: Harry Wolcott, *Ethnography: A Way of Seeing* (Lanham, MD: AltaMira Press, 2000); H. Lloyd Goodall, *Writing the New Ethnography* (Lanham, MD: AltaMira Press, 2000); George E. Marcus, *Ethnography Through Thick and Thin* (Princeton, NJ: Princeton University Press, 1998); Paul Rabinow, George E. Marcus, James Faubion, Tobias Rees, *Designs for an Anthropology of the Contemporary* (Durham, NC: Duke University Press, 2008); and Allaine Cerwonka and Liisa H. Malkki, *Improvising Theory: Process and Temporality in Ethnographic Fieldwork* (Chicago: University of Chicago Press, 2007).

18. Lewis R. Gordon, *Disciplinary Decadence: Living Thought in Trying Times* (Boulder, CO: Paradigm, 2007) reminds us of the difference between "eternal" and "immortal." One has always been and always will be; the other hasn't always been but will be from now on.

19. Lewis Gordon has reminded me (personal communication) that such a consequential link between sin and death has resonances with the Rastafari and other groups. He also points out how this might be likened to the "God Complex" of empires, another potential variation on Sartre's claim that human beings have a misplaced desire to be God, another *will to immortality*. Rock band Fishbone has a 1993 album title that captures a similar idea: "Give a Monkey a Brain and He'll Swear He's the Center of the Universe."

20. The AHIJ community is also unabashedly against homosexuality, which, along with Riggs's omnivorous diet (as flagged by his film's use of a gumbo metaphor), would be part of what Saints would use to explain his physical mortality. These are manifestations, they argue, of a disregard for our ancestors' covenant with Yah, a disregard that directly translates into the certainty of death. Eternal life, saints argue, is only possible by repairing the links to Yah (i.e, obeying his Edenic commandments).

21. These preoccupations with beating back death are a function, perhaps, of what literary theorists Stephen Best and Saidiya Hartman describe as "the ongoing production of lives lived in intimate relation to premature death (whether civil, social ,or literal) . . ." Stephen Best and Saidiya Hartman, "Fugitive Justice," *Representations*, 92: 13. Some of this talk about how ethnographic data unfurls was made quite poignantly in *Writing Culture*.

22. Bill Laurer, *Mutual Life, Limited: Islamic Banking, Alternative Currencies, Lateral Reason* (Princeton, NJ: Princeton University Press, 2005).

23. See Johannes Fabian, *Time and the Other: How Anthropology Makes Its Object* (New York: Columbia University Press, 2002); Alfred Gell, *The Anthropology of Time: Cultural Constructions of Temporal Maps and Images.* (London: Berg, 2001); Adam

Kuper, *The Invention of Primitive Society: Transformations of an Illusion*. (London: Routledge, 1988). For a discussion of the "savage slot" as another take on this anthropological propensity for denying coevality, see Michel-Rolph Trouillot, *Global Transformations: Anthropology and the Modern World* (New York: Palgrave, 2003), chap.1.

24. Jane I. Guyer, "Prophecy and the Near Future: Thoughts on Macroeconomic, Evangelical, and Punctuated Time," *American Ethnologist* 34(3): 409–421.

25. Vicky Kirby, *Quantum Anthropologies: Life at Large* (Durham, NC: Duke University Press, 2011), 25, 31, and 27. Physical life, Kirby claims, is a kind of meaning-making of a piece with the linguistic. Some of this might be read as a classic phenomeno-logical point; for a kind of primer on how those connections might be mapped, see Robert Sokolowski, *Introduction to Phenomenology* (New York: Cambridge University Press, 2000).

26. Saints believe that the planet and everything on it has a kind of Yah-given agency. Of course, many other groups, communities, and cultures all around the world posit similar ideas. I won't attempt to flag all the points of convergence between the AHIJ's beliefs and other groups, but some of the resonances should be clear throughout.

27. For a discussion of the ontologies/catholicisms that ground much Christian thought, see William Cavanaugh, "The World in a Wafer: A Geography of the Eucharist as Resistance to Globalization," *Modern Theology* (15)2 (April 1999): 181–196.

28. David Edwards, *Artscience: Creativity in the Post-Google Generation*. Cambridge, (MA: Harvard University Press, 2010).

29. Gordon, *Disciplinary Decadence*.

FOUR ▪ MEGIDDO

1. Hebrew Israelite groups in the United States that are unaffiliated with the AHIJ are labeled "camps," as opposed to AHIJ "extensions" and "jurisdictions."

2. Steven Thrasher, "Black Hebrew Israelites: New York's Most Obnoxious Prophets," *The Village Voice,* March 30, 2011, 8.

3. Rebecca Alpert reminded me (personal communication) that this is a classic trope in many religious conversion stories. I can conjure a gospel version (with singer Mary J. Blige's voice in my ears): *I once was lost, but now am found/ was blind but now I see.* For a fascinating rendition of this personal journey to Hebrew Israelite identity, see Andre Key, "What's My Name? An Autoethnography of the Problem of Moral Evil and Ethnic Suffering in Black Judaism" (PhD diss., Temple University, 2011).

4. Ahmadiel means "I stand for God" in Hebrew. Saints call their non-Hebrew names "slave names" or more commonly "Jake names," a reference to Jacob, the Old Testament figure whose name God changed to Israel. In Ahmadiel's eyes, his grand-mother's whiteness wasn't mitigated at all by her Jewishness.

5. For two differently pitched anthropological discussions of how people negotiate the changed/changing/contested borders of the Israeli state, see Avram Bornstein, *Crossing the Green Line Between the West Bank and Israel* (Philadelphia: University of Pennsylvania Press, 2002) and Rebecca L. Stein, *Itineraries in Conflict: Israelis,*

Palestinians, and the Political Lives of Tourism (Durham, NC: Duke University Press, 2008).

6. A reference to the "ships of Tarshish" is found in Ezekiel 27:25

7. The short film—Reginald Hudlin, *Space Traders* (Home Box Office, 1994)—was one segment in a larger film, *Cosmic Slop* (Home Box Office, 1994). The full short story is online: http://web.archive.org/web/20100404123611/http:/edweb.tusd.k12.az.us /uhs/APUSH/1st%20Sem/Articles%20Semester%201/Artiles%20Semester%201 /Bell.htm.

FIVE ▪ CHICAGO

1. For a new and innovative treatment of these historical figures, see Jacob Dorman, *Chosen People: The Rise of American Black Israelite Religions* (Oxford: Oxford University Press, 2012).

2. The work of many of these scholars has been invaluable to this book, including James E. Landing, *Black Judaism: Story of an American Movement* (Durham, NC: Carolina Academic Press, 2002); Howard Brotz, *The Black Jews of Harlem* (New York: Schocken, 1970); Yvonne Chireau and Nathaniel Deutsch, eds., *Black Zion: African American Religious Encounters with Judaism* (Oxford: Oxford University Press, 2000); Arthur Huff Fauset, *Black Gods of the Metropolis: Negro Religious Cults of the Urban North* (Philadelphia: University of Pennsylvania Press, 1944); and Andre Key, "What's My Name? An Autoethnography of the Problem of Moral Evil and Ethnic Suffering in Black Judaism" (PhD diss., Temple University, 2011).

3. Merrill Singer, "Saints of the Kingdom: Group Emergence, Individual Affiliation, and Social Change Among the Black Hebrews of Israel" (PhD diss., University of Utah, 1979), 73.

4. For an overview of the ebbs and flows that define the long history of African American attraction to emigration, see James T. Campbell, *Middle Passages: African American Journeys to Africa, 1787–2005* (New York: Penguin, 2006).

5. For a recent reprint of some of Faitlovich's work, see Jacques Faitlovich, *The Falashas* (Central, Hong Kong: Forgotten Books, 2012). Falashas is considered a derogatory term. The majority of the community goes by the name Beta Israel now. Also, for an overview of Faitlovich's relationship to the study of Ethiopian Jewry, see Emanuela Trevisan Semi, *Jacques Faitlovitch and The Jews of Ethiopia* (Portland, OR: Vallentine Mitchell, 2007).

SIX ▪ EXILES

1. Engagement with the anthropological "arrival scene" has been discussed and rethought in a lot of locales, including James Clifford and George E. Marcus, eds., *Writing Culture: The Poetics and Politics of Ethnography* (Berkeley: University of California Press, 1986).

2. Bronislaw Malinowski, *Argonauts of the Western Pacific* (New York: Dutton, 1950), 4, includes this classic and often-quoted line: "Imagine yourself suddenly set down surrounded by all your gear, alone on a tropical beach close to a native village, while

the launch of the dinghy which has brought you sails away out of sight." Malinowksi is usually called the father of anthropological fieldwork. Tom Boellstorff, *Coming of Age in Second Life: An Anthropologist Explores the Virtually Human* (Princeton, NJ: Princeton University Press, 2008) plays with this classic articulation of things in his examination of the online world of Second Life. Also, one of the first books I read during the crucial moments when I decided to get a PhD in anthropology, was Nigel Barley, *The Innocent Anthropologist: Notes from a Mud Hut* (Prospect Heights, IL: Wavelenth Press, 1983), which is usually deemed a "popular" book (not a scholarly one) at least in part, I think, because it does begin with the anthropologist running around at his home institution, not just plopped down into the field.

3. Miceala di Leonardo, *Exotics at Home: Anthropologies, Others, and American Modernity* (Chicago: University of Chicago Press, 1998) does a compelling job res-ituating anthropological inquiry into a larger "modern" context that has always included work in the United States. She would take issue with too fine a point being made about ethnography having not been designed to study modern life. It has been doing that kind of work, she'd argue, for a very long time, even if some of its practi-tioners might seem to deny that fact. For an argument about how this pith-helmet imagery also traffics in imperialist longings, see Lewis Gordon, *Disciplinary Decadence: Living Thought in Trying Times* (Boulder, CO: Paradigm Publishers, 2007), especially the final chapter, as well as Lewis Gordon and Jane Gordon, *An Introduction to Africana Philosophy,* (Cambridge: Cambridge University Press, 2008), 22, 196, 204.

4. For a discussion of "headnotes" and how other scholars, including Simone Ottenberg and Margaret Mead, have used the term and the idea it encapsulates, see Roger Sanjek, "A Vocabulary for Fieldnotes," in *Fieldnotes: The Makings of Anthropology,* ed. Roger Sanjek (Ithaca, NY: Cornell University Press, 1990).

5. See Erica Moiah James, "Speaking in Tongues: Metapictures and the Discourse of Violence in Caribbean Art," *Small Axe* 16 (1 37): 119–143. For another new and com-pelling rendition of diasporic black family photography, see Tina M. Campt, *Image Matters: Archive, Photography and the African Diaspora in Europe* (Durham, NC: Duke University Press, 2012).

6. This began long before even the most seemingly isolated and "backward" of non-Western communities were considered "remotely global," linked and linkable by cell phone, laptop, or television screen to the very same social exchanges that Western anthropology was traditionally designed to leave behind. For an articula-tion of this newly appreciated anthropological reality, see Charles Piot, *Remotely Global: Village Modernity in West Africa* (Chicago: University of Chicago Press, 1999). Also, this short-circuiting of the researching-writing binary is not necessarily just another way to describe the rabid inductive process that is "grounded theory," but it does help to explain the purported benefits of going back and forth between theoretical re-conceptualizations and ethnographic data-gathering as demonstrated in A. Cerwonka and L.H. Malkki, *Improvising Theory: Process and Temporality in Ethnographic Fieldwork* (Chicago: University of Chicago Press, 2007).

7. For one classic critique of such a dynamic, see W. E. B. Du Bois, *The Autobiography of W. E. B. Dubois: A Soliloquy on Viewing My Life from the Last Decade of Its First*

Century (New York: International Publishers, 1968), specifically his reflections on his time in Philadelphia.

8. The notion of "grounded theory" is predicated on recursivity, but it is usually framed as a reworking of hypotheses once in the field and less as an ongoing feedback loop of data retrieval and analysis, data retrieval and representation. See Brian Glaser and Anselm Strauss, *Discovery of Grounded Theory: Strategies for Qualitative Research* (Chicago: Aldine, 1967).

9. For a staging of this debate's two sides (one virtualist and emphasizing the newness of new media technologies, the other materialist and critiquing any discussion of digital media that presupposes a rupture with earlier cultural processes, practices, and technologies), see Christine Hine, *Virtual Ethnography* (London: Sage, 2000) and Daniel Miller and Michal Slater, *The Internet: An Ethnographic Approach* (London: Berg, 2001). For an ethnography that is exclusively online, see Tom Boellstorff, *Coming of Age in Second Life* (Princeton, NJ: Princeton University Press, 2008).

10. Mary Catherine Bateson, "Participant Observation as a Way of Living," in *Transforming Ethnographic Knowledge,* eds., Rebecca Hardin and Kamari Maxine Clarke (Madison: University of Wisconsin Press, 2012).

SEVEN ▪ BACKSTAGE

1. For a discussion of "serious games" as a way to think about the political implications of cultural practice and analysis, see Sherry B. Ortner, *Making Gender: The Politics and Erotics of Culture* (Boston: Beacon Press, 1996).

2. "Things are what they are," the phrase implies. "You can't change it, so no use fretting." The AHIJ would critique a kind of "everything is everything" attitude as the very "anything goes" nihilism destroying black America. Their version of everyday ethnography would actually critique the relatively blasé position that "everything is everything" usually captures. (And then there is always the "everything is political" mantra that feminism helped popularize.)

3. That is, provided the group being researched isn't on the other side of the so-called "digital divide," as many scholars remind us, including Faye Ginsburg, "Rethinking the Digital Age," in *The Media and Social Theory,* ed. David Hesmondhalgh and Jason Toynbee (New York: Routledge, 2008).

4. John Durham Peters, *Speaking into the Air: A History of the Idea of Communication* (Chicago: University of Chicago Press, 2001) spends a lot of time explaining how anxieties about the imperfections of communication enervate many classic and contemporary debates. One of my former students has a tale of ethnographic research subjects reading her unpublished dissertation and, consequently, making the actual publication of her book based on that material even more difficult to complete.

5. Several works explicitly tackle the underanalyzed intimacies of ethnographic research, including a couple of interesting edited collections that frame the selfsame fundamental question very differently: Fran Markowitz and Michael Ashkenazi, eds., *Sex, Sexuality, and the Anthropologist* (Champaign, IL: University of Illinois Press,

1999) and Andrew Shryock, ed., *Off Stage/On Display: Intimacy and Ethnography in the Age of Public Culture* (Palo Alto, CA: Stanford University Press, 2004).

6. Johannes Fabian, *Ethnography as Commentary: Writing from the Virtual Archive* (Durham, NC: Duke University Press, 2008).

7. Bambi Schieffelin relayed this point to me in a conversation we had after a presentation of my earlier work on race and sincerity. Some of her research on language ideologies—for instance, Miki Makihara and Bambi B. Schieffelin, *Consequences of Contact: Language Ideologies and Sociocultural Transformations in Pacific Societies* (Oxford: Oxford University Press, 2007)—helps to unpack such culturally specific assumptions. Similarly, according to Webb Keane, "Sincerity, 'Modernity', and the Protestants," in *Cultural Anthropology* 17 (1) (February 2002): 65–92, overinvestments in such sincerity are often a kind of Christian (specifically Protestant) predilection/borrowing.

8. Many scholars studying identity issues in the United States argue that self-representation/misrepresentation is not the only way to understand Western selves and notions of subjecthood. That is quite true, but my goal is simply to maintain that "ethnographic sincerity" points toward a slightly different kind of real/unreal in a mediatized global landscape—and toward an ethnographic field-site that is concomitantly getting reconfigured as a function of newfangled media technology and the digitalizing of ethnographic research. Sincerity is potentially relevant for the anthropological project, even if it isn't relevant in all times and places.

9. This is a notion of fieldwork as fellowship that is only a different version of the same dynamic that grounds traditional ethnographic research. It is part of what is meant by the idea that "ethnography remains vital, not because ethnographic methods guarantee certain knowledge of others but because ethnographic fieldwork brings us into direct dialogue *with* others," Michael Jackson, ed., *Things As They Are: New Directions in Phenomenological Anthropology* (Bloomfield: Indiana University Press, 1996), 8.

EIGHT ▪ ANALOGIES

1. See Tudor Parfitt, *Journey to the Vanished City* (New York: Vintage, 1992) and Tudor Parfitt, *The Lost Ark of the Covenant: The Remarkable Quest for the Legendary Ark* (London: HarperCollins, 2008). For another look at the Lemba vis-à-vis debates about genetic markers for identity and the construction of religio-racial difference, see Noah Tamarkin, "(Lost) Tribes to Citizens: Lemba 'Black Jews' Engage the South African State" (PhD diss, University of California, Santa Cruz, 2011). For another description of Lemba Judaic traditions, see Rabson Wuriga, *Of Sacred Times, Rituals, and Customs: Oral Traditions of the Lemba Jews of Zimbabwe* (New York: Kulanu, Inc. and EpicCenter Stories, 2012).

2. Seth Sanders, "Invisible Races," *Transition* 85 (2000), 76–97, assumes the easy acceptance of other races into the Jewish fold, an easy acceptance that is belied by the self-published memoirs of Kush Miri, *Season in Sheol: A Black Women's Nightmare Journey through Synagogue Culture* (New York: iUniverse, Inc., 2009), and Tamar

Manasseh, *Chai-Me: My Exploration of Race, Religion, and Spirituality in America* (Chicago: Tamar Manasseh, 2012), two examples of African American Jews chronicling slights from European members of their respective synagogues and from the larger Jewish community.

3. Mark G. Thomas, Tudor Parfitt, Deborah A. Weiss, et al., "Y Chromosomes Traveling South: The Cohen Modal Haplotype and the Origins of the Lemba—the 'Black Jews of Southern Africa,'" *American Journal of Human Genetics* 66, no. 2 (February 2000), 674–86.

4. For a musicological discussion about African drums as part of a larger ethnographic story about African musicality and cultural practice, see John Miller Chernoff, *African Rhythm and African Sensibility: Aesthetics and Social Action in African Musical Idioms* (Chicago: University of Chicago Press, 1981); Yaya Diallo, *The Healing Drum: African Ceremonial and Ritual Music* (Rochester, VT: Destiny Recording, 1994).

5. Anthropologist Noah Tamarkin is working on a fascinating book, *Jewish Blood, African Bones: Belonging in South Africa,* which unpacks the experiences of citizenship and belonging, race and religiosity, that frame the identity-claims and political/politicized landscape of those DNA-tested Lemba in South Africa.

6. For a summary of Carey's case, see Brycchan Carey, "Olaudah Equiano: A Critical Biography," http://www.brycchancarey.com/equiano/biog.htm. It should be noted that many scholars take issue with Carey's claim—for instance, Nigerian writer Remy Ilona. I invoke it not as a point of fact. Instead, I want to argue that Equiano's story of Igbo-Jewish similarities is remarkable whether or not Carey's theory is right.

7. For powerful excerpts from *The Interesting Narrative of the Life of Olaudah Equiano* (1789), excerpts that include the sections I've quoted here, see Olaudah Equiano, *Sold as a Slave* (New York: Penguin 2007), 17.

8. Many writers have tackled the curse of Ham. Three valuable (and relatively recent) examples of serious engagement with this idea are Colin Kidd, *The Forging of Races: Race and Scripture in the Protestant Atlantic World, 1600–2000* (Cambridge: Cambridge University Press, 2006): Jonathan Schorsch, *Jews and Blacks in the Early Modern World* (Cambridge: Cambridge University Press, 2004); and David M. Goldenberg, *The Curse of Ham: Race and Slavery in Early Judaism, Christianity, and Islam* (Princeton, NJ: Princeton University Press, 2003). Also, Stacy Davis, *This Strange Story: Jewish and Christian Interpretation of the Curse of Canaan from Antiquity to 1865* (Lanham, M.D: University Press of America, 2008) and David Whitford, *The Curse of Ham in the Early Modern Era: The Bible and the Justifications for Slavery. St. Andrews Studies in Reformation History* (Farnham, England: Ashgate , 2009).

9. All phrases in quotations are taken directly from official AHIJ literature, either the exhibit itself or Kingdom-produced flyers and pamphlets about the exhibit. Or they are quotes taken from saints themselves.

10. Robert R. Edgar and Hilary Sapire, *African Apocalypse: The Story of Nontetha Nkwenkwe, a Twentieth-Century South African Prophet* (Athens: Ohio University Press, 2000).

11. For a few different takes on these relocation projects, see Tudor Parfitt, *Operation Moses: The Untold Story of the Secret Exodus of the Falasha Jews from Ethiopia* (Lanham, MD: Stein and Day Publishing, 1986); Shmuel Yilmah, *From Falasha to Freedom: An Ethiopian Jew's Journey to Jerusalem* (Cedarhurst, NY: Gefen Publishing House, 1996); and Stephen Spector, *Operation Solomon: The Daring Rescue of the Ethiopian Jews* (Oxford: Oxford University Press, 2006). For a discussion of the role that racialization has played in the incorporation of Ethiopians into the Jewish fold, see Bruce D. Haynes, "People of God, Children of Ham: Making Black(s) Jews," *Journal of Modern Jewish Studies* 8(2): 237–254.

NINE ▪ ASIEL

1. For a classic discussion of the culture of poverty argument (as conceptualized by Oscar Lewis and later redeployed by other social scientists and politicians), see Ulf Hannerz, *Soulside: Inquiries into Ghetto Culture and Community* (Chicago: University of Chicago Press, 1969).

2. Ben Ammi, *Physical Immortality—Conquering Death* (Washington, DC: Communicators Press, 2010), 96.

3. This is cited from an unpublished interview conducted by Morris Lounds Jr. Two decades later, Ben Ammi would travel to the United States carrying a message called "Deliver Us From Evil" in which he would remind us that Yeshua's famous prayer asks for deliverance from evil, "not a bigger share of it."

4. David Swift, *Black Prophets of Justice: Activist Clergy Before the Civil War*, (Baton Rouge, LA: Louisiana State University Press, 1989), 354. See also St. Clair Drake, *The Redemption of Africa and Black Religion* (Chicago, IL: Third World Press, 1970).

5. This kind of argument has also long animated versions of Afrocentrism, a critique of false black cultural practices and assumptions as the byproduct of American (or Western, or European) "miseducation" and assimilation.

6. John L. Comaroff and Jean Comaroff, *Ethnicity Inc.* (Chicago: University of Chicago Press, 2009).

TEN ▪ HUSTLING

1. All new saints go through a year-long "absorption process" that includes learning the Kingdom's fundamental beliefs, rereading the Bible with those beliefs as interpretive lenses, and studying the writings of Ben Ammi.

2. This took place during the Second Intifada (2000–2005), which is considered the second major Palestinian uprising against Israel. The First Intifada (1987–1993) raged while the AHIJ's were still fighting for permanent residency in the country.

3. See this expansive critique (of more than just "rational man") in David Graeber, *Debt: The First 5,000 Years* (Brooklyn, NY: Melville House, 2011).

4. I've heard several saints link the Kingdom's philosophy to the Bible, Acts 2:44–45: "And all that believed were together, and had all things common; And sold their possessions and goods, and parted them to all men, as every man had need." See

also Acts 4:32: "And the multitude of them that believed were of one heart and of one soul: neither said any of them that ought of the things which he possessed was his own; but they had all things common." For a discussion of the earliest connections between and among socialism, politics, and Christianity (subsequently posited as mutually exclusive domains in Marxist critiques of religion as an opiate), see Roger Lancaster, *Thanks to God and the Revolution: Popular Religion and Class Consciousness in the New Nicaragua* (New York: Columbia University Press, 1988).

ELEVEN ▪ IGNORANCE

1. In his articulation of a new "anthropology of the contemporary," Paul Rabinow discusses the dynamic of "chronicling observations," an ethnographic world of "first-order," "second-order," and "second, second order" observers determining how much of themselves and the outside world they can fit in their ethnographic frames, in *Marking Time: On the Anthropology of the Contemporary* (Princeton, NJ: Princeton University Press, 2007), 66.

2. I'm reusing another anthropologist's memorable phrasing here: Roger Sanjek, *The Future of Us All: Race and Neighborhood Politics in New York City* (Ithaca, NY: Cornell University Press, 1998).

3. For a discussion of the complicated calculus of partial divulgences, see Eve Kosofsky Sedgwick, *Epistemology of the Closet* (Berkeley: University of California Press, 1990). See also, for a discussion of the transparency of sexualized closets, C. Riley Snorton, *The Glass Closet: Black Sexuality and Panoptical Imagination* (Minneapolis: University of Minnesota Press, forthcoming).

4. Marcel Griaule, *Conversations with Ogotemmeli: An Introduction to Dogon Religious Ideas* (Oxford: Oxford University Press, 1975) is a book that always struck me as demonstrating this dynamic (whether my graduate-student-self read it into their "conversations" or not). Ogotemmeli seemed keen on making sure his anthropological interlocutor understood the "deep knowledge" he was willing to share, even with Europeans.

5. For a discussion of the "public secret," see Michael Taussig, *Defacement: Public Secrecy and the Labor of the Negative* (Palo Alto, CA: Stanford University Press, 1999).

6. The quote comes from Lewis Gordon, *Disciplinary Decadence: Living Thought in Trying Times* (Boulder, CO: Paradigm Publishers, 2007), 80. For a discussion of "risky practice" in anthropology, see Paul Rabinow, *Marking Time.*

7. Laura Bohannan, *Return to Laughter: An Anthropological Novel* (New York: Doubleday and the American Museum of Natural History, 1954), 70.

8. For a discussion of the fundamental role of chance in ethnographic research, see Michael Taussig, *I Swear I Saw This: Drawings in Fieldwork Notebooks, Namely My Own* (Chicago: University of Chicago Press, 2012). Taussig calls for drawing over writing as one way to beat back the will to full and complete knowledge—"to butt against realism, with its desire for completeness" (13). Ethnographic knowledge is "all the more 'complete,'" says Taussig, "because it cannot be completed." Chance is another way of articulating the role of "improvisation" in ethnographic research.

For a version of that discussion on chance as a dance with the improvisational nature of ethnographic fieldwork (along with a related take on the subjective and punctuated unfurling of ethnographic time in the field), see A. Cerwonka and L. H. Malkki, *Improvising Theory: Process and Temporality in Ethnographic Fieldwork* (Chicago: University of Chicago Press, 2007).

9. My understanding of haptography comes from an examination of some of the work being done by a few of my Penn Engineering colleagues: http://haptics.grasp.upenn .edu/index.php/Research/Haptography.

10. Giorgo Agamben, *Nudities* (Palo Alto, CA: Stanford University Press, 2010), 114. For a differently pitched discussion about the ethnographic value of nonknowing, see Casey High, Ann H. Kelly, and Jonathan Mair, *The Anthropology of Ignorance* (New York: Palgrave, 2012).

TWELVE ▪ YMCA

1. See Roger Lancaster, *Sex Panic and the Punitive State* (University of California Press, 2011).

2. See Jean-Paul Sartre, *Anti-Semite and Jew: An Exploration of the Etiology of Hate* (New York: Schoken Books, 1948).

3. See Jonathan Boyarin and Daniel Boyarin, *Powers of Diaspora: Two Essays on the Relevance of Jewish Culture* (Minneapolis: University of Minnesota Press, 2002).

THIRTEEN ▪ UNAFRICAN

1. "Don't be a sucker all your life" is pretty close to a verbatim quote (at least in the film reel of this event pierced into my subconscious). These quotation-marked-off words are what I have always heard him say when I have replayed the exchange in my mind.

2. For a discussion of the institutional history of the ICUPK in the United States, see James E. Landing, *Black Judaism: Story of an American Movement* (Durham, NC: Carolina Academic Press, 2002).

3. Many of the Israelite camps call African Americans "so-called Negroes," a phrasing made famous by Malcolm X in the 1950s and 1960s.

4. For a discussion of these varied Israelite identities, see James E. Landing, *Black Judaism: Story of an American Movement* (Durham, NC: Carolina Academic Press, 2002).

5. For a recent discussion and overview of African Jewry, see Edith Bruder, *The Black Jews of Africa: History, Religion, Identity* (New York: Oxford University Press, 2012).

6. It is important to note that the ICUPK do locate all twelve tribes (not just ten) in different parts of the Americas, even the tribes of Judah and Benjamin, which are linked to African Americans and West Indians, respectively. For a discussion of how Israel is reframed as Africa by the AHIJ, see Fran Markowitz, "Israel as Africa, Africa as Israel: 'Divine Geography' in the Personal Narratives and

Community Identity of the Black Hebrew Israelites," *Anthropological Quarterly* 69(4): 193–205.

FOURTEEN ▪ EMPRESS

1. The film, *Bad Friday: Rastafari After Coral Gardens* (Third World Newsreel, 2011) is based on a chapter from Deborah A. Thomas, *Exceptional Violence: Embodied Citizenship in Transnational Jamaica* (Durham, NC: Duke Univerity Press, 2011) . Deborah Thomas is my wife and was one of my collaborators on the film, along with Rastas Junior Wedderburn and Junior Manning. *Exceptional Violence,* her second book, actually extends an argument that she made in her first one (about how and why some Jamaican communities are more or less prone to violence than others), an argument that she didn't fully realize she had been making until she started to work on the second project after the peaceful mountaintop community where she conducted her research erupted into violence several years later. See Deborah A. Thomas, *Modern Blackness: Nationalism, Globalization, and the Politics of Culture in Jamaica* (Durham, NC: Duke University Press, 2004).

2. Thomas, *Exceptional Violence.*

3. This phenomenon is theorized in John L. Comaroff and Jean Comaroff, *Ethnicity, Inc.* (Chicago: University of Chicago Press, 2009).

4. For an overview of Rastafarian beliefs, see Barry Chevannes, *Rastafari: Roots and Ideology* (Syracuse, NY: Syracuse University Press, 1994) and Douglas R. A. Mack, *From Babylon to Rastafari: Origin and History of the Rastafarian Movement* (Chicago: School Times Publications, 1999).

FIFTEEN ▪ CAMPS

1. There are several important books that lay out some of this historical landscape, especially James Landing, *Black Judaism: Story of a an American Movement* (Durham, NC: Carolina Academic Press, 2002); Yvonne Chireau and Nathaniel Deutsch, eds., *Black Zion: African American Religious Encounters with Judaism* (Oxford: Oxford University Press, 2000); Arthur Huff Fauset, *Black Gods of the Metropolis: Negro Religious Cults of the Urban North* (Philadelphia: University of Pennsylvania Press, 1944).

2. Howard Brotz, *The Black Jews of Harlem* (New York: Schocken, 1970). For differently pitched discussions about Ethiopian Jews, see Tudor Parfitt and Emanuela Semi, *Judaising Movements: Studies in the Margins of Judaism in Modern Times* (London: Routledge, 2002); Steven Kaplan, *The Beta Israel: Falasha in Ethiopia: From Earliest Times to the Twentieth Century* (New York: New York University Press, 1995); Yosef A. A. ben-Jochannan, *We, the Black Jews: Witness to the 'White Jewish Race' Myth,* vols. 1 and 2 (New York: Black Classic Press, 1993). For an evocative discussion of African American investments in Jewishness (including a short discussion on Ben Ammi), see Eric J. Sundquist, *Strangers in the Land: Blacks, Jews, Post-Holocaust America* (Cambridge, MA: Harvard University Press, 2005),

especially chapter 2. For one of the most theoretically rich and ambitious treatments of what it means to be black and Jewish at the same time (with the political and decidedly personal coefficients of that discussion front and center), see Katya Gibel Azoulay, *Black, Jewish and Interracial: It's Not the Color of Your Skin, but the Race of Your Kin, and Other Myths of Identity* (Durham, NC: Duke University Press, 1997).

3. Jacob Dorman, *Chosen People: Black Jews, Israelites, and Polyculturalism from Slavery to Black Power* (Oxford: Oxford University Press, 2011). For a discussion of "hidden transcripts" see James Scott, *Weapons of the Weak: Everyday Forms of Peasant Resistance* (New Haven, CT: Yale University Press, 1987).

4. See my discussion of this in John L. Jackson Jr., *Real Black: Adventures in Racial Sincerity* (Chicago: University of Chicago Press, 2005).

SIXTEEN ▪ LIBERIA

1. This story is found in Gavriel HaGadol and Israel Odehyah, *The Impregnable People* (Washington, DC: Communicators Press, 1992).

2. Merrill Singer, "Saints of the Kingdom: Group Emergence, Individual Affiliation, and Social Change Among the Black Hebrews of Israel" (PhD diss., University of Utah, 1979).

3. M. B. Akpan, "Liberia and the Universal Negro Improvement Association: The Background to the Abortion of Garvey's Scheme for African Colonization," *Journal of African History*, 14, no. 1(1973): 105–127.

4. An undergrad thesis on this Liberian moment, see Johanna Bard Richlin, "Liberating Medusa: Strategies of Accommodation and The Elasticity of Culture "(Wesleyan, 2008). http://wesscholar.wesleyan.edu/cgi/viewcontent.cgi?article=1175 &context=etd_hon_theses

5. "Negro Jews Who Fled America Trying For New Life in Liberia," Danville Register, (January 18, 1968), 26: http://newspaperarchive.com/danville-register/1968-01-18/page-26.

6. Several different saints have told me, in passing, that "Roebuck was a black man."

SEVENTEEN ▪ VISITATIONS

1. My earliest visits to Dimona found me constantly fending off the anxieties of friends and family members. Israel seemed so far away to some of them, so fraught with exotic dangers. They invoked the figure of the suicide bomber to stand in for much of that distance. And I had to admit that going to Israel for the first time did feel unlike any of my previous anthropological escapades in urban America. Just the plane ride from Kennedy to Ben Gurion and its lesson in phylacterial praying was a crash course in Judaic difference that even my upbringing in the predominantly Jewish neighborhood of Canarsie, Brooklyn, hadn't quite prepared me for.

2. This is arguably a permutation of what anthropologist Nadia Abu El-Haj argues has been part of the Israeli state's explicit project of producing historically minded

Jewish citizen-subjects for a long time, producing these subjects through control over how the Israeli landscape and its most important landmarks are interpreted. See Nadia Abu El-Haj, *Facts on the Ground: Archaeological Practice and Territorial Self-Fashioning in Israeli Society* (Chicago: University of Chicago Press, 2001).

3. For a discussion of "media events," see Daniel Dayan and Elihu Katz, *Media Events: The Live Broadcasting of History* (Cambridge, MA: Harvard University Press, 1994).

4. As several colleagues have reminded me, many Israelis engage in this discourse about Israel being much safer (and less crazy) than America.

5. David Graeber, *Debt: The First 5,000 Years* (Brooklyn, NY: Melville House, 2011). He links this to a related contention that the ethnographic record documents the fact that many traditional societies recognize the singular and individual irreplaceability of every human being, no matter what cultural rituals of compensation for loss of life might obtain.

6. The AHIJ use the term "fifth quarter" to describe an area occupied by Africans in Jerusalem's Old City, one of the places where they take visitors during "sacred visitations." Their point is that the area doesn't even have a designation in official representations of the city, representations that invisibilize, they argue, the history of Africans in the area. Sar Ahmadiel would add that the "Western Wall" Plaza—a rather pristine open plaza—was formerly identified as the Moorish (or Moor's) Quarter, invoking a 1928 photograph that ostensibly shows an area densely packed with homes and shops.

7. The designation *Jew* or *Jewish* is also meant to reference far more than just religion. It invokes culture, nationality, and even race. But Israelites would still argue that the Jewish culture at play is both European (not African/Edenic) and far afield from the cultural practices of the Old Testament. For a discussion of how definitions of religion are debated (for instance, whether the emphasis should be on orthodoxy or orthopraxy), see Tomoko Masuzawa, *The Invention of World Religions, or, How European Universalism Was Preserved in the Language of Pluralism* (Chicago: University of Chicago Press, 2005). Of course, anthropologists have long debated whether too-easy characterizations of religious traditions are more practice-based or belief-based. Using debates on mediation among anthropologists of media and religion, Aisha Mahina Beliso-De Jesús challenges this scholarly tradition with her research on Santeros in the United States and Cuba.

EIGHTEEN ▪ IMMORTATILITY

1. Rob Bell, *Love Wins: A Book About Heaven, Hell, and the Fate of Every Person Who Ever Lived* (New York: HarperOne, 2011). Ben Ammi has written about hell as a "social construct," a term that describes not a lake of hellfire but the disobedient ways in which humanity chooses to live here and now. See Ben Ammi, *The Resurrection: From Judgment to Post Judgment* (Washington, DC: Communicators Press, 2005).

2. Linda Carroll, "Scientists Say They're Close to Unlocking the Secrets of Immortality," *USA Today,* December 12, 2011. The saints included a link to the actual article: http://today.msnbc.msn.com/id/45654223/ns/today-today_health/t/scientists-say-theyre-close-unlocking-secrets-immortality/.

3. Carlo Caduff, "The Semiotics of Security: Infectious Disease Research and the Biopolitics of Informational Bodies in the United States," *Cultural Anthropology* 27 (2) (May 2012): 333–357.

4. See Adriana Petryna, *Life Exposed: Biological Citizens After Chernobyl* (Princeton, NJ: Princeton University Press, 2002); Paul Stoller, *Sensuous Scholarship* (Philadelphia: University of Pennsylvania Press, 1997). Kirby, of course, challenges conventional divisions between nature and culture. For many, her reconceptualization is a tough sell—kind of like telling African Americans that they aren't African (the ICUPK's project).

5. Swiftboating is a term used to describe what happens when a political campaign transforms an opponent's ostensible strength into a weakness, going after that issue in a seemingly irrational and ironic effort to make that person's most important attribute his or her Achilles' heel. It comes out of the Bush campaign's attacks on John Kerry's military service, which might have been considered his advantage over Bush (since Bush didn't see any active combat).

NINETEEN ▪ JUNGLE

1. Era Bell Thompson, "Are Black Americans Welcome in Africa?" *Ebony,* January 1969, 50.

2. For a popular overview of the many African Americans who have made treks, permanent or temporary, back to Africa, see James T. Campbell, *Middle Passages: African American Journeys to Africa, 1787-2005* (New York: Penguin, 2006).

3. For a discussion about the history of Liberia, including the frictions and tensions that electrify the castelike borders between Americo-Liberian leaders and other groups, see Mary H. Moran, *Liberia: The Violence of Democracy* (Philadelphia: University of Pennsylvania Press, 2006); Tim Heatherington, *Long Story Bit by Bit: Liberia Retold* (Brooklyn, NY: Umbrage, 2009), which includes riveting photos; and Claude Andrew Clegg, III, *The Price of Liberty: African Americans and the Making of Liberia* (Chapel Hill: University of North Carolina Press, 2003). My rendition of the AHIJ's history (of the community's departure from Chicago) is cobbled together from interviews with current saints and already-published accounts found in several books and articles, including Merrill Singer, "Saints of the Kingdom: Group Emergence, Individual Affiliation, and Social Change Among the Black Hebrews of Israel" (PhD diss., University of Utah, 1979); Gavriel HaGadol and Israel Odehyah, *The Impregnable People* (Washington, DC: Communicators Press, 1992); and Israel J. Gerber, *The Heritage Seekers: American Blacks in Search of Jewish Identity* (New York: Jonathan David Publishers, 1977).

4. See Taylor Branch, *At Canaan's Edge: America in the King Years, 1965-68* (New York: Simon and Schuster, 2006).

TWENTY ▪ THIN

1. For more details about the exhibit, go to http://www.quaibranly.fr/en/musee/areas/the-ramp/the-other-walk.html.

2. Giorgio Agamben, *Nudities* (Palo Alto, CA: Stanford University Press, 2011), 114; Trinh T. Minh-ha and Jean-Paul Bourdier, *Night Passage* (New York: Women Make Movies, 2005). I only caught a portion of Minh-ha's talk. I reconstructed what I missed from students' notes.

3. Alan Klima, *The Funeral Casino: Meditation, Massacre, and Exchange with the Dead in Thailand* (Princeton, NJ: Princeton University Press, 2002).

4. Marc Auge, *Non-Places: An Introduction to Supermodernity* (New York: Version, 2009). These nonplaces might also be primary sites for the temporal invasions and recalibrations that Guy Standing warns about, a warning that could frame an "everything is ethnography" formulation of things as another potential example of how "abstract time" dangerously and imperceptibly cannibalizes "process time." See Guy Standing, "Tertiary Time: The Precariat's Dilemma," *Public Culture* 25, no. 1 (2013): 5–23.

5. Clifford Geertz, *The Interpretation of Cultures* (New York: Basic Books, 1971), 8–9.

6. Bruce Knauft, "Anthropology in the Middle," *Anthropological Theory,* 6 no. 4 (2006), 407–430.

7. George E. Marcus, *Ethnography Through Thick and Thin* (Princeton, NJ: Princeton University Press, 1998), 18.

8. William Shaffir, *Ethnographies Revisited: Constructing Theory in the Field* (New York: Routledge, 2009), 81. The canonized Geertzian distinction between twitches, winks, and fake winks can be productively read as further highlighting the analytical purchase of sincerity (especially on the part of those winking and fake-winking informants).

9. James Boon, "Showbiz as a Cross-Cultural System: Circus and Song, Garland and Geertz, Rushdie, Mordden . . . and More," *Cultural Anthropology* 15, no. 3 (2000), 436.

10. For a nice framing of the logic that might be said to animate these global interconnections, see Jean Comaroff and John L. Comaroff, "Millennial Capitalism: First Thoughts on a Second Coming," in *Millennial Capitalism and the Culture of Neoliberalism,* eds. Jean Comaroff, John L. Comaroff, and Robert P. Weller (Durham, NC: Duke University Press, 2001).

11. Lewis Carroll's *Sylvie and Bruno Concluded* (New York: Macmillan and Co., 1894), which included a story of this fictional map that was the exact size of what it was mapping.

12. Michael Jackson, ed., *Things As They Are: New Directions in Phenomenological Anthropology* (Bloomfield: Indiana University Press, 1996), 8. Emphasis in the original.

13. Just because we are having a dialogue, doesn't mean that I can trust everything you tell me as the truth or even that I can verify its truthfulness. In fact, there are some conversations (not all, but some) for which such vetting might even be beside the

point. The anthropological job isn't always to adjudicate whether or not research subjects have their facts right. For a version of this discussion in a reading of Africana anthropology (particularly the work of anthropologist Richard Price), see David Scott, "That Event, This Memory: Notes on the Anthropology of African Diasporas in the New World," *Diaspora: A Journal of Transnational Studies* 1, no. 3(1991): 261–284.

14. For two particularly prescient critiques of American anthropology's instutionalized and intellectualized racial exclusions, see Faye Harrison, *Outsider Within: Reworking Anthropology in the Global Age* (Champaign, IL: University of Illinois Press, 2008) and Mwenda Ntarangwi, *Reversed Gaze: An African Ethnography of American Anthropology* (Champaign, IL: University of Illinois, 2010).

15. For a discussion of such "anti-Americanism" within U.S.-based anthropology (and a discussion of its factual inaccuracy), see Micaela de Leonardo, *Exotics at Home: Anthropologies, Others, and American Modernity* (Chicago: University of Chicago Press, 1998).

16. Brent Edwards, *The Practice of Diaspora: Literature, Translation, and the Rise of Black Internationalism* (Cambridge, MA: Harvard University Press, 2003).

17. Sterling Brown's famous response to Robert Penn Warren's line from "Pondy Woods": "Nigger, your breed ain't exegetical." Brown's response, "Cracker, your breed ain't exegetical." Henry Louis Gates unpacks this exchange a bit in the introduction to *Figures in Black: Words, Signs, and the "Racial" Self* (Oxford: Oxford University Press, 1987), xix.

18. Adolph Reed, "What are the drums Saying, Booker?: The Current Crisis of the Black Intellectual " *Village Voice* 11, April 1995, 31–36. Consider also the famous Elijah Muhammad line: "Those who tell, don't know. Those who know, don't tell." This may be a quintessential ethnographic secret.

TWENTY-ONE ■ CARREL

1. *Rofeh* is a title meaning doctor or healer in Hebrew.

2. See David M. Friedman, *The Immortalists: Charles Lindbergh, Dr. Alexis Carrel, and Their Daring Quest to Live Forever* (New York: Harper Perennial, 2007).

3. Medical historians consider the experiment misleading in the sense that Carrel's assistants were actually doing more than just replenishing nutrients with their interventions. They were also ostensibly introducing new cell material, even though the scientist and his assistants may have sincerely believed otherwise.

4. For a discussion of Carrel's life and work, see David M. Friedman, *The Immortalists: Charles Lindbergh, Dr. Alexis Carrel, and Their Daring Quest to Live Forever* (New York: Harper Perennial, 2007) and Andres Horacio Reggiani, *God's Eugenicist: Alexis Carrel and the Sociobiology of Decline* (New York: Berghahn, 2006). See also Alexis Carrel, *Man, The Unknown* (London: Burns and Oates, 1961), which is, among other things, his celebration of white/European supremacy.

5. T. Colin Campbell and Thomas M. Campbell II, *The China Study: The Most Comprehensive Study of Nutrition Ever Conducted and the Startling Implications for Diet, Weight Loss, and Long-term Health* (Dallas, TX: BenBella Books, 2006).

6. Of course, the Nation of Islam is also famous for its commitment to healthy eating—for example, Elijah Muhammad, *How to Eat to Live—Book 1* (Phoenix, AZ: Secraterius MEMPS, 1997) and Elijah Muhammad, *How to Eat to Live—Book 2* (Phoenix, AZ: Secraterius MEMPS, 2008). The similarities between the NOI's arguments about what foods to eat and how they combat diseases are actually quite a bit like AHIJ claims. Of course the NOI and the AHIJ are part of a long tradition of institutionalized projects linking nutrition and health to the political, social, cultural and biological wellbeing of African Americans. For a discussion of the Black Panthers, a canonical part of that tradition, see Alondra Nelson, *Body and Soul: The Black Panther Party and the Fight against Medical Discrimination* (Minneapolis: University of Minnesota Press, 2011).

TWENTY-TWO ■ ORIENTALISM

1. The term "Euro-gentile" comes from the many books published by Ben Ammi.
2. For a discussion about the inadequacy and biases endemic to anthropological notions of "the primitive," see Adam Kuper, *The Invention of Primitive Society: Transformations of an Illusion* (London: Routledge, 1988).
3. For some constantly invoked discussions of Africana transnationalities, see Paul Gilroy, *The Black Atlantic: Modernity and Double Consciousness* (Cambridge, MA: Harvard University Press, 1993); Brent Hayes Edwards, *The Practice of Diaspora: Literature, Translation, and the Rise of Black Internationalism* (Cambridge, MA: Harvard University Press, 2003); Michelle Stephens, *Black Empire: The Masculine Global Imaginary of Caribbean Intellectuals in the United States, 1914–1962* (Durham, NC: Duke University Press, 2005); Frank Andre Guridy, *Forging Diaspora: Afro-Cubans and African Americans in a World of Empire and Jim Crow* (Chapel Hill: University of North Carolina Press, 2010); Penny Von Eschen, *Race Against Empire: Black Americans and Anticolonialism, 1937–1957* (Ithaca, NY: Cornell University Press, 1997); J. Lorand Matory, *Black Atlantic Religion: Tradition, Transnationalism, and Matriarchy in the Afro-Brazilian Candomblé* (Princeton, NJ: Princeton University Press, 2005); Bayo Holsey, *Routes of Remembrance: Refashioning the Slave Trade in Ghana* (Chicago: University of Chicago Press, 2008).
4. Cheik Anta Diop, *Civilization or Barbarism: An Authentic Anthropology* (Chicago: Lawrence Hill Books, 1991) and Chancellor Williams, *The Destruction of Black Civilization: Great Issues of Race from 4500 B.C. to 2000 A.D.* (Chicago: Third World Press, 1987).5. George James, *Stolen Legacy* (New York: Philosophical Library, [1954]1973). Martin Bernal, *Black Athena: The Afroasiatic Roots of Classical Civilization*. Vol. 1, *The Fabrication of Ancient Greece 1785–1985* (New Brunswick, NJ: Rutgers University Press, 1987).
6. Mary Lefkowitz, *How "Afrocentrism" Became an Excuse to Teach Myth as History* (New York: Basic Books, 1996). Lefkowitz argues that James gets all of his dates wrong and that things couldn't have transpired the way he lays them out. Martin Bernal, *Black Athena: The Afroasiatic Roots of Classical Civilization*. Vol. 1, *The*

Fabrication of Ancient Greece 1785-1985 (New Brunswick, NJ: Rutgers University Press, 1987).

7. Molefi Kete Asante, *Kemet, Afrocentricity and Knowledge* (Trenton, NJ: Africa World Press. 1990), 5.

8. For a discussion of standpoint theory, see Sandra Harding, *The Feminist Standpoint Theory Reader: Intellectual and Political Controversies* (New York: Routledge, 2003).

9. Asante, *Kemet,* 12.

10. Asante, *Kemet,* 90.

11. Asante, *Kemet,* 88.

12. I want to thank Lewis Gordon for pointing out that the ancient Greeks could be quite mystical, too. Pythagoreanism, he says, would be labeled "mythic thought" today.

13. Richard Iton, *In Search of the Black Fantastic: Politics and Popular Culture in the Post-Civil Rights Era* (Oxford: Oxford University Press, 2008), examines the undeniable creativities at the center of black political work of all kinds.

14. Sherman A. Jackson, *Islam and the Blackamerican: Looking Toward the Third Resurrection* (Berkeley: University of California Press, 2005).

15. Edward Said, *Orientalism* (New York: Vintage, 1979).

16. Jackson, *Islam and the Blackamerican,* 109.

17. The Southern Sudanese call themselves Kushites and make the same case about their own sense of belonging vis-à-vis Arabicized Africans in Northern Sudan.

18. Jackson, *Islam and the Blackamerican,* 109.

19. For another foundational discussion of how Africa is constructed in the West, see V. Y. Mudimbe, *The Invention of Africa: Gnosis, Philosophy, and the Order of Knowledge* (Bloomington, IN: Indiana University Press, 1988) and Achille Mbembe, *On the Postcolony* (Berkeley, CA: University of California Press, 2001).

20. He coauthored it with his Temple University colleague from the school's Cartography Lab, Mark Mattson. The piece was titled,"Rediscovering the African Homeland."

21. See Paul Berman, *Blacks and Jews: Thirty Years of Alliance* (New York: Delacorte, 1994); James Salzman and Cornel West, *Struggles in the Promised Land: Toward a History of Black-Jewish Relations in the United States* (New York: Oxford University Press, 1997); Eric J. Sundquist, *Strangers in the Land: Blacks, Jews, Post-Holocaust America* (Cambridge, MA: Harvard University Press, 2005): and Rebecca T. Alpert, *Whose Torah? A Concise Guide to Progressive Judaism* (New York: Free Press, 2009). See also, Eric Goldstein, *The Price of Whiteness: Jews, Race, and American Identity* (Princeton, NJ: Princeton University Press, 2006); Cheryl Lynn Greenberg, *Troubling the Waters: Black-Jewish Relations in the American Century* (Princeton, NJ: Princeton University Press, 2010); Jeffrey Melnick, *Black-Jewish Relations on Trial: Leo Frank and Jim Conley in the New South* (Jackson: University Press of Mississippi, 2000); Michael Rogin, *Blackface, White Noise: Jewish Immigrants in the Hollywood Melting Pot* (Berkeley: University of California Press, 1996).

22. See Lewis R. Gordon, *Existentia Africana: Understanding Africana Existential Thought* (New York: Routledge, 2000), 7. This project is linked to excavating, circulating, and extending ongoing Africana engagements with questions of

"freedom, anguish, agency, dread, responsibility, embodied agency, sociality, and liberation."

23. Melville Herskovits, *The Myth of the Negro Past* (Boston: Beacon Press, 1990); Wilson Jeremiah Moses, *Afrotopia: The Roots of African American Popular History* (Cambridge: Cambridge University Press, 1998).

24. William Grimshaw, *Official History of Freemasonry Among the Colored People of North America* (New York: Broadway Publishing, 1903); Wilson Jeremiah Moses, *Afrotopia: The Roots of African American Popular History* (Cambridge: Cambridge University Press, 1998). And then you have contemporary figures such as Chicago-based Rabbi Capers Funnye and Ben Ammi Ben Israel, two men whose lives differently exemplify the lie of Black-Jewish incommensurability.

25. See Penny M. Von Eschen, *Race Against Empire: Black Americans and Anti-colonialism, 1937–1957* (Ithaca, NY: Cornell University Press, 1997); Gerald Horne, *Black and Red: W. E. B. DuBois and the Afro-American Response to the Cold War, 1944–1963* (Albany, NY: State University of New York, 1986); Bernard Makhosezwe Magubane, *The Ties That Bind: African-American Consciousness of Africa* (Chicago: Africa World Press, 1987).

26. For discussions of African American links to communism, see Cedric Robinson, *Black Marxism: The Making of the Black Radical Tradition* (Chapel Hill: University of North Carolina Press, 1983); Robin D. G. Kelley, *Hammer and Hoe: Alabama Communists During the Great Depression* (Chapel Hill: University of North Carolina Press, 1990); Carol Boyce Davies, *Left of Karl Marx: The Political Life of Black Communist Claudia Jones* (Durham, NC: Duke University Press, 2008).

27. Alaine Locke, "The New Negro," in *The New Negro: Voices of the Harlem Renaissance,* Alaine Locke, ed., (New York: Albert and Charles Boni, 1925), 14.

TWENTY-THREE ▪ DIGITAL

1. See Anna Everett, *Digital Diaspora: A Race for Cyberspace* (Albany, NY: State University of New York Press, 2009) and Faye Ginsburg, "Rethinking the Digital Age," in *The Media and Social Theory,* eds. David Hesmondhalgh and Jason Toynbee (New York: Routledge, 2008). Many scholars remind us that this purported universality is far from universal.

2. See Michael Taussig, *The Nervous System* (New York: Routledge, 1992); Homi Bhabha, *The Location of Culture* (New York: Routledge, 1994); James Clifford, *Travel and Translation in the Late Twentieth Century* (Cambridge, MA: Harvard University Press, 1997). Also, for a discussion about how some global connections are muted by Western hubris and ethnocentrism, see Susan Buck-Morss, *Hegel, Haiti, and University History* (Pittsburgh: University of Pittsburgh Press, 2009).

3. Kara Keeling, "Passing for Human: Bamboozled and Digital Humanism," *Women and Performance: A Journal of Feminist Theory* 29, no. 1 (2005): 237–250.

4. See Brian Keith Axel, "The Context of Diaspora," *Cultural Anthropology* 19, no. 1 (February 2004): 26–60.

5. For a powerful formulation of diaspora itself, particularly the African Diaspora, as a product of constitutive differences (not just romantic notions of sameness),

differences that function a bit like the gaps invoked here, see Brent Hayes Edwards, *The Practice of Diaspora: Literature, Translation, and the Rise of Black Internationalism* (Cambridge, MA: Harvard University Press, 2003).

6. Vicky Kirby, *Quantum Anthropologies: Life at Large* (Durham: Duke University Press, 2011), 1.

TWENTY-FOUR ▪ CHILDREN

1. Daphna Berman, "Hebrew Israelite Youths Gear up for Draft," *Haaretz,* June 4, 2004, http://www.haaretz.com/misc/article-print-page/hebrew-israelite-youths-gear-up-for-draft-1.124303?trailingPath=2.169%2C.

2. The community's official policy is that physical immortality is even obtainable for their elders, even if their bodies have been previously abused (before life in the Kingdom).

3. Yaakov Katz, "Distrust in Dimona," *Jerusalem Post,* December 8, 2005, http://www.jpost.com/Magazine/Features/Article.aspx?id=6928.

4. Some Penn colleagues and I are preparing to conduct a new version of this study on the community's health.

TWENTY-FIVE ▪ EDEN

1. "Message from the Minister of Health," *Health Foresight!* (Legon, GH: Foresight Media, 2007), 2.

2. But Quashigah went even further, importing a fifteen-member team of saints who were part of a three-year effort to educate trainers, to sensitize the local communities of more than a dozen targeted districts in all ten regions, and in effect to assist in the execution of a paradigm-shift in Ghana's health care system: from a focus on curative to preventive efforts. The Regenerative Health and Nutrition Program remains at the core of the Ghana Health Services ideology.

TWENTY-SIX ▪ DISCIPLINING

1. For more on the Black Berets, see Quito Swan, *Black Power in Bermuda: The Struggle for Decolonization* (New York: Palgrave, 2009). The Bermuda police website < http://www.bermuda.org.uk/bermuda_police.htm> describes what happened with Cohane Ahbir's case many years later: "[S]ome may still remember the Ottiwell Simmons Jr. case (the son of the PLP MP and union leader) allegedly linked to Buck Burrows , Larry Tacklyn (accused of the Governor's murder in 1973) and others—despite an extensive manhunt—managed to get off the island, stay at large (in the USA?) and when he voluntarily returned all the paperwork was missing, therefore no charges, no proceedings, nothing!"

2. Israel J. Gerber, *The Heritage Seekers: American Blacks in Search of Jewish Identity* (New York: Jonathan David Publishers, 1977).

3. Back in the 1970s, the AHIJ approached Yahweh Ben Yahweh's group, in an attempt to build an alliance. They were always interested in forming ties with other African

American Israelites, even attempting to see if some of them would be willing to join them in Israel. They were rebuffed by Yahweh Ben Yahweh's Florida-based group, and they never formed any substantive relationship with them.

TWENTY-SEVEN ▪ ZIMREEYAH

1. Actually, I must be misremembering this. Deborah and I went to Portugal in the summer of 2002, but Houston's visit to Dimona was at the end of May in 2003, when we would have been overseas at a different academic conference. I must be confusing the two, but I swear that I have such a strikingly vivid memory of watching images of Houston's entourage from the bedroom of a quite charming *pousada* outside Lisbon. The distance between my recollections and the temporal facts reminds me of the discrepancies between one author's memories of his father's death and the actual date of that occurrence. See Samuel R. Delany, *The Motion of Light in Water: Sex and Science Fiction Writing in the East Village 1960–1965* (Minneapolis: University of Minnesota Press, 2004). It also reminds us of the potential distances separating sincerity from truth.

2. Joan Borsten, "Rustin Says Leader of Black Cult is 'Dictator,'" *Jerusalem Post*, January 28, 1981, 1–2. I've kept the "Ami" spelling of Ben Ammi's name, though the community has never used it (only journalists and other non-Kingdom authors).

3. "BASIC Leaders Tell Israel: Ban More Black Hebrews and Airport Discrimination," *Jewish News*, January 30, 1981, 6.

4. Joan Borsten, "Rustin Says Leader of Black Cult is 'Dictator,'" *The Jerusalem Post*; "Odyssey in Israel: Summing Up," *Baltimore Afro-American*, May 23, 1981, 5. Named after David Glass, member of the Knesset, the 300-page report the committee produced basically concluded that the AHIJ was not "ominous and dangerous."

5. Borsten, "Rustin Says Leader of Black Cult is 'Dictator.'"

6. The reporter, Joan Borsten, responded by admitting that she had missed the actual report, which they mentioned in their letter, and saying that the paper ran a more substantive story on the delegation the following day, January 29, 1981. She also apologized to the delegation members for the snafu.

7. Representative and Congressional Black Caucus member Mervyn Dymally visited Israel several times over the years advocating for the community.

8. Another important political figure was Jewel LaFontant, an undersecretary of state for President George H. W. Bush and someone who helped to bring about the building of the community's school in Israel.

TWENTY-EIGHT ▪ SINCERE

1. Ethnography penned by nonanthropologists is often called "para-ethnography." And everyone is doing ethnography these days, another version of the "everything is ethnography" idea. As much as number crunchers seem hegemonic, ethnography seems ubiquitous. Everyone wants it. Maybe it is also because it seems too straightforward and commonsensical that everybody thinks they can do it. It seemingly

doesn't demand the same kind of methodological training as rigorous quantitative analysis.

2. See Anna Lowenhaupt Tsing, *Friction: An Ethnography of Global Connection* (Princeton, NJ: Princeton University Press, 2005).

3. See Johannes Fabian, *Time and the Other: How Anthropology Makes Its Object* (New York: Columbia University Press, 1983).

4. For a discussion of partialities intrinsic to the ethnographic process, see Marilyn Strathern, *Partial Connections* (Lanham, MD: AltaMira Press, 2005).

5. Max Weber, *The Protestant Ethic and the Spirit of Capitalism: and Other Writings* (New York: Penguin, 2002). Weber highlighted a religious version of this existential angst in his classic discussion of how Calvinists used public and observable signs to stand-in for their preordained status as members of the "elect." What we can see and count (and differentially value) is a good proxy for what would otherwise be terrifyingly invisible.

6. For one useful discussion of how the faithful query the would-be academic researcher, see James S. Bielo, *Words upon the Word: An Ethnography of Evangelical Group Bible Study* (New York: New York University Press, 2009).

TWENTY-NINE ■ CASEIN

1. The school can be accessed through their website at http://instituteforregenerative truth.com/.

2. Merrill Singer, "Saints of the Kingdom: Group Emergence, Individual Affiliation, and Social Change Among the Black Hebrews of Israel" (PhD diss., University of Utah, 1979).

3. Of course, saints recognize that other animals are made up of the same 102 minerals. Nevertheless, saints contend, Yah mandates that humans "go to the source" as opposed to the "udder foolishness" of dealing with a "middle man" [some other animal].

THIRTY ■ PRODIGAL

1. In many ways, the entire history of anthropology is about trying to determine when and why the social response to an infraction/action is death versus a chuckle and a shake of the head.

2. Here is a posting on the induction of young saints into the Israeli military: http://www.skyscrapercity.com/showthread.php?t=122260

THIRTY-ONE ■ ESAU

1. Again, many Jews, Muslims, Hindus, and others also discuss their identities and spiritual commitments as similarly irreducible to narrow notions of religion.

2. This is an excerpt from an interview with sociologist Morris Lounds Jr., someone who visited the community and interviewed several saints in the 1970s.

3. See David M. Goldenberg, *The Curse of Ham: Race and Slavery in Early Judaism,*

Christianity, and Islam (Princeton: Princeton University Press, 2003), 138. Goldenberg and others have critiqued the idea that Jews were particular proponents of the Hamitic Curse idea, and it is generally understood today that the medieval Christians had no access to rabbinic commentaries.

4. The Nation of Islam offers a narrative about an evil scientist who creates white people in a test tube as their explanation for racial differences.

5. Colin Kidd, *The Forging of Races: Race and Scripture in the Protestant Atlantic World*, 1600–2000 (Cambridge: Cambridge University Press, 2006), 3.

6. I am borrowing the term *colormute* from Mica Pollock, *Colormute: Race Talk Dilemmas in an American School* (Princeton, NJ: Princeton University Press, 2004).

7. For a discussion of links between African American commitments to Exodus and notions of nationality, see Eddie Glaude, *Exodus!: Religion, Race, and Nation in Early Nineteenth-Century Black America* (Chicago: University of Chicago Press, 2000).

8. See Genesis 27–29.

9. The full story can be found in Genesis 25–28.

10. W. E. B. Du Bois, "Jacob and Esau," *The Talladegan* 62, no. 1(November 1944): 1–6.

11. For a discussion of Orthodox Jewish readings of Jacob and Esau (which read Esau and Edomites as the progenitors of hostility and all things non-Jewish), see Henry Goldschmidt, *Race and Religion Among the Chosen People of Crown Heights* (Piscataway, NJ: Rutgers University Press, 2006). There are also midrashic and rabbinical readings of Jacob (as peaceful and "dwelling in tents") versus Esau (deemed a warlike, violent hunter who disdains God).

THIRTY-TWO ▪ SOUL

1. Era Brown Thompson, "Are Black Americans Welcome in Africa?" *Ebony*, January 1969, 46.

2. There are actually quite a few Israelite/black Jewish groups (in Chicago and elsewhere) with musical backgrounds and a history of commercial success as recording artists. For example, the Five Echoes was a famous recording act from the 1950s composed entirely of members from the Church of God and Saints of Christ, one of the Black Jewish groups profiled in Arthur Huff Fauset, *Black Gods of the Metropolis: Negro Religious Cults of the Urban North* (Philadelphia, PA: University of Pennsylvania Press, 1944). For more on this musical group, see "Tommy Hunt: The Door Is Open," *In the Basement* 42 (May–July 2006): 19.

3. Ben Ammi, *God, the Black Man and Truth* (Washington, DC: Communicators Press, 1982).

4. This is a quote from the record company's website: http://www.numerogroup.com/about.php and liner notes.

5. Thompson, "Are Black Americans Welcome in Africa?" *Ebony*, January 1969, 50.

THIRTY-THREE ▪ LAUGHING

1. Ruth Behar, *The Vulnerable Observer: Anthropology That Breaks Your Heart* (Boston: Beacon, 1997).

2. George Marcus, *Ethnography Through Thick and Thin* (Princeton, NJ: Princeton University Press, 1998).

3. Again, see Michael Taussig, *I Swear I Saw This: Drawings in Fieldwork Notebooks, Namely My Own* (Chicago: University of Chicago Press, 2012) for a discussion about the power of chance in ethnography.

4. For a much more poetic and powerful rendering of these proposal-based conceits, see Taussig, *I Swear I Saw This*, 48.

5. Vincent Crapanzano, "Reflections on Hope as a Category of Social and Psychological Analysis," *Cultural Anthropology* 18, no. 1(2003): 3-32.

6. Crapanzano, "Reflections on Hope," 7. There have been several relatively recent scholarly reclamations of hope as an analytic, including Mary Zournazi, *Hope: New Philosophies for Change* (New York: Routledge, 2002), which is staged as a series of dialogues with progressive scholars, dialogues aimed at (among other things) countering narrow, reactionary, and cynical deployments of hope from the political Right. Hirokazu Miyazaki, *The Method of Hope: Anthropology, Philosophy, and Fijian Knowledge* (Stanford: Stanford University Press, 2004) attempts to think about how a focus on hope might allow us to re-imagine exactly "what knowledge is for," 9. This resonates with anthropologist Michael Jackson's distinction between ethnographic "knowing" and ethnographic "showing," a difference predicated on the idea that ethnographers can often show much more than they unequivocally know. That suggestive claim strikes me as quite a different starting point from the one that Geertzian thick description might champion. Indeed, thick descriptions pivot on knowing much more than one can simply show, knowing more than can be shown to the naked eye. Deploying hope as a way of knowing, Miyazaki also wants us to think about how hope recalibrates (and collaborates with) time. Hope is "prospective," Miyazaki argues, unfurling, unfolding. We do its fundamental organizing principle a disservice when we give it a "retrospective treatment" as simply "a product or a strategic moment in a language game or semiotic process[.]" A similar emphasis on temporal perspective and its centrality to questions of anthropological knowing/nonknowing drives the internal logics of "thin description." Thick description is weighed down with absolutist retrospectivity on all sides, leaving very little left for anthropologists to actually hope for. (In a different sense, of course, thin description is also about showing less than you sometimes know, which would be predicated on different forms of hopefulness entirely.)

7. Kathleen Stewart, *Ordinary Affects* (Durham, NC: Duke University Press, 2007), 15.

8. Virginia Dominguez, "For a Politics of Love and Rescue," *Cultural Anthropology* 15, no. 3 (2000): 388.

9. Lionel Trilling, *Sincerity and Authenticity* (Cambridge, MA: Harvard University Press, 1971).

THIRTY-FOUR ■ OCCULTED

1. For a very detailed and fascinating biography of Randolph, see John Patrick Deveney, *Paschal Beveral Randolph: A Nineteenth Century Black American Spiritualist, Rosicrucian, and Sex Magician* (Albany: State University of New York Press, 1997).

2. Historians of religion have characterized the rise of occultism (mesmerism, animal magnetism, etc.) in nineteenth-century America as an instantiation of "the flight from reason," a time of increasingly irrational commitments to mysticism and superstition (as a function, at least in part—and somewhat ironically—of advances in scientific technology). But I am particularly interested in the political service to which sex magic, spiritualism, and even (to a different extent) occultism were put by the likes of Randolph. Also, see the discussion of that era in Molly McGarry, *Ghosts of Futures Past: Spiritualism and the Cultural Politics of Nineteenth-Century America* (Berkeley: University of California Press, 2008).

3. See the Black Public Sphere Collective, *The Black Public Sphere: A Public Culture Book* (Chicago: University of Chicago Press, 1995) for an assortment of fascinating articles on what the public sphere means in an Africana context. Also, for a new and pointed discussion about how African Americans understand their own place in America's political and public sphere, see Salamishah Tillet, *Sites of Slavery: Citizenship and Racial Democracy in the Post–Civil Rights Imagination* (Durham, NC: Duke University Press, 2012).

4. Russ Castronovo, *Necro Citizenship: Death, Eroticism, and the Public Sphere in the Nineteenth Century United States.* (Durham, NC: Duke University Press, 2001).

5. For a discussion of this same theme (about the supposed incommensurabilities between democracy, on the one hand, and race or religion on the other, see David Kyuman Kim and John L. Jackson Jr., "Introduction: Democracy's Anxious Returns," *The ANNALS of the American Academy of Political and Social Science* 637 (2011); 6–16.

6. David Kyuman Kim, "The Public Life of Love," *The Good Society* 19, no. 2 (2010): 37–43.

7. Jeffrey Sconce, *Haunted Media: Electronic Presence from Telegraphy to Television* (Durham, NC: Duke University Press 2000). The invention and public introduction of new media technologies often have the shimmer of supernaturalism imposed upon them, but they also come with revamped definitions to scientificity and rational technical training. For one particularly useful take on the kinds of public discourse (and newfangled institutionalizations of expertise) that emerged with the advent of devices like the telegraph and the telephone, see Carolyn Marvin, *When Old Technologies Were New: Thinking About Electric Communication in the Late Nineteenth Century* (Oxford: Oxford University Press, 1988).

8. See John Tagg, *Burden of Representation: Essays on Photographies and Histories* (Minneapolis: University of Minnesota Press,1993).

9. Lauren Berlant, *Cruel Optimism* (Durham, NC: Duke University Press, 2011), examines the kinds of longings that are self-thwarting, frustrating, and affectively magnetic.

10. Roland Barthes, *Camera Lucida: Reflections on Photography*. (New York: Hill and Wang, 1981). There are many books that are in interesting conversation with Barthes. Barbie Zelizer, *About to Die: How News Images Move the Public* (New York: Oxford, 2010), is just one of them—and one of the most recent. Whereas Barthes makes a case for how all photographs are depictions, in a sense, of human mortality, Zelizer's book is a powerful treatment of photographic images that capture much more imminent deaths, images that circulate in decidedly public ways via news media outlets (as compared to the more private forms of reception foregrounded by Barthes).

11. Mary Poovey, *A History of the Modern Fact: Problems of Knowledge in the Sciences of Wealth and Society* (Chicago: University of Chicago Press, 1998).

12. According to Deveney's biography, Randolph was one of the first to propagate the occultist idea that there aren't just dead people's souls out there waiting to dialogue with mortals. That there are other beings, he argued, "passing" for dead people, taking over mediums like Randolph, and sometimes controlling them even if the medium ostensibly isn't in a trance. That, Randolph says, is what happened to him during the entire first-half of his career, helping to explain his infamous reputation as odd, unpredictable, and "angular."

13. Peter Schwenger, *The Tears of Things: Melancholy and Physical Objects* (Minneapolis: University of Minnesota Press, 2006).

14. For a recent look at the Civil War and the longings its misery unleashed, see Drew Gilpin Faust, *This Republic of Suffering: Death and the American Civil War* (New York: Vintage, 2008).

15. John Durham Peters, *Speaking into the Air: A History of the Idea of Communication* (Durham, NC: Duke University Press, 1999).

THIRTY-FIVE ■ ORDER

1. Ben Ammi, *The Resurrection: From Judgment to Post Judgment* (Washington, DC: Communicators Press, 2005), 48.

2. Merrill Singer, "Saints of the Kingdom: Group Emergence, Individual Affiliation, and Social Change Among the Black Hebrews of Israel." (PhD diss., University of Utah, 1979).

3. Cohane Michael Ben Levi, head of the West Indian jurisdiction, was an Israelite priest before he joined the Kingdom, so he didn't get his early training at the School of the Prophets.

4. There have been some exceptions to the male exclusivity of these positions. In the early days, when the community first arrived in Liberia, wives of the Princes automatically became "Princesses," but that was eventually deemed too unwieldy since it was not based on merit (or even potential/commitment) and was soon discontinued in favor of the Crowned Sisters designation (which is an official order of leadership). Some of the wives of the Princes were "crowned" and they continue to receive that honorific today. There was a female Minister (of Education) who was "set down" (a version of being placed on sabbatical) and eventually lost her post. She has since been reinstated to the Crowned Sisters order and functions at a high level in "dedication"

(education) arenas. Finally, there is a body of women—the *Lamdahneeote*—who are charged to work alongside the Prophetic Priesthood. They serve as teachers of the law in areas where the law applies to women, the feminine side of Adam. They, along with some Crowned Sisters, also form part of the teams that work with the Priests in their many counseling responsibilities. Also, "Sister" and "Brother" are formal titles carried by all adult males and females in the Kingdom.

5. For a closer look at the dynamics of relations between the "sister-wives" of the AHIJ, see Patricia Dixon, *We Want for Our Sister What We Want for Ourselves: African American Women Who Practice Polygyny by Consent* (Baltimore, MD: Black Classic Press, 2009).

6. Ben Ammi, *The Resurrection*, 27.

7. This is the AHIJ's official definition of the Kingdom.

8. Two of the characteristics of the black poor's supposed culture of poverty are matriarchal families and the multiplicity of familial households. For a canonical reclamation of these multiunit families, see Carole Stack, *All Our Kin: Strategies for Survival in a Black Community* (New York: Basic, 1974). For counterexamples of "traditional" African gender roles/norms, see Nkiru Nzegwu, *Family Matters: Feminist Concepts in African Philosophy of Culture* (Albany: State University of New York Press, 2006); Oyèrónké Oyewùmi, *The Invention of Women: Making an African Sense of Western Gender Discourses* (Minneapolis : University of Minnesota Press, 1997).

9. *The Munir Muhammad Show*, October 2, 2011.

10. These details are documented throughout the AHIJ literature.

11. Sar Ahmadiel, a spokesperson for the Kingdom, offered specific responses to each of Asiel's accusations:

    1) Asiel's initial sabbatical letter encouraged him to spend time at home and explicitly left open a channel for communication with Ben Ammi.

    2) Removal of the asbestos roofing panels would have presented a far greater hazard to the community than for it to remain undisturbed for the next hundred years. The staff of the Ministry of Building and Maintenance, in their capacity as those with such knowledge and expertise, made that decision (which was corroborated from consultations with other municipalities in the country with similar materials). To have embarked on such a project in an existing residential area would have been unprecedented, and we were not willing to be guinea pigs.

    3) Several plans for our relocation to a new housing compound have been thwarted by the often-transient nature of the Israeli political structure and scene. On more than one occasion, years of negotiations which brought us to the very doorstep of a resolution came to naught when early elections brought in a new government who "knew not Joseph." We are in just such a situation at the moment, but are confident that plans have moved beyond the political phase and are looking any day for ground to be broken on our new compound.

    4) The Holy Council has not been disbanded or even marginalized (quite the contrary with the ever-increasing reach into Edenic areas and subsequent workload of the Kingdom). The Princes continue to meet with Ben Ammi on average two or three times a week. The Ministers sit with him virtually on a daily basis.

5) Charges of the complicity of leadership in a cover-up involving pedophilia are baseless. An isolated case of molestation has to be distinguished from a pattern of pedophilia (at the far end of the sexual perversion spectrum in our view) and clearly differentiated from sexual experimentations and shenanigans committed by adolescents. However, to be perfectly clear, none of these behaviors are condoned in any way. Such matters, along with the usual multiplicity of mitigating components, circumstances and consequences that each case brings, have historically been dealt with by the Priesthood and/or other leadership entities, and always in conjunction with the parents of those children involved. As painful as such matters are, they need not be aggravated by the insensitive nature of a public spectacle.

6) Often issues and specific problems are referred for discussion in the local Brotherhood and Sisterhood meetings, which serve to augment the role of the Holy Council in any decision-making that impacts on the saints. Ben Ammi makes a point of consulting with these bodies in order to tap the collective wisdom of the saints in making such decisions.

7) Charges that we have deified Ben Ammi are grossly inaccurate. Except for us knowing that ignorance often prevails in the absence of a proper historical/cultural understanding of the role of the Hebraic messianic personage, we would be insulted. For those who would insist that Ben Ammi is "just a man," we would ask "was not Moses a man?!"

8) To be critical of our youth serving in the IDF (Israel Defense Forces), even to suggest that our children are "traumatized" from such, seems disingenuous to say the least, particularly given the many thousands of African Americans who have and continue to serve in the U.S. military—often on battlefields and for geopolitical motives that they have absolutely no awareness of. But to make such a statement from the environs of Chicago—where entire neighborhoods live under the shadow of a daily routine of violence that rivals the worst of war zones, would be laughable, save for being so deadly serious (an environment that Prince Asiel has attempted to lure some of our youth to). Common sense would inform even a detached observer that we wouldn't hesitate to defend ourselves against, say incoming Scud missiles from a neighboring country (as indeed was the case during the Gulf Crisis). Our sons and daughters remain aligned with our peaceloving preferences and posture, but are not raised to be naïve. They are also expected to maintain their respect for ALL humanity and to always be an influence, for good, of course, upon the larger Israeli society that they interact with.

9) Finally, aside from his actions being most unfortunate, most unbecoming and above all, most untruthful, we have simply chosen not to engage Prince Asiel and others in a manner that would play into the motives and machinations that have driven past, and presumably present, policies of global entities which would seek our demise. Besides, with man obviously bent on the destruction of our planet, we deem it more important that our energies be directed toward that struggle. As with all of the other tribulations we have had to endure on this path, we rest with the fact that "Truth has no master" and that "Truth crushed to earth, will surely

rise again". Time has a way of revealing all things . . . and with immortality as our ultimate goal, we've got nothing but time!

12. "If anything, Ben Ammi's isolation is self-imposed," Sar Ahmadiel says, "one wherein he is bound to a workload—and an accountability—that none of us aspires to and which most of us can scarcely imagine. However, because a daily interaction with one another is an essential part of our culture—our 'people-to-people ecology'—Ben Ammi counts such opportunities as his chief joy."

THIRTY-SIX ▪ GENESIS

1. For details about the Nasik Asiel court case, see https://bulk.resource.org/courts .gov/c/F2/823/823.F2d.591.86-3075.86-3073.86-3065.html.

2. For example, the U.S. government used this law to prosecute the Yahweh Ben Yahweh group in Florida. For a discussion of that group (and the law enforcement's approach to indicting them), see Sydney P. Freedberg, *Brother Love: Murder, Money and a Messiah* (New York: Pantheon, 1994).

3. Saints also claim that there was evidence of FBI interactions with the dismissed juror in violation of anti–jury tampering guidelines.

4. This "deal" (permanent residency for saints already residing in Israel in exchange for those saints promising not to sneak in any more believers from the United States) is said to be an unwritten and unofficial agreement between the Kingdom and Israeli state officials.

5. For a discussion of Senegalese successes in the fight against sickle cell anemia as a kind of excuse for global nonresponsiveness, see Duana Fullwiley, *The Enculturated Gene: Sickle Cell Health Politics and Biological Difference* (Princeton, NJ: Princeton University Press, 2011). The idea that Western governments and NGOs might be looking for excuses to ignore or downplay urgent health concerns in Africa helps to spur on the AHIJ's efforts on that continent (as a response to such neglect).

6. For a discussion of the varied ways in which theories of race and Jewishness have intersected in scientific discourse, see Nadia Abu El-Haj, *The Genealogical Science: Genetics, the Search for Jewish Origins, and the Politics of Epistemology* (Chicago: University of Chicago Press, 2012). For a very different take on Jews and race, a version critiqued by El-Haj, see Jon Entine, *Abraham's Children; Race, Identity and the DNA of the Chosen People* (New York: Grand Central, 2007). See also David B. Goldstein, *Jacob's Legacy : A Genetic View of Jewish History* (New Haven, CT: Yale University Press, 2008); Harry Ostrer, *Legacy: A Genetic History of the Jewish People* (New York : Oxford University Press, 2012).

7. Paschal Beverly Randolph, *Pre-Adamite Man: Demonstrating the Existence of the Human Race Upon This Earth 100,000 Years Ago* (Whitefish, MO: Kessinger Publishing, [1888] 1997).

8. Randolph, *Pre-Adamite Man,* 93.

9. Randolph, *Pre-Adamite Man,* 94. This kind of rhetoric also gets critiqued for anti-Semitism, the same charge leveled at many Israelite groups for similarly dismissive language about Jewish thought and culture.

10. Randolph, *Pre-Adamite Man,* 97. Ben Ammi, *An Imitation of Life: Redefining What Constitutes True Life and Living in the New World* (Washington, DC: Communicators Press, 1999).

11. There are many interesting roads that might link Randolph's theories to various forms of black gnosticism. For example, the Moorish Science Temple's Holy Koran or Circle Seven Koran included some material from earlier forms of Rosicrucianism that Randolph was also versed in. The Moorish Science Temple adherents in urban America in the early twentieth century had ties to the Nation of Islam and various black Israelite groups. Brotz, Fauset, Landing, Dorman, and other authors I cite throughout this text help to fill in connections among these black groups.

12. Randolph, *Pre-Adamite Man,* 34, 89.

13. This idea of the masculinist and patriarchal model of black political mobilization is not exclusive to the AHIJ. Indeed, it is a critique of black struggles of all kinds, from the radical to the accommodationist. Saints believe that any invocation of "Adam" in Genesis is inclusive of Eve, unless the narrative explicitly excludes her (see Genesis 5:2).

THIRTY-SEVEN ▪ INSINCERITIES

1. For a classic philosophical critique of sincerity, see Jean-Paul Sarte, *Being and Nothingness: An Essay in Phenomenological Ontology* (New York: Citadel Press, 1956). See also Lewis R. Gordon, *Bad Faith and Antiblack Racism* (Amherst, NY: Humanity Books, 1995); Lewis R. Gordon, *Fanon and the Crisis of European Man: An Essay on Philosophy and the Human Sciences* (New York: Routledge, 1995).

2. Saba Mahmood, *Politics of Piety: The Islamic Revival and the Feminist Subject* (Princeton, NJ: Princeton University Press, 2005); Wendy Brown, *States of Injury.* (Princeton, NJ: Princeton University Press, 1995). Both authors make differently framed arguments about the blind spots and ethnocentrisms of Western (human rights) discourses.

3. Again, Vicky Kirby, *Quantum Anthropologies: Life at Large* (Durham: Duke University Press, 2011) is a fundamental reformulation of this problematic.

4. Karen Fields, "Witchcraft and Racecraft: Invisible Ontology in Its Sensible Manifestations," in *Witchcraft Dialogues,* eds. George C. Bond and Diane M. Ciekawy (Athens, OH: Ohio University Center for International Studies, 2001), 283–315.

5. See Stephan Palmié, "Genomics, Divination, "Racecraft," *American Ethnologist* 34, no. 2 (2007): 205–222, which is followed by responses from several scholars.

6. Duana Fullwiley, "The Molecularization of Race: Institutionalizing Racial Difference in Pharmacogenetics Practice," *Science as Culture* 16, no. 1(2007): 1–30.

7. Lanita Jacobs-Huey, "The Arab Is the New Nigger," *Transforming Anthropology* 14, no. 1 (2008): 60–64.

8. Marla Frederick, *Between Sundays: Black Women and Everyday Struggles of Faith.* (Berkeley, CA: University of California Press, 2003); Andre Key, "What's My Name?: An Autoethnography of the Problem of Moral Evil and Ethnic Suffering in Black Judaism" (PhD diss., Temple University, 2011).

9. Roxanne Varzi, *Warring Souls: Youth, Media and Martyrdom in Post-Revolution Iran* (Durham, NC: Duke University Press, 2006).

10. Bronislaw Malinowski, *A Diary in the Strict Sense of the Term* (Palo Alto, CA: Stanford University Press, 1967).

11. Diane M. Nelson, *Reckoning: The Ends of War in Guatemala* (Durham, NC: Duke University Press, 2009); Derek Freeman, *The Fateful Hoaxing of Margaret Mead: A Historical Analysis of Her Samoan Research* (Boulder, CO: Westview, 1999); Margaret Mead, *Coming of Age in Samoa* (New York: First Quill. 1973).

12. David Stoll, *Rigoberta Menchú and the Story of All Poor Guatemalans* (Boulder, CO: Westview Press, 1999); Patrick Tierney, *Darkness in El Dorado: How Scientists and Journalists Devastated the Amazon* (New York: Norton, 2000). Irving Lewis Horowitz, *The Rise and Fall of Project Camelot: Studies in the Relationship Between Social Science and Practical Politics* (Cambridge, MA: MIT Press, 1967); David Price, *Anthropological Intelligence: The Deployment and Neglect of American Anthropology in the Second World War* (Durham, NC: Duke University Press, 2008).

13. Annelise Riles, *The Network Inside Out* (Ann Arbor: University of Michigan Press, 2001).

THIRTY-EIGHT ▪ SUMERIANS

1. Prince Gavriel is currently in the final stages of *The Impregnable People, Part 2*, which picks up the story when the early saints' first arrive in Israel in 1969 and chronicles their journey through 1990, when their legal status changed (from "temporary residents" to "permanent residents").

2. Michel Foucault, "Technologies of the Self," *Technologies of the Self* , ed. L. H. Martin, H. Gutman, and P. H. Hutton (Amherst, MA: University of Massachusetts Press, 1988), 16–49.

3. Era Bell Thompson, "Are Black Americans Welcome in Africa?" *Ebony,* January 1969.

4. For a discussion about the Sumerian practices of Yah's chosen people, see Thomas Cahill, *The Gifts of the Jews: How a Tribe of Desert Nomads Changed the Way Everyone Thinks and Feels* (New York: Nan A. Talese/Anchor Books, 1998). This might seem like a bit of an odd analogy, especially since Jewish folklore is so much about leaving past (Egyptian) culture/life behind. But many scholars try to make a case for why cultural diffusion would mean that the group that originally left Sumer for Ur (if you believe the historicity of the Old Testament/Torah) must have had the same cultural practices as other Sumerians. Many would protest that there is no historical evidence for the figure Moses (outside of the Hebrew Bible), but saints point to several texts that recalibrate the archaeological evidence in ways that serve as proof for the historical accuracy of the story. For instance, the AHIJ read David Rohl, *Pharoahs and Kings: A Biblical Quest* (New York: Crown, 1995).

5. Giorgio Agamben, *Homo Sacer: Sovereign Power and Bare Life* (Palo Alto, CA: Stanford University Press. 1998). Agamben also famously describes Foucauldian takes on "the archive" as a "system of relations between the said and the unsaid," a pithy characterization that pivots on this book's central premise about the

ethnographic's resonances with the archival. See Giorgio Agamben, *Remnants of Auschwitz: The Witness and the Archive* (Brooklyn, NY: Zone Books, 1999), 144.

THIRTY-NINE ▪ MUNIR

1. Jonathan Boyarin and Daniel Boyarin, *Powers of Diaspora: Two Essays on the Relevance of Jewish Culture* (Minneapolis: University of Minnesota Press, 2002).
2. Boyarin and Boyarin, *Powers of Diaspora,* 55.
3. Henry Louis Gates Jr., *The Signifying Monkey: A Theory of African American Literary Criticism* (Oxford: Oxford University Press, 1988).
4. Kevin Young, *The Grey Album: On the Blackness of Blackness* (Minneapolis: Graywolf Press, 2012).
5. Ethnographers might embrace some of this same sensibility, even if mostly in vain, trying as much as possible to trouble the waters of cultural representation with full knowledge of that project's probable (even inevitable) failure. It means an acceptance of such failure, maybe even claiming the "power to define" it as success.
6. For a discussion of his critiques of white racist assumption of superiority and black subhumanity, see Lewis R. Gordon, *Bad Faith and Antiblack Racism* (Amherst, NY: Humanity Books, 1995). Gordon extends and elaborates on his discussion of bad faith Eurocentrism by deploying Fanonian phenomenologics, in *Fanon and the Crisis of European Man: An Essay on Philosophy and the Human Sciences* (New York: Routledge, 1995). Gordon makes a point about how Jews are signified as "hyper-rational" and blacks as "hyper-somatic," which is part of the reason why the "Afro-Jew" seems so confounding to some people. He also reminds us of Fanon's powerful and relevant suggestion of imagining Rodin's *The Thinker* with an erect penis.
7. Munir Muhammad is a Chicago businessman and a former member of the Nation of Islam who has had a close relationship with Nasik Asiel for many years. He founded the Committee for the Remembrance of Elijah (CROE), which is dedicated to the teachings of Elijah Muhammad. Throughout the 1970s and 1980s, the Nation of Islam's periodicals provided some of the most consistent media coverage of saints in Israel, much of it quite supportive. In fact, as one story goes, the community had to demonstrate (to the Israeli state) a willingness to reject the embrace of Farrakhan and the Nation Of Islam to further prove its sincere commitments to contemporary Israel. Saints maintain that Munir Muhammad is quite decidedly biased in his representation of the Kingdom's disputes with Asiel. One saint even wondered if Muhammad was being "played or paid, maybe both, in the long and honored tradition of Chicago politics."

FORTY ▪ BROCHURE

1. Admittedly, there are also relatively few photographs in this book. I fear that it is my own investment in (and pushback against) the supposed flatness of the photographic

image, the same phobia about its inability to render context that Franz Boas once marked (and that I don't want to simply accept at face value).

2. See Wilton Martinez, "Who Constructs Anthropological Knowledge? Toward a Theory of Ethnographic Film Spectatorship," in *Film as Ethnography*, eds. David Turton and Peter Ian Crawford (Manchester: Manchester University Press, 1992), 130–161.

3. John L. Comaroff and Jean Comaroff, *Ethnicity, Inc.* (Chicago: University of Chicago Press, 2009).

4. Yafah Asiel, *The New Soul Vegetarian Cookbook* (Atlanta, GA: Divine Universal Sisterhood, 2005).

5. All the quotations come from the same Kingdom-produced pamphlet/brochure.

6. Ben Ammi, *Everlasting Life: From Thought to Reality* (Washington, DC: Communicators Press, 1994), iii.

7. Ben Ammi, *The Resurrection: From Judgment to Post Judgment* (Washington, DC: Communicators Press, 2005), 92.

FORTY-ONE ▪ RABBI

1. Israel J. Gerber, *The Heritage Seekers: Black Jews in Search of Identity*, (New York: Jonathan David Publishers, 1977), 35. Several of the original émigrés returned to Chicago and eventually became a part of Beth Shalom.

2. As quoted in Gerber, *The Heritage Seekers*, 35.

3. Zev Chavet, "Obama's Rabbi," *New York Times*, April 2, 2009, http://www.nytimes .com/2009/04/05/magazine/05rabbi-t.html?pagewanted=all.

4. Thanks to Lewis Gordon, who asked me to think about the extent to which Jews as "people of color" might have also been a less odd proposition in Chicago during the early twentieth century. It is a very important point.

5. I told Tamar about a book I'd just read from another black Jewish woman with similar complaints who had also self-published her work: Kush Miri, *Seasons in Sheol: A Black Women's Nightmare Journey Through Synagogue Culture*, (New York: iUniverse, 2009). Also, see Tamar Manasseh, *Chai-ME: My Exploration of Race, Religion, and Spirituality in America* (Chicago: Tamar Manasseh, 2012).

6. This is taken from the Temple's website: http://bethshalombz.org/blog2/history/

FORTY-TWO ▪ HEBREWS

1. For a short discussion of Felton, see John L. Jackson Jr., *Real Black: Adventures in Racial Sincerity* (Chicago: University of Chicago Press, 2005) and John L. Jackson Jr., *Racial Paranoia: The Unintended Consequences of Political Correctness* (New York: Basic Civitas, 2008).

2. John Patrick Deveney, *Paschal Beverly Randolph: A Nineteenth Century Black American Spiritualist, Rosicrucian, and Sex Magician* (Albany: State University of New York Press, 1997), 160. Even though the "stupid" is in quotes, Randolph still seemed to think that blacks were always destined to be below whites.

3. Tudor Parfitt, personal communication, April 2012.

4. Eliza Slavet, *Racial Fever: Freud and the Jewish Question* (New York: Fordham University Press, 2009).

5. Literary theorist Hortense Spillers highlights the fact that even claiming the relevance of psychoanalysis for studies of African American life is a hard sell in many popular and scholarly circles. Hortense Spillers, "'All the Things You Could Be by Now if Sigmund Freud Was Your Mother': Psychoanalysis and Race," *Critical Inquiry* 22, no. 4: 710–734. See also Jean-Paul Rocchi, "Dying Metaphors and Deadly Fantasies: Freud, Baldwin and Race as Intimacy," *Human Architecture: Journal of the Sociology of Self-Knowledge* 7, no. 2 (Spring 2009): 159–178.

6. For an expansive and inclusive notion of Jewish authenticity, see Rebecca T. Alpert, *Whose Torah? A Concise Guide to Progressive Judaism* (New York: New Press, 2008); Melanie Kaye/Kantrowitz, *The Colors of Jews: Racial Politics and Radical Diasporism* (Bloomington, IN: Indiana University Press, 2007).

7. See Walter Benn Michaels, "Race into Culture: A Critical Genealogy of Cultural Identity," *Critical Inquiry* 19, no.4 (1992): 665–685. The argument here is that any truly anthropological definition of culture as "practice" (as what people do) should come without any precultural identificatory grounding, which Michaels claims is never the case (not even for anthropologists who claim to challenge biological assumptions about race).

8. When philosopher Lewis Gordon read Sar Ahmadiel's formulation, he found it odd. "Hebrew," Gordon wrote, "means 'from the other side of the river.' Israelite means 'from Sara' and with 'el signifying G-d's covenant. Thus, upholding Torah was considered a call to Israelites. Jew actually didn't exist. 'Judean' simply meant someone from Judah. But the complex story of the expansion of Judah, its destruction, and then its continuation through mitzvoth led to 'Judaism,' and eventually 'Jews,' but this happened specifically within the Roman Empire. Outside of it, there were Israelites, Judeans, and a variety of related groups." And here is Sar Ahmadiel's emailed response to Gordon:

> The word/name "Hebrew" is drawn from "eber" or "avar," which basically means having "crossed over" (a river, as in Avram's coming out of Ur . . . or anything for that matter in our extended translation of it), so he's right on that. (Of course, we DO claim the right to do some REtranslating—via the Power to Define. Being back again at the Genesis—and in A beginning, not THE beginning—we, like the first Adam, have the right to name all things (the Power to Define). His interpretation, which connects "Israel to Sarah," no doubt is one that is promulgated in *yeshivot*. But in consulting with our resident Hebrew experts, it really should be *yi-sar-el* (and not *yis-ra-el*, an easy mistake to make when considering the way that Hebrew vowels are determined), which would mean "one who shall become a prince" (the son of a king, who, in this case, is the Creator). In ancient Hebrew "Sar" was a "Prince." It can also mean "one who will repel and overcome great challenges" (or as we freely translate and interpret that, "one who has power with man and the Creator," which is related to Jacob's "wrestling" with the

angel—who is also related to be God Himself in another verse—and the reason why his name was changed).

9. The Kingdom's shift from racial motives is a refinement of past views in favor of an immediate and pressing priority (more than a recanting). What they called "racial pride" (which is quite different from racial prejudice) was an important part of their search for identity (individually and collectively). But once they reclaimed that identity and were reoriented accordingly, even resituated in Northeast Africa, the question became "Now what?" And the answer was "We had to do something." Being African—in a world where all humans were shown to have come from Africa and were hence Africans too—took on a secondary importance. They decided to move from a narrow Afrocentric perspective to a "universal Truth-centered" one in which the relationship that they were to have with the Creator and His Creation was of primary concern.

FORTY-THREE ▪ ZOMBIE

1. For a discussion of Foucaldian biopower and its connection to questions of sovereignty and the nation-state, see Giorgio Agamben, *Homo Sacer: Sovereign Power and Bare Life* (Palo Alto, CA: Stanford University Press, 1998). Or for a conceptualization of the nanopolitics of race, see Paul Gilroy, *Against Race: Imagining Political Culture Beyond the Color Line* (Cambridge, MA: Harvard University Press, 2000). For a discussion of state racism's biopolitical moorings, see Michel Foucault, *Society Must Be Defended: Lectures at the College de France, 1975–1976,* trans. David Macey (New York: Picador, 2003).

2. See Adriana Petryna, *Life Exposed: Biological Citizens After Chernobyl* (Princeton, NJ: Princeton University Press, 2002).

3. Elaine Scarry, *The Body In Pain: The Making and Unmaking of the World* (Oxford: Oxford University Press, 1987). Scarry attempts to explain the challenges and necessities of capturing pain (and its brutal inflictions) in semiotic and artistic registers.

4. According to Ben Ammi, hell "is a social construct." For this argument, see Ben Ammi, *The Resurrection: From Judgment to Post Judgment* (Washington, DC: Communicators Press, 2005).

5. Orlando Patterson, *Slavery and Social Death: A Comparative Study* (Cambridge, MA: Harvard University Press, 1982).

6. Zora Neal Hurston, *Tell My Horse: Voodoo and Life in Haiti and Jamaica* (New York: Harper and Row, 1938).

7. For a discussion of these themes, see Jane Gordon and Lewis Gordon, *Of Divine Warning: Reading Disaster in the Modern Age* (Boulder, CO: Paradigm, 2009).

8. See Eduardo Bonilla Silva, *Racism Without Racists: Color-Blind Racism and the Persistence of Racial Inequality in America* (New York: Rowman and Littlefield, 2006). For a recent formulation of Ahmadiel's discussion about the difference between consensus/choice/voluntarism and blood/genealogy/chosen-ness as the underlaying basis for Hebrew identity, see Michael Walzer, *In God's Shadow: Politics in the Hebrew Bible* (New Haven, CT: Yale University Press, 2012).

9. Lewis R. Gordon, *Existentia Africana: Understanding Africana Existential Thought* (New York: Routledge, 2000), 3–4, argues that "Calibanistic thought" (a revolutionary striving for freedom) and "language is infused with forces of magic." Michael Taussig, *I Swear I Saw This: Drawings in Fieldwork Notebooks, Namely My Own* (Chicago: University of Chicago Press, 2011) is a recent attempt to theorize ethnography as a kind of divination.

10. And it might all just be so much more smoke and mirrors, some claim. So that even when Sar Ahmadiel says that the community must unlearn its racial logics, the real antiracists question his sincerity and chalk the move up to a cunning realpolitik that is gambling on the idea that a politically correct and inclusive discourse might convince the Israeli state to finally grant all AHIJ saints full citizenship.

11. For a similar discussion, see the final chapter of Lewis R. Gordon, *Bad Faith and Antiblack Racism* (Amherst, MA: Humanity Books, 1995).

FORTY-FOUR ▪ MLK

1. To hear Cohane Michael tell it, perhaps the Israelites should be weaned off of Jesus altogether. The New Testament is hardly a book to trust, he says.

2. The AHIJ suggest that Israel changed its "Right of Return" laws right after they began to arrive, specifically to disqualify them.

3. The Liberian government had already shelled out some money to support the group, which they wouldn't have necessarily wanted redirected to this second emigration project. And the Israeli government would not know what to do about a group of African Americans from Chicago claiming to be the Lost Tribes of Israel and requesting citizenship as a function of that fact.

FORTY-FIVE ▪ SECONDS

1. Ben Ammi, interview by Morris Lounds, 1973.

2. Merrill Singer, "Saints of the Kingdom: Group Emergence, Individual Affiliation, and Social Change Among the Black Hebrews of Israel." (PhD diss., University of Utah, 1979).

3. Israel Gerber, *The Heritage Seekers: American Blacks in Search of Jewish Identity* (New York: Jonathan David Publishers, 1977). The characterization of Gerber's reading comes from James Landing, *Black Judaism: Story of an American Movement* (Durham, NC: Carolina Academic Press, 2002).

4. Ben Ammi, *Physical Immortality–Conquering Death* (Washington, DC: Communicators Press 2010), 24–25.

5. There is a long literature on what such groups tend to do when their prophecies don't come true. In a nutshell, the argument goes, they cling to one another all the more tightly. Another discrepant recapitulation of the community's backstory has to do with whether or not Liberia was always supposed to be a temporary sojourn, a short time for cleansing in the wilderness (with Israel the predetermined finish line). That's how the saints tell the West African portion of their story now, as little more than a pit stop on the way to what was always supposed to be their final destination,

Northeast Africa. Or was the latter storyline crafted later on, Israel framed as their ultimate endgame with little more than retrospective certainty (as many of the AHIJ's academic chroniclers maintain)?

6. Just as New World Passover can be said to represent a rearticulation or continuation of the Passover story found in Exodus, there are examples of what might be called "cyclical instantiation" in versions of Rastafari wherein Abraham, Moses, David, Jesus, and Haile Selassie are reappearances of the same person. A similar notion seems at work in Ben Ammi's discussions from the early 1970s.

7. This is the name for the Chicago-based Israelite group that Ben Ammi was a part of when he was visited by Gabriel.

8. Ben Ammi, interview by Morris Lounds, 1973.

Acknowledgments

This can only be a very partial list of the many people who have helped me to think through this project (in big and small ways) over the years. Several individuals were generous enough to read early drafts of the entire manuscript. Lewis R. Gordon, Rebecca Alpert, Noah Feldman, Ahmadiel Ben Yehuda, and Kamari Maxine Clarke each read the entire thing and provided me with incredibly valuable feedback. The book is much, much better for their substantive engagements with it. Clarke incorporated the manuscript into the final week of her Penn graduate seminar at the end of 2012, and the graduate students also offered me very compelling suggestions for how I might improve and clarify key points. One of those students, Diana Burnett, also proffered written comments that were amazingly helpful.

I have been able to present portions of this book at several academic institutions, including the American University, the City University of New York, Rutgers University, the University of Chicago, Harvard University, UCLA, Haverford College, University of California, Berkeley, Duke University, University of Connecticut, Lincoln University, Stanford University, Carnegie Mellon University, Temple University, Northwestern University, Yale University,

Princeton University, Williams College, Rice University and the University of Texas, Austin (for the New Directions in Anthropology Conference), and the University of Delaware. I've also presented this research at the New York Academy of Sciences, the American Academy of Religion, and the American Anthropological Association, which included a very engaging and helpful discussion with the Committee for the Anthropology of Jews and Judaism.

I also want to thank my colleagues at the University of Pennsylvania's Annenberg School, the Department of Africana Studies, the Department of Anthropology, and the Graduate School of Education. Many individuals (at Penn and elsewhere) have read portions of the manuscript or provided advice on aspects of the project, including David Kyuman Kim, Wahneema Lubiano, Stanton Wortham, Heather Sharkey, Derek Hicks, Monica Miller, Barbara Savage, Anita Allen, Salamishah Tillet, Adriana Petryna, Philippe Bourgois, Kathy Hall, Brian Spooner, Asif Agha, Edith Bruder, Tudor Parfitt, Anthea Butler, Lisa Lewis, Yulia Egorova, Cohane Michael Ben Levi, Rabbi Capers Funnye, Sharrona Pearl, Elihu Katz, Marwan Kraidy, Carolyn Marvin, Barbie Zelizer, Michael X. Delli Carpini, Betsy Rhymes, Marla Frederick, Mark Anthony Neal, Thadious Davis, Leith P. Mullings, Charlie Piot, Anne Allison, Lee Baker, Bayo Holsey, Orin Starn, Ajantha Subramanian, Vincent Brown, Sherry Ortner, Jessica Fishman, Greg Bisson, Kellie Jones, Elizabeth Alexander, J. Lorand Matory, Setha Low, Jacqueline Nassy Brown, Roxanne Varzi, E. Patrick Johnson, Richard Iton, Dawn-Elissa Fischer, Savannah Shange, Marc Lamont Hill, Jacob Dorman, Jasmine Cobb, C. Riley Snorton, Noah Tamarkin, Carolyn Rouse, Guthrie Ramsey, Jean Comaroff, John Comaroff, Netta Van Vliet, Faye Ginsburg, Donald Robotham, Bambi Schieffelin, Susan McDonic, Leith Mullins, Joy Williams, Imani Williams, Sar Elyashuv, Sar Levi, Levi Ben Levi, Aturah Khazriel, and many others.

Several graduate students (and former graduate students) helped with the research and preparation of this manuscript, including Lyndsey Beutin, Diana Burnett, Tim Fallis, Emily LaDue, Jasmine Salters, Krystal Smalls, Khadijah White, and Imani Williams.

I would like to thank my HUP editor, Sharmila Sen, and her assistant, Heather Hughes, for shepherding this book so expertly (and patiently) through the process. Sam Spofford coordinated the book's production process, and Stephanie Magean was a very careful copyeditor. Thanks for all of your work on this book.

Deborah A. Thomas read the entire manuscript with a wonderfully encouraging and inspiring criticality that spurred me on to the finish line. Thanks for always supporting my endeavors, no matter how quirky. And for doing it all with so much love and grace.

And I especially want to thank all the saints in the Kingdom for allowing me to look over their shoulders for so long.

Chapters, 9, 14, and 23 of the present volume include portions of "Ethnography Is, Ethnography Ain't" (from *Cultural Anthropology*). Chapters 28, 33, and 34 incorporate portions of "On Ethnographic Sincerity" (from *Current Anthropology*). Most of Chapter 22 has been excerpted from "All Yah's Children: Emigrationism, Afrocentrism, and the Place of Israel in Africa" (from *Civilisations*). Most of Chapter 3 is a revised version of the opening section of "Return of the Reflexed: Filmmaking and the Aesthetics of Social Science" (from *Ethnic and Racial Studies*).

Index